A SECOND CHICAGO SCHOOL?

D1557439

A SECOND CHICAGO SCHOOL?

The

Development

of a Postwar

American

Sociology

Edited by
Gary Alan Fine

The University of Chicago Press
Chicago and London

GARY ALAN FINE is Professor of Sociology at the University of Georgia and author of *Shared Fantasy: Role-Playing Games as Social Worlds* and *With the Boys: Little League Baseball and Preadolescent Culture*, both published by The University of Chicago Press.

THE UNIVERSITY OF CHICAGO PRESS, CHICAGO 60637
THE UNIVERSITY OF CHICAGO PRESS, LTD., LONDON

Printed in the United States of America
04 03 02 01 00 99 98 97 96 95   1 2 3 4 5

ISBN: 0-226-24938-7 (cloth)
      0-226-24939-5 (paper)

Library of Congress Cataloging-in-Publication Data

A second Chicago school? : the development of a postwar American
  sociology / edited by Gary Alan Fine.
      p.   cm.
  Includes bibliographical references and index.
    1. Sociology—Study and teaching—United States.   2. Chicago
  school of sociology—History.   3. Sociology—United States—History.
  I. Fine, Gary Alan.
  HM47.U62C47   1995
  301'.0973—dc20   94-46877

To the Second School

CONTENTS

viii   Contents

THE SECOND CHICAGO SCHOOL?

Joseph R. Gusfield

It is surprising and satisfying to see one's friends, oneself, and so many onetime fellow graduate students accorded the degree of recognition implied in the concept of a school. My preface to this book cannot avoid mixing personal memoir with analytical judgments. We were subject to many experiences, influences, and colleagues after we left the womb of the Midway yet a seeming unity of thought and procedure, a tacit understanding about sociology is implied in the idea of a "Second Chicago School." In these few pages I want to place our cohort of sociologists in the historical time and context of their student days and to consider those preconceptions, sensitivities, and feelings that have given some perceived unity to their work since then. My contribution is impressionistic, personal, and colored by my experiences rather than by any sample survey. As such it is clearly affected by all of the ills and wellnesses of a participant observing forty years of life and thought retroactively.

THE CHICAGO SCHOOL

In the postwar world of the late 1940s and early 1950s American sociology, and American higher education, were in an expansive mode. The University of Chicago had been *the* center of sociological research and graduate study before the war. Its graduates, its research, its concepts had dominated the field. As Anselm Strauss once remarked to me, "We didn't think symbolic interaction was a perspective in sociology; we thought it was sociology." In the postwar atmosphere this was no longer the case. The advent of general theory at Harvard under Talcott Parsons and the development of survey research and functionalism with Robert Merton and Paul Lazersfeld at Columbia was where the new and exciting mainstreams were flowing. Chicago was an aging giant, only beginning to

I am grateful to Bennet Berger for a critical reading of this preface and to Howard Becker and Anselm Strauss for the same and for sharing graduate experiences with me. They, of course, do not necessarily agree with my observations in all parts. My apologies to all those whose names I should have mentioned but for time and space constraints.

be conscious that the eastern barbarians had surmounted the gates of their once impregnable midwestern fortress.

The sense of an embattled tradition hung over the lecture rooms of Chicago's Sociology Department. The ghost of Robert Park stalked the halls, looking over the shoulders of his Chicago graduates who now had ascended to faculty status—Blumer, Hughes, and Wirth and the remaining member of that earlier generation, Ernest Burgess. We graduate students whom they taught were sensitive to the fact that we descended from that heroic period in American sociology. It was a period of the great case studies: Zorbaugh's *Gold Coast and the Slum;* Wirth's *The Ghetto;* Reckless's *Vice in Chicago,* and Faris and Dunham's *Mental Disorders in Urban Areas.* We were conscious heirs to the Chicago school and its defense.

In her chapter in this volume, Jennifer Platt is quite right that this was not the only sociological stream in Chicago's postwar department; that in this period the same department that credentialed Erving Goffman credentialed Otis Dudley Duncan. Yet insofar as the Chicago school of prewar sociology was the "Chicago school," the members of the group discussed in this volume saw themselves in a line of that tradition. They were, in a sense, committed to "keeping the faith" in a period of challenge.

THE FACULTY

As most contributors to this volume recognize, Herbert Blumer and Everett Hughes, with Louis Wirth to a lesser extent, formed the dominant intellectual influences on the second Chicago school. Yet in their teaching and in their published writings they were by no means all of a piece. Blumer's general criticisms of what was the mainstream of American sociology were important in his programmatic development of symbolic interactionism. Though Blumer left for Berkeley in 1952, most of the cohort had been exposed to his courses earlier and his influence remained through Tom Shibutani's classes. Hughes's orientation was less definitive but no less important. He was much more the social anthropologist than Blumer; less given to theory or methodological programs than to empirical observation of substantive concerns. Hughes was no self-styled symbolic interactionist, but he was deeply committed to the observation of behavior in a natural setting, a view shared with symbolic interactionists. His orientation had more in common with the methods of anthropologists than with sociological practice. His sociology was more eclectic and more functionalist than was Blumer's. Yet both shared a cluster of values and of sensitivities to the pursuit of sociological work.

The relations to social anthropology were strong with Hughes and W. Lloyd Warner on the faculty, with a term of anthropology required, with Robert Redfield's general influence in social science at Chicago. Hughes, Blumer, and Wirth, although from different intellectual positions, all contributed to a skeptical orientation toward the emergent mainstream of a quantitative sociology heavily dependent on survey, questionnaire, or official records as data or, alternatively, wedded to the quest for abstract general theory that was then attracting attention and dominance.

This does not mean that the cohort was not open to other influences or did not change directions or ideas during their careers. To a great extent we were, especially the veterans, older and more affected by life experiences than was true of graduate students in general. As Helena Lopata points out in her insightful postscript, this was also true of several of the women. I was an instructor in the University of Chicago College while a graduate student in sociology and exposed to a far more macro, more theoretical group of intellectuals than was the case in the department.

THE SECOND CHICAGO SCHOOL

As a group of sociologists we have often been identified as "symbolic interactionists," yet that description fails to catch the rhythm and sensibility of the approaches. Hughes and Blumer might be thought to have utilized different theoretical viewpoints, but they shared a unity of sociological culture which united them in their skeptical view of what was becoming the mainstream of American sociology. Certainly there was much sympathy to symbolic interaction, but neither Goffman nor Becker (in my estimation the two most influential sociologists of our crew) were Blumer students. What we shared were tacit perspectives without a great deal of concern for rigorous theoretical justifications or deductions. These perspectives reflected a culture of sociological practice which played a part in the dominant sociology of the 1960s and 1970s.

While diversely stated and applied, these perspectives had much in common with that first Chicago school and the tradition it formed. There was, and remained, a certain indifference, even disdain, for the endless efforts of sociologists to develop refined theory or methodological rigor. Perhaps Everett Hughes crystallized it best in his opposition to the professionalization of the field (summarized in something I have reported elsewhere). He felt a great deal was lost when the American Sociological Society renamed itself the American Sociological Association. The initials of the earlier title possessed a needed humility and irony that was lost by professional organization and the search for a sociology fashioned in the model of natural science.

The Sociological Culture of the Second Chicago School

The work of the cohort here labeled the "Second Chicago School" appeared in publications and gained attention during the late 1950s, through the 1960s and 1970s. Goffman's *The Presentation of the Self in Everyday Life* appeared in an Anchor edition in 1959; *Boys in White* (Becker, Geer, Hughes, and Strauss) in 1961; Becker's *Outsiders* in 1963; my *Symbolic Crusade* in 1963; Freidson's *Profession of Medicine* in 1972, to mention some of the studies discussed here. During this period many of us also became significant as graduate teachers and important in shaping the policies of a number of major departments. The influence of the group was exercised both through their teaching and their research.

Any effort on my part to produce a list of the contents of the second Chicago school must be personal and tentative. I do so with a mixture of temerity and courage. Even this attempt to organize implies a consistency that is alien.

What stands out for me is the intensive focus on the empirical world; on seeing and understanding behavior in its particular and situated forms. Data that do not stay close to the events, actions, or texts being studied are always suspect. There is a hostility to generalizations at any level that are not connected to description, to immersion in substantive matter. What Geertz called "thick description" is the ideal, not always achieved but always to be aimed at. Other data and other methods were acceptable but more as concessions to practicality than as preferred ways to study human behavior.

The preference for descriptive material and observation made us suspicious of records and questionnaires—of data torn from the context of their creation. Action was too situated, too contextual to be understood at the high levels of much macroanalysis. Meanings were not often assuredly understandable without an experience with those we were describing. The sample survey, probably the major contribution of sociology to American life, is still viewed with a degree of doubt and humility.

Perhaps the best of the few programmatic statements of the cohort is found in Barney Glaser and Anselm Strauss's *Discovery of Grounded Theory.* It emphasizes the inductive character of sociology; building general statements from the accumulation of specific cases in much the way jurists and legal scholars use analogy to develop concepts and legal principles.

These principles were hardly systematized as guidelines. "Methodology," as a subject of sociology, was hardly an organized subject matter. Fieldwork has yet to develop a casuistry or a text that is much beyond simple cautions and the advice of experienced hands. In this respect, the Chicago school was open to a more artistic, improvised, and situated mode of sociology than implied in the tenets of research design.

The Political Culture of the Chicago School

Beyond the unstated programs of research lie the felt commitments and antagonisms to the institutions and groups that make up society. They are the cultural frames within which sociological work occurs. The second school shared with the first an identification with the less respected, less established elements in the society and a notable dose of skepticism and disrespect for the well-off, the authoritative, and the official. No one has captured this better than the non-Chicagoan Alvin Gouldner. He had studied at Columbia and was a great admirer of his mentor, Robert Merton. In 1962 he wrote with equal admiration for what he termed the contemporary "Chicago school":

> A case in point can be found in the recent studies of medicine conducted by Columbia or Harvard or Chicago-trained men. It is difficult to escape the feeling that the former are more respectful of the medical establishment than the Chicagoans, that they more readily regard it in terms of its own claims, and are more prone to view it as a noble profession. Chicagoans, however, tend to be uneasy about the very idea of a "profession" as a tool for study, believing instead that the notion of an "occupation" provides more basic guide-lines for study, and arguing that occupations as diverse as the nun and the prostitute, or the plumber and the physician, reveal instructive sociological similarities. . . . Epitomizing this difference are the very differences in the book titles that the two groups have chosen for their medical studies. Harvard and Columbia have soberly called two of their most important works *The Student Physician* and *Experiment Perilous,* while the Chicagoans

have irrevently labelled their own recent study of medical students *Boys in White.* (*Social Problems,* Winter 1962)

These aspects of culture have often been commented on in the work
of the Chicago cohort. In the conflicts between the great abstractions of
"society" and the "individual," the Chicago cohort was more often on the
side of the latter than the former. Gary Fine's analysis of this tension in
the work of Erving Goffman is one of the most valuable parts of this
volume. Goffman's study *Asylums* stands as superb example of the differences between the view of the patient seen from the perspective of the
psychiatrist and the view of the patient's action seen from his/her perspective as a response to the institutions of treatment. We did not look at
events and behavior from the standpoint of order and function; we were
hostile to the idea of "society" and feared being taken in by institutions
and their purposes and assertions. Becker's development of labeling theory
and Freidson's analysis of medical knowledge are two examples of how
these cultural presuppositions helped frame new ways of analysis.

It is not that these orientations to human behavior were specific or
unique to Chicago graduates, a recognition confirmed by Jennifer Platt's
study of journal articles in this volume. The perception of a unity to the
work of the Chicago cohort, however, is at another level. Platt ignores
the significance of books as major sources of influence and leadership in
sociology. Becker's *Outsiders,* I venture to write, has had far more influence
on the study of deviance than a decade of the *American Sociological
Review.*

The continued attention to the Chicago school during the 1970s and
1980s is not only a result of continuing work but was also aided by the
shift in sociological thinking that has its sources in intellectual movements
elsewhere. The "coming of age" of the postwar cohort coincided with intellectual streams unrelated to that source. In a variety of ways and origins
the presuppositions of the Chicago school were in harmony with other
work that overlapped, affected their study, and reinforced some of the
orientations. Ethnomethodology, German critical theory, phenomenology,
French focus on cultural *mentalités*—all these, as well as major currents
of thought in linguistics, anthropology and literary theory, were at work.
The abstract theory, quantitative method, and survey research that dominated the 1950s, 1960s, and 1970s was now itself only a part of those intellectual tensions summarized in the conflicts surrounding that vague term
"postmodern".

THE SOCIAL BASIS OF COHORT FORMATION

Who were we? Most of the contributors to this volume recognize the imprecise nature of any definitive boundaries to inclusion and exclusion. We can think of them in terms of chronology or in terms of the social and intellectual networks in which they were included during the graduate years of the postwar University of Chicago department. That the group contained a high percentage of Jews and veterans is noted by the contributors. But this was also true of departments at other major universities and does not shed much light on the unique character of the school. What I see as significant is the particular character of the University of Chicago community in the late 1940s and early 1950s. The geographical ecology of Chicago's Hyde Park, the existence of the G.I. Bill, and the housing units committed to veteran residence made for factors which reinforced the classroom and helped to form an aggregate of graduate students into a social group with distinctive cultural traits.

Most of the cohort mentioned here lived within a few blocks of each other—blocks that constituted the University of Chicago community huddled close to a clearly demarcated campus. The slumlike character of many of the old apartment buildings made it possible for most graduate students to afford housing close to campus. The G.I. Bill and the housing for veterans supplied by the university added to their ability to choose Hyde Park as a place of residence. The large, parklike expanse of the Midway made a boundary between the community and the city to the south. The Illinois Central elevated tracks separated the student community from the high-rent areas close to Jackson Park and the lakefront to the east. Within this area there were common hangouts and meeting places—Jimmy's Bar and the University Tavern on 55th Street; the Tropical Hut eatery on 57th; the bookstores of 57th Street. The closeness of places, the then-safety of the streets, and the proximity of residence helped us to form friendships and events of solidarity that have been lasting. The classroom spilled over onto the streets and, of course, into the living rooms and kitchens. My wife still remembers the night she thought I had met foul play when a search of the streets at 1:00 A.M. found me and Erving Goffman "talking shop" under a lampost. During one or two years there was an ongoing softball game in a 57th Street schoolyard. The Social Science building had a daily interdisciplinary coffee hour. There were the frequent parties and, above all, the talk-talk-talk.

I cannot know whether or not these experiences were more salient for this cohort than for other graduate student groups elsewhere. But they did provide a basis for the continuing relationships fed by annual A.S.A. meetings, in part attractive because they meant a regrouping of a graduate cohort that has perhaps overly romanticized its own formation. They may have also helped establish the networks which in later years were important to the institutional journeys of the group. More significantly, it developed and reinforced those partially articulated "domain assumptions" that I have described above.

Such considerations are important to the formation of schools of thought. This volume's focus on research and theory necessarily slights such considerations. They are, however, important to the understanding of how culture and knowledge may be generated and continued even after the initially formative experiences. The first Chicago school was a contributory to the tacit assumptions of the Park-influenced faculty that taught us. Yet that is insufficient to explain both the continuance of the culture and the retention of close friendships and networks through the decades. Did these continuing networks reinforce the cultural presuppositions of our graduate studies?

* * *

I have no conclusion to offer. Were the experiences of graduate work and life significant to the continuing networks that gave a massed quality to the publications of the second Chicago school? Is the very idea of a "second Chicago school" only a self-serving idea, a social construction that is more shadow than substance? I am too close to its subject matter to be more than a self-interested participant-observer. One of the virtues of this book is that it offers no definitive answer to these questions but instead may make us reflect on the ways in which ideas occur and gain recognition and influence.

A SECOND CHICAGO SCHOOL?

THE DEVELOPMENT OF A POSTWAR AMERICAN

SOCIOLOGY

Gary Alan Fine

The question seemed so simple, at first. Was there a "second" Chicago school of sociology, a postwar school of qualitative sociologists and symbolic interactionists? How could such an obvious claim be doubted? We had read Howard Becker, Fred Davis, Eliot Freidson, Erving Goffman, Joseph Gusfield, Robert Habenstein, Lewis Killian, Helena Lopata, Hans Mauksch, Gregory Stone, Ralph Turner: friends and colleagues. These scholars were role models for that younger generation of symbolic interactionists trained in the past quarter-century. This cohort received their Ph.D. degrees at the University of Chicago, and were trained by such inspiring teachers and scholars as Herbert Blumer, Everett Hughes, W. Lloyd Warner, Robert Redfield, David Riesman, Anselm Strauss, Ernest Burgess, and Louis Wirth, in the period immediately following the Second World War. For a generation of qualitative sociologists this group produced our intellectual charter, our legitimation, our Golden Age.[1] History is a means by which one's right to exist can be settled.

This volume was originally conceived of as a valorization, a vindication of that period, of that place, and of those scholars. The original impulse was imbued with a rosy romanticism for a time that had passed, since the present intellectual concerns of the Department of Sociology at the University of Chicago no longer represent that remembered past. Our goal was to make a case that there was a *second* Chicago school, one that rivaled or even outshone the *first* (that of Thomas, Mead, and Park) in its impact on the discipline, creating a label for a period of great symbolic meaning. Yet, the real world is rough, even when one brings an axe to grind. Complexity is a mighty cure for hubris.

In dealing with the question of whether there was a "second" Chicago school, we needed to ask, what do we mean by a "school"?—a question which has become more complicated as it has been addressed by sociologists of science and intellectual life (e.g., Platt 1993). The problematizing of the concept of "school" is particularly applicable to those of an interactionist bent, who find it "contrary to the very spirit of pragmatism and symbolic interactionism to formalize and focus all into the pigeon-hole of 'a' school in a positivist sense" (Eliot Freidson, letter to Gary Fine, May 22, 1990). Schools, paradigms, and traditions float in unmapped intellectual space. Diana Crane (1972) and others have spoken of "invisible colleges," networks of like-minded scholars, often working on similar sets of problems. The reason that these colleges are invisible is that they do not require spatial proximity. In contrast, there are physical colleges—of stone and Gothic spires. These are places where scholars and scholars-in-training physically gather together. By the ideology, structure, and politics of American social sciences, these places typically offer diverse training to students. Eclecticism is seen as virtuous. In few places do all students learn the same things from the same faculty. Indeed, it is quite possible that—except for a few required courses—two graduate students in the same department may have entirely non-overlapping sets of professors, and may socialize with a different group of friends and colleagues. American social science departments tend to be sufficiently large and pluralistic, imbued with the idea of choice and wide coverage of disparate disciplines, that diversity characterizes them more than focus. The historical linkage of individuals in an institutional space does not suggest a similarity of theoretical development (Platt 1993).

This is not to suggest that all departments have the same set of orientations, or that one cannot characterize distinctive departmental contributions to a discipline. The recognition of the reality of diversity should not deny the special contributions that can arise from particular places. A school—as meant here—refers to a collection of individuals working in the same environment who at the time and through their own retrospective constructions of their identity and the imputations of intellectual historians are defined as representing a distinct approach to a scholarly endeavor (Platt 1993). The existence of a school within a department is, then, not especially problematic, although one must be careful not to conflate the "school" with the department within which it is located. Several intellectual traditions may exist within an academic unit, but we may choose only to give the label of "school" to one, because of its distinctive orientation to a problem or methodology, or because of the subsequent fame of several of its participants. Within a department lines separating those who are inside and outside the "school" are—and should be—somewhat fluid.

CENTRAL TENDENCY AND DIVERSITY

Intellectual historians are prone to label periods, organizations, and groups, focusing on the central tendency, rather than the variance. Our emphasis in this volume is to elaborate the distinctive contributions that University of Chicago sociology faculty and, most particularly, graduate students made to qualitative sociology, ethnographic methodology, and symbolic interaction in the postwar era. Although it is impossible to define precisely and narrowly the reference of this perspective, it became clear that among many graduate students and some faculty there was a self-consciousness at Chicago among those present; particularly those students who took a qualitative, ethnographic, or interactionist approach saw themselves as making a distinctive, unique contribution (Gusfield 1990). Further, despite the substantial contributions of those Chicagoans who were applied researchers, demographers, or who addressed any of the substantive branches of macrosociology, the qualitative sociologists have been seen as having a particularly notable effect on the discipline, perhaps a function of the reality that there were other equally prominent training centers for macrosociology, applied research, and demography, whereas Chicago has traditionally been defined as unique in its commitment to qualitative sociology. We are not attempting a complete history of the department, and of the ideas that were prominent among the faculty, but rather attempting to find common themes among a group of people in a particular place and time.

The reality that the department was perceived both by insiders and by outsiders as distinctive provides a prima facie legitimacy for our analysis. However, because of the existence of other strong intellectual interests in the department and because of the hazy boundaries surrounding this approach, we recognize as authors that this volume does not represent the history of a department, or of the ideas of the faculty in that department, but only of a group (i.e., a "school") with some degree of intellectual coherence, a point emphasized by Helena Lopata in her Postscript. Indeed, Andrew Abbott and Emanuel Gaziano note quite correctly, in chapter 7, that the images of graduate students (on whom we focus) did not necessarily represent the politics and alliances among the faculty. When we contributors analyze the second Chicago school as an intellectual entity throughout this volume we emphasize the contributions of a particular subset of scholars. An examination of the faculty of the period might well look quite different from an examination of the students.

If we analyze the existence of a school, it becomes clear that some individuals are core contributors to the approach, both intellectually and socially. Among Chicago faculty in the postwar era Herbert Blumer, Everett Hughes, and Anselm Strauss made up such a group; others were marginally tied to the group, as with Ernest Burgess, W. Lloyd Warner, Louis Wirth, David Riesman, or, later, Morris Janowitz; while still others in the same department had a relatively minor direct influence on this intellectual approach—W. F. Ogburn, Philip Hauser, or Leo Goodman. Those who are marginal or outside of one grouping might well be central to another.[2] Similarly, intellectual impact or relations to students do not necessarily provide an accurate template of departmental politics (Abbott and Gaziano, this volume).

In speaking of a second Chicago school of sociology, we run a danger of neglecting the reality that, at the time, many sociologists did not comfortably fit within the "interactionist, interpretivist, qualitative" central tendency that the label suggests, and that, according to some, the department was factionalized (Fred Davis and Anselm Strauss, transcribed tape, 1990). The recognition of objective diversity, coupled with symbolic focus, most emphatically applies to postwar sociology at the University of Chicago. Not all Chicago Ph.D.'s during the period, and probably not even a majority, defined themselves or were defined by others as symbolic interactionists, qualitative sociologists, or participant-observers. Thus, Leo Bogart (letter to Gary Fine, May 29, 1990) could write that "there was no shared community of theoretical orientation in this post-war period," and others suggested that this was the period in which Chicago sociology joined mainstream American sociology (Eugene Uyeki, letter to Gary Fine, June 13, 1990).

In commemorating an intellectual school, we recognize that we are being both cautious and inexact. Of the contributions in this volume, the chapter by Jennifer Platt is the most explicit in calling into question the validity of labeling a school on the basis of a narrowly contained perspective on sociological research. Platt argues effectively against the claim that qualitative research was the *dominant* methodology employed by students in the Department of Sociology during this period. Hers is a compelling case, forcing us to recognize that our use of the image of a second Chicago school represents a subset of the sociology conducted during this period. In a similar vein, a letter, written as we were compiling information and memories for the book from Ph.D. graduates of the Department of Sociology at the University of Chicago, from Nathan Keyfitz (letter to Gary Fine, June 25, 1990) chastized us:

> Statistics and demography were going strong during the period that you are interested [in], with Don Bogue, Phil Hauser, Evelyn Kitagawa, Leo Goodman, and a number of very bright young people graduated. . . . *Should not some of this get into the volume?*

Keyfitz is correct, of course, both in noting the emphasis of the volume and in raising the question of whether in a fully adequate and balanced treatment of a particular *period,* the statisticians and demographers should not be given more weight. One might further ask whether those many students who were involved in applied sociology are being given their due (Charles W. Nelson, letter to Gary Fine, May 22, 1990).[3] The honest, if uncomfortable, response is that this volume is not designed to be historically balanced. The further reality is that it is not only the statisticians and demographers who are downplayed, but those who arrived later in the period, those who were not later to obtain prominence in the discipline, those who labored in applied settings, and those who contributed to mainstream macrosociology.

The existence of diversity, even within a program that is labeled as distinctive by insiders and outsiders poses two questions: one general and one specific.

The *general* question is whether any period labeling is justified. By focusing on one group, the labeling inevitably directs attention away from others who do not fit so well into that intellectual tendency or social grouping. The label is a social construction, used for local political ends. Choosing to emphasize some portion of a group as characteristic of the whole—intellectual synedoche—has virtues in that it allows us to emphasize what is unique and what has long-lasting consequences. This labeling forever alters history to the extent that the past consists of the way in which we memorialize it—memory is intellectual destiny (Maines, Katovich, and Sugrue 1983; Halbwachs 1992).

The *specific* question is whether labeling *this* period as the second Chicago school is justified. Such a label is clearly unfair in that it shapes history; yet, in another sense, that labeling helps us to remember some of the special contributions of that cohort of men and women in affecting the discipline. Whatever the statistical reality of the *number* and *proportion* of qualitative sociologists and symbolic interactionists in the cohort (Platt, this volume), there can be little doubt that this period at this place has been defined as a font of a compelling type of outsider sociology. The evidence from the students themselves, memories that are admittedly retrospective reconstructions, indicates that for a significant number of individuals the Department of Sociology at the University of Chicago was seen as an intellectually distinct locale, one that posed a challenge to the remainder of the discipline. Joseph Gusfield, one of those in the cohort who most emphasized the central tendency of the "school,"[4] noted in a taped communication:

> The Park tradition and the Chicago School of field observations was . . . a major model of what sociologists do best. That emphasis had its newer model in William Whyte's *Street Corner Society* and we were all imbued more or less with a great fondness for it . . . that model was, in many ways, an ideal. . . . George Herbert Mead was, as we referred to it, the *Bible*. We read Mead with great intensity, discussed it with great intensity and the symbolic interactionist orientation seemed to us at the center of what sociology was. A few years ago, Anselm Strauss remarked to me that "We didn't think symbolic interaction was a perspective in sociology; we thought it was sociology." (Transcribed taped communication, 1990)

Lee Braude (letter to Gary Fine, May 15, 1990), noting that the department "fell apart" in the 1950s, also claims that there were some important characteristics of Chicago sociology that, perhaps, transcend intellectual labels:

> What *was* Chicago sociology, and what is its continuing influence as the twentieth century wanes, is its clarity and consistency regarding an interpretation . . . of the empirical social world; a strategy of knowledge-gathering appropriate to that interpretation; and (perhaps most important) a thoroughgoing commitment to the idea that knowledge makes a difference not only to the discipline but in the lives of those whom the sociologist studies. . . . The humble or the proud (as Hughes would put it) was fit grist for the sociologist's mill, for problems and processes would continually assert themselves regardless of venue. I would submit, then, that what was Chicago sociology is precisely that singularity and, withal, catholicity of orientation.

Recognizing the limitations of this treatment, we believe that theoretical components of qualitative sociology at Chicago at this period make it worthy of examination. Certainly this research tradition was both powerful and prominent, looking at social order in a way that was distinct in tone and methodology from much of what had gone before, emphasizing the processes by which an average citizen creates a social space in which to operate. This approach also took the description of social settings as fundamental to the sociological enterprise, deliberately choosing modest settings for ethnographic focus. The presence of both Herbert Blumer and Everett Hughes, the one providing a theoretical grounding and the other a demand for ethnographic detail, coupled with middle-level concepts, proved to be highly stimulating and productive for the cohorts they instructed. The linkage between a distinctive theoretical outlook and a model of how data should be collected and analyzed proved enormously influential. While there may be a tendency to give priority to Blumer the theorist, Hughes the empirical sociologist may in reality have been more influential for the discipline as a whole. After Blumer relocated to Berkeley in 1952, Hughes (with the collaboration, for a time, of Anselm Strauss) held the qualitative, interactionist group together. While both Blumer and Hughes have their partisans, attesting to each one's centrality in student training, the program would look quite different without either of these two scholars, even for those students who had contact with only one, or neither.[5]

The existence of this group of young scholars, and the associated faculty, at the University of Chicago became an effective charter for work that was carried on at other institutions that were defined, in comparison, as distinctly less supportive of this methodological tradition and theoretical perspective. The sociology of the past thirty years would have had a very different complexion without this graduate training. The Department of Sociology at the University of Chicago served both as a normative and a comparative reference group for qualitatively oriented scholars at other institutions. This claim represents another instance of the belief in the reality of a "Golden Age."

The label of *second* Chicago school has political ramifications within the discipline; it is designed to suggest a continuity with the *first* Chicago school. While there has been an enormous literature on the first Chicago school, there has not yet been a comparable literature on the postwar graduates of Chicago. The debate over what the first Chicago school meant is a lively and disputatious one. As in our view of the second school, some sociologists have effectively claimed that the original Chicago school (a school with several periods and generations—see Deegan, this volume) provided a charter for qualitative sociology and symbolic interaction. George Herbert Mead and Robert Park serve much the same roles in this version of Chicago sociology as Herbert Blumer and Everett Hughes would for a later generation. Some researchers have noted that Chicago sociology was always diverse intellectually and methodologically (Harvey 1987), and that the casual labeling does not adequately apply to the objective circumstances of intellectual life. In this introduction I do not intend to determine the legitimacy of the conflicting readings of Chicago sociology in its first half-century; the charge to chapter authors is to examine the following fifteen years.

The goal of the contributors to this volume is to provide pieces of a picture. Our collective belief is that Chicago sociology at midcentury provides the roots from which much (though by no means all) qualitative sociology in subsequent decades grew. Each author, in some way, believes that this time and place were special in the production of contemporary qualitative sociology, particularly the symbolic interactionist perspective. To understand the strands of thought in the writings of these midcentury scholars, and in some measure to understand the milieu in which they were trained, is to expand our insight into the basis of their sociological vision.

In sum, we emphasize that our choice of an uncertain label, the second Chicago school, to refer to an intellectual stance within sociology, must not be taken to refer to the totality of the faculty, students, or research at the University of Chicago in the postwar years. This label is not meant to suggest that those who fit most comfortably within are the *best*, but that we see their contributions as particularly distinctive and cohesive. Although some who were defined as interactionists were among the best and brightest of the period, so were some who were not so defined.

Yet, because of the presence of Herbert Blumer (until 1952), Everett Hughes, and to some extent, for portions of the period, W. Lloyd Warner, Ernest Burgess, Robert Redfield, William Foote Whyte, Joseph Lohman, David Riesman, and Anselm Strauss, sociological training at Chicago had an emphasis distinct from that at other training centers, notably Columbia and Harvard.[6] Certainly, in retrospect, faculty and students at Chicago have made unique, important, and lasting contributions to the development of an interactionist and qualitative sociology, as we shall show in this volume, despite our recognition of the power of other styles of research in the period. In defense of the idea of a "second school," we should note that the University of Chicago produced an enormous proportion of the subsequently prominent qualitative sociologists—those whose works collectively rewrote and reframed the discipline.

CHANGE

A key feature that complicates our attempt to label the fifteen years after World War II as the second Chicago school is the historical reality that the department changed substantially in the early 1950s when Herbert Blumer moved to Berkeley, Louis Wirth died, and William Ogburn and Ernest Burgess retired. For some, 1952 was the watershed year: for certain romantics, an annus horribilis. In 1960 the department was a very different place in which to be trained than it had been in 1946, with what many perceived as a much changed intellectual and methodological milieu. For some this represented a necessary coming of scientific, modern, positivist sociology to a department increasingly out of the "mainstream." For others it represented a misdirection of energy; these critics contended that the department "fell apart" in the 1950s, when "the department [attempted] to reconstruct itself by attracting 'wise men' from the East [i.e., Columbia]." (Lee Braude, letter to Gary Fine, May 15, 1990). Even though there were important qualitative researchers studying at Chicago throughout the period (Kai Erikson, for instance, received his Ph.D. in 1963), a sea change swamped the department during the early 1950s. Although it might be reasonable to speak of the central intellectual contribution of the department as involving qualitative research in the first half of the postwar period, by the second half such a claim makes less sense, except that qualitative students who had been trained earlier in the period were completing their degrees later in the 1950s. The core of the second-school period was the time from 1946 to 1952, not the longer time-frame of 1946–1960. In practice, if not by definition, many of the chapters in this volume limit their focus to these earlier years. Most chapters give particular emphasis to the contributions of graduate students from the earlier period.

In considering these episodes of strong, memorable, and influential academic community—and by all reasonable definitions postwar Chicago would have to be among them—we recognize that such times and places rarely last long and rarely are unchanging. "Schools" are typically unable to institutionalize themselves. Neither are these episodes as homogeneous as our confident and memorable labels suggest. The web of connections between Harvard, Columbia, and Chicago—each school central to the development of sociology as we recognize the discipline today—was real, and in some measure it eclipses the distinctive traditions of those schools, particularly later in the period.[7] At the same time that rivalry and joking were directed at the programs of the other schools, there was also a movement of personnel, a network, among them. At Chicago, this process—exemplified in the additions to the faculty of James Coleman, Peter Rossi, Peter Blau, and Fred Strodtbeck—was felt by some "true believers" in the interactionist faith to have contributed to the decline of Chicago as a unique training center.

Ultimately in preparing this volume we were left with an unsettling sense that the objective existence of a second Chicago school was more problematic than the existence of the volume might suggest; thus, the question mark in the title of this volume is a mark of both honesty and intellectual doubt. Nor did we reach full consensus on when this school existed. Did it truly begin in 1946 with the arrival of G.I. Bill veterans? Did it end about 1952 with the transformation of the Chicago faculty, even though many subsequently prominent sociologists remained as graduate students? Did it end in 1962 when Everett Hughes finally retired from Chicago and moved to Brandeis, ending the direct linkage with Park's legacy?

Such questions tie nicely into an interactionist analysis of intellectual history, which questions the "objective" and determined reality of meaning, and points to the social construction of texts through the process of response by audiences. Even our doubts are a lagniappe from those we study. Chicago-trained sociologist Fred Davis in his book *Yearning for Yesterday* (1979) has effectively underlined the subtle and dramatic ways in which memory is constructed. Nostalgia results from what we need to believe in light of the emotional demands of the present. Likewise, Davis argues that the process of decade labeling is a social construction, one that gives social meaning to arbitrary temporal divisions and creates boundaries by symbolic means. The recent interest in the process of commemoration describes the same set of phenomena.

A Festschrift for a Golden Age

This book might be said, on one level, to serve as a collective festschrift. Each author agreed to participate because of intellectual curiosity, scholarly engagement, and personal admiration for the department, the faculty, and the students. We wished to explore how we might characterize this period of intellectual ferment, how it came to be, and how these parti-

cipants were influenced by and influenced others. In this respect, we hope
that the chapters have a measure of intellectual candor and coherence.
The desire for balance can be difficult, particularly when one is writing
about live and active scholars who have more personal knowledge about
the events and works in which they were involved than we do, and may
not hesitate to demonstrate this knowledge (recall, for instance, Erving
Goffman's vigorous attempt to preserve his interpretation of *Frame Analysis* against a markedly different reading by Norman Denzin). In addition,
we have chosen to analyze the writings and, in some passages, the lives of
men and women who represent the pinnacle of their profession, and who
hardly need others speaking for them. Can we upstarts ever be correct
when dissenting from the interpretations of these luminaries? The audience of the present and future must decide when scholars are no longer to
be given tight control over their own works and lives. We believe that our
readings are valuable, but we do not claim that ours are the only reasonable interpretations. Distance and perspective may permit us to see this
period and these works in valuable ways, but in ways that were not intended by those involved.

Because each author here has a set of specific goals, some are less
limited than others in their selection of key actors. Authors differ, for instance, in the degree to which they focus upon the (subsequently defined)
"stars," as opposed to a larger population. They also differ in the degree
to which they limit their focus to those of a particular intellectual stripe.
For Deegan, exploring the position of women at Chicago, the intellectual
distinctions are not central: gender, not theoretical perspective, is the
dominant focus. Platt's question is the extent to which one can say on the
basis of methodology that Chicago was distinct: her findings are that this
is only partially true, raising the question of the degree to which this group
is a "school." Colomy and Brown, and Galliher, examining intellectual
issues in the sociology of work and deviance, bring in some of those nor-
mally considered outside the standard interactionist orbit. Snow and
Davis, Fine and Ducharme, Wacker, and Reinharz are more directly focused on the substantive traditions of Chicago sociology. Reinharz, in particular, attempts to explain how the qualitative, Hughesian tradition in the
second Chicago school became diffused to other institutions, particularly
Brandeis, in her case study. This analysis, while it addresses one locale, is
important in that the justification for speaking of the second Chicago
school is precisely in the extent of its diffusion beyond the Midway into

other academic precincts. Abbott and Gaziano remind us that the image of a department from the student perspective may differ substantially from the image among the faculty or the administration.

As is proper, visions differ. Disagreements have been particularly evident in response to the chapter written by Mary Jo Deegan, "The Second Sex and the Chicago School: Women's Accounts, Knowledge, and Work, 1945–1960." Deegan argues that systematic gender bias and sexism characterized sociological training at Chicago, an argument with which some of those to whom she sent a draft of the chapter take issue. Deegan carefully compiled the responses to her chapter and worked those contrary analyses into her text, but despite the revisions the chapter remains controversial. Rather than attempting to erase her images, I include them as a statement which others may challenge. Some graduate students of the period find that picture compelling; others do not fully recognize their department; and still others feel betrayed by the reading. Informing people that they were oppressed is a difficult business. Throughout the volume the work of female sociologists of the second Chicago school is cited, although, as with men, there are some influential figures whose work is barely touched upon. Helena Lopata's postscript attempts to place the careers of these women in perspective, in light of the contributions of this cohort of men and women. She emphasizes the pieces of the puzzle missing from the other chapters.

The role of women and the recognition of their contributions are not the only possible points of contention in the volume. Some might argue that Jennifer Platt understates the contribution that qualitative research and symbolic interaction made to the Department of Sociology. Some disagree with the argument that Lori Ducharme and I put forward that the cultural discourse of the 1950s is reflected in ethnographies of the period. Sociologists may doubt that the zeitgeist can be determined as easily and casually from texts, designed for other purposes, as we have done. None of the chapters presents a final word on the subject; all are seen as contributions to a debate.

In inviting a set of scholars to contribute chapters, one depends on separate intellectual agendas. As editor, I attempted to avoid extensive overlap in the chapters. Yet with a large subject and a relatively small number of contributors, it was inevitable that many topics were not covered and some were covered too often. In organizing the volume I dissuaded contributors from focusing on any one scholar in detail, and, so we do not have specific chapters on Blumer, Hughes, Goffman, or Becker, as a differently structured volume might have had. The volume begins with a trio of chapters that cover the larger issues in the second Chicago school: theory (Colomy and Brown), methodology (Platt), and metaphor (Fine and Ducharme). The next set of chapters addresses a set of substantive issues. Here authors examine race and ethnicity (Wacker), deviance (Galliher), and collective behavior (Snow and Davis). These are followed by three chapters which address not only substantive issues of research but the social organization of the second Chicago school. Andrew Abbott and Emanuel Gaziano present a portrait of a divided faculty and of an administration that was none too certain of the value of sociology as practiced on the Midway. Shulamit Reinharz describes how the traditions of the second Chicago school became diffused, focusing on the building of the Department of Sociology at Brandeis University, an institution heavily influenced by Chicago sociology. Mary Jo Deegan, as noted above, describes the position of women in the second Chicago school. We were delighted that Helena Znaniecka Lopata agreed to contribute a postscript that placed some of the arguments of the volume in perspective, particularly by examining the subsequent lives led by the female cohorts at the University of Chicago. The volume closes with two appendices. The first lists the Ph.D.s from the Department of Sociology (a list provided by the University of Chicago), the year of their graduation, and the title of their Ph.D. dissertation. We also include a list of the faculty on staff at the University of Chicago during the years 1946–60.

At various points in the creation of the manuscript, a few colleagues had to withdraw because of other commitments. With each change in personnel the content of the finished product changed. Topics such as writing style, reflexivity, and organizational theory might have been in the final manuscript, but are not. We make no claim to have recognized or described all dimensions of this period and this place, but we have contributed to the process by which this generation of scholars can be understood and integrated into the historical development of the discipline of sociology.

Unfortunately we did not emphasize much of an "ethnography" of graduate life at the University of Chicago and in Hyde Park, although that is a valuable topic for future research. Some chapters do touch lightly on this issue, such as Mary Jo Deegan's discussion of the experiences of women in this group and Helena Lopata's discussion of her experiences in midcentury Hyde Park. Many correspondents shared excellent information, which can provide the basis for such a discussion, although in-depth interviews would be necessary to supplement the compiled documents. A balanced organizational, intellectual, and historical treatment still needs to be written.

* * *

Many sociologists have been involved in the preparation of this volume. The book could not have taken the form that it did without the collaboration and kind support of numerous members of this academic cohort. Each time one reads the phrase "personal communication" or "letter to the author" this debt of gratitude is being acknowledged. More than this, the personal support of these senior scholars meant much to us. The robust criticism we occasionally received was not easy to accept, but it did what it was intended to: insure that the chapters were better than they had been before the critique and make us rethink what we wrote. The members of this cohort who contributed to this volume by responding to my letter (in many cases in great length and often with much additional material that would have been otherwise unavailable) were: Samuel C. Adams, Jr., Howard S. Becker, Reinhard Bendix, Rhoda Blumberg, Leo Bogart, Lee Braude, Jean Burnet, Wilmoth Carter, Harvey Choldin, John Clausen, Phillips Cutright, Fred Davis, Robert Dentler, Otis Dudley Duncan, Reynolds Farley, Bernard Farber, Eliot Freidson, Daniel Glaser, Joseph Gusfield, A. Paul Hare, Charles Hawkins, David Heise, Wolf Heydebrand, Nathan Keyfitz, Lewis Killian, Charles E. King, Orrin Klapp, Louis Kriesberg, Gladys Lang, Kurt Lang, Donald Levine, Stanley Lieberson, Fred Lindstrom, Helena Lopata, Elizabeth Lyman, Hans Mauksch, Bevode McCall, Frank Miyamoto, David Moore, Joan Moore, Charles W. Nelson, Terrence Nosanchuk, Margaret Peil, W. M. Phillips, Jr., Peter C. Pineo, Jyotirmoyee Sarma, W. Richard Scott, Tamotsu Shibutani, James Short, Rita Simon, Robert C. Stone, Anselm Strauss, Ralph Turner, Eugene Uyeki, Murray Wax, Harold Wilensky, Eugene Wilkening, and Everett Wilson. Others contributed through their contacts with individual chapter authors, and these individuals are acknowledged where appropriate. It has become joyfully and painfully clear that this cohort is very eager to know what we have written about them, and they will have no hesitation in pointing out errors of omission and commission. While we cannot do each of them the justice they deserve, we are proud of what we have to contribute and believe that it opens an important period of sociology to other interpretations. We believe that through contemporary understandings of social theory, the sociology of science, and oral history and documentary analysis our studies will contribute to a better understanding of a crucial period of sociological development and that we have addressed issues of the development of educational institutions and theoretical diffusion. We have attempted to situate the writings of these scholars in their period and to draw linkages to other writings, both contemporaneous and previous. No scholar works in isolation. Further, we have attempted to address linkages and distinctions between Chicago and other locales. The issues raised in Shula Reinharz's chapter on diffusion deserve to be expanded by others who will examine schools not as isolated entities but as nodes of intellectual networks. The effects of zeitgeist on scholarship, explored in Fine and Ducharme's chapter, also deserve to be treated in a more detailed and systematic way in additional research reports. Surely cohort effects exist, but to what degree do they derive from forces from within the academic world and to what extent do they originate outside ivory towers? Colomy and Brown, by questioning the intellectual presuppositions of Chicago sociology, demand a similar treatment of all sociological training. Questions flow from answers, not merely the reverse.

Whether we can justly speak of this postwar period as representing a *school* of sociological inquiry at this place—a "second Chicago school"—we share an opinion that this time in this location was important for the development of a postwar American sociology. Along with Harvard and Columbia, Chicago represented the zenith of midcentury sociology. As at Columbia and Harvard, the department changed markedly over the decades, and change is vital to continued growth. Change does not erase the department's centrality. Each chapter attempts to deal with the significance of this time and place, and what it meant for sociology, providing an admittedly broken and distorted mirror of the remembered "reality" that our mentors, friends, and colleagues experienced.

To borrow from Harvard-trained, Columbia-affiliated Robert Merton, we stand on the shoulders of giants.

NOTES

This volume was completed while I was a Fellow at the Center for Advanced Study in the Behavioral Sciences. I am grateful for financial support provided by National Science Foundation #SBR-9022192.

1. This view seems not to have been shared by the administration of the University of Chicago (see Abbott and Gaziano, this volume).

2. We do not explicitly discuss the connections between the Department of Sociology and other units on campus, as, for example, the Committee on Human Development, which produced several graduates who later became prominent so-

16   Gary Alan Fine

ciologists, including Julius Roth (see Fine and Ducharme's chapter), Lee Rain-water, and Gerald Handel.

3. Charles Nelson writes (letter to Gary Fine, May 22, 1990): "the decline [at Chicago] was on the academic side which kept repeating the concepts and replicating the studies of the earlier leaders but failed to catch their spirit of inquiry. . . . I was told by Hughes when I accepted a half-time appointment with the Industrial Relations Center that 'it was the kiss of death' and that proved to be true from the publishing point of view but 'it was the kiss of life' from the inquiry point of view." In our chapter Lori Ducharme and I note that many of the most prominent scholars of the generation were involved in applied research in the years immediately preceding and following their degrees.

4. Similar comments were made by Fred Davis, Donald Levine, Bevode McCall, and Anselm Strauss.

5. After Hughes departed in the early 1960s, it was left to Morris Janowitz to serve as the connection with the earlier Chicago traditions, particularly those associated with the examination of urban life, as distinct from the symbolic interactionist focus (Andrew Abbott, personal communication, 1994).

6. Fred Davis (transcribed tape communication, 1990) explicitly contrasts the Blumerian tradition at Chicago with the sociology taught at Columbia, Wisconsin, and Washington. Davis acknowledges that, although there were exemplars of positivism at Chicago, they played a less central role.

7. This does not suggest, of course, that this was the only connection. Leo Goodman and Harrison White were both connected with Princeton, before moving to Chicago (Andrew Abbott, personal communication, 1994).

REFERENCES

Crane, Diana. 1972. *Invisible Colleges.* Chicago: University of Chicago Press.
Davis, Fred. 1979. *Yearning for Yesterday.* New York: The Free Press.
Gusfield, Joseph. 1990. "My Life and Soft Times." Pp. 104–29 in Bennett M. Berger, ed., *Authors of Their Own Lives.* Berkeley: University of California Press.
Halbwachs, Maurice. 1992. *On Collective Memory.* Chicago: University of Chicago Press.
Harvey, Lee. 1987. *Myths of the Chicago School of Sociology.* Aldershot: Avebury.
Maines, David, Michael Katovich, and Noreen Sugrue. 1983. "G. H. Mead's Theory of the Past." *American Sociological Review* 48: 161–73.
Platt, Jennifer. 1993. "What Is a School?" Paper presented to Cheiron Conference, Durham, New Hampshire.

CHAPTER ONE

ELABORATION, REVISION, POLEMIC, AND

PROGRESS IN THE SECOND CHICAGO SCHOOL

Paul Colomy and J. David Brown

This chapter examines a school of thought with powerful ties to sociology as taught and practiced at the University of Chicago in the postwar period. That school of thought is interactionism, and our referent for the second Chicago school is the theorizing and research conducted under the aegis of the most prominent wing of the interactionist tradition during the postwar years.[1] We readily concede that using interactionism and the second Chicago school interchangeably reflects more a disciplinary collective representation than accurate intellectual history: several interactionists have no affiliation with Chicago while many members of Chicago's sociology department work in social scientific traditions hostile to interactionism. But it would be equally misleading to suggest that the connection between Chicago and the interactionist tradition is pure fabrication. To the contrary, several of interactionism's most revered figures were trained at or closely identified in other ways with the University of Chicago. Our concern is to elucidate the scholarly infrastructure beneath the symbolism.

The discussion begins with some general considerations about the structure and dynamics of social scientific traditions. An examination of the second Chicago school's generalized discourse follows, with particular attention given to the work of Herbert Blumer and the methodological contributions of Everett Hughes. We also review two research programs—work and occupations and the interactionist approach to role dynamics. A concluding section speculates about the challenges confronting contemporary proponents of Chicago sociology.

THE STRUCTURE AND DYNAMICS OF
SOCIAL SCIENTIFIC TRADITIONS

Employing a postpositivist perspective, we treat the second Chicago school as a tradition rather than as a cohort or specific theory.[2] Traditions make several inter-related intellectual commitments that range from the abstract, general, and metaphysical, on the one hand, to the concrete, empirical, and factual, on the other (Alexander 1982). Additional elements of social scientific discourse, including ideologies, models, concepts, laws, propositions, methodological assumptions, and observational statements, fall between these endpoints.

An exhaustive treatment of a single tradition would require a detailed and tedious analysis of work carried out at each of these levels. It is useful therefore to introduce a simplifying distinction between two genres. Generalized discourse refers to debates about presuppositions, the methodological underpinnings of social scientific practice, general models purporting to describe and explain social processes and systems, and ideological commitments, explicit or otherwise. Within the context of research programs, by contrast, these generalized issues are assumed to be relatively unproblematic. What propels this mode of scientific inquiry is the attempt to explain or interpret specific empirical structures and processes.

Both generalized discourse and research programs are problem-solving activities, but the problems addressed by the two genres differ in dramatic ways. Research programs are organized around relatively concrete problems with readily specifiable empirical referents, while generalized discourse is preoccupied with relatively abstract issues—e.g., the problems of order and action—whose empirical referents are not always immediately apparent. In formulating and attempting to solve general problems, generalized discourse supplies its home tradition with a framework of relevance and plausibility (Parsons 1937). That framework identifies fundamental features and dynamics of the social world, characterizes the nature of human action, highlights crucial social processes, and proposes methods or procedures of analysis. It is in this discursively constituted context that research programs identify and endeavor to resolve particular empirical problems.

Conflict and competition between and within traditions fuel the development of sociological knowledge. Competition is structured around debates over the relative merits of contesting research programs and general theories. At the level of research programs, competition is organized around rival attempts to explain or interpret empirical structures and processes regarded as significant by the discipline. A program (and its parent tradition) is accorded greater scientific stature when it devises explanations and interpretations deemed superior relative to comparable work produced by other schools. Competition in generalized discourse revolves around producing better solutions to more significant general problems.[3]

The primary reference points for measuring progress in sociological knowledge are established by the relations between traditions and by signposts internal to a given tradition itself. Implicitly or explicitly every scientific statement claims to be more incisive or compelling on some point(s) than rival formulations associated with contending schools or previous work in the same tradition, and is partially assessed by comparison to these reference points. Instead of speaking about theoretical or empirical progress per se, one must speak of relative discursive and programmatic success vis-à-vis one's own tradition or competing ones.

Advances in discourse or research programs can be discussed in terms of several ideal typical patterns. Relative to established work in a social scientist's home school or in a rival one, an *elaborative* statement is more comprehensive, more precise, more rigorous, or possesses more empirical support or fertility. *Proliferation* involves applying an existing framework to previously unexamined discursive or substantive problems, frequently establishing an intellectual beachhead in a new area and enlarging a framework's range of applicability.[4] Whereas elaborative work and proliferative work proceed from the presumption that the original tradition is internally consistent and relatively complete and is directed principally at refining and expanding its scope or demonstrating its advantages over competing schools, *revisionist* work is more attuned to the vulnerabilities of the established paradigm and in the guise of loyal specification makes an often implicit effort to address these strains and to suggest formulations that can resolve them. *Reconstruction* introduces substantial shifts in the core assumptions of a tradition's discourse or its affiliated research programs without, however, abandoning allegiance to the overarching tradition. Reconstruction differs from elaboration, proliferation, and revision in that differences with the founder(s) of the tradition are clearly acknowledged and openings to other traditions are explicitly made.[5]

There is considerable consensus among a tradition's adherents, but this does not prevent serious disputes from arising. Indeed most schools contain two or more tradition segments that while affiliated with the same encompassing framework and pledging scientific fealty to the same classic progenitor(s) nevertheless make disparate commitments on one or more dimensions of sociological thought. Personal considerations undoubtedly play an important role and the availability of resources such as stable employment, students, funding, and publishing outlets exert a powerful conditioning effect, but the fault lines along which tradition segments appear and the intellectual grounds used to support them are most readily understood as fundamental disagreements about the school's generalized discourse and research programs. Virtually every enduring tradition generates competing segments, and the longer a school persists the more segments it creates.

This framework is used to highlight core contributions of the second Chicago school. In the postwar period, interactionists elaborated and revised work conducted by proponents of the first Chicago school. The second Chicago school was also influenced by significant alterations in the disciplinary field and the larger society. The ascendance of rival traditions, particularly functionalism and positivism, provided interactionists with an incentive and a constraint to frame their theorizing and research as a critical and superior alternative. Our thesis, then, is that the generalized discourse and research programs of the second Chicago school represent an effort to elaborate and revise the intellectual legacy of the tradition's founding generation as well as an attempt to demonstrate the conceptual and empirical merits of their approach vis-a-vis competing formulations.

HERBERT BLUMER ON THE PROBLEM OF ACTION AND NATURALISTIC INQUIRY

Herbert Blumer was an inspiring teacher, engaging writer, talented administrator, charismatic personality, and forceful intellectual. Blumer's scholarly work features pattern-setting statements in diverse substantive areas, but his most enduring contribution resides in elaborating interactionism's fundamental assumptions (Becker 1988).[6] In this vein we agree with Collins's (1988, p. 267) characteristically bold proclamation that "Herbert Blumer is the central figure in creating a symbolic interactionist position within sociology." Blumer portrayed his generalized discourse as a faithful exposition of Mead's perspective[7] and a distillation of core ideas advanced by other prominent first generation Chicagoans. This elaborative stance, and particularly the classic status it imparted to Mead's thought, introduced a fateful dynamic to subsequent interactionist discourse. No less consequential was the polemical posture Blumer adopted toward what in the immediate postwar years was regarded as mainstream theory and methodology.

Blumer insisted that social action is sociology's most significant general problem. Social action constitutes social science's "primary subject matter" (Blumer 1969, p. 55) because "[h]uman groups or society *exist in action*" and "action must be the starting point (and the point of return) for any scheme that purports to treat and analyze human society empirically" (ibid., p. 6; emphasis in original). Therefore, to be understood, "a society must be seen and grasped in terms of the action that comprises it" (ibid., p. 71). Blumer's generalized discourse is chiefly concerned with the nature of social action, the environment in which action unfolds, and the character of acting units.

Social action is mediated by an interpretive process. Consequently, interactionism's foundational premise is that human beings act toward things, whether physical entities, other people, social institutions, or cultural ideals, on the basis of the meanings those objects have for them (ibid., p. 2). Meanings do not inhere in the thing itself, neither are they merely an expression of psychological elements, nor do they represent a simple application of culturally standardized symbol systems. Meanings are social creations "formed in and through the defining activities of people as they interact" (ibid., p. 5), and they operate and are modified through an interpretive process, "a formative process in which meanings are used and revised as instruments for the guidance of action" (ibid., p. 5).

Human behavior has an indeterminant and contingent quality: actors construct their acts in terms of what they take into account. Lines of action may be initiated or terminated, abandoned or postponed, and if begun they may be transformed (ibid., p. 64–65). In this way, social action is "built up step by step through a process of self-indication" (ibid., p. 81).

The social act, or what Blumer variously refers to as joint action, the interlinkage of action, and collective action, is sociology's fundamental unit of analysis, and its examination "lays bare the generic nature of society" (ibid., p. 70). Ranging from social acts in dyads to transactions between corporations and nation-states, joint action involves participants fitting together their distinct lines of behavior. Aligning discrete behaviors in this fashion is dependent on interpretive processes wherein participants identify the encompassing social act in which they are about to engage and interpret one another's conduct in light of that frame. Collective action is built up over time, has a career, and is subject to unforeseen contingencies. When a recurring social act assumes a patterned, regularized, and orderly character this is due not to internalized norms or the complementarity of expectations attached to social roles but to a common definition of the joint act. Since "uncertainty, contingency, and transformation are part and parcel of the process of joint action," the career of joint acts is open to alteration at any time (ibid., p. 72). Because interpretive processes inform both stable, recurrent patterns of joint action as well as innovative forms of collective action and since the analysis of these processes are a central concern of interactionism, this perspective can explain both stability and change without shifting conceptual gears.

Human action transpires within environments or social worlds constituted by objects that the given human beings recognize and know. Formed through the processes of definition and interpretation, objects are anything that can be indicated, pointed to, referred to, and designated. People live not in an environment of stimuli or self-constituted entities but in a world of meaningful objects. The nature of an object consists of the meaning it has for the person(s) for whom it is an object, this meaning establishing the way the individual sees the object, the way he or she is organized to act toward it, and the way he or she is prepared to talk about it. Common objects—those having the same meaning for a given group and seen in the same way by its members—arise from a process of mutual indication. However, objects have a fixed status only insofar as their meaning is sustained through the definitions people make of them. Different groups fashion different worlds and these worlds are transformed as the objects that comprise them change in meaning. Accordingly, "human group life is a process in which objects are being created, affirmed, transformed, and cast aside" (ibid., p. 11).

Given this conception of the social environment, it is hardly surprising that Blumer criticizes those who treat human action as an expression of a self-contained social system propelled by its own dynamics. Social organization is nothing more than "an interlinkage of action" (ibid., p. 59) and should be "explained in terms of the process of interpretation engaged in by the acting participants as they handle the situations at their respective positions in the organization" (ibid., p. 58). Consequently, social roles, status positions, class relations, bureaucratic organizations, and other structural elements are significant "only as they enter into the process of interpretation and definition out of which joint actions are formed" (ibid., p. 75).[8]

Human beings have a self and, because they do, social action assumes a reflexive character. Not a structure but a process, the self enables people to communicate with themselves, to be an object of their own actions; people can act toward themselves as they might act toward others (ibid., p. 79). The process of self-indication imbues human action with considerable autonomy. Self-interaction "places the person over against his world instead of merely in it, requires him to meet and handle his world through a defining process instead of merely responding to it, and forces him to construct his action instead of merely releasing it" (ibid., p.

63–64). Human beings stand over against the objects that constitute their world "in both a logical and psychological sense," and this stance frees actors from a coercive response to those objects (ibid., p. 69). By virtue of indicating things to him- or herself, the individual is able to act back against those things, accepting them, rejecting them, or transforming them in accordance with how they are defined or interpreted.

Blumer's presentation of interactionism's premises and root imagery is more than a skillful, if controversial, elaboration of the views of Mead and other earlier Chicagoans. His discussion is also a powerful response to significant changes on sociology's disciplinary field during the postwar period. In reaction to the eclipse of the Chicago school by the ascendant functionalist project, Blumer went on the offensive, becoming "the spokesman for a small minority of dissidents" (Shibutani 1988, p. 25) and propounding a position that "is a scarcely concealed polemic against Parsons" (Alexander 1987, p. 216). Functionalism was not, of course, the only object of Blumer's incisive criticism, but as the era's leading school and interactionism's chief intellectual rival it was widely regarded as a primary target.[9]

Blumer's critique proceeds by highlighting deficiencies in functionalism's underlying theoretical logic and identifying conceptual anomalies that afflict both its generalized discourse and research programs. His indictment included several specific charges. First, though human society consists of individuals and groups interacting with one another and within their respective environments and therefore must be conceptualized first and foremost in terms of social action, functionalism devotes more attention to devising reified concepts, such as social system and culture, whose connection to human action is at best ambiguous. Attributing agentic qualities to these constructs compounds the error by implying that systems, subsystems, and formal organizations, rather than individuals and concrete collectivities, are the central acting units. Second, when functionalists do examine action they ignore the interpretive dimension of human conduct, explaining behavior by reference to internal or external factors that play upon the individual or group rather than in terms of the meanings people ascribe to objects. Third, functionalists presume that individual behavior and social interaction are mere forums through which social and psychological determinants operate and thereby neglect action's contingent, formative, and emergent properties as well as the fact that individual and joint acts have careers that are always subject to interruption, alteration, and abandonment and whose constructed character cannot be explained away by recourse to initiating factors. Fourth, functionalism portrays people as merely responding organisms, submitting compliantly to cultural or systemic directives and socialized need-dispositions rather than as creative, independent, acting organisms endowed with the capacity for self-indication and the ability to stand over, against, and apart from their environment. Fifth, Blumer maintained that the problem of order (i.e., the patterned, nonrandom character of social life), *the* general problem for functionalists, presupposes a persuasive answer to the conceptually prior problem of action. He added that functionalists, with their emphasis on values, norms, and system requisites and their inattentiveness to the interpretive process, had not answered adequately the issue of action and, given their current intellectual commitments, could not provide an adequate answer. Blumer charged that functionalists frequently conflate the general problem of order with the empirical issue of stability, a conflation that makes it difficult to explain change without introducing such suspect notions as social strain or an immanent systemic drive toward adaptive upgrading. By contrast, interactionism explains change with the same notions used to account for enduring forms of action. Finally, functionalism's conflation of order with stability encourages a preoccupation with consensual or cooperative forms of action whereas interactionism's more ecumenical stance spawns investigations of every form of human conduct known to social science. Issued at the height of functionalism's influence, Blumer's criticisms struck at the very core of that tradition's scientific authority (Bourdieu 1991) and by contending that the Chicago alternative provided a better solution to sociology's most significant problem, relegitimated interactionism's claim to provide a more useful discursive foundation for sociological theorizing and research.

In conjunction with the effort to resolve the problem of action, and to demonstrate the debilities of solutions proposed by rival approaches, another crucial element in Blumer's generalized discourse is an attempt to articulate a distinctive interactionist methodological orientation. He presents interactionism's methodological position as a logical extension of its foundational premises about the nature of social action, a rigorous and authentically scientific approach to the study of the empirical social world, and a superior alternative to conventional procedures for collecting and analyzing sociological data.

In Blumer's view there are direct and incontrovertible links between interactionism's approach to social action and its strategy for investigating social life. Because human group life and society exist in action, Blumer

(1969, p. 55) reasons, sociological concepts can be meaningful only if they are "seen and cast ultimately in terms of social action." People act on the basis of the meanings they ascribe to objects in their world, and if social scientists wish to understand actors' behavior, they are obliged to get inside people's worlds of meaning and to see those objects as the individuals under investigation see them. To capture the insider's perspective requires taking both the role of specific individuals and the group's generalized other, accurately describing how actors see the objects that comprise their world, subjecting those descriptions to the probing reflection of informed participants, and subjecting the investigator's preconceptions to relentless critical test against a social reality that can talk back. Failure or refusal to heed these directives, Blumer warns, results in substituting the scholar's conception of the participants' social world for the individual's and group's standpoint, with disastrous results for the study's validity. And if one assumes that group life consists of a process in which action is built up step by step as individuals make indications to one another and draw inferences about the other's conduct to make adjustments in their own behavior, the corresponding methodological stricture is to identify how the process of "designation and interpretation is sustaining, undercutting, redirecting, and transforming the ways in which the participants are fitting together their lines of action" (Blumer ibid., p. 53). Since formal organizations, institutions, the division of labor and the like represent complex interlinkages of action, it is essential to study how members "define, interpret, and meet the situations at their respective points" (ibid.,p. 58) in the larger structure while also giving attention to the historical connection between past and current interpretations through which participants "form and maintain their organized relations" (ibid., p. 60).

Blumer portrays interactionism as a perspective in empirical social science designed to produce "verifiable knowledge of human group life and human conduct" (ibid., p. 21). In contrast to the constricted and erroneous conception of science that equates methodology with sophisticated quantitative procedures, Blumer proposes an inclusive methodological strategy which demands that every phase of the scientific act—initial premises, formulating problems for study, identifying data pertinent to the problem and the most viable means of securing them, drawing connections between the data, interpreting the findings in terms of an analytic framework, and, in each of these steps, carefully scrutinizing the concepts employed in the investigation (ibid., pp. 24–28)—be "subject to the test of the empirical world . . . and validated through such a test" (ibid., p. 27).

Decrying most social scientists' unfamiliarity with their subject matter and contending that no theory, however ingenious, and no scientific protocol, however meticulous, can substitute for direct examination of ongoing group life, Blumer outlines a naturalistic alternative that involves "lifting the veils that obscure or hide what's going on" (ibid., p. 39) in order to "get close to the empirical social world and dig deeply into it" (ibid., pp. 39–40).

During exploration, the first step in naturalistic inquiry, the scholar produces a wealth of descriptive information about the social world or process under examination. At this juncture preconceptions are critically assessed by the researcher asking seemingly ludicrous questions, recording observations inconsistent with the investigator's working assumptions, and noting phenomena not immediately relevant to the research problem (ibid., pp. 40–42).

The data unearthed by exploration are analyzed in the inspective phase of naturalistic inquiry. In contrast to the customary means of assessing relationships between analytic components (e.g., hypothesis testing, adherence to a conventional scientific protocol, operational procedures, and replication studies), inspection involves posing the problem in theoretical form, identifying generic relations, specifying the connotative referents of the concepts, and presenting theoretical propositions (ibid., p. 43). Subjecting analytical elements to detailed examination by intensive, imaginative, and flexible scrutiny of both the empirical instances covered by the general category and those instances designated by the postulated relations between analytic elements, inspection produces meaningful and useful concepts and a richly nuanced understanding of the inter-relations between concepts (ibid., pp. 42–46).

For Blumer, naturalistic inquiry represents not only the best method for generating verifiable social scientific knowledge; it is also essential for improving social theory. Though concepts occupy a crucial position in social theory, most sociological concepts, Blumer avers, are vague and ambiguous. Consequently, sociological theory is enervated by several deficiencies, e.g., it is divorced from the empirical world and empirical research, and it benefits little from empirical observation and studies. Naturalistic inquiry can correct these deficiencies provided that an important distinction is accepted. Blumer recommends that definitive concepts, which clearly define a term by identifying the attributes or fixed traits common to a class of objects (ibid., pp. 147–48), must be separated from sensitizing concepts, which do not specify common attributes but provide "a general sense of reference and guidance in approaching empirical instances," "suggest directions along which to look," and "rest on a general sense of what is relevant" (ibid., p. 148). Sociological concepts are necessarily sensitizing, and naturalistic research is designed to test, refine, and improve those concepts, and thereby redirect and improve much sociological theory through careful examination of the empirical instances they are presumed to cover.

Just as Blumer's statement on the problem of social action represents, in part, a critical reaction to functionalism's increasing prominence, so his naturalistic methodology represents a riposte to the ascendance of the conventional, quasi-natural scientific approach to methodology,[10] and consequently must be situated in disciplinary and departmental context to be fully appreciated.[11] Though some first-generation Chicagoans (e.g., Anderson 1923; Cressey 1932; Hayner 1936; Thrasher 1927; Young 1932; Zorbaugh 1929) relied to a degree on firsthand observation and sought in part to unveil the subjective dimension of action whose sociological significance Thomas and later Park had underscored, and while the informal interviews and observations reported in early Chicago monographs can be construed as pioneering techniques that subsequently became elements of naturalistic field methods (Adler and Adler 1987; Bulmer 1984), it is a mistake to equate this school's methodological approach with contemporary field research (Platt 1983). The studies conducted by Chicagoans in the 1920s and early 1930s employed a variety of research methods and resources—spot maps, census data, rudimentary statistics, newspaper files, police, court, and social agency records, personal documents (including diaries, life histories, and letters, which were frequently elicited by the investigator who asked those under study to put their recollections, thoughts, and feelings on paper), informal interviews with both subjects and those presumed to possess expert knowledge about a particular group or social context, and observations, participant and otherwise (e.g., Bulmer 1984; Hammersley 1989).[12] Further, while unequivocally committed to empirical research, early Chicagoans, like other American sociologists of their generation, did not articulate a systematic methodology (Adler and Adler op. cit.; Bulmer op. cit.).[13]

Beginning in the late 1920s and continuing through the next several decades a discipline-wide movement toward quantitative techniques and statistical reasoning blossomed, a movement buttressed epistemologically by the emergence of logical positivism, operationism, and behaviorism. Attracting several prominent adherents (Stuart Chapin, Luther Bernard,

Read Bain, and George Lundberg) (Hammersley 1989, p. 98), this movement inaugurated a shift towards survey research, quantification, positivism, and methodological self-consciousness that challenged the case-study
method advocated by some Chicagoans, a method the more vitriolic adherents of rigorous, quantitative social science dismissed none too gently.[14]

Stung by the charge that qualitative studies were scientifically suspect, Blumer set out to show that interactionism's supposedly soft methodology was in fact hard and demanding while the purportedly exacting
regimen of hard social science was in practice soft and sloppy. Responding
to the disciplinary ascendance of a positivist philosophy of science and
quantification, Blumer and other interwar and postwar faculty members
at Chicago (Hughes, Warner, Strauss, and Riesman) and their students
(e.g., Becker, Geer, Junker, Miller, Schwartz, Vidich) recast the methodological rationale and practice of the case study and life history. In fact,
the discursive foundation of qualitative methodology and the more concrete strictures that guide its practice reflect in large measure the efforts of
second-generation Chicagoans. This reconstructed version of qualitative
research established the canons of contemporary fieldwork and, relative
to both the underdeveloped methodological principles and practices of
the first-generation Chicagoans and the one-sided positions staked out by
the more extreme proponents of positivism and quantification, represented a highly significant advance in social scientific methodology.

For his part, Blumer inveighs against social scientists' uncritical
adoption of the trappings and paraphernalia of the natural sciences and
their fetish for sophisticated quantitative technique. Mimicking the practices of more established disciplines can never satisfy sociology's longing
for scientific respectability because the methods and procedures touted in
this strategy violate a cardinal principle of empirical science, namely, respect for the nature and obdurate character of the empirical world (in this
case the social world of everyday life) under investigation. Moreover, in
comparison to the inclusive model of the scientific act devised by naturalistic inquiry, mainstream methodologists promote a truncated rendition
of methodology, core elements of which lack empirical validity. The latter
can only be secured by going "directly to the empirical social world"
(1969, p. 32), an option discouraged by conventional methodology.

The path to empirically verifiable knowledge of the social world,
Blumer holds, cannot be found in emulating the procedures of the physical
sciences, embracing the newest mathematical and statistical techniques,
elaborating new forms of quantitative analysis, or enlisting still greater

adherence to the established canons of research design. Rather, the road to verifiable knowledge, as charted by the method of naturalistic inquiry, lies in the direct examination of the empirical social world (ibid., p. 34).[15]

EVERETT C. HUGHES ON FIELDWORK AND THE INQUIRING ATTITUDE

Though Blumer assumed leadership in establishing the discursive foundation of interactionist methodology, this report would be incomplete if it failed to discuss the intellectual and pedagogical contributions of Everett Hughes to ethnographic studies.[16] More eclectic than Blumer, Hughes used a wide variety of data in his own research, insisted that his students be literate in statistics (Becker et al. 1968, p. vii), and believed that ultimately every methodological instrument "must be valued by its results" (Hughes 1971, p. 436).[17] Nevertheless, Hughes preferred the direct observation of social phenomena, played a crucial role in elaborating the Chicago fieldwork tradition, and trained several of its most adept practitioners.[18]

Hughes's preference for fieldwork stemmed, first, from his personal connections with anthropology (his closest colleague and friend at Chicago was Robert Redfield, noted anthropologist and son-in-law of Robert Park, after whom Hughes appears to have modeled himself) and his intimate "familiarity with the studies, the problems, and the methods of anthropology in the post-Malinowski era" (Chapoulie 1987, p. 266).[19] Second, with Blumer he held that fieldwork enabled investigators to penetrate and understand social worlds different from their own.[20] Unlike survey research, which presumes a universe of discourse shared by researcher and respondents (a condition difficult to satisfy even in Western literate societies), fieldwork does not have to limit itself to minor variations of behavior within large homogeneous populations. Hughes seems to be arguing that, compared to survey research, fieldwork is better able to give voice to those excluded from consideration. In addition, he maintains that whereas survey research typically accounts for its statistical concentrations and correlations with largely uninformed speculation, fieldwork provides for more grounded explanations of observed patterns and relationships.

In his fieldwork courses Hughes trained students to become effective and versatile observers. Because the circumstances in which field observation is conducted are highly variable Hughes did not prepare a manual of detailed rules. Rather, with some general words of introduction, instruction, encouragement, and relatively little direct supervision, Hughes sent students into the field to observe and record "the sights and sounds" of humanity "on the hoof" (Gans 1968, p. 301). This lack of structure generated some confusion, but according to one of Reinharz's (this volume) informants, students were urged to continue taking "copious field notes and not to worry about what they meant or might mean"; the meaning, they were assured, would emerge after they reviewed their notes. Hughes's careful reading of those notes and his incisive feedback eased novitiates' frustration and consternation. "He read students' and colleagues' field notes and encouraged the fieldworkers by his own example and by letter, insisting that, if one persisted, every episode might become significant. Invariably, Everett found something good in the material in which the fieldworker had been mired. He was the star to pull the wagon of fieldwork through the mud of dailiness" (Riesman 1983, p. 481). He also underscored the intersection of biography and sociology, advising students to use their origins, background and experience, jobs, and communities as bases for ethnographic studies (Becker et al. 1968, pp. vii–viii).[21]

Hughes's treatment of the concrete issues, problems, and dilemmas confronting fieldworkers supplements Blumer's discussion of the epistemological bases of qualitative research. Adopting a Simmelian perspective, Hughes describes the fieldworker's position as an uneasy synthesis of opposites: "the outstanding peculiarity of this method is that the observer, in greater or lesser degree, is caught up in the very web of social interaction which he observes, analyzes, and reports" (Hughes 1971, p. 505). This peculiarity introduces an "unending dialectic" between the role of member (participant) and stranger (observer and reporter). As group member the fieldworker is privy to shared secrets and sentiments. But as reporter and observer, the social scientist is obliged to analyze what has been recorded in an objective way that frequently affronts those under study. This dialectic is never fully resolved and the struggle to maintain a good balance between these standpoints lies at the heart of fieldwork (ibid., p. 503). The fieldworker role is also structured around related oppositions, including insider and outsider, participation and detachment, and involvement and dispassionate analysis. In this vein, Hughes suggests that the fieldworker occupies a position similar in many respects to marginal (wo)men and cultural hybrids.

Hughes draws attention to the explicit or implicit bargain fieldworkers invariably strike with those they observe (ibid., p. 462), noting that the terms of exchange are conditioned by the researchers' status relative to those studied (ibid., p. 511). In addition, the ability to gain entree, establish rapport, and secure reliable information depends largely on the degree to which the interviewer role is institutionalized in a society or group (ibid., pp. 507–15). When the level of institutionalization is low or non-existent, the fieldworker must rely on a social circle's existing repertoire of roles and social conventions to establish a relationship with group members.

Through his teaching and publications Hughes links fieldwork to a distinctive sociological sensibility. That sensibility, which, following Hughes (ibid., p. 460), we will call "the inquiring attitude," has several components. First, he stresses the importance of comparisons, both historical and contemporaneous. The sociological significance of an event or process, Hughes says, could be partially determined by noting its similarities with and differences from events or processes occurring in other times and institutional contexts. Hughes was a master of "comparative free associations," which frequently revolved around what Riesman (1983, p. 480) characterizes as "ironic juxtapositions." Becker et al. (1968, p. 272) recollect that Hughes "taught us to compare parts of our society with one another, to compare one time with another, to see the small differences between closely related phenomena that had great theoretical import."

Second, he insists on a mutually enriching connection between the timely and the timeless, the specific and general, the news and theory. His mastery of what was then called general sociology enabled him to identify the universal significance of particular, seemingly small events. Such observations serve not only to illuminate an existing or emerging middle-range conceptual scheme; when the facts cannot be fitted into extant frameworks they spur revision of an established scheme or the creation of a new one.

Third, Hughes disdained narrow and largely arbitrary academic boundaries,[22] read extensively in sociology, anthropology and history, and was enamored of German novels and those written by French Canadians (Riesman 1983, p. 477). The ability to make poignant comparisons and to intuit the universal in the particular, Hughes apparently believed, depends largely on the breadth of knowledge and experience the fieldworker brings to his or her research. The richly furbished mind is well equipped to provide a comprehensive and incisive analysis of what has been seen and recorded.

Lastly, he calls for a freeing of the sociological imagination. Conceptually, sociologists should use their license to "break the bonds of ordinary thought and moral inhibition so as to conceive a great variety of human situations, even the most outrageous" (Hughes 1971, p. 494). There must also be constant methodological innovation to keep pace with "a world in which changes are happening on a scale and at a rate unknown in history" (ibid., p. 477). Hughes himself was "all for the sociological adventure; it will require travel, the eating of strange food, the speaking of strange languages, the tolerance of queer ideas, and the adventure of finding the means and methods suited to the problem" (ibid., p. 477). He criticizes the increasing professionalization of sociology and the excessive rigidity of career lines largely because, in his view, they pose a threat to the unfettered imagination and are a potential source of theoretical and methodological ethnocentrism.

* * *

Blumer and Hughes championed the interactionist tradition at a time when rival schools prospered. Their success in sustaining this approach is due to several considerations. First, and most important, Blumer's forceful statement on the nature of social action and the distinctive methodology advanced by both men provided a provocative social scientific vision that appealed to several generations of sociologists. Sharply contrasting his view of social science with the purportedly arbitrary strictures of an un-imaginative positivism and propounding a voluntaristic view of action that emphasized individuals' capacity to forge new lines of conduct, Blum-er's interactionism contains a humanistic thrust that is equally apparent in Hughes's emancipatory and humanizing conception of fieldwork, a hu-manism that appealed to those not enamored of a theoretically and meth-odologically narrow scientistic sociology.[23] Whereas the then dominant perspectives and procedures seemingly portrayed human beings as but a shadow of the real thing, Blumer and Hughes recognized that people were complex, flesh-and-blood agents, and devised modes of inquiry that re-spected these qualities. Finally, the unmistakably insurgent stance Blumer assumes toward the discipline and its practices,[24] Hughes's interest in those all too frequently left out of consideration, and the attention both Blumer and Hughes devoted to self powerfully resonated with the diffuse anti-establishment, democratic sensibility and the concern for personal identity that marked the 1960s and early 1970s and proved enormously attractive to those who came of age in that era.

Relative to earlier work in this tradition and competing formulations in rival approaches, Blumer's and Hughes's elaborations of interactionist discourse represent important advances. Through monographs, textbooks, and readers several other scholars, most of whom were strongly influenced by Blumer's and Hughes's teaching and published work, elaborate this perspective's conception of social action along similar lines. Lindesmith and Strauss (1956 [1949]), for example, present an interactionist approach to human language, its embeddedness in social groups, language acquisition, motivation, selective perception, and the life cycle. Shibutani (1961) discusses meaning, the symbolic organization of experience, the communicative process, and the nature of concerted action. For his part, Hewitt (1976) outlines an interactionist position on self, social interaction, deviance, and collective behavior. Rose's (1962a) edited collection complements statements on symbolic interactionism's working assumptions by Rose (1962b) and Blumer (1962) with a host of empirically oriented studies on such topics as identity, occupations, role processes, and deviance. Similarly, Manis and Meltzer (1967, 1972) assemble both classic and contemporary discussions of the tradition's theory and method, its treatment of society, self, and mind, and its research implications. Lindesmith and Strauss's (1969) reader examines symbolic processes, language acquisition, interaction, and deviance, and the Stone and Farberman volume (1970a; also see 1981), which is dedicated to Blumer, features nearly seventy chapters that in addition to a review of the school's basic premises, investigate symbolic transformations, definitions of the situation, social worlds, interaction processes, conceptualizations of the self, empirical tests of the perspective, and treatments of motivation, socialization, and personal development.

The formulation by Blumer and Hughes of a distinctively interactionist methodology has also been elaborated. One line of elaboration is pitched at the same high level of abstraction that characterizes Blumer's methodological approach and proceeds by extending his logic of procedure. For instance, in a broad ranging discussion for which Blumer wrote the foreword, Bruyn (1966) portrays sociology as a third culture standing between the culture of the literary intellectual and scientific culture, and clarifies the foundations and objectives of what he calls the human perspective in the social sciences. The method of analytic induction[25] as formulated and applied by Lindesmith (1947 [1937], 1968), Cressey (1950, 1953), and Becker (1953, 1955) also constitutes both a partial elaboration of Blumer's methodological stance, particularly its treatment of what Blumer eventually called the inspective phase of data analysis and an extension of Hughes's comparative method, as does Williams's (1976) pattern model that envisions description and explanation as an indivisible whole. Widely regarded as one of the best analyses of inductive theory and interactionism's logic of procedure, Glaser and Strauss's (Glaser 1978; Glaser and Strauss 1967; Strauss 1970, 1987; Strauss and Corbin 1990) approach to sampling, data collection and analysis represents, in part, an extension of the Chicago tradition of research, an effort to close the gap between theory and research identified by Blumer, and a means for generating theory consistent in many respects with Hughes's emphasis on "comparative associations." They outline a four-stage, constant comparative method of coding and analysis for creating grounded theory: (1) compare incidents applicable to each category; (2) integrate categories and their properties; (3) delimit the theory; (4) write the theory (Glaser and Strauss 1967, p. 105). Glaser and Strauss recommend using this method in conjunction with theoretical sampling, a process of data collection for generating theory whereby the investigator jointly collects, codes, and analyzes data and determines what data to collect next and where to find them in order to develop a theory as it emerges (ibid., p. 45), with the data collection process controlled by the emerging theory. Relative to Blumer and Hughes, they articulate a more nuanced conception of theory, which includes discovering significant categories and their analytic properties, their conditions and consequences; developing these categories at different levels of conceptualization; hypothesizing relations of varying scope and generality between categories (and their properties); and "above all" integrating the total theoretical framework (ibid., pp. 168–69). Two variants of grounded, middle-range theory are distinguished: substantive and formal. Formal theory is especially important, and is usually assembled from a combination of direct data collection on pertinent comparison groups, reflection on existing ethnographic and other empirical studies, and abstracting more general categories from established substantive theory. The distinction between substantive and formal theory also informs Glaser and Strauss's conception of how sociological knowledge and theory cumulate; they envision "a progressive building up from the facts through substantive to grounded formal theory" (ibid., p. 35).

Blumer's general orientation toward empirical examination of the social world supplied little in the way of detailed instructions for the practicing social scientist (Athens 1984). And though Hughes, by contrast, gave more attention to the specifics of conducting qualitative research, his published work provides little more than an orienting stance toward fieldwork. Accordingly, a second line of elaboration[26] is organized around the concrete problems researchers confront in conducting fieldwork and analyzing qualitative data. Lohman's (1937) early article, for example, advocates participant observation as a method for eliciting meanings and insights, Miller (1952) examines how rapport is established between researcher and subject, Gold (1958) identifies the different roles field workers assume, Becker (1958, 1964a) like Schwartz and Schwartz (1955), addresses problems of inference and proof in participant observation and ethical dilemmas in publishing field research, and Junker (1960), in a book for which Hughes wrote the introduction, describes the immediate situational constraints and opportunities from the individual field worker's perspective. Wax (1971) offers a detailed account of her fieldwork experiences and, finally, attempting both to improve the "low social prestige" accorded qualitative studies and "to provoke those who measure everything and understand nothing," Filstead's (1970, p. vii) collection showcases classic interactionist statements on the directions of sociology, field work roles, data collection and analysis, validity and reliability, ethical problems, and the connections between theory and method, as does McCall and Simmon's (1969) edited volume. Indeed, Adler and Adler (1987, p. 10) maintain that the most important methodological contribution of the second Chicago school "lay in the development and codification of the technique of participant observation." The proof, of course, is in the pudding, and what imbues these discussions of qualitative method with special significance is not only their connection to a particular tradition but also their association with several classic empirical studies, e.g., Becker's *Outsiders* (1963), Becker et al.'s *Boys in White* (1961), and Davis's *Passage Through Crisis* (1963), Goffman's *Asylums* (1961a), and Roth's *Timetables* (1963) (see Fine and Ducharme, this volume).[27]

Elaboration, whether in generalized discourse or research programs, is typically coupled with other ideal-typical patterns of knowledge cumulation, and it is not difficult to discern significant lines of revision alongside the elaborative thrust so prominent in the work just described. For instance, while Blumer presumed that individuals were conscious of the meanings imputed to social objects, Shibutani (1961) draws on the psychoanalytic work of Freud, Horney, and Sullivan to highlight the unconscious sources of meaning and the influence of personality on social action.[28] In addition, he claims that societies are moral orders and that such "external" considerations as social values and norms are internalized and exert a profound influence on human conduct. Lindesmith and Strauss (1956 [1949]) are also concerned with the impact of external constraints and devote considerable attention to how class structure affects conduct, linguistic conventions, perception, and self conceptions. Though in partial agreement with Blumer's emphasis on the contingent and transformative potential of human conduct, Stone and Farberman (1967a, 1967b, 1970b) intuit a point of convergence between Mead's discussion of significant symbols and Durkheim's treatment of collective representations, and suggest that the symbolic environment confronting individuals exerts a constraining influence on social action. The second edition of Manis and Meltzer's (1972) reader explicitly recognizes the contributions of adherents to the Iowa school and other tradition segments in symbolic interactionism that challenge the Blumerian position in important ways.

Elaboration and revision also figure prominently in Goffman's contributions. Like Blumer, Goffman highlights the centrality of interpretive processes and the contingent features of social action. Further, he portrays the pertinent environments of human action as consisting of meaningful objects, and presumes that a degree of autonomy inheres in the capacity for self indication. But Goffman also gives more attention to how hegemonic definitions of the situation constrain action, the ways in which environments pattern conduct, and the institutional and situational conditions that powerfully affect and inform the self.[29]

An important strand of Goffman's work extends the Blumerian principle that social action is mediated by interpretive processes. Goffman's (1959) discussion of the working consensus, for example, describes how participants' interpretive work sustains face-to-face interaction. Similarly, his analysis of frames describes the interpretive schemata actors use for rendering events or strips of activity meaningful (Goffman 1974). A complementary study of embarrassment (1967, pp. 97–112) elucidates how events which undermine the working consensus and prove recalcitrant to tactful repair can result in the breakdown of an encounter. In a more strategic vein, Goffman (e.g., 1972) indicates how individuals deploy fronts, lines, face, and fabrications to manipulate others' definitions of the situation.

At the same time, however, a revisionist thrust underscores the obligatory and collective cast of reigning definitions of the situation. The working consensus, for instance, requires actors to suppress their immediate thoughts and feelings behind statements or nonverbal expressions that assert or imply views to which those present feel obliged to give lip service (Goffman 1959). Further, because sustaining the definition of the situation is usually a collective enterprise, the appropriate unit of analysis is not the solitary actor but a team, which consists of a set of individuals whose intimate cooperation is essential if a given, projected definition of the situation is to be maintained. Team members are constrained to support the party line, conceal team secrets, and refrain from sanctioning derelict teammates frontstage.

A similar mixture of elaboration and revision informs Goffman's treatment of the environments of action. Though presupposing environments comprised of meaningful objects and acknowledging the contingent nature of action, Goffman highlights a panoply of conditions, particularly situational ones, that produce a recognizable orderliness in human conduct. As Hochschild (1979, pp. 555–56) notes, Goffman scrutinizes how, moment to moment, the individual actively negotiates a course of action that, ironically, sustains social convention. Especially germane in this context is Goffman's characterization of the interaction order as an analytically distinguishable domain that is profitably examined in its own right.

The social situation is the basic working unit in the interaction order. Social interaction, Goffman (1983, p. 2) maintains, occurs in environments where two or more individuals "are physically in one another's response presence." Action's situated quality imbues it with distinctive characteristics and effects, e.g., it is markedly circumscribed in time and space, and its communicable, expressive features are preeminently promissory and evidential. Moreover, human behavior is conditioned by personal and territorial vulnerabilities that give rise to techniques of social management designed to cope with them or, as Goffman would have it, ritual vulnerabilities engender a complementary body of ritual resources.

A diverse constellation of social and psychological conditions contributes to the patterned nature of the interaction order: an ostensibly pan-human need for face-to-face interaction rooted in the universal preconditions of social life, the psychological untenability of participating in encounters that regularly break down, and, more immediately, in what Goffman variously refers to as trans-situational regulations and expectations, information about situational proprieties in conjunction with individual and categoric frameworks for classifying coparticipants, the cognitive relations between actors (what each can effectively assume the other knows), and a large storehouse of shared understandings and self-imposed restraints. But if situated conduct is orderly, it is also highly contingent. The working consensus established in any encounter requires the participants' sustained collaboration and is easily violated, intentionally or inadvertently.

The interaction order's distinctive effects can be examined in terms of the forms and processes particular to it. In this regard Goffman identifies several interactional entities, ranging in size from "human ambulatory units" to celebrative social occasions. The interaction order is also associated with a distinctive, though vast and variable, constellation of interactional roles and conventions. Thus, one commentator claims that a moral commitment to the working consensus for its own sake is one of the ground rules of interaction (Rawls 1987, 1988). Moreover, interactional obligations—duties interactants owe to the interaction order per se—are tied to the interaction order irrespective of the institutional status or role an individual may hold.

Goffman proposes a loose coupling approach to describe the relation between the interaction order and other social orders. The essential elements of this position are, first, that though the interaction order impinges on encompassing patterns of social organization (e.g., work done in large organizations is partially dependent on face-to-face interaction and so is vulnerable to face-to-face effects), social structure cannot be reduced to, nor should it be translated into, the forms and processes particular to the interaction order. On the other hand, though material and cultural conditions constrain the interaction order, the latter is by no means a mere reflection of macroenvironments. In this context, Goffman (1983, p. 11) maintains that "what one finds, in modern societies, at least, is a non-exclusive linkage—a loose coupling—between interactional practices and social structures . . . , a set of transformation rules, or a membrane selecting how various externally relevant social distinctions will be managed within this interaction."

The analytic autonomy Goffman imparts to the interaction order should not be construed as a rampant situationalism. In contrast to Blumer, Goffman argues that the sources for the orderliness observable in particular settings are not, in most circumstances, generated in them at the moment. These patterns partly reflect the prior experience of participants and the cultural assumptions actors bring with them to the encounter. Because it is penetrated by macrosociological conditions and traditions that reach across time and space, the interaction order is not entirely a local production.

Finally, Goffman modifies and extends Blumer's discussion of the self. A revisionist impulse is evident, for example, in his contention that not only is the individual's freedom limited by external constraints but that the self is partly constituted by institutional and situational exigen-

cies. The autonomy attendant on an individual's capacity for self indication is conditioned by an obdurate social world that limits what he or she
can do and be. In an important sense the self is "not a property of the
person to whom it is attributed" but rather is "something that resides in
the arrangements prevailing in a social system for its members" (Goffman
1961a, p. 168). For Goffman the self is an object that others, including
institutions, organizations, teams, roles, routines, and alters, can fashion
and act upon, often with powerful effects. Whether discussing the interactional rituals (Goffman 1967) that support and reaffirm a sacred self or
examining the mortification and reconstitution of identity inmates experience in total institutions (Goffman 1961a), the largely coercive dynamics
that propel mental patients' moral career (ibid., pp. 125–69), and the vulnerabilities of those with stigmatized or spoiled identities (1963), Goffman
vividly portrays how a virtual self can be generated or recast by conventions and procedures over which the actor exercises little control.

Though rarely challenging dominant institutional arrangements in a
direct way, Goffman's actor, like Blumer's, remains capable of asserting an
autonomous self and engaging in various, albeit frequently symbolic,
forms of resistance. Accordingly, Goffman supplements his analysis of the
organizational, situational, and ritual determinants of self with an examination of secondary adjustments (1961a), the underlife of public institutions, and role distance (1961b). The latter concepts assume that the individual is "a stance-taking entity, a something that takes up a position
somewhere between identification with an organization and opposition to
it," and that the self can emerge only against something (Goffman 1961a,
p. 320). In this regard, Fine and Ducharme (this volume) highlight the
thematic dialectic of institutional domination and individual (and group)
resistance, of organizational control and individual agency, evident in
Goffman's work (and in other Chicago ethnographies published in the
early 1960s).

Other second-generation Chicagoans revised Blumer's methodological position. Thus, in contrast to Blumer's naturalistic inquiry, analytic
induction devises definitive concepts, posits deterministic relationships,
and postulates universal laws. For his part, Lofland (especially 1970) is
explicitly critical of interactionism's preoccupation with sensitizing rhetoric and generalized imagery, particularly pronounced, he avers, in Blumer's
work, and the conceptual poverty it engenders. Glaser and Strauss (1967)
temper the polemic Blumer directed against quantification, asserting that
there is no fundamental opposition between the purposes of qualitative

and quantitative methods and data. They propose a cooperative division
of labor, with quantitative approaches, which "come later in the scientific
enterprise" (ibid., p. 103), providing partial tests of theories produced with
the constant comparative method. Finally, they incorporate elements of
the Columbia survey research tradition, particularly Lazarsfeld's treatment of concepts and their empirical indicators, the interchangeability of
indices, and elaboration analysis, to demonstrate how quantitative analysis can be redeployed to generate theory.

* * *

An elaboration and revision of first-generation Chicagoans' work and a
critical rejoinder to rival, ascendant traditions, postwar interactionist discourse engendered critical assessments that in turn spurred further elaboration and revision. The criticisms assumed a variety of forms. The divergence thesis, for example, questions Blumer's disciplinary position as *the*
authoritative interpreter of Mead, usually combining an effort to de-
Blumerize Mead with an ostensibly more accurate rendition of Mead's
contributions. In this fashion rival interpretations attempt to advance a
competing segment or tradition by appropriating the symbolic capital
attached to a disciplinary classic. One of the most vigorous statements of
the divergence thesis contends that Blumer presents Mead's own social
realist position as subjective nominalism and thereby distorts and deletes
core elements of Mead's thought (Lewis 1976, 1977, 1979; Lewis and
Smith 1980, 1983). According to this argument Mead maintained that the
meanings of significant symbols are universal, collective, and objective,
but Blumer, claiming to follow Mead's led, asserts they are individual and
subjective, a product of the interpretations an actor chooses to assign
them. Moreover, Blumer's conception of the "spontaneous actor whose
dispositions to act are not subject to social control" lead him to reject
Mead's theories of the me and the generalized other as "guiding influences
upon human behavior" (Lewis and Smith 1980, p. 176). There is a complementary methodological turn to the divergence thesis, and it contrasts
Mead's understanding of science and the form of scientific inquiry best
suited to the study of human conduct with Blumer's stance on these issues
(e.g., Lewis 1976). Thus, in McPhail and Rexroat's (1979, p. 449) words,
"Naturalistic inquiry neither complements nor extends Mead's methodological perspective." For Mead, the primary aim of scientific study is not
accurate description or progressive refinement of sensitizing concepts but
the formulation and assessment of hypotheses and theories purporting to

explain scientifically (and societally) important problems. This methodological de-Blumerization of Mead undercuts the polemic Blumer waged against conventional research practices, asserting that Mead's position is fully consistent with the procedures (e.g., experimentation, statistical manipulation of systematically garnered data) of mainstream social science, questions the purportedly incontrovertible link Blumer forged between interactionism's foundational premises and naturalistic inquiry, and proposes that the tradition's core tenets are readily assessed and extended by methodological strategies very similar to those Blumer and other interactionists assailed.[30]

Others insist that action is not the only general problem sociologists must address and that the problem of order, namely, accounting for the patterned or nonrandom character of social life, is every bit as significant. Whatever the merits of Blumer's approach to social action, critics charge, his conception of order is enervated by inconsistencies. Alexander (1985) argues that Blumer is caught in an individualist dilemma structured around an irresolvable choice between the randomness of pure contingency and the indeterminacy of residual categories. In a similar vein, others claim that interactionist discourse suffers from an astructural bias allegedly manifest in an inadequate conceptualization of social organization, a failure to come to grips with the "master institutions of market society that profoundly influence people's lives," and a neglect of the broader structuring principles of class, power, age, and gender around which social systems are organized (Reynolds 1993, p. 153; also see Reynolds and Reynolds 1973).

Critics also detect an objectionable absence of ideological vigor in some of interactionism's leading formulations. The central charge is that by neglecting social inequality, power differentials, the structural bases of conflict and coercion, and the purportedly pervasive sense of alienation in contemporary societies while simultaneously making bland references to negotiations, working compromises, and a moving pattern of accommodative adjustments, interactionists evince a noxious naiveté about fundamental features of the modern world and an unwarranted and quintessentially American optimism that somehow things will work out okay (e.g., Alexander 1987; Gouldner 1970; Huber 1973a).

These rebukes provoked spirited rejoinders that, in some cases, introduced significant elaborations and revisions of interactionism's generalized discourse. Blumer (1966, 1967, 1973, 1977, 1980, 1983), of course, questioned the merits of every argument that drove a wedge between his own theoretical and methodological position and Mead's views. Though his ripostes were not always persuasive (see, for example, the counter-arguments by Huber 1973b; Lewis and Smith 1983; McPhail and Rexroat 1980), they supported the notion that even if not definitive, Blumer's Mead was, at the very least, plausible and defendable.[31] The criticism that inter-actionism ignores the problem of order, like the charges that it suffers from an astructural bias and is ideologically anemic, prompted important extensions of the school's discourse. Far from being oblivious to the prob-lem of order, Shalin (1986, p. 13) argues, pragmatists and the first- and second-generation Chicagoans have been preoccupied with the paradox of a social reality that is simultaneously patterned and emergent, a para-dox that compelled the perspective's proponents to devise a dialectical stance which recognized the structural properties of social life without glossing over its fluid characteristics and envisioned the individual as both "product and producer of society."[32] A reconsideration of Blumer's and other Chicagoans' discursive and substantive work in light of inter-actionism's alleged astructural bias has lead some students (e.g., Lyman 1984, 1988; Maines 1988, 1989; Maines and Morrione 1990) to contend that Blumer's sociology contains an impressive arsenal of concepts well-suited for the study of such macrosociological issues as social, economic, and political hierarchies, racial stratification and conflict, power and resis-tance, industrialization, and industrial organization. Wood and Wardell (1983) and Shalin (1986) present a somewhat different case, asserting that Blumer's polemic against functionalism and rival macrosociologies pro-pelled him toward a hypervoluntaristic position that is not as evident in the work of Mead, Park, Thomas, and other first-generation Chicagoans, who provide powerful intellectual tools for exploring structural conditions and constraints. These discursive attempts to elaborate an interactionist macrosociology have been supplemented by a burgeoning research pro-gram that, anchored around the concept of negotiated order, analyzes so-cial organization (e.g., Maines 1977, 1979, 1982; Maines and Charlton 1985; Strauss 1978). Finally, Lyman and Vidich (1988) claim that Blumer's ideological stance, largely implicit in his substantive and theoretical con-tributions, is neither complacent nor naive as critics charge but is more accurately characterized as a public philosophy committed to democracy, equity, and freedom, while Shalin (1986) Fisher and Strauss (1978a, 1978b, 1979), and Joas (1987) highlight the pragmatists' and early Chicagoans' advocacy of social reconstruction and progressive change.

Research Programs

Generalized discourse is an indispensable feature of every enduring social scientific tradition. However, a tradition that does not simultaneously devise research programs to complement its generalized discourse cannot long survive. Moreover, although the generalized discourse produced by the second Chicago school is undeniably an important part of the interactionist legacy, the school will be remembered just as much, if not more, for its contributions to several empirical specialty areas.

Typically, research programs depend on assumptions explicated and defended in a tradition's generalized discourse that researchers themselves take more or less for granted. What enables the programs reviewed below to cohere is precisely their shared presuppositions about the nature of social reality, action, and order. In addition, these presuppositions structure the critiques issued by a school's proponents against rival traditions and their associated programs. Consequently, there is a family resemblance not only in the content of a school's research programs but also in the criticisms directed at competing programs, a resemblance emanating from presuppositions at the paradigm's core. For instance, the themes in the second Chicago program on collective behavior and social movements—symbolization, cognitive and affective transformation, emergence, fluidity, and interactive determination—as well as the criticisms directed against rival approaches are informed by interactionism's discursive assumptions about the interpretive process and the preeminence of meaning, the contingent and constructed character of social action, and the reflexive nature of human conduct (Snow and Davis, this volume). Further, broadly similar themes and critiques of contending approaches are apparent in other interactionist programs, including work and occupations, deviance, social problems, role theory, and formal organizations.

Research programs do not only specify a school's generalized discourse to substantive areas. Every social scientific school's discourse contains ambiguities, inconsistencies, and residual categories, and a tradition's most adept practitioners often address and attempt to resolve these discursive deficiencies in their more empirically oriented work.[33] In this vein we argue that the research programs reviewed here simultaneously specify and revise interactionist discourse.

Five additional nuances must be introduced. First, each research program is partially autonomous, and a tradition's programs do not unfold in lockstep fashion. A particular program confronts distinct empirical issues, different competing formulations and disciplinary reactions, exudes variable degrees of appeal to potential adherents, and meets with strikingly different degrees of success.

Second, research programs are influenced by more than the overarching tradition's generalized discourse. A school's later generations regularly find that they must address, whether appreciatively or not, the previous programmatic advances introduced by an earlier cohort in their specialty area. Consequently, the younger generation often adopts an elaborative, revisionist or reconstructive stance toward previous work. Wacker (this volume), for example, indicates that while elaborating the processual perspective of early Chicagoans to ethnic and racial relations, the work of Shibutani, Gusfield, and Gans revises their predecessors' optimistic assumptions about progressive change in ethnic inequality and the race-relations cycle, supplanting them with a more differentiated, inclusive, and critical account of marginality, subcultures, and symbolic and instrumental dimensions of modern ethnic identity.

Third, the unexplicated assumptions of earlier programs that directly inform a subsequent generation's research are sometimes partially inconsistent with the tradition's formal discourse. Thus, Fisher and Strauss (1978a) argue that Thomas's and Park's middle-range work rests on an implicit dialectic of freedom and constraint that is decidedly less evident in Blumer's discourse with its (over)emphasis on the voluntaristic and creative aspects of action.[34] Consequently, second Chicagoan programs influenced by Thomas and Park give more attention to structural conditions and constraints than would be anticipated had these programs relied solely on Blumer's theorizing.

Fourth, a specific research program can also be influenced by developments in a school's other programs. Thus, while Galliher (this volume) notes that the labeling theory program on deviance was premised on interactionist, and largely Blumerian and Hughesian, discourse and methodology, he indicates that many of this program's key notions—e.g., deviant careers and moral entrepreneurs—reflected the proliferation of middle-range concepts from other programs, particularly the study of work and occupations and social movements. Hughes's recommendation that users of illegal drugs and other deviants could be examined in the same fashion as physicians or engineers proved instructive for the scholarly investigation of deviance. Similarly, labeling theorists who took to heart Hughes's dictum that an occupation must be understood from the workers' standpoint demonstrated that new light could be shed on deviance if it too were understood from the actors' perspective.

Finally, research programs vary in their level of generality. Redeploying Glaser and Strauss's distinction between substantive and formal theories, we suggest that more substantive research programs are closely tied to a single specialty area while more formal ones draw on work in two or more specialties.[35] The interactionist program of work and occupations, which we examine next, represents a substantive program, while interactionist role theory constitutes a formal program.

WORK AND OCCUPATIONS

The second Chicago school's program on work and occupations represents both an elaboration of studies undertaken by early Chicago sociologists and a critical response to the functionalist approach to the professions. Both the elaborative thrust and the critical rejoinder to functionalism were informed by interactionism's, particularly Blumer's, generalized discourse about meaning and the nature of social action. At the same time, the extension of this research program did not rigidly adhere to Blumer's general theory, and it gave more attention to how social structure conditions action. Alongside this apparent tension between the second generation's emphasis on social structure and the more polemical features of Blumer's discourse is a significant continuity between first and second Chicago school studies of work and occupations.[36]

The first Chicago school's study of occupations arose from a concern with the dynamics of social change and social control and the interdependence between social organization and the trajectories of individual lives (Janowitz 1966; Kurtz 1984; Rock 1979). According to Kurtz (1984, p. 48), the study of social organization involved three broad categories: "the relationship between individuals and social institutions, systems of social stratification, and the study of occupations." Under the rubric of social organization, one crucial theoretical and empirical challenge for first-generation sociologists involved articulating the processes through which society imposed itself upon individuals in the form of socially systematized schemes of behavior.

The interrelationship among social structure, contingency, and the work world reverberated throughout the first Chicago school's program. Though W. I. Thomas's "definition of the situation" underscored the contingent nature of social action, its usage within the first Chicago school's study of work and occupations was tempered by an understanding that social structure profoundly influenced and circumscribed the meanings individuals attributed to social situations. The definition of the situation was portrayed as an interpretive compromise between the contingent and structural elements of a situation. In Hughes's (1952, p. 426) view these interrelated elements served to articulate "the work drama" as it unfolds in a variety of occupations while simultaneously identifying a general "set of problems and processes applicable to the whole range of cases."

Thomas and Znaniecki's *The Polish Peasant in Europe and America* (1918–1920) was a pattern-setting statement for Chicago sociologists. Research inspired by that path-breaking document identified the formal properties of primary groups, cooperative and voluntary associations, the press, occupational communities, the residential community, and social institutions including the family and education (cf. Janowitz 1966). Though the examination of occupations and formal organizations was closely tied to broader studies of urban institutions and social organization, Hughes and the Human Relations in Industry Group laid much of the intellectual groundwork for the second Chicago school's study of occupations. Beginning with his dissertation on the Chicago Real Estate Board, Hughes's analysis of institutional development was extended into the areas of social roles, careers, professions and occupational types (Kurtz 1984). Hughes and the Human Relations in Industry Group were also instrumental in launching a series of studies that described the structural and interactive processes among members of work groups (Gardner and Whyte 1946; Hughes 1946). Composed of an interdisciplinary team of social scientists from sociology, anthropology, human development, economics, and business administration, the Human Relations in Industry Group examined the relationships between workers, industrial organizations, and management styles (Whyte 1987). Its more well-known research includes studies conducted on the Western Electric and the Relay Assembly Test Room, the Bank Wiring Observation Room, the Restaurant Study, and the Sears, Roebuck and Company. In addition to its social scientific analyses of human relations and organizational behavior, the Human Relations in Industry Group sought to apply its findings to the practical problems confronting employees, management, and industrial organizations in general.

While such scholars as W. Lloyd Warner, Burleigh B. Gardner, and William F. Whyte made significant contributions to the knowledge produced and applied by the "Group," it was the pioneering work and unique sociological imagination of Hughes that provided the succeeding generation of Chicago sociologists with a distinct perspective for studying the work world.[37] As their mentor, Hughes insisted that the study of occupations was both important in itself and a critical medium for understanding society as a whole. In Hughes's view occupations could not be studied in isolation but had to be understood in terms of their social environments. His students investigated how occupations were influenced by such factors as the structure of the work organization, families, living arrangements, health, gender, culture, and historical circumstances (Abbott 1988; Holmstrom 1984).

The second Chicago school's program on work and occupations also represents a critical response to the ascendant functionalist view of professions. Part of the functionalist interest emanated from general theoretical concerns. Thus, Parsons's (1939; also see Parsons 1940) groundbreaking article on the professions sought to demonstrate the limitations of utilitarian thought, particularly its contention that concrete, instrumental motives were the primary sources of human action. Stressing the institutionalized patterns that informed and regulated behavior, Parsons claimed that modern professionals' conduct was shaped not by the norms encouraging self-interest, as in business, but by standards prescribing a collective orientation. Barber (1963; also see Goode 1957; Moore 1970), for instance, characterized professional behavior in terms of four dimensions: a high degree of generalized and systematic knowledge; primary orientation to community interest; a high degree of self-control attained through codes of ethics internalized during professional socialization and sanctions administered by professional voluntary associations; and, finally, a system of symbolic rewards primarily organized around professional achievement.

Hughes and his students played key roles in critiquing functionalism's program and reformulating the interactionist research agenda (Abbott 1988).[38] Critical theorists argued that functionalism was conservatively biased, took professional ideologies on trust, and failed to examine the historical conditions under which occupational groups became professions (Daniels 1971; Elliott 1972; Gouldner 1962).[39] Interactionists added their own charges. Hughes and Becker, for example, challenged the functionalist claim to objectivity. Hughes's (1958) comparison of "professional" and other occupational groups refuted the value assumptions promoted by self-interested professionals and uncritically accepted by functionalist social scientists. Freidson (1971) claimed that the most salient features of professionalism were dominance and autonomy rather than trust and collegiality. Becker (1962) argued that the label "profession" was not a scientific or neutral concept and, consequently, a social scientific approach, like functionalism, that simply incorporated presuppositions regarding the professions' ostensibly distinctive characteristics is necessarily suspect. As an alternative, Becker maintained that the term "profession" was a folk concept with no precise definition, which various groups claimed for themselves under certain conditions and at particular times. Similarly, Bucher and Strauss (1961) contested Goode's (1957) characterization of a profession as a "community within a community" by arguing that occupational groups contained antagonistic segments with often conflicting identities, values, and interests. Contention, competition and differentiation, not homogeneity, are typical and recurrent features of professional groups.

Interactionists portrayed professional training as the fundamental process by which novices abandoned their lay world for the universe of discourse and the identity of the professional (Davis 1968; Hughes 1945, 1958). They rejected the "empty vessel" model (Olesen and Whittaker 1968) proposed by Merton et al. (1957), who argued that training was a vehicle that poured skills, values, norms, and professional identities into its newest members. *Boys in White* (Becker et al. 1961; also see Becker and Geer 1958) drew attention to the contingencies and negotiations associated with medical students' training. These studies emphasized how students subordinated their ideological commitments to medicine, negotiated the enormity of knowledge to be consumed, and reconciled their underdog status through membership in a student culture partly organized around conflict and resistance.

Treating the training organization as problematic, interactionists were wary about taking its goals, values, and culture at face value. As Atkinson (1983, p. 229) noted, they focused on ". . . the hidden curriculum which informs the actual daily practices of teachers and students." Since professional training and socialization experiences were considered crucial in shaping the individual's self conception, the task of exposing the "hidden curriculum"—the innumerable problematic interactions and contingencies facilitating or impeding trainees' acquisition of skills and professional identities—became a critical topic. Olesen and Whittaker's (1968) examination of student nurses, for example, introduced the notion of "lateral role socialization" to refer to enculturation issues that hindered professional socialization. By contrast, Davis's (1968, p. 248) study of doctrinal conversion among nurses suggested that the employment of professional rhetoric provided student nurses with an "interpretive scheme for appraising [their] performances and for communicating their 'meaning' to significant others."

Though embracing interactionism's standard, processual view of social structure (e.g., Shibutani and Kwan 1965; Gusfield to Fine), second-generation students of work and occupations also highlighted, in a more compelling fashion than did Blumer, institutions' powerful constraints on actors' interpretive and agentic capacities. Fine and Ducharme's (this volume) account of select ethnographies emphasizes work organizations' capacity to undermine their respective clienteles' initial definition of situation, self, and setting. Further, these studies suggest that it is largely organizational power and inequities and/or structurally generated uncertainty that precipitate individual and group efforts to redefine the situation and blunt, control, subvert, or challenge professionals' authority.

Partially in response to the rise of conflict approaches to the study of work (and to their charge that the interactionist program's examination of the conditions and constraints on work was premised on an anemic conception of social structure), Chicago sociologists have directed attention to the political-economy of work and professions. Interactionists increasingly recognize that occupations, particularly those aspiring to professional status, have material as well as ideal interests at stake (Gusfield 1967), seek to monopolize the production and transmission of knowledge (Freidson 1970a, 1970b, 1986; Zola 1972, 1975), attempt to attain market power by transforming the scarce resource of knowledge into social and economic rewards (Freidson 1971), and are shaped by powerful institutions, particularly the state (Freidson 1986).

ROLE THEORY

The second Chicago school's program on role dynamics combined an elaborative and revisionist stance toward earlier work with a polemic directed against the structuralist conception of social roles.[40] The tradition's generalized discourse on the meaningful, innovative, and contingent dimensions of social action structured both the elaborative and revisionist thrust and the indictment of rival approaches. However, this program, like the second generation Chicagoans' examination of work and occupations, also challenged certain elements of interactionist discourse while incorporating select concepts from other perspectives. Finally, though the elaboration of a distinctively interactionist conception of roles continues, increasing attention is now being given to the synthesis of structural and interactionist role theories.

Mead's (1934) analysis of role-taking, Cooley's (1902) examination of the social self, Park's (1926, 1927, 1931) observations on the ubiquity of role playing and how roles mediate perception of self and other, Thomas's (1921) and Wirth's (1928) descriptions of recognized immigrant and Jewish types, and Znaniecki's (1940, 1954, 1965) characterization of roles as sets of interdependent relations between persons and their social circles supplied the foundation for an interactionist role theory. Extending this early work, second-generation Chicagoans clarified and altered key concepts and demonstrated their utility for empirical research. Coutu (1951), for example, distinguished role-taking from role-playing and playing at a role. Lindesmith and Strauss (1956 [1949], pp. 386–388) and Turner (1956) differentiated the Meadian characterization of role-taking from the related concepts of role-taking capacity, sympathy, empathetic ability, the psychodramatic analysis of role playing and the then new concept of reference groups. Turner also expanded Mead's original model of the relations between the imputed other role and the enactment of the self role by identifying three standpoints ego may adopt in role-taking, distinguishing between reflexive and nonreflexive role-taking, and combining these two axes to delineate several different ways in which the self-other relation shapes conduct. Complementing Mead's analysis of role-taking, interactionists introduced the concept of identification to explain both actors' motivation to enact particular roles (Foote 1951; Cressey 1962) and to describe how individuals place one another into recognizable roles, a process ordinarily facilitated by an actor's appearance (Stone 1962).

Empirical studies identified and substantiated several dimensions of role-taking. Cottrell's (1950) and Cottrell and Dymond's (1949) exploratory study suggested that role-taking presumes empathy, and that high levels of empathy foster insight into one's own conduct and cooperative relations with others. Stryker (1956, 1962)[41] maintained that accurate role-taking requires a shared universe of discourse and is more likely in relationships marked by high levels of rationality, utilitarianism, and organization. His research on married couples and their parents also questioned the widely held assumption (and the preliminary findings reported by Cottrell and Dymond) that accurate role-taking invariably promotes satisfactory adjustment between interactants (Stryker 1957). Glaser and Strauss (1964) claim that Mead's discussion of role-taking presumed an open-awareness context in which each interactant is cognizant of the other's true identity and his or her own identity in alter's eyes. Their research on dying patients indicates that in other awareness contexts—closed, suspicion, and pretense—accurate role-taking is more problematic (for at least one of the interactants). O'Toole and Dubin (1968) hypothesize that Mead's concept of role-taking denoted two distinct processes (i.e., responding to self cues from the standpoint of other and responding to other cues from the standpoint of the other), a thesis corroborated in their investigation of baby-feeding and body sway.

Others explored the developmental issues raised by Mead and Cooley of how children learn to see themselves from another's standpoint. Lindesmith and Strauss (1956, pp. 390–97, 418–27) discuss how children develop the ability to take the role of particular and generalized others and to exercise self-regulation, Shibutani (1961, pp. 502–23) identifies mechanisms (e.g., imitation and vicarious identification) and relationships (e.g., primary groups and organized activities) through which children acquire the capacity for role taking and self-control. Stone (1962, pp. 104–16; 1965) refines Mead's discussion of how role-taking emerges during the play and game stages, arguing that by taking the role of another in dramatic play and gaining a reflected view of himself or herself as different from but related to that other, the child begins to establish a separate identity.

Park's conjecture that social roles comprise the framework for an individual's self-conception, in conjunction with Mead's discussion of social objects (and the inference made by some of his students that the self shares many properties with other objects), and Cooley's metaphor (borrowed from Emerson) of the looking-glass self, supplied a starting point for examining connections between role dynamics and the self concept. Miyamoto and Dornbusch (1956; also see Reeder et al. 1960; Kinch 1963; Quarantelli and Cooper 1966), for instance, found that subjects' self-conceptions closely correspond to the perceived attitudes or responses of group members and are even more closely tied to their estimates of the generalized other's attitude. The processes and conditions—e.g., socialization, ceremonies, side-bets, shifts in role clusters, availability of other roles, gratifications in occupying and enacting a role, consistent altercasting by a person's social circles, investment expended in gaining or maintaining a role, and the prestige and power attached to a role—fostering identification with a particular role or complex of roles have also been examined (e.g., Becker 1962, 1964b; Lopata 1971; Turner 1978).[42]

Thomas's (1921) and Wirth's (1928) respective discussions of immigrant and Jewish social types intimated that roles represent a comprehensive pattern for behavior and attitudes and a strategy for adapting to recurrent types of situation. Extending this logic, Strong (1943, 1946) sketches several social types or modes of adjustment that arose in Chicago's African American community in response to its forced exclusion from the larger society. Klapp (1949, 1954, 1962) treats the fool, hero, and villain as social types, describing their roles, the situations in which they arise, and their impact on social organization.

Elaborating Znaniecki's early work, Lopata (1971, 1973, 1991, this volume) portrays a social role as a set of negotiated, interdependent relations between an individual and a social circle. Since roles are responsive to the person's changing dispositions and broader societal and cultural developments that impinge on the person and social circle, the content of roles is constantly modified and new roles regularly emerge. Lopata (1971) uses this framework to examine transformations in role relations associated with becoming a housewife and the expanding and shrinking social circle associated with different stages of the housewife role and the accompanying shifts in priorities and patterns of involvement.

The Chicago school's generalized discourse on the nature of social action also informs interactionist role theory. Specifying interactionism's conceptualization of meaning, Turner (1957) characterizes roles as phenomenological units of meaning or "folk concepts" that individuals use to categorize and orient themselves toward others. Roles are meaningful groupings of behavior, sentiment, motive, and value. Specific actions are interpreted as meaningful expressions of a larger pattern, with ego's conduct understood as an expression of the role he or she is presumed to be performing; the same behavior can mean different things when interpreted as the expression of different roles (Turner 1962, 1968; Turner and Shosid 1976).[43]

Interactionist discourse underlines the creative aspects of human conduct, an emphasis carried over into its role theory. Ego is presumed to understand the perspectives of other participants well enough to improvise a role that will mesh effectively with roles that are simultaneously being improvised by others (Turner 1962, 1985). Because roles are typically understood in terms of general aims or sentiments, innovative conduct is readily seen as an expression of an existing role, and incumbents who do the unexpected often receive the highest ratings of role adequacy. Competent role behavior frequently involves departures from standardized prescriptions, and the greater an individual's mastery of a role the more likely the performer is to deviate from its stereotypical execution (Stone 1984, pp. 12–3).

Contingency also figures prominently in interactionist role theory and is manifest in an interactant's assessing and reassessing the conception he or she has of the other's role. Ego infers alter's role based on the latter's presumed status and personal attributes, conduct, and/or cues from situational others. Alter's subsequent behavior reinforces or challenges this conception. Actors regulate their own action in accord with this testing process: If alter appears to be playing a role different from the one originally imputed, then ego is likely to change his or her conduct in a complementary fashion (Turner 1968).

In addition to the elaboration and revision of the founders' initial statements and the specification of interactionism's generalized discourse, a polemic shaped the development this research program. The rival structuralist[44] approach to social roles drew inspiration from Linton (1936, pp. 113–31) who, in the context of a more refracted understanding of culture, presented a highly influential examination of status and role.[45] Linton's statement became the point of departure for several distinctive versions of structuralist role theory, including the preeminent functionalist approach (e.g., Bates 1956; Gross et al. 1958; Merton 1957a, 1957b; Parsons 1951; Nye 1976; Bates and Harvey 1975). The central concerns of the functionalist program included an interest in incumbents' willingness and ability to conform to institutionalized role expectations, a preoccupation with the conflict generated by incompatible expectations held by different elements of ego's role set, a proclivity for studying highly formalized roles, and an assumption that role allocation is fixed early in an encounter.

Interactionist role theory questioned these assumptions. Whereas functionalists portrayed roles as cultural givens and role behavior as a matter of conformity to role prescriptions, interactionists insisted on the innovative dimensions of role behavior. Objecting to structuralist imagery of mechanistic compliance to detailed role expectations,[46] McCall and Simmons (1978 [1966], p. 7) contend that no script exists for the great majority of role relationships and therefore "the individuals involved must somehow improvise their roles within very broad limits." Because role definitions are often ambiguous and constantly changing, role conduct is necessarily contingent, constructed, and negotiated (Strauss 1959, pp. 54–64). Having imputed a role to alter, ego improvises his or her role in light of alter's putative role.

Charging structuralists with presenting an oversocialized conception of role-person dynamics, second generation Chicagoans maintained that autonomous interactional and self processes condition role performance and influence the elements that comprise a particular role. Even highly conventionalized roles are enacted in a distinctive style reflecting each individual's unique self-conception or personal orientation (and eliciting correspondingly distinctive responses from role alters) (Shibutani 1961, pp. 324–31; Stone 1984, p. 13), a thesis supported by research describing Chicago housewives' three distinct styles of role enactment—passive, reactive, and initiative-prone (Lopata 1969). Further, the contents of roles are partially shaped by incumbents' efforts to secure a viable balance of rewards and costs; failure to provide a favorable balance is one impetus to role reallocation or change (e.g., Dornbusch 1955, pp. 319–20; Roy 1952, 1953, 1960; Turner 1990; Turner and Colomy 1988). Most of the industrial workers Dubin (1956) examined ranked their work roles and informal work relations as secondary to other central life-interests, exhibiting adequate but not superior job performance. Goffman (1961b) underscores the possibility of self-role disjuncture: through discordant gestures, attitudes, and symbols, actors actively distance themselves from the virtual self implied by a role. Turner (1976) speculates that the conventional pattern of structuring the self concept around select institutional roles in an individual's repertoire is giving way to a self anchored in impulse, a shift which may undermine traditional forms of role commitment and concerns for high role adequacy.

Their emphasis on conformity prompted structuralists to portray socialization into roles as a one-way process through which members acquire the knowledge, skills, dispositions, and motivations necessary to fulfill expectations. By contrast, interactionists highlight the reciprocity between person and social organization, describing how persons actively negotiate and restructure their socialization outcomes and sometimes resist attempts to "coach" them into a new status and identity (Goffman 1961a, pp. 173–320; Strauss 1959, pp. 109–18).

Critical of functionalism's penchant for examining roles in highly formalized organizational contexts, interactionists contend that formal systems restrict free operation of the role-making process, "limiting its repertoire and making role boundaries rigid" (Turner 1962, p. 22). Moreover, structuralists' (over)reliance on the formally defined roles that arise in tightly structured organizations—a type of role which is atypical—represents a kind of sampling bias that produces a misrepresentation of role dynamics. This bias impedes consideration of the role dynamics and interaction processes (e.g., bargaining) that regularly modify organizationally defined roles (e.g., Becker and Geer 1960; Roth 1962, 1963), spawn informal organization within formal structures (e.g., Gross 1953; Zurcher 1965), and contribute to the transformation of the environing social structure (Strauss 1978; Strauss et al. 1963).

Contesting the functionalist assumption that once interaction has begun role allocation is set, interactionists suggested that the allocation of roles is negotiated and renegotiated. The continuous monitoring of self and other roles and shifts in the reigning awareness context (Glaser and Strauss 1964) lead interactants to reassess and modify their respective roles. The appropriateness of formal role allocation is constantly under question in any organization (Turner 1962, 1985), and the notions of altercasting (Weinstein and Deutschberger 1963), status forcing (Strauss 1959, pp. 76–84), and impression management (Goffman 1959) indicate that role assignment is continuously negotiated among goal-directed actors attempting to assume or assign roles in accord with their particular ends.

Core tenets of interactionist role theory, then, were established through elaboration and revision of earlier work, specification of the tradition's generalized discourse, and critique of the functionalist approach. At the same time, this program borrowed useful concepts from other traditions and challenged, often implicitly, select elements of interactionism's discourse. For instance, psychoanalytic principles animate Shibutani's discussion of role-taking capacity and self-control, Piaget's learning theory is redeployed in Lindesmith and Strauss's account of role taking, and Gestalt psychology informs Turner's characterization of roles as frameworks of meaning. Pertinent concepts from macrosociological traditions—e.g., the Durkheimian treatment of symbol systems in Turner and Colomy's (1988) discussion of the representational grounds of role differentiation, Lopata's (1971) use of social class to account for variation in the types of role relations women develop with their husbands and with other members of their social circles, Strauss's (1978) examination of the structural contexts within which negotiations over roles and role allocation occur, and Stone's (1965) reliance on Veblen's analysis of the leisure class and Aries's sociohistorical treatment of childhood to sketch the macrosociological context in which analyses of children's play and games must be situated— also inform interactionist role theory. Even functionalist notions, modified and revised, (re)appear in Turner's (1980; Turner and Colomy 1988) formulation of a functionality principle to explain role differentiation and his redeployment of Merton's idea of role set (e.g., Turner 1962).

And while qualitative research (e.g., Turner 1947; Goffman 1961a,

1961b; Roth 1963; Roy 1952; Zurcher 1983) has made important contributions to interactionist role theory, several of those advancing this program adopt a relatively inclusive approach to methodology and theory construction. Thus, Weinstein and Deutschberger (1963), O'Toole and Dubin (1968), and Turner and Shosid (1976) utilize experimental or quasi-experimental designs to assess and elaborate interactionist notions, Shibutani (1961) uses clinical data and reports to support his discussion of role-taking and self-control, Miyamoto and Dornbusch (1956) employ pencil-and-paper rating scales to test the postulated link between role taking dynamics and self conception, and Lopata's (1971, 1973) data on housewives and widows were secured in part through probability sampling and interviews containing both open-ended and pre-coded items. Similarly, Turner's (1980) protocol for building an axiomatic role theory rejects Glaser and Strauss's grounded theory approach and is implicitly critical of Blumer's equation of theory and sensitizing concepts, while Weinstein and Deutschberger, O'Toole and Dubin, and Miyamoto and Dornbusch use conventional hypothesis-testing procedures to examine select elements of interactionist role theory.

Since its crystallization in the postwar era, interactionist role theory has developed along two distinct lines. First, proponents have elaborated the program in a variety of analytic and empirical domains. Shott (1979), for example, argues that particular emotions (shame, guilt, embarrassment, sympathy, pity) presuppose reflexive and empathetic role-taking. Interactionist role theory has been used to examine adjustment to old age as well as challenges to reigning conceptions of the elderly (e.g., Mahoney 1994), and Turner (1972) underscores parallels between imputing self and other roles and the labeling theory of deviance. In addition, this program has been used to examine involuntary role loss and the ensuing role transitions and transformations of self-concept (Gordon and Gordon 1982), to investigate the constraints and opportunities for role making among married, Hispanic, working-class, and professional women (Williams 1989), to underscore the autonomy, creativity, and purposefulness in a diverse array of settings and roles (Zurcher 1983), and to conceptualize research on the family (e.g., Turner 1970, pp. 185–215) and person perception (e.g., Colomy and Rhoades 1983).

Second, several recent substantive studies as well as more formal theorizing about role dynamics highlight lines of convergence between interactionist role theory and ostensibly competing approaches. Thus, Baker and Faulkner's (1991, forthcoming) analysis of how roles are used as a resource to create new positions and social structures joins elements of interactionist, structural, and network approaches, while research on role exiting among nuns (Ebaugh 1984, 1988) and substance abusers (Brown 1991), like Adler and Adler's (1991) treatment of athletes' experience of role engulfment, deploy both interactionist and structuralist ideas. This turn toward synthesis is equally apparent in more formal statements. Handel (1979), for example, maintains that structuralist and interactionist conceptions of role are complementary: the former analyze structurally produced conflicts without examining the processes through which they are reconciled, while interactionists emphasize the negotiation of emergent meanings but neglect macro constraints. Heiss (1981, p. 101) outlines an integrated role theory that combines "the macroanalysis of the structuralists with the microanalysis of the interactionists." Stryker (1968, 1980; Stryker and Statham 1985) asserts that a viable interactionist perspective on role processes must incorporate structuralist explanations of the routine, habitual, and customary aspects of role enactment, models of highly differentiated social systems, and accounts of how structure organizes behavior. Powers (1981) maintains that the role processes conceptualized by interactionists and structuralists operate simultaneously but that their relative scope varies; a compelling synthesis must specify the conditions under which either set of dynamics exerts a more powerful effect. Finally, Callero (1986, p. 344) argues for a Meadian conceptualization of role as social object and perspective "that transcends traditional structural and interactionist concerns."

It is reasonable to expect that in the near term a distinctive interactionist role theory will continue to be extended and revised. A large portion of this elaborative work will treat the second Chicago school's program as a point of departure for subsequent empirical and conceptual studies, while another strand will rely on innovations in interactionism's generalized discourse (e.g., new frames of reference for understanding the problem of action, the identification and resolution of new general problems, new interpretations of Mead, other pragmatists and of Blumer, and newly designated classics and methodological breakthroughs) to reassess and revise the program. Criticisms directed at interactionist role theory, particularly its putative neglect of structural constraints, power, and macro-environmental conditions, will spur additional revisions. A final impetus to revision, and a potential source for the creation of a new program on social roles, stems from attempts to synthesize interactionist role theory with competing approaches.

CONCLUSION

We have suggested that relative to the efforts of first-generation Chicagoans and to the pertinent statements of competing schools and rival segments, the contributions of postwar interactionists represent significant progress. Second generation Chicagoans advanced the interactionist tradition by elaborating and revising previous work and demonstrating how these formulations provided tenable solutions to important discursive and empirical problems either neglected or unresolved by other approaches.

At this juncture it may be appropriate to speculate about the issues likely to confront the next generation of interactionists. Four challenges seem particularly crucial. First, a less equivocal position on the role of generalized discourse must be devised. While a portion of his work can be construed as a discursive statement on the problem of social action, Blumer, like many interactionists, frequently assumed a skeptical, even hostile, stance toward the entire genre of generalized discourse. This leads Blumer to embrace a contradictory position that conflates theoretical presuppositions with empirical observations: on the one hand arguing that interactionism's key tenets faithfully (re)present the central sociological insights of a philosopher (Mead) who conducted no original research and who exemplifies the type of armchair theorist Blumer disdained, and on the other characterizing the tradition's core assumptions as empirically grounded and obvious to any who would but open their eyes and look. But general problems do not disappear if they are not addressed, nor can they be adequately resolved through empirical examination alone. And despite his own ambivalence about the value of generalized discourse, Blumer himself was an effective general theorist, who outlined in stark, dramatic form the basic assumptions and imagery that informed much of the second Chicago school's research. An important task for contemporary interactionists, then, is to formulate a conception of social science that combines previous cohorts' emphasis on research with a more affirmative posture toward generalized discourse. There are promising signs that the discursive side of the interactionist project is beginning to receive the attention it merits. Recent interpretive work on Mead (Joas 1985, 1987), other pragmatists and first-generation Chicagoans (Shalin 1986; Rochberg-Halton 1986; Strauss 1993), and Blumer (Lyman and Vidich 1988) explicitly recognizes that the discursive foundations of a school are crucial to its scholarly fortunes.

An equally consequential issue is articulating a persuasive conception of sociological knowledge. Early Chicagoans envisioned their project
as thoroughly scientific. Postwar interactionists' criticisms of those social
scientists who mimicked the practices of the established sciences were *not*
a rejection of science per se but insisted that a genuine social science must
respect the character of the empirical world and devise procedures suited
to its examination. The appropriate procedures, it was believed, would
generate objective, valid, and verifiable solutions to important empirical
problems. However, some contemporary proponents, particularly those
influenced by postmodernism, reject even this modified view of social science. Adler and Adler (1987, p. 86), for example, characterize scientific
canons and the second generation's concern for objectivity and detachment as "shackles," while Denzin (1989, p. 6) advises abandoning the mod-
ernist foundation that has supported the interactionist project since 1937,
proclaiming that, "There can be no science of the real, no theory of the
totality, and no cumulation of verified knowledge. There is only situated,
practical activity organized and legitimated under the heading of one theory or another." Clearly, then, the ontological and epistemological bases
and character of the "knowledge" produced by interactionist theorizing
and research must be clarified.

Third, the legitimate objections, discursive and empirical, to second-
generation work need to be addressed. Perhaps the single most ramifying
criticism is interactionism's alleged astructural bias, a charge leveled
against both this tradition's (and particularly Blumer's) theorizing and several of its research programs. Whether the predominant response to that
charge involves elucidating the extant but heretofore neglected structuralist moment in first- and second-generation work or borrowing pertinent
models and concepts from other traditions to bolster interactionism's understanding of structural conditions and constraints, the ultimate outcome
is likely to be more explicit theorizing and research on the relations between macro environments and social action.

Finally, interactionists now confront a very different intellectual
field. A series of polemics against rival schools (especially functionalism
and positivism) that some feared and others predicted were about to dis-
place Chicago-style sociology fueled the formulation of a distinctively interactionist approach in the postwar years. But sociology is no longer
dominated by a single paradigm and interactionists are no longer constrained to frame their efforts as a critical riposte to a preeminent school.
In the contemporary multiparadigmatic field the stances taken toward

other schools and disciplines will vitally affect the direction of future interactionist work. A consistently competitive stance toward other approaches insures the maintenance of a distinctively interactionist approach but risks preserving orthodoxy at the expense of producing new
knowledge. A series of rapprochements with other schools can generate
significant advances but may also erode the tradition's defining intellectual
commitments and transform interactionism into little more than a label
of convenience (Fine 1993). And a reconstructionist posture (e.g., Denzin
1992) that retains interactionism's core tenets but combines them with
purportedly consistent elements of other traditions could revitalize the
interactionist imagination and/or dilute interactionist energies by creating
a new segment that vies for prominence with established segments in the
same school.

We stand at an important juncture in the Chicago school's history.
A generation is passing and a new one waits in the wings. A legacy is
bequeathed but no one can say precisely how it will be honored. We do
know that if a tradition is to persist it must change. These changes are
frequently precipitated by unresolved problems within a tradition and by
the challenges and opportunities presented by rival segments and competing schools. There are problems, challenges, and opportunities aplenty for
contemporary interactionists, and this tradition's future depends on how
the new generation shoulders the burden.

NOTES

We thank Patricia Adler and Peter Adler, Gary Alan Fine, Jennifer Platt, and the
reviewers for their comments and suggestions on this chapter.

1. There is ample precedent for using the second Chicago school and interactionism interchangeably (e.g., Collins 1985, pp. 185–204; Meltzer and Petras
1970; Reynolds 1993; Rock 1979; J. Turner 1991, pp. 391–409). This usage presupposes, as we do, that the primary unit of analysis is a tradition, not a department
or cohort. Accordingly, we recognize that not everyone associated with Chicago's
sociology department in the postwar years contributed to the interactionist tradition (Platt; Galliher, this volume) and that interactionism was practiced elsewhere
(Reinharz, this volume).
2. This discussion condenses an argument elaborated at greater length elsewhere (Alexander and Colomy 1992; Colomy 1991).
3. The significance of a general problem is not given in the nature of things
but is established through contentious debate.
4. The notions of elaboration and proliferation are borrowed from Wagner's

(1984) and Wagner and Berger's (1985) discussion of growth in sociological theories.

5. A final pattern of knowledge cumulation, which will not receive sustained attention in this chapter, is *tradition-creation,* which involves generating new schools organized around the synthesis of elements drawn from several existing and often competing frameworks with the aim of crystallizing the discursive and programmatic core of a new tradition.

6. We contend that Blumer's generalized discourse supplied an analytic framework for second-generation interactionists, most of whom were immersed in more empirically oriented research programs. Our discussion of Blumer's generalized discourse draws on the articles reprinted in his *Symbolic Interactionism* (1969). In particular, we refer liberally to the book's introductory chapter, specially prepared for that volume. Our reliance on that lengthy essay prompted one reviewer to question whether the ideas appearing in a paper published in 1969 could influence students taught years earlier. As Blumer's (1969, p. viii) preface to the book clearly indicates, however, the notions advanced in that chapter convey in written form the unified practice of interactionist theory and method which he "sought to present to graduate students over four decades of instruction." In his contribution to *Symbolic Interaction*'s special issue on Herbert Blumer's legacy, Tamotsu Shibutani (1988, p. 24) corroborates the fundamental continuity of Blumer's teaching and writing on symbolic interactionism: "For more than five decades Blumer reiterated [the] same basic position." Alongside the elaboration of a generally consistent position, however, there are instances of discontinuity in Blumer's theorizing and they will be noted later in this discussion.

7. An important aspect of Blumer's contributions is demonstrating the sociological implications of a system of thought primarily oriented to philosophical issues.

8. There is some ambiguity in Blumer's position on this issue. The preceding paragraph emphasizes, for the most part, that portion of Blumer's work which portrays social organization as a form of joint action mediated by interpretive processes. But another strand of Blumer's theorizing suggests that social organization "is the framework inside of which social action takes place" though it is not the determinant of that action (ibid., p. 87). In the same vein, Blumer holds that components of social structure (e.g., culture, social systems, social institutions) set the conditions for action but do not determine it (ibid., pp. 87–88). Thus, Blumer seems to vacillate between a position that by equating social organization with interpretive and reflexive human action questions the causal influence mainstream sociology imparts to the macro environments of action and one which concedes that social organization supplies a framework inside of which action unfolds or imposes conditions that inform but do not dictate the course of social action. Apart from the apparent inconsistency in these two positions is the issue of whether *either* alternative is formulated in a completely satisfactory way.

9. Fisher and Strauss (1978a, p. 484) suggest that interactionist discourse, including new interpretations of Mead, has developed "in contest with the ideas of other traditions," especially, we would add, traditions that are highly acclaimed

when a new formulation is being constructed. In the 1920s and 1930s, they observe, behaviorism constituted the negative intellectual reference group, and later Freudian and other psychoanalytic paradigms were widely perceived as the paramount antagonist. We suggest that in the postwar period, functionalism was the primary rival and interactionist discourse was partially articulated as a critical rejoinder to that school.

10. Blumer was by no means the first or even the most vitriolic critic of the quantification and positivism that began to dominate the discipline in the 1930s and 1940s. Other noteworthy opponents of these developments include Ellwood, Lynd, MacIver, Sorokin, and Znaniecki (Hammersley 1989, pp. 106–11).

11. Blumer's formulation of a distinctively interactionist methodology was partially framed as an alternative to what he and others construed as a constrictive but ascendant positivism. But it should also be noted that in a well-known, early essay he turned a critical eye on Thomas and Znaniecki's (1918–20) "qualitative" work (particularly their use of human documents), questioning the generalizability of their findings, the representativeness and reliability of their data, and the use of that data to verify and validate their theoretical interpretations (Blumer 1969 [1930], pp. 117–26). Denzin (1992, pp. 46–56) notes the irony in critics' subsequent (re)application of these same objections to Blumer's mature methodological position.

12. Students of the Chicago school suggest that participant observation as now understood played a rather small role in early Chicago research. Quoting from a personal interview conducted with Blumer in (September) 1982, Platt (1983, p. 392) notes that at Chicago in the 1920s, "Participant observation was thought of as being a contributory device, and for that very reason not studied carefully."

13. At this time research strategies were not formalized, courses on methods were not offered (though between 1918 and 1933 Park and Burgess offered a seminar on field research), few methodology texts were available, and graduate students learned how to do research through informal apprenticeships with their supervising professor, usually Park or Burgess or both (Anderson 1983; Cavan 1983).

14. It should be noted that the tilt toward quantification and positivism had powerful representatives in the Chicago sociology department and in Chicago's other social science departments as well (Bulmer 1984, pp. 151–89). Though Burgess was "a career-long proponent of the case study method" (Platt, personal communication), he also displayed a keen and enduring interest in spot maps, census tract data, and statistics. The employment of quantitative techniques was also promoted by faculty members in economics (e.g., Field, who in the early and mid-1920s taught statistics to sociology graduate students), political science (e.g., Merriam and Gosnell), and psychology (e.g., Thurstone). Ogburn's appointment as a senior professor in 1927 gave quantitative work in the sociology department a decisive push and reflected the department's commitment to methodological diversity and the realization that a first-rate quantitative sociologist was essential for sustaining the department's preeminence. In this vein, Platt (this volume) points out that almost half of the dissertations produced at Chicago between 1946 and 1962 were quantitative in character, a not terribly surprising finding given the pres-

ence of such outstanding, quantitatively oriented faculty as Ogburn, Hauser, Kitagawa, Duncan, Goodman, Bogue, Rossi, Coleman, and Davis. At the same time, however, Platt (personal communication) notes that many of these faculty members did not remain at Chicago throughout the 1946–62 period and implies that this mobility diluted their impact on students' work.

Deegan (this volume, chap. 9) contends that the battle between conventional positivism and qualitative approaches was overlaid with an exclusionary stance toward woman sociologists. She notes, for instance, that mathematical contributions were initially defined as part of women's work in sociology and not coincidentally denigrated as technical, repetitive, and uninteresting. Following the Depression, however, quantitative work was recast as a male domain and increasingly lauded as creative, powerful, and sophisticated because it used hard science. Deegan also claims that women were formally and informally excluded from "the powerful inner circle of qualitative, male sociologists" and consequently from the tradition of qualitative research.

15. As noted earlier, Blumer is highly critical of those who would draw upon the symbolic capital of the mature sciences to buttress sociology's claims to scientific respectability by unreflectively mimicking the practices of more highly esteemed disciplines. It seems clear, however, that the phrase "naturalistic inquiry" is designed, in part, to conjure up an affinity between Charles Darwin, "perhaps the greatest naturalistic scientist" (Denzin 1970, p. 9), and Blumerian methodology. Thus, in Blumer's view, Darwin "exemplified" the essence of authentic scientific method, which involves getting close to the empirical world and digging deeply into it (Blumer 1969, pp. 39–40). Darwinian imagery also informs Blumer's characterization of the inspective phase of naturalistic inquiry: "The prototype of inspection is represented by our handling of a strange physical object; we may pick it up, look at it closely, turn it over as we view it, look at it from this or that angle, raise questions as to what it might be, go back and handle it again in the light of our questions, try it out, and test it one way or another" (ibid., p. 44). Darwin is the natural-scientist-as-exemplar most frequently invoked by Blumer, but he is not the only one. Other scientists cited approvingly by Blumer include Galileo, Newton, and Pasteur (Hammersley 1989, p. 137).

16. According to the Adlers (1987, p. 10), "Two younger faculty members, Anselm Strauss and David Riesman, were also instrumental in encouraging and sponsoring participant observation fieldwork."

17. Though Hughes and Blumer were absolutely crucial to sustaining the interactionist tradition, they apparently did not collaborate on a regular basis. Prus (forthcoming, chap. 3, p. 12) observes, "In contrast to Park and Burgess who often worked much more as a team . . . , Blumer and Hughes worked quite independently." Becker (1988, p. 19) makes a significant point: "Students in the department at Chicago, in the 1950s thought of themselves as Hughes students *or* Blumer students, but not both." However, Blumer's and Hughes's similar intellectual commitments appear to have outweighed their differences. Thus, the very next sentence in Becker's (ibid., p. 19) essay reads, "Most people learned, some sooner than others, that we were almost always both."

18. Indeed, Hughes has been described as "perhaps the strongest driving

64   Paul Colomy and J. David Brown

force behind the development of participant observation as a distinct methodology" (Adler and Adler 1987, p. 10). That assertion may be contested, but it is clear
that in the context of the often acrimonious methodological disputes in the postwar years Hughes became a living symbol of qualitative research and a powerful
legitimating force for this type of work.

19. Hughes decried the splintering of sociology and anthropology departments, arguing that it led to the "dehydration" of sociology. Despite this departmental split Hughes maintained close personal and working relationships with
several anthropologists, and a number of them, including William Lloyd Warner
and Robert Redfield, directly influenced some Chicago graduate sociology students in the postwar period.

20. In contrast to Blumer, Hughes (1971, pp. 436, 496) noted parallels between fieldwork (particularly the interviewing component) and the psychoanalytic
method. Both procedures, he argued, are concerned with discovering meanings
people attach to individuals, events, and interpersonal processes. The uncovering
of meaning, through either psychoanalysis or "the prolonged sympathetic interview of the social investigator" (ibid., p. 436), can prompt sometimes difficult personal and social revelations.

21. An important part of Hughes's not so hidden agenda was to convey the
message that through fieldwork students might emancipate themselves from the
prejudices and practices of their backgrounds, though this emancipation need not
entail complete alienation from their origins (Hughes 1971, p. 574). In this manner,
sociological study fosters an enlargement of perspective and a humanizing of the
mind. Of course, Hughes was well aware that realizing a fuller understanding of
self, other, and society was contingent on specific social and historical circumstances, and toward the end of his career he implied that the circumstances which
once made this possible were being eroded (ibid., pp. 574–76). He also conceded
that the optimistic assumption that personal emancipation would precipitate appropriate collective action and social reform was sociologically naive.

22. He claimed that existing departments were largely the product of historic social movements and were not based on genuine differences in logic, theory,
or method.

23. This contrast conception is contestable. There are innumerable instances of highly imaginative positivistic research advancing humanistic and
emancipatory ends.

24. In this vein, one attempt to chart the course of theoretical developments
in symbolic interactionism observes, "The trajectory of the last 70 or 80 years has
been from the super straight into the underground with Blumer's critique of official
sociology as the turning point" (Collins 1985; p. 202). Several chapters in this volume discuss interactionism's critical position toward elites and authority, whether
in sociology or outside the academy. Galliher, for example, highlights labeling theorists' penchant for aligning themselves with the underdog, while Fine and Ducharme (p. 115) describe the "swaggering, debunking stance, a subversive analogy-
building" that infuses the work of several second generation Chicagoans.

25. Znaniecki (1928, 1934, 1969), of course, is customarily credited with the

initial formulation of analytic induction. According to Hammersley (1989, p. 166), Lindesmith denies any influence from Znaniecki, though they present rather similar notions about the process of inquiry. However, in a letter to Jennifer Platt (January 30, 1985), Lindesmith indicates that his ideas of scientific method "were largely derived from what I read on the logic of natural sciences." The very next sentence in his letter reads, "I read and was influenced by Znaniecki, and also by George Herbert Mead. . . ." He also credits Blumer, whom he describes as "The Chicago Professor who had the greater influence on me in these matters than any other," and Dewey, Marenau, and Keynes. Whatever the exact origins of this method, it is clear that Lindesmith was among the first (also see Angell 1936) to demonstrate its utility in systematic empirical research, a lead subsequently advanced by Cressey's and Becker's studies of the violation of financial trust and becoming a marijuana user, respectively. (For further discussion of these points and for an assessment of the strengths and weaknesses of analytic induction, see Hammersley (1989, pp. 163–72, 195–98; also see Manning 1982).)

26. It would be a mistake to draw a hard-and-fast line between these two lines of elaboration. Thus, though Glaser and Strauss (1967) outline a general logic for analysis, they also provide specific recommendations for conducting research, while Wax's (1971) practical advice for doing qualitative research is prefaced with a discussion of the theoretical presuppositions of fieldwork.

27. Our discussion implies an affinity but not an exclusive relationship between the Chicago segment of interactionism and the method of participant observation, particularly in the postwar period. Obviously, other sociological traditions and, for that matter, other social scientific disciplines, especially anthropology, employ fieldwork methods, while several Chicago interactionists use strategies other than participant observation.

28. Earlier we noted that Hughes was more sympathetic to psychoanalysis than Blumer. However, Hughes does not discuss psychoanalysis in a systematic way or attempt to integrate it with interactionist principles. Compared to Hughes, Shibutani presents a much more elaborate treatment of the unconscious sources of meaning and their significance for interactionist theory.

29. There are significant parallels between Goffman's general treatment of how hegemonic definitions of the situation constrain action and the institutional and situational conditions affecting the self, and the more empirically oriented studies of work and occupations conducted by Hughes and his students. It should also be noted that Goffman's work draws extensively on other sociological traditions and other disciplines, with some commentators (e.g., Collins 1985) contending that Goffman is more Durkheimian than interactionist.

30. The theoretical and methodological objections to Blumer's generalized discourse we have described are intimately tied to a tradition segment one observer calls the Illinois school (Rochberg-Halton 1986, p. 64), an approach which insists that social behaviorism is the true Meadian legacy. The more general point, however, is that every competing segment in the interactionist tradition—whether the Illinois school (e.g., Lewis and Smith 1980), the old or new Iowa schools (e.g., Meltzer and Petras 1970; Buban 1986), or Stryker's (1980) structuralist inter-

actionism—provides a distinctive rendition of the divergence thesis, pointing to discrepancies between Mead and Blumer and providing new and non-Blumerian or anti-Blumerian readings of interactionism's classic texts.

31. More important, for practicing interactionists concerned primarily with substantive problems, Blumer's generalized discourse proved empirically fertile. Perhaps the strongest case for Blumer's discursive efforts is the fact that they informed several compelling research programs in a diverse array of specialty areas. Whatever their intellectual merits, rival segments' renditions of interactionism's core theoretical and methodological tenets have yet to inspire either the quantity or quality of research produced by the second Chicago school. At the same time, perfect congruence between Blumer's discourse and the second Chicago school's research programs never obtained, a point we will examine later.

32. Shalin (1986, p. 26) also suggests that a failure of dialectical nerve has split interactionism into "more voluntaristically and less voluntaristically oriented branches," and intimates (n. 6) that Blumer advances a relatively extreme voluntaristic position. Also see Fisher and Strauss (1978a).

33. These advances in research programs, in turn, can prompt significant revisions in a tradition's generalized discourse.

34. Fisher and Strauss temper this contrast by noting that Blumer's substantive contributions in race relations and collective behavior elaborate Thomas's and (especially) Park's work in these areas and consequently exhibits a greater awareness of the constraints on social action.

35. Generalized discourse is considerably more abstract than a formal research program, and a particular tradition's discourse frequently informs (and responds to developments in) several substantive and formal programs.

36. The first Chicago school's focus on social structure was distinctively anthropological and emphasized the study of whole social systems. Their study of human behavior proceeded by examining its interconnectedness to the larger system of social action of which it was a part. Describing this emphasis on social systems, Moore (1982, p. 49) noted that it, "required detailed attention to the structure of societies, the positions constituting the structure, and the expected and actual role behavior characterizing the various positions."

37. Due to the constraints of space and time it is impossible to credit the many influential social scientists associated with the Human Relations in Industry Group. A partial list of Whyte's associates, for example, would include the studies of restrictions of output among production workers conducted by Collins, Dalton, and Roy. Their findings were subsequently presented in *Money and Motivation* (Whyte 1955).

38. Abbott (1988) suggests that the second Chicago school's research agenda subsequently divided into "institutionalist" and "individualist" strands. The institutionalist agenda follows most closely the foundation laid by the first Chicago school and Everett Hughes. The individualist agenda, by contrast, is informed by the Blumerian directive that organizations, social structure, culture, and power are crucial only to the degree "they enter into the process of interpretation and definition out of which joint actions are formed" (Blumer 1969, p. 75). These

thickly descriptive studies highlight the processes and contingencies associated with professional socialization and identity transformation.

39. Interestingly, the criticisms leveled at functionalism's study of the professions were similar to the criticisms leveled at the first Chicago school's Human Relations in Industry Group. More specifically, the empirical validity of the Human Relations in Industry Group's findings were challenged on the grounds that (1) they were conservatively biased as a result of the financial support received from many of the industries they studied, (2) they supported the status quo since their findings were intended to assist management in manipulating workers and undermining unions, and (3) by arguing that problems could be resolved by "good communications" between workers and management they naively assumed that workers accepted the authority and legitimacy of the organization (cf. Whyte 1987).

40. Our use of the term "theory" to designate the research program organized around the study of role dynamics is at odds with more restrictive conceptions of what qualifies as a theory. The interactionist program on role processes consists of a loosely joined set of models, concepts, propositions, and empirical studies that have not yet congealed into the sort of axiomatic structure (but see Turner [1980] for an initial attempt in this direction) that for some constitutes the heart and soul of an authentic social scientific theory. Our usage corresponds, we believe, to the imprecise and rather optimistic convention common in sociological discourse.

41. Though Stryker's commitment to a quantitative, natural-science model of sociological inquiry is clear, his early work is discussed here because he had not yet tied his methodological position to a competing segment of interactionist thought. Subsequently, Stryker (1980, 1981; Stryker and Serpe 1982; Stryker and Statham 1985) explicitly wedded his conception of scientific method to a critique of Chicago, and largely Blumerian, interactionism for its purported failure to recognize structural constraints and the recurrent, habitual, customary aspects of social action and to the formulation of a rival discourse organized around a reinterpretation of Mead, other pragmatists, and the Scottish moral philosophers (Hume, Hutcheson, Smith, and Ferguson).

42. The connection between role and self has also been examined by scholars identified with "structuralist" segments of interactionism. Kuhn (1960; Kuhn and McPartland 1954; also see Couch 1958) maintains that a significant part of an actor's self-definition reflects the internalization of commonly recognized group membership roles and social statuses. McCall and Simmons (1978[1966]) portray the self as a constellation of role identities arranged in a prominence hierarchy and describe the factors (e.g., investment, commitment, self- and social support, intrinsic and extrinsic gratifications) that determine a given identity's location in the hierarchy. For Stryker (1968, 1980) the self comprises differentiated identities (largely derived from ego's repertoire of roles) organized into a salience hierarchy. The position of a particular identity in the hierarchy is a function of such considerations as the degree of ego's commitment to that identity and the prestige attached to it.

43. Cicourel (1974) and others writing from an ethnomethodological perspective (e.g., Hilbert 1981; Halkowski 1990) assert that interactionists' treatment of role as an interpretive framework used by actors to make sense of their own and others' conduct does not go far enough. Indeed, the use of an abstract concept like role, Cicourel (1974, p. 27) charges, actually masks the interpretive procedures whereby actors produce behavioral displays which others and the observer label "role behavior." "Without a model of the actor that specifies such procedures or rules, we cannot reveal how behavioral displays are recognized as 'role taking' or 'role making.'" Wilson (1970), however, presents a more favorable assessment of interactionist role theory, emphasizing the theoretical and methodological parallels between this program and ethnomethodology.

44. The structuralist approach is actually a composite of several distinct traditions, including functionalist theory (Parsons 1951; Merton 1957a, 1957b), structuralist/positional theory (Nadel 1957; Burt 1976, 1982; White et al. 1976; Boorman and White 1976), and organizational theory (Kahn et al. 1964). Of these competing renditions, functionalist role theory posed the most significant, enduring, and intellectually coherent challenge to the second Chicago school (Biddle 1986).

45. Lopata (1964) charges Linton with conflating status and role, arguing that the two terms designate distinct dynamics. Status processes are evaluative and involve ranking comparable physical objects, actions, persons, roles, and groups. Role, on the other hand, refers to the diverse forms of patterned relations and interdependence between persons and their social circles. Though roles are often ranked, their placement in a status system represents but one dimension of a role.

46. This critique also reflects an ideological commitment to the voluntaristic and creative dimensions of social action, a commitment consistent with interactionism's valorization of individualism and freedom. Interactionist role theory rejects as less than fully human a structuralist perspective that portrays conduct as either conformity or nonconformity to normative expectations, noting that the most highly evaluated role performances frequently involve unexpected, surprising, and strikingly out-of-the-ordinary behavior. The interactionist program advances a role theory "that more accurately describes social interaction as human behavior, and less as the programmed performance of bureaucratic robots whose circuits sometimes get overloaded and which behave in aberrant fashion when contradictory messages are relayed to their control boxes" (Turner 1985, pp. 34–35).

REFERENCES

Abbott, A. 1988. *The System of Professions: An Essay on the Division of Expert Labor.* Chicago: University of Chicago Press.

Adler, P. A., and P. Adler. 1987. *Membership Roles in Field Research.* Newbury Park, Calif.: Sage.

———. 1991. *Backboards and Blackboards: College Athletes and Role Engulfment.* New York: Columbia University Press.

Alexander, J. C. 1982. *Theoretical Logic in Sociology,* Volume 1: *Positivism, Presup-*

positions, and Current Controversies. Berkeley: University of California Press.

———. 1985. "The Individualist Dilemma in Phenomenology and Interactionism: Toward a Synthesis with the Classical Tradition." Pp. 25–57 in *Perspectives in Sociological Theory,* vol. 1, edited by S. N. Eisenstadt and H. J. Helle. Beverly Hills: Sage.

———. 1987. *Twenty Lectures.* New York: Columbia University Press.

Alexander, J. C., and P. Colomy. 1992. "Traditions and Competition: Preface to a Postpositivist Approach to Knowledge Cumulation." Pp. 27–52 in *Metatheorizing in Sociology,* edited by G. Ritzer. Newbury Park, Calif.: Sage.

Anderson, N. 1923. *The Hobo.* Chicago: University of Chicago Press.

———. 1983. "A Stranger at the Gate: Reflections on the Chicago School of Sociology." *Urban Life* 11: 396–406.

Angell, R. 1936. *The Family Encounters The Depression.* New York: Scribner's.

Athens, L. H. 1984. "Blumer's Method of Naturalistic Inquiry: A Critical Examination." *Studies in Symbolic Interaction* 5: 241–57.

Atkinson, P. 1983. "The Reproduction of the Professional Community." Pp. 224–41 in *The Sociology of the Professions,* edited by R. Dingwall and P. Lewis. London: Macmillan.

Baker, W. E., and R. R. Faulkner. 1991. "Role as Resource in the Hollywood Film Industry." *American Journal of Sociology* 97: 279–309.

———. Forthcoming. "The Dynamics of Role Enactment." In *Self, Collective Action, and Society: Essays Honoring the Contributions of Ralph H. Turner,* edited by G. Platt and C. Gordon. Greenwich, Conn.: JAI Press.

Barber, B. 1963. "Some Problems in the Sociology of Professions." *Daedalus* 92: 669–88.

Bates, F. L. 1956. "Position, Role, and Status: A Reformulation of Concepts." *Social Forces* 34: 313–21.

———. and C. C. Harvey. 1975. *The Structure of Social Systems.* New York: Gardner.

Becker, H. S. 1953. "Becoming a Marijuana User." *American Journal of Sociology* 59: 235–42.

———. 1955. "Marijuana Use and Social Control." *Social Problems* 3: 35–44.

———. 1958. "Problems of Inference and Proof in Participant Observation." *American Sociological Review* 23: 652–60.

———. 1960. "Notes on the Concept of Commitment." *American Journal of Sociology* 66: 32–40.

———. 1962. "The Nature of a Profession." Pp. 27–46 in *Education for the Professions,* Sixty-First Yearbook of the National Society for the Study of Education, Part II. Chicago: University of Chicago Press.

———. 1963. *Outsiders: Studies in the Sociology of Deviance.* New York: The Free Press.

———. 1964a. "Problems in the Publication of Field Studies." Pp. 267–85 in *Reflections on Community Studies,* edited by A. J. Vidich, J. Bensman, and M. R. Stein. New York: John Wiley and Sons.

———. 1964b. "Personal Change in Adult Life." *Sociometry* 27: 40–53.

————. 1988."Herbert Blumer's Conceptual Impact." *Symbolic Interaction* 11: 13–21.

————, and B. Geer. 1958. "The Fate of Idealism in Medical School." *American Sociological Review* 23: 50–56.

————. 1960. "Latent Culture: A Note on the Theory of Latent Social Roles." *Administrative Science Quarterly* 5: 304–313.

————, B. Geer, E. Hughes, and A. Strauss. 1961. *Boys in White: Student Culture in Medical School.* Chicago: University of Chicago Press.

————, B. Geer, D. Riesman, and R. Weiss. 1968. "Everett C. Hughes—An Appreciation." In *Institutions and the Person,* edited by H. S. Becker, B. Geer, D. Riesman, and R. Weiss. Chicago: Aldine.

Biddle, B. 1979. *Role Theory: Expectations, Identities, and Behaviors.* New York: Academic Press.

————. 1986. "Recent Developments in Role Theory." *Annual Review of Sociology* 12: 67–92.

Blumer, H. 1962. "Society as Symbolic Interaction." Pp. 179–92 in *Human Behavior and Social Processes,* edited by A. Rose. Boston: Houghton Mifflin.

————. 1966. "Reply to Bales." *American Journal of Sociology* 71: 547–48.

————. 1967. "Reply to Woelfel, Stone and Farberman." *American Journal of Sociology* 72: 411–12.

————. 1969. *Symbolic Interactionism: Perspective and Method.* Englewood Cliffs: Prentice-Hall.

————. 1973. "A Note on Symbolic Interactionism" [Reply to Huber]. *American Sociological Review* 38: 797–98.

————. 1977. "Comment on Lewis's 'The Classic American Pragmatists as Forerunners to Symbolic Interactionism.'" *Sociological Quarterly* 18: 285–89.

————. 1980. "Mead and Blumer: The Convergent Methodological Perspectives of Social Behaviorism and Symbolic Interactionism: [Reply to McPhail and Rexroat]. *American Sociological Review* 44: 409–419.

————. 1983. "Going Astray With a Logical Scheme" [Reply to Lewis and Smith]. *Symbolic Interaction* 6: 127–37.

Boorman, S. A., and H. C. White. 1976. "Social Structure from Multiple Networks. II. Role Structures." *American Journal of Sociology* 81: 1384–1446.

Bourdieu, P. 1991. "The Peculiar History of Scientific Reason." *Sociological Forum* 6: 3–26.

Brown, J. D. 1991. "The Professional Ex-: An Alternative for Exiting the Deviant Career." *Sociological Quarterly* 32: 219–30.

Bruyn, S. 1966. *The Human Perspective in Sociology.* Englewood Cliffs: Prentice-Hall.

Buban, S. 1986. "Studying Social Process: The Chicago and Iowa Schools." *Studies in Symbolic Interaction* 2 (Part A): 25–38.

Bucher, R., and A. Strauss. 1961. "Professions in Process." *American Journal of Sociology* 66 (January): 325–34.

Bulmer, M. 1984. *The Chicago School of Sociology: Institutionalization, Diversity, and the Rise of Sociological Research.* Chicago: University of Chicago Press.

Burgess, E. W. 1926. *The Urban Community.* Chicago: University of Chicago Press.

Burt, R. S. 1976. "Positions in Networks." *Social Forces* 51: 93–122.

―――. 1982. *Toward a Structural Theory of Action: Network Models of Social Structure, Perception, and Action.* New York: Academic.

Callero, P. 1986. "Toward a Meadian Conceptualization of Role." *Sociological Quarterly* 27: 343–58.

Cavan, R. S. 1983. "The Chicago School of Sociology, 1918–1933." *Urban Life* 11: 407–20.

Chapoulie, J. M. 1987. "Everett C. Hughes and the Development of Fieldwork in Sociology." *Urban Life* 15: 259–298.

Cicourel, A. V. 1974. "Interpretive Procedures and Normative Rules in the Negotiation of Status and Role." Pp. 11–41 in *Cognitive Sociology.* New York: The Free Press. (Originally published in 1972 in *Studies in Social Interaction,* edited by D. Sudnow. New York: The Free Press.)

Collins, R. 1975. *Conflict Sociology.* New York: Academic Press.

―――. 1985. *Three Sociological Traditions.* New York: Oxford University Press.

―――. 1988. *Theoretical Sociology.* San Diego: Harcourt Brace Jovanovich.

Colomy, P. 1991. "Metatheorizing in a Postpositivist Frame." *Sociological Perspectives* 34: 269–86.

―――, and G. Rhoades. 1983. "Role Performance and Person Perception: Toward an Interactionist Approach." *Symbolic Interaction* 6: 207–27.

Cooley, C. H. 1902. *Human Nature and the Social Order.* New York: Charles Scribner's Sons.

Cottrell, L. S. 1950. "Some Neglected Problems in Social Psychology." *American Sociological Review* 15: 705–12.

Cottrell, L. S., and R. F. Dymond. 1949. "The Empathic Responses." *Psychiatry* 12: 355–59.

Couch, C. J. 1958. "Self-attitudes and Degree of Agreement with Immediate Others." *American Journal of Sociology* 63: 491–96.

Coutu, W. 1951. "Role-Playing vs. Role-Taking: An Appeal for Clarification." *American Sociological Review* 16: 180–87.

Cressey, D. R. 1950. "The Criminal Violation of Financial Trust." *American Sociological Review* 15: 738–43.

―――. 1953. *Other People's Money.* Glencoe, Ill.: Free Press.

―――. 1962. "Role Theory, Differential Association, and Compulsive Crimes." Pp. 443–67 in *Human Behavior and Social Processes,* edited by A. M. Rose. Boston: Houghton Mifflin.

Cressey, P. 1932. *The Taxi Dance Hall: A Sociological Study in Commercialized Recreation and City Life.* Chicago: University of Chicago Press.

Daniels, A. K. 1971. "How Free Should Professions Be?" Pp. 39–58 in *The Professions and Their Prospects,* edited by E. Freidson. Beverly Hills: Sage.

Davis, F. 1963. *Passage Through Crisis.* Indianapolis: Bobbs-Merrill.

―――. 1968. "Professional Socialization as Subjective Experience: The Process of Doctrinal Conversion Among Student Nurses." Pp. 235–251 in *Institutions and the Person,* edited by H. S. Becker, B. Geer, D. Riesman, and R. Weiss. Chicago: Aldine.

Denzin, N., ed. 1970. *Sociological Methods.* Chicago: Aldine.

————. 1989. "Thoughts on 'Critique and Renewal in Symbolic Interactionism.'" *Studies in Symbolic Interaction* 10: 3–8.

————. 1992. *Symbolic Interactionism and Cultural Studies.* Cambridge, Mass.: Blackwell.

Dornbusch, S. M. 1955. "The Military Academy as An Assimilating Institution." *American Sociological Review* 33: 316–321.

Dubin, R. 1956. "Industrial Workers' World: A Study of the Central Life Interests of Industrial Workers." *Social Problems* 3: 131–142.

Ebaugh, H. R. F. 1984. "Leaving the Convent: The Experience of Role Exit and Self-Transformation." Pp. 156–76 in *The Existential Self in Society* edited by J. A. Kotarba and A. Fontana. Chicago: University of Chicago Press.

————. 1988. *Becoming an EX.* Chicago: University of Chicago Press.

Elliott, P. 1972. *The Sociology of the Professions.* New York: Herder & Herder.

Filstead, W., ed. 1970. *Qualitative Methodology.* Chicago: Markham.

Fine, G. A. 1993. "The Sad Demise, Mysterious Disappearance, and Glorious Triumph of Symbolic Interactionism." *Annual Review of Sociology* 19: 61–87.

Fisher, B., and A. Strauss. 1978a. "Interactionism." Pp. 457–98 in *A History of Sociological Analysis,* edited by Tom Bottomore and Robert Nisbet. New York: Oxford University Press.

————. 1978b. "The Chicago Tradition and Social Change: Thomas, Park, and Their Successors." *Symbolic Interaction* 1: 5–23.

————. 1979. "George Herbert Mead and the Chicago Tradition of Sociology." *Symbolic Interaction* 2: 9–25.

Foote, N. N. 1951. "Identification as the Basis for a Theory of Motivation." *American Sociological Review* 16: 14–21.

Freidson, E. 1970a. *Profession of Medicine.* New York: Dodd, Mead.

————. 1970b. *Professional Dominance.* Chicago: Aldine.

————, ed. 1971. *The Professions and Their Prospects.* Beverly Hills: Sage.

————. 1986. *Professional Powers: A Study of the Institutionalization of Formal Knowledge.* Chicago: University of Chicago Press.

Gans, H. J. 1968. "The Participant-Observer as a Human Being: Observations on the Personal Aspects of Field Work." Pp. 300–317 in *Institutions and the Person,* edited by H. S. Becker, B. Geer, D. Riesman, and R. Weiss. Chicago: Aldine.

Gardner, B., and W. F. Whyte. 1946. "Methods for the Study of Human Relations in Industry." *American Sociological Review* 11: 506–11.

Glaser, B. 1978. *Theoretical Sensitivity.* Mill Valley, Calif.: Sociology Press.

Glaser, B. G., and A. L. Strauss. 1964. "Awareness Contexts and Social Interaction." *American Sociological Review* 29: 669–79.

————. 1967. *The Discovery of Grounded Theory.* Chicago: Aldine.

Goffman, E. 1959. *Presentation of Self in Everyday Life.* Garden City: Anchor.

————. 1961a. *Asylums.* New York: Anchor.

————. 1961b. *Encounters: Two Studies in the Sociology of Interaction.* Indianapolis: Bobbs-Merrill.

————. 1963. *Stigma: Notes on the Management of Spoiled Identity.* Englewood Cliffs: Prentice-Hall.

————. 1967. *Interaction Ritual: Essays on Face-to-Face Behavior.* Garden City: Anchor.

————. 1972. *Strategic Interaction.* New York: Ballantine.

————. 1974. *Frame Analysis: An Essay on the Organization of Experience.* New York: Harper Colophon.

————. 1983. "The Interaction Order." *American Sociological Review* 48: 1–17.

Gold, R. L. 1958. "Roles in Sociological Field Observations." *Social Forces* 36: 217–23.

Goode, W. 1957. "Community Within a Community: The Professions." *American Sociological Review* 22 (April): 194–200.

Gordon, C., and P. Gordon. 1982. "Changing Roles, Goals, and Self-Conceptions: Process and Results in a Program for Women's Employment." Pp. 243–83 in *Personality, Roles, and Social Behavior,* edited by W. Ickes and E. S. Knowles. NY: Springer-Verlag.

Gouldner, A. 1962. "Anti-Minotaur: The Myth of Value Free Sociology." *Social Problems* 9: 209–17.

————. 1970. *The Coming Crisis of Western Sociology.* New York: Basic Books.

Gross, E. 1953. "Some Functional Consequences of Primary Controls in Formal Work Organizations." *American Sociological Review* 18: 368–73.

Gross, N., W. S. Mason, and A. W. McEarchern. 1958. *Explorations in Role Analysis.* New York: John Wiley and Sons.

Gusfield, J. 1967. "Moral Passage: The Symbolic Process in the Public Designations of Deviance." *Social Problems* 15: 175–88.

Halkowski, T. 1990. "Role as an Interactional Device." *Social Problems* 37: 564–77.

Hammersley, M. 1989. *The Dilemma of Qualitative Method.* London: Routledge.

Handel, W. 1979. "Normative Expectations and the Emergence of Meaning as Solutions to Problems: Convergence of Structural and Interactionist Views." *American Journal of Sociology* 84: 855–81.

Hayner, N. 1936. *Hotel Life.* Durham: University of North Carolina Press.

Heiss, J. 1981. "Social Roles." Pp. 94–129 in *Social Psychology,* edited by M. Rosenberg and R. H. Turner. New York: Basic Books.

Hewitt, J. 1976. *Self and Society.* Boston: Allyn and Bacon.

Hilbert, R. A. 1981. "Toward an Improved Understanding of Role." *Theory and Society* 10: 207–26.

Hochschild, A. R. 1979. "Emotion Work, Feeling Rules, and Social Structure." *American Journal of Sociology* 85: 551–75.

Holmstrom, L. L. 1984. "Everett Cherrington Hughes: A Tribute to a Pioneer in the Study of Work and Occupations." *Work and Occupations* 11: 471–81.

Huber, J. 1973a. "Symbolic Interaction as a Pragmatic Perspective: The Bias of Emergent Theory." *American Sociological Review* 38: 274–84.

————. 1973b. "Reply to Blumer: But Who Will Scrutinize the Scrutinizers?" *American Sociological Review* 38: 798–800.

Hughes, E. 1945. "Dilemmas and Contradictions of Status." *American Journal of Sociology* 50: 353–59.

————. 1946. "The Knitting of Ethnic Groups in Industry." *American Sociological Review* 11: 512–19.

———. 1952. "The Sociological Study of Work: An Editorial Foreword." *American Journal of Sociology,* 57 (5): 423–26.

———. 1958. *Men and Their Work.* Glencoe: The Free Press.

———. 1971. *The Sociological Eye: Selected Papers.* New York: Aldine-Atherton.

Janowitz, M., ed. 1966. *W. I. Thomas, On Social Organization and Social Personality.* Chicago: University of Chicago Press.

Joas, H. 1985. *G. H. Mead: A Contemporary Re-examination of His Thought.* Cambridge: MIT Press.

———. 1987. "Symbolic Interactionism." Pp. 82–115 in *Social Theory Today,* edited by A. Giddens and J. Turner. Stanford: Polity Press.

Junker, B. H. 1960. *Field Work.* Chicago: University of Chicago Press.

Kahn, R. L., D. M. Wolfe, R. P. Quinn, and J. D. Snoek. 1964. *Organizational Stress: Studies in Role Conflict and Ambiguity.* New York: John Wiley and Sons.

Kinch, J. W. 1963. "A Formalized Theory of the Self-Concept." *American Journal of Sociology* 68: 481–86.

Klapp, O. E. 1949. "The Fool as a Social Type." *American Journal of Sociology* 55: 157–62.

———. 1954. "Heroes, Villains, and Fools, As Agents of Social Control." *American Sociological Review* 19: 56–62.

———. 1962. *Heroes, Villains, and Fools: The Changing American Character.* Englewood Cliffs: Prentice-Hall.

Kuhn, M. H. 1960. "Self-Attitudes by Age, Sex, and Professional Training." *Sociological Inquiry* 1: 39–55.

———, and T. S. McPartland. 1954. "An Empirical Investigation of Self-Attitudes." *American Sociological Review* 19: 68–76.

Kurtz, L. 1984. *Evaluating Chicago Sociology.* Chicago: University of Chicago Press.

Lewis, D. J. 1976. "The Classic American Pragmatists as Forerunners to Symbolic Interactionism." *Sociological Quarterly* 17: 347–59.

———. 1977. "Reply to Blumer." *Sociological Quarterly* 18: 291–92.

———. 1979. "A Social Behaviorist Interpretation of the Meadian 'I'." *American Journal of Sociology* 84: 261–87.

——— and R. L. Smith. 1980. *American Sociology and Pragmatism.* Chicago: University of Chicago Press.

———. 1983. "Putting the Symbol in Symbolic Interactionism: A Rejoinder." *Symbolic Interaction* 6: 165–74.

Lindesmith, A. R. 1947. *Opiate Addiction.* Bloomington, Ind.: Principia Press. (Originally written in 1937 as *The Nature of Opiate Addiction,* Chicago: University of Chicago Libraries).

———. 1968. *Addiction and Opiates.* Chicago: Aldine.

———, and A. Strauss. 1956 [1949]. *Social Psychology.* Revised edition. New York: Holt, Rinehart, and Winston.

———, eds. 1969. *Readings in Social Psychology.* New York: Holt, Rinehart, and Winston.

Linton, R. 1936. *The Study of Man.* New York: D. Appleton-Century.

Lofland, J. 1970. "Interactionist Imagery and Analytic Interruptus." Pp. 35–45 in *Human Nature and Collective Behavior,* edited by T. Shibutani. New Brunswick: Transaction Books.

Lohman, J. D. 1937. "The Participant Observer in Community Studies." *American Sociological Review* 2: 890–98.

Lopata, H. Z. 1964. "A Restatement of the Relation between Role and Status." *Sociology and Social Research* 49: 58–68.

———. 1969. "Social Psychological Aspects of Role Involvement." *Sociology and Social Research* 53: 285–98.

———. 1971. *Occupation: Housewife.* New York: Oxford University Press.

———. 1973. *Widowhood in an American City.* Cambridge, Mass.: Schenkman.

———. 1991. "Role Theory." Pp. 1–11 in *Social Roles and Social Institutions: Essays in Honor of Rose Lamb Coser,* edited by J. R. Blau and N. Goodman. Boulder: Westview.

Lyman, S. 1984. "Interactionism and the Study of Race Relations at the Macrosociological Level: The Contribution of Herbert Blumer." *Symbolic Interaction* 7: 107–20.

———. 1988. "Symbolic Interactionism and Macrosociology." *Sociological Forum* 3: 295–301.

Lyman, S., and A. Vidich. 1988. *Social Order and the Public Philosophy: An Analysis and Interpretation of The Work of Herbert Blumer.* Fayetteville: University of Arkansas Press.

Mahoney, A. R. 1994. "Change in the Older-Person Role: An Application of Turner's Process Role and Model of Role Change." *Journal of Aging Studies* 8: 133–48.

Maines, D. 1977. "Social Organization and Social Structure in Symbolic Interactionist Thought." *Annual Review of Sociology* 3: 235–59.

———. 1979. "Mesostructure and Social Process." *Contemporary Sociology* 8: 524–27.

———. 1982. "In Search of Mesostructure." *Urban Life* 11: 267–79.

———. 1988. "Myth, Text, and Interactionist Complicity in the Neglect of Blumer's Macrosociology." *Symbolic Interaction* 11: 43–57.

———. 1989. Repackaging Blumer: The Myth of Herbert Blumer's Astructural Bias." *Studies in Symbolic Interaction* 10 (Part B): 383–413.

———, and J. Charlton. 1985. "The Negotiated Order Approach to the Analysis of Social Organization." *Studies in Symbolic Interaction* 1: 271–308.

———, and T. Morrione. 1990. "On the Breadth and Relevance of Blumer's Perspective: Introduction to His Analysis of Industrialization." Pp. xi–xxiv in *Industrialization as an Agent of Social Change: A Critical Analysis,* by Herbert Blumer. Edited and with an introduction by David R. Maines and Thomas J. Morrione. New York: Aldine de Gruyter.

Manis, J., and B. Meltzer, eds. 1967. *Symbolic Interaction.* First edition. Boston: Allyn and Bacon.

———, eds. 1972. *Symbolic Interaction.* Second edition. Boston: Allyn and Bacon.

Manning, P. K. 1982. "Analytic Induction." Pp. 273–302 in *A Handbook of Social Science Methods,* Vol. 2, edited by R. Smith and P. Manning. Cambridge, Mass.: Ballinger.

McCall, G. J. and J. L. Simmons, eds. 1969. *Issues in Participant Observation.* Reading, Mass.: Addison-Wesley.

———. 1978 [1966]. *Identities and Interactions.* Second edition. New York: The Free Press.

McPhail, C., and C. Rexroat. 1979. "Mead vs. Blumer: The Divergent Methodological Perspectives of Social Behaviorism and Symbolic Interactionism." *American Sociological Review* 44: 449–67.

———. 1980. "Ex Cathedra Blumer or Ex Libris Mead?" *American Sociological Review* 45: 420–30.

Mead, G. H. 1934. *Mind, Self, and Society,* edited by C. W. Morris. Chicago: University of Chicago Press.

Meltzer, B. N. and J. W. Petras. 1970. "The Chicago and Iowa Schools of Symbolic Interactionism." Pp. 3–17 in *Human Nature and Collective Behavior,* edited by T. Shibutani. New Brunswick: Transaction Books.

Merton, R. K. 1957a. *Social Theory and Social Structure.* New York: The Free Press.

———. 1957b. "The Role Set: Problems in Sociological Theory." *British Journal of Sociology* 8: 106–20.

———, G. Reader, and P. L. Kendall, eds. 1957. *The Student Physician.* Cambridge: Harvard University Press.

Miller, S. M. 1952. "The Participant Observer and Over-Rapport." *American Sociological Review* 17: 97–99.

Miyamoto, S. F. and S. M. Dornbusch. 1956. "A Test of Interactionist Hypotheses of Self-Conception." *American Journal of Sociology* 51: 399–403.

Moore, W. E. 1970. *The Professions.* New York: Russell Sage Foundation.

Nadel, S. F. 1957. *The Theory of Social Structure.* Glencoe: The Free Press.

Nye, I. F. 1976. *Role Structure and Analysis of the Family.* Beverly Hills: Sage.

Olesen, V., and E. Whittaker. 1968. *The Silent Dialogue: The Social Psychology of Professional Socialization.* San Francisco: Jossey-Bass.

O'Toole, R., and R. Dubin. 1968. "Baby Feeding and Body Sway." *Journal of Personality and Social Psychology* 10: 59–65.

Park, R. E. 1926. "Behind Our Masks." *Survey Graphic* 56: 135–39.

———. 1927. "Human Nature and Collective Behavior." *American Journal of Sociology* 32: 695–703.

———. 1931. "Human Nature, Attitudes and Mores." Pp. 17–45 in *Social Attitudes,* edited by K. Young. New York: Holt.

Parsons, T. 1937. *The Structure of Social Action.* 2 Vols. New York: The Free Press.

———. 1939. "The Professions and Social Structure." *Social Forces* 17: 457–67.

———. 1940. "The Motivation of Economic Activities." *Canadian Journal of Economics and Political Science* 6: 187–203.

———. 1951. *The Social System.* New York: The Free Press.

Platt, J. 1983. "The Development of the Participant Observation Method in Sociology: Origin, Myth and History." *Journal of the History of the Behavioral Sciences* 19: 379–93.

Powers, C. 1981. "Role-Imposition or Role-Improvisation: Some Theoretical Principles." *Economic and Social Review* 12: 287–99.

Prus, R. Forthcoming. *Studying Human Lived Experience.*

Quarantelli, E. L., and J. Cooper. 1966. "Self-Conceptions and Others: A Further Test of Meadian Hypothesis." *Sociological Quarterly* 7: 281–97.

Rawls, A. 1987. "The Interaction Order Sui Generis: Goffman's Contribution to Social Theory." *Sociological Theory* 5: 136–49.

———. 1988. "Interaction vs. Interaction Order: Reply to Fuchs." *Sociological Theory* 6: 124–29.

Reeder, L. G., G. A. Donohue, and A. Biblarz. 1960. "Conceptions of Self and Others." *American Journal of Sociology* 66: 153–59.

Reynolds, J., and L. Reynolds. 1973. "Interactionism, Complicity, and the Astructural Bias." *Catalyst* 7: 76–85.

Reynolds, L. 1993. *Interactionism: Exposition and Critique.* 3d edition. Dix Hills, N.Y.: General Hall.

Riesman, D. 1983. "The Legacy of Everett Hughes." *Contemporary Sociology* 12: 477–81.

Ritzer, G. 1990. "The Current Status of Sociological Theory: The New Syntheses." Pp. 1–30 in *Frontiers of Social Theory,* edited by G. Ritzer. New York: Columbia University Press.

Rochberg-Halton, E. 1986. *Meaning and Modernity.* Chicago: University of Chicago Press.

Rock, P. 1979. *The Making of Symbolic Interactionism.* Totowa, N.J.: Rowman and Littlefield.

Rose, A. M., ed. 1962a. *Human Behavior and Social Processes.* Boston: Houghton Mifflin.

———. 1962b. "A Systematic Summary of Symbolic Interaction Theory." Pp. 3–19 in *Human Behavior and Social Processes,* edited by A. Rose. Boston: Houghton Mifflin.

Roth, J. 1962. "The Treatment of Tuberculosis as a Bargaining Process." Pp. 575–88 in *Human Behavior and Social Processes,* edited by A. M. Rose. Boston: Houghton Mifflin.

———. 1963. *Timetables.* Indianapolis: Bobbs-Merrill.

Roy, D. F. 1952. "Quota Restriction and Goldbricking in a Machine Shop." *American Journal of Sociology* 57: 427–42.

———. 1953. "Work Satisfaction and Social Reward in Quota Achievement: An Analysis of Piecework Incentive." *American Sociological Review* 18: 507–14.

———. 1960. "Banana Time: Job Satisfaction and Informal Interaction." *Human Organization* 18: 156–68.

Schwartz, M. S., and C. G. Schwartz. 1955. "Problems in Participant Observation." *American Journal of Sociology* 60: 343–53.

Shalin, D. 1986. "Pragmatism and Social Interactionism." *American Sociological Review* 51: 9–29.

Shibutani, T. 1961. *Society and Personality.* Englewood Cliffs: Prentice-Hall.
———. 1988. "Herbert Blumer's Contributions to Twentieth-Century Sociology."
    Symbolic Interaction 11: 23–31.
———, and K. Kwan. 1965. *Ethnic Stratification.* New York: Macmillan.
Shott, S. 1979. "Emotion and Social Life: A Symbolic Interactionist Analysis."
    American Journal of Sociology 84: 1317–34.
Stone, G. P. 1962. "Appearance and the Self." Pp. 86–118 in *Human Behavior and
    Social Processes,* edited by A. Rose. Boston: Houghton Mifflin.
———. 1965. "The Play of Little Children." *Quest* 4: 23–31.
———. 1984. "Conceptual Problems in Small Group Research." *Studies in Sym-
    bolic Interaction* 5: 3–21.
Stone, G., and H. Farberman. 1967a. "On the Edge of Rapprochement: Was
    Durkheim Moving Toward the Perspective of Symbolic Interaction?" *Socio-
    logical Quarterly* 8: 149–64.
———. 1967b. "Further Comment on the Blumer-Bales Dialogue Concerning the
    Implications of the Thought of George Herbert Mead." *American Journal
    of Sociology.* 72: 409–10.
———, eds. 1970a. *Social Psychology Through Symbolic Interaction.* First edition.
    Waltham, Mass.: Xerox College Publishing.
———. 1970b. "Social Process as Symbolic Transformation." Pp. 89–92 in *Social
    Psychology Through Symbolic Interaction,* edited by G. Stone and H. Farber-
    man. Waltham, Mass: Xerox Publishing.
———, eds. 1981. *Social Psychology Through Symbolic Interaction.* Second edi-
    tion. New York: John Wiley and Sons.
Strauss, A. 1959. *Mirrors and Masks.* Glencoe: The Free Press.
———. 1970. "Discovering New Theory from Previous Theory." Pp. 46–53 in *Hu-
    man Nature and Collective Behavior,* edited by T. Shibutani. New Brunswick:
    Transaction Books.
———. 1978. *Negotiations: Varieties, Contexts, Processes, and Social Order.* San
    Francisco: Jossey-Bass.
———. 1987. *Qualitative Analysis for Social Scientists.* New York: Cambridge
    University Press.
———. 1993. *Continual Permutations of Action.* New York: Aldine De Gruyter.
———, and J. Corbin. 1990. *Basics of Qualitative Research.* Newbury Park, Ca-
    lif.: Sage.
———, L. Schatzman, D. Ehrlich, R. Bucher, and M. Sabshin. 1963. "The Hospi-
    tal and Its Negotiated Order." Pp. 147–69 in *The Hospital in Modern Society,*
    edited by E. Freidson. New York: The Free Press.
Strong, S. M. 1943. "Social Types in a Minority Group." *American Journal of Soci-
    ology* 48: 563–73.
———. 1946. "Negro-White Relations as Reflected in Social Types." *American
    Journal of Sociology* 52: 23–30.
Stryker, S. 1956. "Relationships of Married Offspring and Parent: A Test of
    Mead's Theory." *American Journal of Sociology* 62: 308–19.
———. 1957. "Role-Taking Accuracy and Adjustment." *Sociometry* 20: 286–96.
———. 1962. "Conditions of Accurate Role-Taking: A Test of Mead's Theory."

Pp. 41–62 in *Human Behavior and Social Processes,* edited by A. M. Rose. Boston: Houghton Mifflin.

———. 1968. "Identity Salience and Role Performance: The Relevance of Symbolic Interaction Theory for Family Research." *Journal of Marriage and the Family* 30: 558–64.

———. 1980. *Symbolic Interactionism: A Social Structural Version.* Menlo Park: Benjamin Cummings.

———. 1981. "Symbolic Interactionism: Themes and Variations." Pp. 3–29 in *Social Psychology,* edited by M. Rosenberg and R. H. Turner. New York: Basic Books.

———, and R. T. Serpe. 1982. "Commitment, Identity Salience, and Role Behavior: Theory and Research Example." Pp. 199–218 in *Personality, Roles, and Social Behavior,* edited by W. Ickes and E. S. Knowles. New York: Springer-Verlag.

———, and A. Statham. 1985. "Symbolic Interaction and Role Theory." Pp. 311–78 in *Handbook of Social Psychology,* vol. 1, edited by G. Lindzey and E. Aronson. New York: Random House.

Thomas, W. I. 1921. *Old World Traits Transplanted* New York: Harper and Brothers.

Thomas, W. I. and F. Znaniecki. 1918–20. *The Polish Peasant in Europe and America.* 5 Vols. Boston: Badger.

Thrasher, F. M. 1927. *The Gang.* Chicago: University of Chicago Press.

Turner, J. H. 1991. *The Structure of Sociological Theory.* 5th edition. Belmont, Calif.: Wadsworth.

Turner, R. H. 1947. "The Navy Disbursing Officer as a Bureaucrat." *American Sociological Review* 12: 342–48.

———. 1956. "Role-Taking, Role Standpoint, and Reference-Group Behavior." *American Journal of Sociology* 61: 316–28.

———. 1957. "The Normative Coherence of Folk Concepts" *Research Studies of the State College of Washington* 25: 127–36.

———. 1962. "Role Taking: Process versus Conformity." Pp. 20–40 in *Human Behavior and Social Processes,* edited by A. M. Rose. Boston: Houghton Mifflin.

———. 1965. Role Theory: A Series of Propositions." Mimeo, Department of Sociology, UCLA.

———. 1968. "Role: Sociological Aspects." *International Encyclopedia of the Social Sciences* 13: 552–57.

———. 1970. *Family Interaction.* New York: John Wiley and Sons.

———. 1972. "Deviance Avowal as Neutralization of Commitment." *Social Problems* 19: 308–21.

———. 1974. "Rule Learning as Role Learning: What an Interactive Theory of Roles Adds to the Theory of Social Norms." *International Journal of Critical Sociology* 1: 52–73.

———. 1976. "The Real Self: From Institution to Impulse." *American Journal of Sociology* 81: 989–1016.

———. 1978. "The Role and the Person." *American Journal of Sociology* 84: 1–23.

————. 1980. "Strategy for Developing an Integrated Role Theory." *Humboldt Journal of Social Relations* 7: 123–39.

————. 1985. "Unanswered Questions in the Convergence between Structuralist and Interactionist Role Theories." Pp. 22–36 in *Micro-Sociological Theory: Perspectives on Sociological Theory,* vol. 2, edited by H. J. Helle and S. N. Eisenstadt. Beverly Hills: Sage.

————. 1990. "Role Change." *Annual Review of Sociology* 16: 87–110.

Turner, R. H., and P. Colomy. 1988. "Role Differentiation: Orienting Principles." *Advances in Group Processes* 5: 1–27.

Turner, R. H., and N. Shosid. 1976. "Ambiguity and Interchangeability in Role Attribution: The Effect of Alter's Response." *American Sociological Review* 41: 993–1006.

Wagner, D. G. 1984. *The Growth of Sociological Theories.* Beverly Hills: Sage.

————, and J. Berger. 1985. "Do Sociological Theories Grow?" *American Journal of Sociology* 90: 697–728.

Wax, R. 1971. *Doing Fieldwork.* Chicago: University of Chicago Press.

Weinstein, E. A. and P. Deutschberger. 1963. "Some Dimensions of Altercasting." *Sociometry* 26: 454–66.

White, H. C., S. A. Boorman, and R. L. Breiger. 1976. "Social Structure from Multiple Networks: I. Blockmodels of Roles and Positions." *American Journal of Sociology* 81: 730–80.

Whyte, W. F. 1955. *Money and Motivation.* New York: Harper and Row.

————. 1987. "From Human Relations to Organizational Behavior: Reflections on the Changing Scene." *Industrial and Labor Relations Review,* 40 (4): 487–500.

Williams, N. 1989. "Theoretical and Methodological Issues in the Study of Role-Making." *Studies in Symbolic Interaction* 10 (Part A): 167–84.

Williams, R. 1976. "Symbolic Interactionism: Fusion of Theory and Research." In *New Directions in Sociology,* edited by D. C. Thorns. London: David and Charles.

Wilson, T. P. 1970. "Conceptions of Interaction and Forms of Sociological Explanation." *American Sociological Review* 35: 697–710.

Wirth, L. 1928. *The Ghetto.* Chicago: University of Chicago Press.

Wood, M., and M. Wardell. 1983. "G. H. Mead's Social Behaviorism vs. the Astructural Bias of Symbolic Interactionism." *Symbolic Interaction* 6: 85–96.

Young, P. 1932. *The Pilgrims of Russian Town.* Chicago: University of Chicago Press.

Znaniecki, F. W. 1928. "Social Research in Criminology." *Sociology and Social Research* 12: 307–22.

————. 1934. *The Method of Sociology.* New York: Farrar and Rinehart.

————. 1940. *The Social Role of the Man of Knowledge.* New York: Columbia University Press.

————. 1954. "Basic Problems of Contemporary Sociology." *American Sociological Review* 19: 519–24.

————. 1965. *Social Relations and Social Roles.* San Francisco: Chandler.

————. 1969. *Florian Znaniecki on Humanistic Sociology,* edited by R. Bierstedt. Chicago: University of Chicago Press.

Zola, I. 1972. "Medicine as an Institution of Social Control." *Sociological Review* 20: 487–504.

———. 1975. "In the Name of Health and Illness: On Some Socio-Political Consequences of Medical Influence." *Social Science and Medicine* 9: 83–87.

Zorbaugh, H. 1929. *The Gold Coast and The Slum.* Chicago: University of Chicago Press.

Zurcher, L. 1965. "The Sailor Aboard Ship: A Study of Role Behavior in a Total Institution." *Social Forces* 43: 389–400.

———. 1983. *Social Roles: Conformity, Conflict, and Creativity.* Beverly Hills: Sage.

CHAPTER TWO

RESEARCH METHODS AND THE

SECOND CHICAGO SCHOOL

Jennifer Platt

Did the "second Chicago school" have a distinctive methodological character? For some, its image is one of overwhelming commitment to symbolic interactionism and qualitative methods, especially participant observation, and that commitment is seen as distinguishing Chicago from other departments. But is this image justified, and can the important qualitative researchers who came from Chicago at that time be seen as representative of the department, or as a product of its character? This chapter argues that the image has as much of myth as it does of history.

There is no doubt that some postwar Chicago graduates were both prominent themselves in the significant revival of interest in "qualitative" methods in the 1960s and 1970s and provided exemplars and methodological writings which inspired others. It does not follow that they were quantitatively dominant within the department, or that their contributions can be seen as due to what they learned there. The facts of the situation are considered more closely below.[1] If the myth is true, the department must have been both distinctive and homogeneous; let us see first how far that was so.

The faculty were notoriously divided on questions of method, and sometimes actually in conflict. In the interwar period, the cleavage had been defined in terms of the case-study versus the statistical method (Platt 1992), and leading members of the faculty who had taken sides on that issue were still active in the earlier part of the period we are considering. After the war, there were those whose work was primarily quantitative in character, in demography and ecology as well as among the users of surveys: Ogburn and Hauser in particular, initially, and then later Kitagawa, O. D. Duncan, Goodman, Bogue, Rossi, and Coleman as well as those such as Hart, Star, and Davis who were based in the National Opinion Research Center (NORC). Those whose work was primarily qualitative included Blumer, Hughes, Warner, and Whyte at an earlier stage, and later added Strauss; a number of junior people such as Becker, Junker, and Roy held short-term instructorships. Ernest Burgess, who retired in 1951, occupied an important intermediate position in that he both championed the case study and conducted large-scale quantitative studies. (Clifford Shaw, based in the Institute for Juvenile Research but also a long-term associate of the department, was also active in both.) Insofar as the department had a methodological tradition which was sustained by faculty representation over the whole period, the demographic-ecological one is as strong a candidate as fieldwork. What this looks like is a continuing tradition of heterogeneity, although with a greater emphasis on survey methods as these became more important nationally.

When we turn from the faculty to the students, it is not surprising that they too were diverse, although the proportion of theses that were predominantly quantitative in method may be found surprising. A sample of theses[2] gives the results summarized in Table 2.1. (The detailed breakdown by year of doctorate is not very informative, since it was not uncommon for students to submit their theses years after they had left the department physically and taken jobs elsewhere and some students took much longer to complete them than others. Later years are combined because fewer theses from them were examined.) This shows that at each date a range of different methods was used, and that at no point were the more richly qualitative methods (quantitatively) dominant. Table 2.2 uses the same material to make the quantitative/qualitative distinction, and shows that at each period about half the theses were quantitative and about a third qualitative.

These basic figures raise the question of distinctiveness. Is a tradition

TABLE 2.1. MAIN METHOD OF DATA-COLLECTION IN CHICAGO THESES

Year of thesis	Census	Other statistics	Survey	Mixed Methods	Intensive Interviews	Fieldwork/ Participant Observation	Other*
1946–48	3	1	4	4	2	2	2
1950	—	6	6	3	1	3	2
1952	1	4	3	5	—	4	—
1954	—	2	2	6	2	1	2
1956–58	2	1	1	1	7	1	—
1960–62	3	—	5	3	—	—	1
Total	9	14	21	22	12	11	7

*"Other" includes historical and documentary sources, one experiment, and one secondary analysis of taped survey interviews.

TABLE 2.2. QUANTITATIVE/QUALITATIVE METHOD, IN CHICAGO THESES

Year of thesis	Quantitative*	Qualitative*	Mixed or Unclassified	N
1946–50	51%	36%	13%	39
1952–54	48%	29%	23%	31
1956–62	54%	33%	13%	24

*Methods were classified as quantitative if the main data came from a survey, the Census, or other official statistics; they were classified as qualitative if the main data came from intensive interviews, fieldwork/participant observation, or documents (without significant quantitative analysis).

of heterogeneity much of a tradition at all? Was Chicago perhaps just a microcosm of a heterogeneous discipline? Or perhaps the department as a whole is not the right unit? We address these questions below.

To consider how far Chicago was just a microcosm of the discipline, we need to compare what was happening at Chicago with what was happening elsewhere at the same time. A comparison of Chicago doctoral methods with those of other universities would require collection of data from a sample of the other theses, which is not practicable. The only practicable possibility is to make the comparison with the methods used in published articles,[3] and this is what has been done.

A sample of articles has been taken from the main journals,[4] and the methods used in the articles have been classified in the same way as those of the Chicago theses. The articles are divided into those by the Chicago cohort in question, and others. This enables us to compare the articles by others with both Chicago articles and Chicago theses. What do we find? Table 2.3 summarizes the data. The differences between the two groups of articles are small. When the two groups of articles are compared with the ambiguous "other" and "mixed" categories excluded, we see that there is slightly more qualitative method from Chicago, and more survey method from elsewhere. This fits the stereotypes, but the differences are not large and still leave two-thirds of the Chicago articles quantitative. Moreover, the influence of the department cannot be responsible for the use of fieldwork or participant observation in some of the Chicago articles, because the work was done before the author joined the department (Adams 1947) or was based on personal experience not undertaken for research purposes. (Turner 1947, Mitra 1947, Becker 1951, Dornbusch 1955, Roth 1957, Davis 1959). However, the departmental style was, of course, involved here in another way; it was seen as acceptable to use personal ex-

TABLE 2.3. MAIN METHODS OF DATA-COLLECTION

	Census	Other Statistics	Survey	Mixed Methods	Intensive Interviews	Fieldwork/ Participant Observation	Other*	N
Chicago theses	9% (13%)	15% (21%)	22% (31%)	23%	13% (19%)	11% (16%)	7%	96 (70)
Chicago articles	9% (15%)	8% (13%)	24% (40%)	9%	7% (12%)	12% (20%)	31%	100 (60)
Other articles	6% (13%)	8% (17%)	24% (53%)	5%	3% (6%)	5% (11%)	49%	850 (386)

*"Other" here includes many instances with no empirical data, as in purely theoretical articles, or with data which do not have a clear source, as well as with data collected from miscellaneous sources. The bracketed figures show the percentages when the "other" and "mixed methods" categories are excluded.

periences as data, and indeed Hughes actively encouraged this. This probably meant that more such work was done at Chicago, even though in the immediate postwar period the journals had from many sources short articles which drew on people's wartime experiences. If the Chicago theses are compared with the articles, the extent by which work done elsewhere leads Chicago in the "survey" category increases, but the overall quantitative/qualitative division remains the same. Thus Chicago shows a small propensity towards more qualitative work, but the overall pattern is such that it would not be unreasonable to conclude that it was, indeed, roughly—if only roughly—a microcosm of the larger discipline.

Our second question was whether the Chicago department as a whole is the right unit to consider in characterizing its methodological traditions. There are a number of excellent reasons why it should not be, arising from the social organization of any large department. First, students become particularly associated with some faculty members rather than others: their mentors or the members of their thesis committees, and ones with whom they work as teaching or research assistants. Second, students form their own friendship groups, both within the department and outside it. Third, students arrive in different cohorts, and their formative experiences may thus differ over time; this can happen both because of faculty presence and course structure, and because of the size and composition of student groups. The information I have about these patterns is fragmentary, but I will piece it together to describe as much as possible of this substructure.

As in other graduate schools, the choice of doctoral topics and methods was often influenced by faculty research interests and funding. Killian (1990) has described how he chose his thesis topic from a list of suggestions provided by the faculty; Vajda (1960) acknowledges the help of Hauser "for his suggestion of Burma as a topic for demographic research and for making the scarce 1953 Burmese Census available to me." Hughes had a whole series of students whom he encouraged to work on occupations, from doctor and funeral director to jazz musician and janitor. These were topics not directly associated with funded research or a project team, as some others were. Orvis Collins, Melville Dalton, and Donald Roy did their theses as part of a project directed by Whyte for the Committee on Human Relations in Industry, with which Warner and Hughes were also associated. Another industrial project from which several theses arose was the one on trade unionism on which London, Karsh, and Tagliacozzo worked. (The foreword to the eventual book suggests that the project was in part a response to the presence on campus of a number of graduate students who already had union experience [Seidman et al. 1958: vii]). The theses of Benson, Bowerman, Lu, and Pineo used data from Burgess's study of the adjustment of married couples, and those of Harlan, Pan, Schmidt, and Shanas were part of his program on "later maturity." Amerman, Becker, McDowell, and Winget worked on studies directed by Hughes and Wirth in the Chicago public schools; Janowitz's work was part of a study directed by Shils and Bettelheim; Beale, Cutright, Greeley, and Star drew their data from NORC projects on which they worked. A number of students also wrote their theses on data from projects or jobs elsewhere: Ohlin and Daniel Glaser used data they worked on in the course of their employment in the Illinois criminal justice system, and Clausen and Miyamoto used data from their wartime work on the American Soldier and on the study of Tule Lake camp, respectively. Some students, like Rainwater (1984), got both their data and some important methodological socialization from working in Social Research, Inc., the market research and consultancy firm run by Burleigh Gardner in which several faculty members were also involved.

Some of these programs, though probably not all of them, created social groupings. For instance, Edward Gross (1984) reports that the industrial sociology group around Whyte met regularly each week over beer to discuss their work and ideas, including those on method. Ray Gold (1984)[5] was closely involved with Hughes and Junker when they worked together on a project on fieldwork. NORC provided a physical location which probably helped to make it a socially meaningful unit for those working on its projects, as did the Institute for Juvenile Research, the Chicago Community Inventory, and the Population Studies Center. Such centers also, of course, provided hands-on apprenticeship training in research methods which was an important learning experience for the students involved.

It cannot be assumed, however, that the choice of a thesis method or topic necessarily implied long-term commitments. For some it did, although they may not have been sure of that at the time. For others, it seems likely that it was an expedient and instrumental matter, a convenient way to achieve a needed qualification before getting on with the rest of life. Turner, for instance, wanted to do a dissertation that would combine his interests in race relations and social psychology but came up against political and practical problems in the work he had started; he was thus led to submit as his dissertation the demographic data on race in the labor force which had been intended as background material (Turner 1991). At any rate, it is clear that some graduate students were not socialized by their thesis work into methodological traditions which they have stayed with in their later careers; if they had been, Sanford Dornbusch would have specialized in labor force demography using Census data rather than social psychology, and Simon Marcson would have worked mainly on prediction from questionnaire data on families rather than on other kinds of study of industrial organizations.

Even after graduation, individual accounts of careers show how subsequent patterns of work are affected by other factors besides personal methodological commitments and interests. No doubt it is always true that present settings interact with prior characteristics to produce current behavior, but the importance of material resources probably intensifies the significance of contemporary opportunities in relation to the choice of research methods. O. D. Duncan (1984) noted the great differences made in his style of work by the growth and increasing sophistication of computer technology. He also said that nearly all the projects he worked on arose accidentally through other people bringing problems to him. Eliot Freidson (1984) describes himself as committed to qualitative field methods in graduate school, but in the jobs he could get in years after that he found himself involved with the use of structural linguistics to analyze taped data and with rat-running psychologists, as well as with carrying out a survey. James Short (1984) did secondary analysis of official statistics for his Ph.D. because he was intellectually enamored of Ogburn; however, his general interest in crime also led to contacts with Lohman and Shaw, through whom he became interested in self-reports as a way of improving on the data in official statistics, and so did some work on that; pursuing the same interest further led to the use of participant observers in delinquent gangs as well as the use of survey data. Albert Reiss (1984) also moved, though by a very different route, from the use of Census data to a large-scale survey and then to systematic observation (of police behavior). Morris Schwartz (1984), while strongly committed to participant observation as a preferred method, found himself doing conventional interviewing when it was required by the nature of his work for the Joint Commission on Mental Health. These examples show members of the cohort, starting with varying levels of skills and commitment in relation to different methodological styles, responding to environments in which they were exposed to new intellectual influences, taking jobs with little scope for personal choice, following substantive concerns which incidentally took them in new methodological directions, being influenced by the resources available—and so on. Such processes are normal.

There is also some reason to question just how important relations with faculty were for many students. Numbers of those in the department in the earlier part of the period, when there were extremely large numbers of graduate students, have described how the faculty seemed swamped by the tide of returning veterans and were hard to meet with. An anecdote which encapsulates this was told by one former student, who describes meeting a faculty member on the stairs in the department and, when the student said "Good morning," getting only the reply "It's the vacation"! Several graduates also report that in 1946 or 1947 there was a student petition of protest at the lack of attention they were getting. Some other comments:

"Wirth repeatedly told his classes that the function of a university was to advance knowledge by providing its faculty with a facility for research; students, he said, should consider themselves very lucky to gather the crumbs of wisdom that fell from the table" (Bogart 1990).

"Nobody taught any of us; I think you'd say we were self-taught, we proceeded from inspiration from people we liked, like I liked Everett Hughes . . ." (Gross 1984).

". . . most of us learned our research largely by doing; you took courses, but what really was the best learning experience was contact with fellow graduate students, particularly those you came into contact with while doing research" (Short 1984).

Where students were involved with other sociology students in ways which were intellectually important to them, there is a little information available about the bases on which groups formed and their composition. Gusfield describes his experience of the ecology of the area in which many students lived as throwing them together in chance encounters, as well as giving a homogeneous social character to particular buildings. He goes on to list other members of his group who have made careers in sociology, and the list includes a high proportion of the key figures associated with qualitative methods; he points out that they were heavily Jewish, which may have provided one basis of solidarity (Gusfield 1990b). This suggests the possibility that such factors may have been a crucial condition for the development of a socio-intellectual grouping within the department which led to longer-term shared concerns. Several other informants mention the Canadian group, to which Everett Hughes was important because of his Canadian connections and towards whom he acted as "mother hen." This

group included Goffman and Gross (Gross 1984), and also David Solomon and Aileen Ross (Becker et al. 1968), Leo Zakuta, Dan Lortie and
Jacques Brazeau (Becker 1990), and Harold Finestone (Galliher, this volume); there were probably others. Several also mention the practice of
preparing for exams in groups, which could have up to ten members
(Gross 1984; Turner 1990); these could be groups of close friends but they
could also be, as with Leo Bogart, Albert Reiss, and Natalie Rogoff (Bogart 1990) a group that got together just because they were going to sit
their prelims at the same time. Some informants (e.g., Freidson 1984) say
that most of those they mixed with were doing the same sort of work,
while others give a quite different impression; no general pattern emerges,
except that the lists given by some of the women suggest that they may
have tended to stick together. Another identity which seems to have been
salient to those who bore it is white Southerner, though they do not mention sticking together for that reason; there is a hint that this highly self-
selected minority group may have mixed more with the small number of
black students.

    Not every student, however, was deeply involved intellectually with
other students. Hare (1990) and Peil (1990), for instance, both mention
that they and others were so busy completing their work in only two years
that they had little time for social relations. Many students worked on
their theses while holding full-time jobs elsewhere, and during that stage
were not available on campus. Many of those who commented stress the
importance of the fact that a lot of students, especially among the veterans, were married, often with children, and therefore spent much of their
spare time with their families and found general sociability with their
neighbors.

    Is it helpful to understand any of the department's methodological
character in terms of the influence of symbolic interactionist theory? It
has often been assumed that this is so, though I do not find the arguments
convincing. This is in part because of the uncertainty about who should
be classified as a symbolic interactionist.[6] Some identify themselves with
the label, and may be taken as unproblematic cases. However, some to
whom the label has most confidently been applied reject it. Goffman, interviewed by Winkin, said that there is no "symbolic interactionism." The
students taught by Hughes, Warner, and Blumer were individuals, not a
movement, and thought of themselves as occupational or industrial sociologists (Winkin 1988: 235). Freidson (1984) says he did not classify himself as one, though sometimes called such. Deutscher (1984: 71) describes

being asked by Arnold Rose to contribute to his reader on symbolic interactionism. He asked what that was, and reports that Rose's "face flushed
as he angrily shouted 'it is what they do at Chicago!'" Becker (1990) says
none of them used that term for a school of thought—it was just one
of several key ideas in Blumer's theory—and he remembers being quite
surprised at having it applied to him. It does not help that there is a tendency to a kind of back-formation in this field: participant observation is
associated by some writers with symbolic interactionism, and those who
do it are therefore defined as symbolic interactionists without any independent evidence that they are such. This operational definition then,
naturally, produces a strong correlation between theory and method. This
sort of approach can be taken even in such subtle and sophisticated accounts as Rock's, in which he sees symbolic interactionism as a theory
implicit in the concrete detail of particular studies rather than stated in
the abstract (Rock 1979: 9,19). However, even those who do claim the
label are not all committed to the same methodological styles. It has been
pointed out (Meltzer and Petras 1967: 8) that Kuhn's Iowa group of symbolic interactionists have typically collected data by the "Twenty Statements Test" rather than by more "qualitative" methods.

But even within the Chicago department it was neither the case that
all those seen as symbolic interactionists confined themselves to participant observation nor that all those actively involved in participant observation were interactionists. Faculty members are considered first. Noone
regards Warner as an interactionist, and it was clear that his participant
observation came out of the anthropological tradition. Whyte is not an
interactionist, and his participant observation seems to have related at the
time to a combination of anthropology and an almost behaviorist conception of the role of direct observation (Platt 1983: 385). Burgess may be
regarded as some sort of interactionist, but he was not involved with participant observation; he was an active proponent of the case study but also
undertook a number of large-scale surveys and used ecological data and
statistical prediction techniques. Hughes was committed to fieldwork, but
those closest to him have emphasized that he was not dogmatic about
methodology, used demographic data, and expected students to be literate
in statistics (Becker et al. 1968: vii). Blumer is the faculty member most
strongly and explicitly associated with symbolic interactionism—a term
he invented—and his ideas are invoked to justify participant observation.
However, he published very little empirical research himself, and so did
not provide exemplars. Even those who admire him and find inspiration

in his ideas may say, as David Wellman and Howard Becker both did at the session in his honor at the ASA meetings of 1984, that he did not provide what are conventionally regarded as methods and that it was not clear how to translate his system into data. (This may go some way to account for the difficulty some of his disciples had in bringing their work to a conclusion and for the "analytic interruptus" described by Lofland (1970).) In my own interview with him (Blumer 1982a), he said that "Participant observation can be very dangerous to scholarship, in the sense that an individual who thinks he's really participating can be only doing so on the surface and misperceiving what's really taking place. In short, one has to be very careful to check up on participant observation and make sure it's not distortive." Norbert Wiley also interviewed him (Blumer 1982b) and asked which empirical studies caught the theory of symbolic interaction best. Blumer apparently had difficulty thinking of examples, and didn't think field research had caught the theory well. (The examples he did come up with were not from Chicago.) He went on to say that there are no fixed fieldwork techniques, but that being a field-worker is like being a good investigative reporter.

What about the students? Much information is missing, but a rough tabulation of those graduates generally regarded as interactionists shows only five out of twenty-one using participant observation as the main source of data for their theses. Three of the five were supervised by Blumer, but one of the three was Miyamoto, whose participation was done not under Blumer but as part of a wartime project supervised by the behavioristically inclined Dorothy Thomas. Those who have shown a longer-term commitment to participant observation, whether or not they used it in their theses, were more often the students and coworkers of Hughes and Warner, who were actively involved themselves in projects based on fieldwork. There is probably a moral to be drawn here about the influence of abstract theoretical positions on empirical work, and about the ways in which many methodological choices and commitments emerge.

One may treat it as problematic that symbolic interactionism should lead especially to participant observation as the most appropriate method, even if the two are highly compatible. The interwar Chicago school did not make that connection; for them the relevant qualitative categories were "case-study method" (consistent with, and even requiring, a variety of methods of data collection) and "life history" or "personal documents." It is interesting that Denzin, one of the contemporaries unequivocally committed theoretically to symbolic interactionism, in his important text-book (Denzin 1970), tried to revive interest in the life history and stressed it more than participant observation, as well as seeing a useful place for surveys and experiments. In this he was following more directly in the tradition of the first Chicago school than have some of those who invoke its name. The modern conception of participant observation is essentially a postwar invention (Platt 1983, 1994), one to whose invention the key contributions were made by some of the postwar Chicago faculty and students. The emphasis on participant observation in the image of Chicago probably reflects the current concerns of those putting forward the image as much as or more than the historical realities. (Any emphasis on it in this paper is in response to that image.)

Despite the diversity we have shown, some graduates do give a general characterization of the department but they do not emphasize a particular methodological style, unless eclecticism is to count as a style. What people are more likely to mention is a general atmosphere of seriousness and excitement about sociology, the pervasive idea that it was possible to be scientific about society, and a strong emphasis on empirical work with a relative lack of interest in theory. (This tends to be contrasted with what they saw as the contemporary Harvard style.) Some, like Charles E. King (1990) or Joseph Gusfield (1990a), put this in terms of an emphasis on science, but it is a conception of science which does not seem to have the connotation of following any particular philosophical or methodological prescription so much as staying close to the data and only making assertions that can be backed up. Some illustrative quotations:

"It was a methodology that held the student firmly to what he/she could see, hear, and experience at first-hand. . . . Abstractions and concepts ungrounded by the experience with concrete observations were suspect" (Gusfield 1982).

"There was a strong strand in Chicago thinking that if you went out and got your feet dirty you would learn the reality" (Reiss 1984).

". . . if anything at Chicago characterized us it was that empiricism, a crass empiricism, you've got to touch it—that was really very strong . . ." (Freidson 1984).

Such statements are not made only by those who prefer one kind of method. O. D. Duncan (1984) describes how he met Erving Goffman at the airport on the way home from the celebrations for the fiftieth anniversary of the Social Science Research Building and they agreed that, despite their totally different styles of work, they both felt like part of Chicago: "it was not a methodological style, but a kind of curiosity they had about human life."

What created this atmosphere? In our emphasis so far on the internal differentiation of the department, we have not yet mentioned some important shared experiences for students. My interviews about research methods (e.g., Gans 1984, Gold 1984, Freedman 1983, Short 1984) repeatedly describe the compulsory fieldwork course, taught first by Burgess and then by Hughes with various junior assistants. (Reinharz in this volume shows how Hughes carried this tradition to Brandeis.) This carried forward the interwar tradition of the department in that it involved work on the city of Chicago. An integral part of it was for each student to be allocated a census tract and told to go out and collect data on it. Guidance seems to have been minimal: "I was asked to choose a partner, assigned a census tract and told to go out and get some data, period. . . . [Hughes] didn't have anything intellectual to say about it, it was all by example and precept" (Freidson 1984).[7] It is clear that many students found this rather traumatic induction to research exciting. The same emphasis on students actually doing research themselves is also mentioned by two graduates in connection with other courses. Wilmoth Carter (Carter 1990) says that one of the great attractions of Chicago for her was that every course she took required a research paper rather than an exam. (She also mentions that one fellow student dropped out of Chicago because he couldn't stand having to interview so many people on the street!) Annabelle Motz Blum (Blum 1990) also emphasizes the importance of term papers and essays, rather than short answers, for final exams, and sees this as linked with a higher level of commitment to sociology than has been shown by other graduate students she has encountered. I do not know that these courses and experiences were unique to Chicago among the major graduate schools, but I do not recall similar accounts in interviews with graduates from elsewhere. The meaning of such experiences was probably intensified by their association with the strengths of the first Chicago school.

These traditions had, however, changed by the later 1950s. Reiss (1984) mentions that, when he taught the fieldwork course, he updated it by moving it more in the direction of survey methods. When I myself reached the department as an M.A. student in 1959–60, the only compulsory course for the M.A. connected with methods was the one on statistics, taught by a statistician; most other M.A. students did not even seem to be collecting their own data for their theses. I heard nothing about the work of the first Chicago school, and did not understand why Hauser (a prewar student) treated it as important in his historical course; indeed, I am ashamed to say that I thought this was just parochialism. The obvious explanation to suggest for this change is that it was part of the rise in importance of survey method and the development of a more national sociology. NORC was established at Chicago, and members of its staff did some teaching; the old members of the prewar faculty retired, left, or died and were replaced by younger people who mostly came from the Columbia survey or demographic traditions. The amount of data now being generated made it less obvious that each sociologist should generate his or her own, and the division of labor in large-scale surveys provided many training opportunities; an established pattern of national sample studies had been made possible by advances in physical and social technology. In addition, a larger profession with more students had by then created a larger and more systematic methodological literature, as well as a larger body of published studies, which probably suggested that more time could and should be spent in the library rather than on the street. Whether or not this explanation is correct, there seems no doubt that there had been a significant change in the department's methodological atmosphere and the experiences it gave its students.

Another important feature of the department was simply that it was a graduate department, with undergraduate work taught by a different faculty in the separately organized college. Gusfield (1982) has described the great differences in atmosphere between the two as he experienced them. This must have contributed towards the very strong emphasis on research. Most faculty had ongoing projects, which they could draw on for examples and in which they frequently involved students. Moreover the tradition of involvement with the city meant that there were many contacts with people in policy positions, perhaps especially in the criminal justice system. Some of them (like Lohman) were also graduates of the department or did some teaching in it, and they gave access to other sources of data as well as providing potential research problems. Students seem frequently to have done quite substantial empirical work even for their M.A. theses, and indeed some familiar examples referred to in the literature are drawn from this work (Becker on jazz musicians, Schwartz on a mental hospital, Gold on janitors). That some of the work was published shows—even if the shortage of other papers in the immediate postwar period may also have had some bearing—that it was taken seriously. This draws attention to a final point: the presence of the *American Journal of Sociology.* It would be unrealistic not to see this as adding to the perception of early publication as a real possibility; even if there was no discrimination in favor of papers by members of the department, the editors would be likely to encourage the submission of articles on work they knew of and thought promising. (In the period 1949–59, 24 percent of the articles in the *American Journal of Sociology* were by the postwar cohort of Chicago graduates.)

A significant change of direction within the department in the 1950s is mentioned above; several of those who were there argue that there was an important caesura in the department's history around 1952. This resulted from two main factors: the end of the large cohort of G.I. Bill veterans on campus and faculty turnover. In the period 1949–57 Wirth died, Burgess and Ogburn retired, Blumer, Becker, and Whyte left; they were replaced by O. D. Duncan, Leo Goodman, Donald Bogue, Peter Blau, Elihu Katz, Peter Rossi, James Coleman, James Davis—and Anselm Strauss, but within another few years Strauss, Warner, and Hughes were gone, and they were not replaced by people with fieldwork interests. This makes it seem unsurprising that fewer students known for their important qualitative work graduated later.

Those attached to the qualitative myth of Chicago often characterize these changes as part of a significant decline of the department. Such accounts, however, tend not to consider the purely numerical features of the situation. Table 2.4 summarizes the lists given every year in the *American Journal of Sociology* of doctoral degrees. Those lists may not be complete, but there seems no reason to believe that they do not give an accurate

TABLE 2.4. DOCTORATES IN SOCIOLOGY, 1945–62

	Chicago Proportion of Total	(Chicago N)	Total N
1945–46	10%	(8)	79
1947–48	24%	(24)	100
1949–50	22%	(46)	205
1951–52	11%	(28)	250
1953–54	14%	(45)	311
1955–56	5%	(15)	274
1957–58	7%	(19)	272
1959–60	8%	(25)	295
1961–62	8%	(22)	272

picture of the general trend—and they surely do not underrepresent Chicago degrees. What the table shows is that Chicago's proportion of doctorates declined markedly after 1950 but that this was to a considerable extent accounted for by the expansion of programs elsewhere. (Since doctoral candidates take a varying number of years to complete their programs after they start on them, these figures cannot be interpreted as saying anything precise about recruitment dates.) We know that the educational benefits for veterans were very important in the expansion of the graduate schools in the 1940s, and inevitably it was the established graduate schools that were likely to feel the effect first; sociology departments were, however, growing and increasing in number over the period, and this was bound to spread the students more widely. The figures in the table show broadly what one would thus expect for what was originally a leading and numerically dominant department which gradually became one among a larger leading group. Against that background, the figures cannot be taken to show decline in any other sense.

This numerical background must also be taken into account in evaluating the vicissitudes of the department's qualitative methodological tradition. The (incomplete) available data on which students were actually present around the department at which time suggest that the maximum number of those associated with qualitative methods (or symbolic interactionism) who were simultaneously present was in 1947–50; the maximum number of staff committed to qualitative methods (some of them the same people as the students counted above) was reached around 1950 (Harvey 1987). This was, however, almost certainly the time when there was the maximum total number of students and staff. A relatively sharp numerical decline after that is simply part of the drop in numbers of the department as a whole, not anything with special significance for one part of its tradition. Moreover, to the extent that Chicago graduates went out and got jobs across the country in other expanding departments, the tradition they carried was becoming more widely diffused.

Why, if the realities were as complex as has been suggested here, does the myth of a golden age of qualitative method at Chicago have the currency that it does? I suggest that, like many other versions of history within or outside the social sciences, this one has served contemporary purposes. It provides a banner around which sympathizers can rally, and an honorable past with which to legitimate their activities. Such functions are beautifully epitomized in the choice, by a group of California-based sociologists around John and Lyn Lofland who were committed to ethnographic styles of work, of the title "Chicago Irregulars." What, then, were the groupings and movements whose purposes this myth served? Fresh research into the wider context has not been done for the purposes of this chapter, but some well-known facts may be drawn on to suggest a plausible interpretation.

At the end of the 1960s the broad New Left/countercultural movement had many sociologists, especially graduate students, as participants, and it was from this generation that the young faculty of the 1970s were recruited. One part of the ethos of the movement was a strong hostility to quantification and to earlier conceptions of science; a version of support for the alternative of fieldwork/ethnography/participant observation could quite easily be constructed which associated itself with a conception of the Chicago tradition. (In this choice it surely helped that the substantive subject-matter of many of the Chicago studies focused on deviant or marginal groups.) Lyn Lofland has suggested (1983: 491) that the "Chicago school" operates as a sort of Rorschach ink-blot to which people impute their own meanings, and we may happily accept that that conception was, as her comment suggests, only one of many possible ones, and that different more-or-less-participants may have had their own versions of it. A particular ambiguity is involved in the question of which period at Chicago is relevant, because "Chicago school" has most often referred to the interwar period, but the methodological writings and working exemplars to which people related themselves were probably more often postwar. It seems likely that the two periods were unconsciously conflated in people's minds, with the relative homogeneity of the earlier monographs associated with the well-known newer substantive and methodological writings. Table 2.5 lists some of the methodological writings that form part of this

TABLE 2.5. DATES IN THE RESURGENCE OF INTEREST IN
"CHICAGO"-STYLE METHODS

1966	S. T. Bruyn, *The Human Perspective in Sociology*
1967	B. G. Glaser & A. Strauss, *The Discovery of Grounded Theory*
1969	G. J. McCall & J. L. Simmons, *Issues in Participant Observation*
1970	N. K. Denzin, *The Research Act in Sociology*
	W. J. Filstead, *Qualitative Methodology*
1971	J. Lofland, *Analysing Social Settings*
1972	Founding of *Urban Life and Culture* (later just *Urban Life*)
1973	L. Schatzman & A. Strauss, *Field Research*

movement of thought. Space does not permit the inclusion of articles, or of the other works which would be necessary to make the case that this was a fairly sudden and novel efflorescence; for that the reader's general knowledge is invoked. (This efflorescence may in part be accounted for as a reaction to the hegemonic claims of survey research, which made it necessary to justify and rationalize practices previously taken for granted.) Strauss is the only main author in the table who was himself at Chicago, although many of the selections in the books of readings are from Chicago authors, Chicago influences are invoked and there are many Chicago editorial connections.

The introductory editorial of *Urban Life and Culture* rather curiously makes no reference to Chicago, but its style is Blumeresque and later writings (e.g., Manning 1978) make it clear that the journal emerged from the "Chicago Irregulars." The eight consulting editors included Roth and Lemert from Chicago, and the twenty-one advisory editors included eleven associated with postwar Chicago. The journal's declared methodological commitment is to "urban ethnography" seeking inside understanding through participant observation or intensive interviewing. It is worth noting here that the dominance of the urban theme belongs more to prewar Chicago, although that tradition was continued in the work of the demographically oriented group (Bogue, B. and O. D. Duncan, Hauser, Kitagawa) at the Chicago Community Inventory, while the methods mentioned better typify what was actually done by some members of the postwar group not especially concerned with urban issues, thus again exemplifying a conflation of rather different periods. Schatzman and Strauss's book (the first of several textbooks by Strauss, with various collaborators, introducing systematic fieldwork methods) has no visible Chicago links other than the inclusion of some works in the symbolic interaction tradition in its suggested general reading. This might perhaps be taken to symbolize the establishment of an independent California base for a self-conscious methodological style no longer requiring historical legitimation. However, some California groupings continued to refer back to Chicago: a transcription of a 1969 occasion when Blumer and Hughes reminisced about classic Chicago was published in *Urban Life* as late as 1980, and the journal had a special issue on "The Chicago School: The Tradition and the Legacy" in 1983 (vol. 11, no. 4). It is arguable that what eventually emerged was a California-based social movement (of which the methodological concerns of this chapter were only one part), in which some of the Chicago cohort by then in California played a role (cf. Gellner 1979). Berkeley in particular, with Blumer at its head, could be seen as important in this, as Reinharz (this volume) hints.

Another factor which probably helped to create the impression we have criticized is that, even if fieldworkers were never dominant at Chicago, there was a noticeable cluster of them when there was no equivalent at other leading schools; their presence could, thus, reasonably be seen as a distinguishing feature of the department. But why were they there? The golden age of homogeneous qualitative commitment may be mythical, but there was indeed some very important qualitative empirical and methodological work done by members of the postwar Chicago cohorts. Should we impute this to the accidental presence there of a small number of exceptional individuals, or can it be explained by departmental characteristics?

There are several different ways in which methodological contributions and reputations can be made: carrying out empirical work treated as exemplary by others, creating innovative methods in substantive work, writing directly about method, researching method. Postwar Chicago contributed in all these ways, with two senior faculty members—Blumer and Hughes—and three graduates—Strauss, Goffman, and Becker—playing leading roles. When one is dealing with such small numbers it is hard to make well-founded generalizations, but it is probable that no other department made a comparable contribution. However, this cannot simply be put down to Chicago's intellectual style, since one could make a similar list (Hauser, Goodman, O. D. Duncan, Lieberson) of people there important in quantitative methods. The sheer size of the department at the time must have something to do with the magnitude of its contribution, but that is paralleled in other fields by other large departments. It is clear that the presence of Blumer and Hughes, and also of Warner and Whyte, was significant in encouraging students into fieldwork and providing them with relevant opportunities to take part in funded research. Becker's early career, under Hughes's sponsorship, would fit well into an account which emphasized that. Goffman, however, provides a striking counterexample. He got bad grades in his first years at Chicago, and did not get on with Blumer. Although he later referred to Hughes as his patron saint, Hughes was not his mentor and did not approve of him or his work. Warner was his mentor and recommended him to the University of Edinburgh, the base for his doctoral fieldwork on Shetland; the idea was that he should do a Warner-type community study, but that is certainly not what he eventually did. He spent about eighteen months there, and then wrote up his thesis in Paris without returning to Chicago. He was very strongly influenced by the work of Kenneth Burke, a nonsociologist not at Chicago, and by members of Toronto University whom he met before he went to Chicago (Winkin 1988, passim). Winkin suggests that some of his enduring substantive concerns arose from his life experience as the upwardly mobile son of Ukrainian Jewish immigrants to Canada. All this makes it hard to impute his special qualities to the influence of Chicago.

Perhaps Goffman should simply be treated as an exception. However, for some other students he was an important part of the intellectual environment, as they, in turn, were for him. This brings us back to the importance of the student group for at least some of the cohort. Perhaps the most plausible general account we can give for the emergence of the important postwar group of qualitative fieldworkers is this. In a very large intake of students, a number had skills and interests which made them at least open to development in that direction. The early course structure gave them active encouragement, some current faculty and earlier departmental tradition provided exemplars, and faculty research provided relevant work opportunities. Ecology and some shared identities such as "veteran" and "Jewish" helped to create groups which provided mutual support and criticism. Consciousness of difference from what was becoming the mainstream led to the elaboration of explicit justifications for what they were doing. Once these justifications were written, they helped to create the rather unbalanced conception of "Chicago" on which we have commented. Writers always tend to draw examples from the work with which they are already most familiar, whether their own or that of colleagues, and so to publicize it as exemplary. (Why is the early work of Blau and Gouldner almost never cited to exemplify participant observation?) Substantive works which stress issues of method are also more likely to have their methods noticed and written about by others, especially if, as at Chicago, the authors write well about striking topics and have many nonspecialist readers.[8] A small number of methodologically self-conscious writers in one place can, thus, have a multiplier effect on public images. It probably also helps in establishing the conception of "school" if, as was true of these key figures, they showed a continuity of commitment and concerns over long periods. It can be noted that contributors to this volume who are more interested in the postgraduation role and influence of our cohort naturally tend to concentrate on those who have become relatively prominent and refer very little to those who have not had academic careers, have returned to home countries abroad, or have had rank-and-file status in U.S. sociology. In this they reflect the general processes of reputation-creation in the discipline. Thus a department's reputation comes to depend on its prominent representatives (cf. Endler et al. 1978), and if there are noticeable contingents of these representatives in rather separate specialist fields, the department may have two or more relatively independent reputations, as I suspect is the case for Chicago.

What, then, may we conclude about the methodological character and contribution of the "second Chicago school"? It has been argued that the homogeneity and narrowness of the methodological commitments of the cohort as a whole have been much exaggerated, in ways which have served the current needs of those who wish to associate themselves with some part of what the cohort can be made to stand for.[9] Although it has indeed been the case that some of them have made important contributions both by writing about participant observation and other qualitative methods and by exemplifying them in their empirical work, other members of the cohort have been equally prominent in work in quite different styles. Those who were there are more likely to emphasize methodological diversity and conflict than uniformity. However, despite this, there is a sense of shared departmental character transcending that diversity: what was shared was a strong emphasis on the importance of going out and getting data—an important continuity with prewar tradition—and a relative lack of interest in more abstract theoretical issues.

There were significant changes in departmental character from the mid 1950s, when several members of faculty left and were replaced from Columbia and elsewhere. To see this as representing a decline is to make a value judgment which may or may not be shared. However, to see the fact that fewer graduates with qualitative and symbolic interactionist commitments emerged later in the period as showing a decline in that tradition is to ignore the general pattern of changes in graduate numbers. Chicago's leading position at an earlier time must have owed something to relative size as well as to purely intellectual hegemony. This size ensured that Chicago graduates were distributed across a wide range of universities, and so took what they had learned at Chicago to fresh audiences. It also meant that any who stayed in the profession were likely to remain in touch with other Chicago graduates; this was further encouraged by the tendency for other midwestern departments to be dominated by Chicago graduates, and by the custom of returning for summer school and meetings of the Society for Social Research (Bulmer 1984: 114–17). More recently, expansion elsewhere diluted Chicago influence. However, some "neo-

Chicagoan" colonies have been founded, at Brandeis, in California around Berkeley, and elsewhere. Such groupings might be better described in terms of units such as the Society for the Study of Symbolic Interaction than of departmental affiliations.

NOTES

Comments on a first draft of this paper were received from Howard Becker, Leo Bogart, O. Dudley Duncan, Ronald Freedman, Eliot Freidson, Lewis Killian, and Stanley Lieberson; these were most helpful, and are acknowledged with thanks. Thanks, too, to Norbert Wiley for giving me a copy of his interview with Herbert Blumer, and to Herbert Gans for providing a copy of Hughes's reading list.

Work on which this paper is based has been funded by grants from the Leverhulme Foundation, the American Philosophical Society, the Economic and Social Research Council (G00242008/1), and the Research Support Fund of the University of Sussex; their support is acknowledged with gratitude.

1. The task of following all the cohort into their later careers would be too onerous, and has not been attempted. This chapter focuses on what happened in the graduate school and the faculty at the time, and on the later careers only of those whose work has been regarded as central to the "school"; this selectivity fits the issue as here defined.

2. The sample was drawn from even-numbered years, 1946–62. The total number of doctorates varied considerably from year to year, and in some years there were very few. Limited time in Chicago prevented me looking at every thesis in the chosen years; about half the relevant theses were, thus, selected for the largest single cohort (1954) and the later years (1960 and 1962) of less central concern to this chapter; in other years every available thesis was taken. It should, therefore, be borne in mind that the total sample cannot be regarded as a representative one, although there seems no reason to believe that it gives a misleading impression as it is used in the text. The table below shows the actual numbers.

	1946	1948	1950	1952	1954	1956	1958	1960	1962
Total theses	5	14	23	17	28	7	7	12	13
Sample	5	13*	21*	17	15	6*	7	5*	7

*One or two theses could not be found in the library.

3. It is possible that a different impression might have been given if books had been taken into account, and it could be suggested that the more qualitatively inclined have a higher ratio of books to articles. However, the Chicago people best-known for qualitative work are heavily represented in the article sample.

4. The journals used were *American Journal of Sociology, American Sociological Review, Journal of Social Issues, Rural Sociology, Social Forces, Social Problems, Sociology and Social Research.* This list includes the recognized main general, regional, and specialist journals which existed at least for most of the period covered. *Public Opinion Quarterly, Social Research,* and *Sociometry* are omitted on the ground that their remit gave them such a pronounced

methodological character that one would expect articles in them to be of the same type. The years used were odd-numbered years, 1945–59; within years, issues 1, 3, and 5 were used when there were six a year, and issues 2 and 4 when there were four a year. All articles, as distinct from editorial introductions, letters, etc., were classified. The "other" category is large because it includes not only purely theoretical or methodological articles but also the many articles from the earlier part of the period which made assertions without documenting them or did not indicate their methods.

5. This interview, along with others dated 1982–84, was carried out as part of a more general program of research on the history of U.S. sociological research methods. In these interviews I asked my respondents to tell me the story of their careers from a methodological point of view, commenting as they did so on the social contexts and influences which they had experienced. The interviews included eighteen from members of our cohort, although only those directly quoted are listed.

6. Clearly I differ here from Colomy and Brown (this volume), who take a reader's rather than an actor's perspective on what it is to be a symbolic interactionist. That too is a legitimate approach. (For discussion of some of the general issues it raises, see Platt 1981, 1986.) Fortunately this difference does not much affect the point at stake here. Those who reject the label cannot have been consciously influenced by the ideas they associate with it, and the lack of methodological homogeneity among those accepting the label remains.

7. The reading list for this course in Fall 1947 (kindly provided by Herbert Gans) shows slightly more structure than this suggests in the tasks set. Students were required to make a general description of their area from published statistics and observation, to do some standard interviews, to compile a genealogy of a family and a description of its household, to report on formal and informal institutions and on a public gathering, and to conduct interviews without a questionnaire on "some problems which you by this time think of some significance in the area." All this in one quarter! It is worthy of note that, although the reading list included many examples of studies using participant observation, there are no works about the method (less surprising when one recalls that hardly any had been written by that time), and the term is not used, while there are works on personal documents and life histories. There is also a long list of statistical sources about Chicago.

8. Eliot Freidson suggests, very plausibly, that explicit writing about methodological issues tends to lead to the dramatized formulation of contrasts between viewpoints, and that this helps to produce the invention of a "school" (Freidson 1990). Howard Becker adds that the development of other graduate schools created a need at Chicago "to define what we were that they weren't," and so the emergence of a clearer sense of collective identity (Becker 1990).

9. Jim Thomas, in his introduction to the special issue of *Urban Life* (Thomas 1983: 387), makes this selection explicit: "Chicago sociology most correctly refers to a particular worldview and fieldwork research method preferred by many, but by no means all, Chicago analysts in the 1920s and 1930s."

REFERENCES

Adams, S. C. 1990. Letter to Fine.

Becker, H. S. 1951. "The Professional Dance Musician and His Audience." *American Journal of Sociology* 57: 136–44.

Becker, H. S. 1990. Letter to Platt.

Becker, H. S. et al. 1968. *Institutions and the Person.* Chicago: Aldine.

Blum, A. M. 1990. Letter to Fine.

Blumer, H. 1982a. Interview with Platt.

Blumer, H. 1982b. Interview with Platt.

Bogart, L. 1990. Letter to Fine.

Bruyn, S. T. 1966. *The Human Perspective in Sociology.* Englewood Cliffs: Prentice-Hall.

Bulmer, M. 1984. *The Chicago School of Sociology.* Chicago: University of Chicago Press.

Carter, W. 1990. Letter to Fine.

Davis, F. 1959. "The Cabdriver and His Fare." *American Journal of Sociology* 65: 158–65.

Denzin, N. D. 1970. *The Research Act in Sociology.* Chicago: Aldine.

Deutscher, I. 1984. "Choosing Ancestors: Some Consequences of the Selection from Intellectual Traditions." In R. M. Farr & S. Moscovici eds., *Social Representations.* Cambridge: Cambridge University Press, pp. 71–100.

Dornbusch, S. 1955. "The Military Academy as an Assimilating Institution." *Social Forces* 33: 316–21.

Duncan, O. D. 1984. Interview with Platt.

Endler, N. S., et al. 1978. "Productivity and Scholarly Impact (Citations) of British, Canadian, and U.S. Departments of Psychology (1975)." *American Psychologist* 33: 1064–82.

Filstead, W. J., ed. 1970. *Qualitative Methodology.* Chicago: Rand McNally.

Freedman, R. 1983. Interview with Platt.

Freidson, E. 1984. Interview with Platt.

Freidson, E. 1990. Letter to Platt.

Gans, H. 1984. Interview with Platt.

Gellner, E. 1979. "Ethnomethodology: The Re-enchantment Industry or the California Way of Subjectivity." In *Spectacles and Predicaments.* Cambridge: Cambridge University Press, pp. 41–64.

Glaser, B. G. & Strauss, A. L. 1967. *The Discovery of Grounded Theory.* Chicago: Aldine.

Gold, R. L. 1984. Interview with Platt.

Gross, E. 1984. Interview with Platt.

Gusfield, J. 1982. "The Scholarly Tension: Graduate Craft and Undergraduate Imagination." In J. MacAloon, ed., *General Education in the Social Sciences.* Chicago: University of Chicago Press.

Gusfield, J. 1990a. "My Life and Soft Times." In B. M. Berger, ed., *Authors of Their Own Lives.* Berkeley: University of California Press, pp. 104–29.

Gusfield, J. 1990b. Tape sent to Fine.

Hare, A. P. 1990. Letter to Fine.

Harvey, L. 1987. *Myths of the Chicago School of Sociology.* Aldershot: Avebury.

Killian, L. 1990. Letter to Fine.

King, C. E. 1990. Letter to Fine.

Lofland, J. 1970. "Interactionist Imagery and Analytic Interruptus." In T. Shibutani, ed., *Human Nature and Collective Behavior.* Englewood Cliffs: Prentice-Hall.

Lofland, J. 1971. *Analysing Social Settings.* Belmont, Calif.: Wadsworth.

Lofland, J., ed. 1980. "Reminiscences of Classic Chicago: The Blumer-Hughes Talk." *Urban Life* 9: 251–81.

Lofland, L. 1983. "Understanding Urban life: The Chicago Legacy," *Urban Life* 11: 491–511.

Manning, P. 1978. "Editor's remarks." *Urban Life* 7: 282–84.

McCall, G. J. & Simmons, J. L. 1969. *Issues in Participant Observation* Reading, Mass.: Addison-Wesley.

Meltzer, B. N. & Petras, J. L. 1967. In J. G. Manis & B. N. Meltzer, eds., *Symbolic Interaction.* Boston: Allyn & Bacon.

Mitra, N. D. 1947. "Mourning Customs and Modern Life in Bengal." *American Journal of Sociology* 52: 309–11.

Peil, M. 1990. Letter to Fine.

Platt, J. 1981. "The Social Construction of 'Positivism' and Its Significance in British Sociology, 1950–1980." In P. Abrams et al., eds., *Practice and Progress: British Sociology 1950–1980.* London: Allen and Unwin, pp. 73–87.

Platt, J. 1983. "The Development of the 'Participant Observation' Method in Sociology: Origin Myth and History." *Journal of the History of the Behavioral Sciences* 19: 379–93.

Platt, J. 1986. "Functionalism and the Survey: The Relation of Theory and Practice." *Sociological Review* 34: 501–36.

Platt, J. 1994. "The Chicago School and First-hand Data." *History of the Human Sciences* 7: 57–80.

Reiss, A. L. 1984. Interview with Platt.

Rock, P. 1979. *The Making of Symbolic Interactionism.* London: Macmillan.

Roth, J. 1957. "Ritual and Magic in the Control of Contagion." *American Sociological Review* 22: 310–14.

Schatzman, L. & Strauss, A. L. 1973. *Field Research.* Englewood Cliffs: Prentice-Hall.

Schwartz, M. 1984. Interview with Platt.

Seidman, J., London, J., Karsh, B. & Tagliacozzo, D. 1958. *The Worker Views His Union.* Chicago: University of Chicago Press.

Short, J. 1984. Interview with Platt.

Thomas, J. 1983. "Chicago Sociology: An Introduction." *Urban Life* 11: 387–95.

Turner, R. H. 1947. "The Navy Disbursing Officer as a Bureaucrat." *American Sociological Review* 12: 342–48.

Turner, R. H. 1990. Letter to Fine.

Turner, R. H. 1991. Letter to Wacker.

Vajda, E. 1960. "Burmese Urban Characteristics: A Size-of-Place Study of a Southeast Asian Urban Population." University of Chicago: Doctoral thesis.

Winkin, Y. 1988. *Erving Goffman: les moments et leurs hommes.* Paris: Editions du Seuil.

CHAPTER THREE

THE ETHNOGRAPHIC PRESENT:

IMAGES OF INSTITUTIONAL CONTROL IN

SECOND-SCHOOL RESEARCH

Gary Alan Fine and Lori J. Ducharme

Robert Nisbet (1976) pointedly notes that the connections among sociological writers, artistic expression, and the spirit of the age are tight and compelling. Social theorists, artists, and publics respond to similar sets of circumstances, create shared images, and have related fears and desires. When a writer attempts to "picture" a scene, the images employed are drawn from social concerns of the time. This does not, of course, mean that the writer is consciously aware of the themes or that all writers will draw upon, much less have the same attitude toward, a set of themes. Within the zeitgeist many alternative readings are possible, even though all respond to central defining issues.[1]

In an examination of a "group" of scholars who see themselves as a group (and are so seen by others), the thematic focus becomes more compelling. Here we explore through their writings certain central images employed by a band of scholars who shared an academic environment (the University of Chicago in the early 1950s). We shall then briefly compare elements of their ethnographies to those of scholars trained in the same "place" two decades later.[2]

On some level our perspective can be applied to all sociological writing with its roots in the 1950s; generational effects are a compelling feature of sociological analysis (Mannheim 1952). Cohort effects are particularly powerful for scholars whose writings are mutually influenced. The ethnographic scholars at the University of Chicago were trained in the same environment, in the same period, and were exposed to similar cultural themes in their upbringing. Each chose a qualitative or descriptive methodology. To understand these themes we select a set of ethnographic "masterworks": works which, at that time and subsequently, were recognized as making important contributions to the discipline. Specifically we examine Erving Goffman's *Asylums* (1961), Fred Davis's *Passage Through Crisis* (1963), Julius Roth's *Timetables* (1963), and Howard Becker, Blanche Geer, Everett C. Hughes, and Anselm Strauss's *Boys in White* (1961).[3]

For the most part, these scholars matured during the Depression, an era of economic insecurity, lived through the Second World War, in some cases serving in the military,[4] and came of age academically in the postwar era, a time obsessed with conformity and security (e.g., Carter 1983; Diggins 1988; Morris and Schwartz 1993). We find these themes echoed in our key texts. Specifically we see implicit in the works: (1) a concern with sudden, dramatic change ("How could a prosperous economy suddenly turn sour?"); (2) a concern with totalitarian control ("How was Hitler possible?"); and (3) a concern with the basis of community and conformity ("How could one be an individual in a period in which cultural order was profound?"). The themes are rarely directly enunciated, but they come through in subtle messages and concerns revealed in the text.

Every cohort, particularly in a media-saturated culture, faces critical "defining" events that serve as the basis of long-time discussion and debate and as models for the cohort's interpretation of the world (Schuman and Scott 1989). These events (the Depression, the war, and the push for conformity in the postwar era, as expressed in the politics of Senator Joseph McCarthy) are the defining coordinates in which the perspective of this group was anchored, even if unknowingly. We do not argue that these writers were consciously aware of these themes. In fact, in their reading of this chapter, several principals distanced themselves from our analysis, notably from its emphasis on conformity. Fred Davis, for instance, finds that this emphasis "rings falsely." He notes that "I, for one, am not in the least aware of any such remote, analytically reified, after-the-fact conditioning circumstance." He adds, "Of course, it is always possible that in ways we were utterly unaware of at the time (or since) what you delineate as the general condition of fifties' socio-political culture did somehow cause us to write as we did" (Fred Davis, personal communication, 1991).[5] His point is well-taken. Yet, he is more willing to concede the formative effects of the Depression and the war than the ethos of conformity (taped conversation, 1991).[6] Conformity was hardly a conscious theme, but then these insightful scholars were attempting to understand their society, a society that, by the time they were writing, had been categorized as "conformist." As Davis (1979, 1984) himself so influentially notes in his examination of nostalgia and decade labeling, after-the-fact themes become socially constructed (Halbwachs 1992). Whether they were *present* originally is unanswerable.

Ultimately, several dimensions must be taken into consideration. First, we must consider the culture of the period for all Americans. Second, we must consider cohort effects. These are children of the Great Depression (e.g., Elder 1974), either soldiers or onlookers during the Second World War, young men (we are examining a group largely segregated by gender [see Deegan, this volume]) who entered the academy together. Of course, a single cohort effect for the entire postwar period does not recognize the changes during this timespan. To lessen oversimplification, we have selected authors from those trained during the first half of this period. Third, we must consider "school" effect. In examining sociology at the University of Chicago, we differentiate it from sociology at Columbia, Harvard, and elsewhere, suggesting that the "second Chicago school" is different.[7] Fourth, we must look at the place of these particular scholars within the wider network of graduate students at the University of Chicago at the time. Our subjects both are and are not representative of their academic cohort, and the divisions within the department (as described by Jennifer Platt, this volume) are real. Fifth, there are the effects of the interest groups or interaction networks in which these students traveled and from which each of them was formed. These friends, colleagues, and relatives affected how the spirit of the age influenced scholarship. Each of these men was of Jewish descent (as were many in their cohorts and in sociology generally). Fred Davis (taped conversation, 1991) suggests that their marginal status and immigrant stock may have contributed to their perspectives as "marginal men." Finally, each of these men worked outside of institutions of higher education in the 1950s: each of their works has an applied, pragmatic, or public-policy component. Their ethnographic experiences brought them into contact with individuals caught in the crossfire between the power of institutional control and the desire for individual freedom.

   In this chapter we discuss four ethnographic texts, each published in the early 1960s, that have become recognized classics of sociological analysis; each work examines a corner of the social institution of medicine.[8] The popularity of these ethnographic sites reflects in part the concern of these scholars with the latent effects and consequences of ostensibly prosocial institutions.[9] We then briefly compare these four works to four major ethnographies published by University of Chicago-trained scholars in the late 1970s and early 1980s. In each case, our concern is less with the explicit substantive analysis than with our thematic reading of the surrounding images and illustrative examples. Through their use of images and examples to convey information, these authors connect one social world to others, linking content-specific analysis to general discussion.[10]

THE ORGANIZATION MAN

Intellectual life in the 1950s centered around debates on the role of conformity and the power and legitimacy of institutions to shape that conformity—for good or for ill, but mostly, according to the authors, for ill (but see O'Neill 1986). David Riesman's *The Lonely Crowd* (1950), William H. Whyte's *The Organization Man* (1956), C. Wright Mills's *The Power Elite* (1956), and Daniel Bell's *The End of Ideology* (1960), stretching through the decade, represent archetypical sociological treatments of the time by a quartet of prominent public intellectuals. These scholars, each in his own way, confront the dual questions of public conformity to normative standards and the power of institutions to shape individual behavior. These writings represent attempts of intellectuals to address the legacy of totalitarianism in a Golden Age of *Pax Americana.* They ask: How can an individual integrate communal, normative demands with personal morality? How can the individual create a personal preserve apart from forces of social order?[11]

The writings we examine in this chapter, and their themes, are a reaction and challenge to American culture in the 1950s.[12] They are indirect, second-order readings of the thirties and forties, coming to terms with these themes through the eyes of a generation that grew up in these eras and was defined by the images of young adulthood and the beginnings of intellectual maturity.

Unlike the works of Riesman, Bell, Mills, and Whyte, the empirical studies we examine are not addressed to a "public" audience. Unlike technical, specialist works, primarily meaningful within a discipline, and unlike works written for a general intellectual audience, the products of these Chicago scholars transcend parochial disciplinary concerns but do not reach into public discourse. They are not for general consumption, but they are readable by nonspecialists and, therefore, differ from much "professional" scholarship of the period.[13] As serious, "scholarly" work they are remarkably free of technical jargon; the concepts created (notably, though not exclusively, Goffman's) are borrowed from public discourse. Goffman's *Asylums,* particularly, has a literary air (Fine and Martin 1990), drawing on tropes of irony, sarcasm, and satire; yet it was not the kind of work that reached audiences beyond the ivory tower and the medical establishment. These works are literature for a professional audience, accessible to those interested in underlying theoretical issues.

While none of these four works directly addresses the questions of conformity and organizational control, we find that these themes run close to the surface and implicitly provide a dialogue with the writings of Riesman and Whyte. Yet, as Harvey (1987, p. 140) notes, these authors abjured questions that might be asked by those taking a fundamentally radical or critical approach to society. In contrast, the authors ask: What are the means by which organization is constructed and how do they produce constraints on individual action and reaction? How are opportunities and degrees of freedom found in these institutions? The ultimate answers are microsociological, personal, and interpretive. In the works examined (Goffman; Davis; Roth; and Becker et al.), the hospital is the social arena; it represents the sunny side of organizational goals—saving lives. But what are the personal costs by which these lives are rescued? When the revolution comes, the hospital may be the institution most likely to be spared, but perhaps this reflects only the power of the metaphor of physician as savior, a metaphor that is subtly being undercut in these texts.

From their examination of a central scene, medicine, these researchers attempt to transcend the structure of that special world to examine general social process, the tethering of the individual to the organization and to the larger social order. Underlying this perspective is the idea that social scientific themes are not only based on individual insight but represent the spirit of an age, as mediated through an organizational context and through interacting small groups. Only in part do these documents reflect the "sociology of the age"; in addition, they contain a representation of that sociology, scholarship mediated through public discourse.

Erving Goffman's Asylums

Erving Goffman (1922–82) was born in Alberta, Canada, of Jewish parents. Despite his prominence, no full treatment of his life has been published in English (but see Winkin 1988). He received his B.A. degree from the University of Toronto in 1946. Of course, as a Canadian, his experiences of the Depression and the war and his images of *American* society differed from those of most of his cohort (Howard S. Becker, personal communication, 1991); his Jewishness and his Canadian upbringing helped to define his outsider status. He attended the University of Chicago, where he received his M.A. degree in 1949 and his Ph.D. in 1953. During the middle 1950s (autumn 1954 to the end of 1957) he was a visiting member of the Laboratory of Socio-environmental Studies of the National Institute of Mental Health in Bethesda, Maryland, where he conducted participant observation at St. Elizabeth's Hospital. His articles began appearing in the early 1950s with the publication of "Symbols of Class Status" in the *British Journal of Sociology* (1951). His first book, *Presentation of Self in Everyday Life* (published in a Scottish edition in 1956 and an American edition in 1959), most clearly made Goffman's reputation, although his brilliance was widely commented on by many in his cohort of graduate students at Chicago. (They elected him most likely to succeed.)[14] While Goffman was just one among many fine scholars at Chicago in this period, his writings have surely had the most extensive impact.

Goffman's first major empirical research was his examination of systems of interpersonal deference and demeanor on the Shetland Islands, which eventually became his doctoral dissertation, "Communication Conduct in an Island Community." *Asylums* was his second significant empirical investigation, based on his participant-observation research at St. Elizabeth's, a large federal mental hospital in Washington, D.C.[15] Goffman's role in the hospital was as an assistant to the athletic director, in which capacity he spent the day in informal interaction with patients. *Asylums* is a collection of four of his essays on the structure of mental institutions, two of them previously published.

Goffman contends that the mental institution, while ostensibly designed for the protection and treatment of patients with mental disorders, works latently to create conformity, professional control, and the socialization of moral order (Manning 1992). In its own terms the book has had considerable effect in goading authorities to deinstitutionalize the mentally ill and to formulate patients' rights (Fine and Martin 1990; Robert Faulkner, personal communication, 1991).

In examining the criticism of mental institutions, one might recognize that *Asylums* is a report conditioned by consideration of concentration camps and political totalitarianism, raising questions of the rights of individuals in totalistic systems. One can hardly miss Goffman's critique of the incorporation of Nazi control techniques into American institutions. The concept of a "total institution" could only have developed from a culture that had been exposed to the cruelty of Nazi atrocities. Goffman implies that the two cultures are more similar than they appear on the surface in terms of their straining for control. More than a collection of essays about the impact of total institutions on inmates, *Asylums* is implicitly a reader's guide to life in institutional Hell, made more compelling by its "benign" American setting and its focus on a profession—psychiatry—that during this period was perceived as remarkably successful as a cultural and therapeutic model.[16] Goffman's work is thoroughly subversive in its discrediting of privileged institutions and its questioning of the value of conformity to standards of social control, even when deviance can plausibly be seen as "crazy."

While drawing most of his data and formulating most of his conclusions from his observations at St. Elizabeth's, Goffman collects examples from other total institutions to illustrate the extension of his argument: prisons, cloisters, ships at sea, and concentration camps. On the last, *Asylums,* particularly the lead essay, "On the Characteristics of Total Institutions," makes extensive use of Eugene Kogon's *The Theory and Practice of Hell,* as well as E. A. Cohen's *Human Behaviour in the Concentration Camp* and D. P. Boder's *I Did Not Interview the Dead.* Goffman's familiarity with the literature and his repeated use of examples from life in the camps testify to their personal influence. Not merely do they fit his theoretical interests, but his theoretical interests fit the debates of the period in which he wrote.

Structurally, concentration camps are not all that different from prisons or cloisters, except that their inmates have neither broken the law (unless the law is specially constructed for them to break through the ordinary course of living), nor did they volunteer for internment. In that sense, concentration camps resemble mental hospitals, for their "clients" are similarly defined as being socially polluting. Within the gates, prisoners and mental patients lead similar lives. As a case in point, Goffman suggests that the whippings that concentration camp prisoners are required to give each other typify how mental institutions force mortification and disidentifying roles upon their patients (p. 23).

Consider the specific institutional attempts cited by Goffman to demonstrate the connections between the two spheres of control—one fascistic and the other paternalistically democratic:

> Loss of self-determination seems to have been ceremonialized in concentration camps; thus we have atrocity tales of prisoners being forced to roll in the mud, stand on their heads in the snow, work at ludicrously useless tasks, swear at themselves, or, in the case of Jewish prisoners, sing anti-Semitic songs. A milder version is found in mental hospitals where attendants have been reported forcing a patient who wanted a cigarette to say "pretty please" or jump up for it. In *all such cases* the inmate is made to display a giving up of his will. (P. 44, emphasis added)

... In total institutions of all three varieties [religious institutions, concentration camps, and other ("instrumental") total institutions], however, the various rationales for mortifying the self are very often merely rationalizations, generated by efforts to manage the daily activity of a large number of persons in a restricted space with a small expenditure of resources. Further, curtailments of the self occur in all three. . . . (Pp. 46–47)

... [W]hen the inmate returns to the free community, he may leave with some limits on his freedom. Some concentration camps required the inmate to sign a release, attesting that he had been treated fairly; he was warned of telling tales out of school. In some mental hospitals an inmate being prepared for discharge is interviewed a final time to discover whether or not he harbors resentment against the institution and those who arranged his entrance into it, and he is warned against causing trouble to the latter. (P. 73)

The irony in Goffman's writing has been noted, most especially because Goffman, a Jew, came of age during the Holocaust. To link concentration camps with mental hospitals, even in a sardonic vein, creates a cutting critique of contemporary society, as well as a potential charge of personal insensitivity. Yet, while some of the tone and content of *Asylums* is due to the perspective that Goffman brings to the material, he simultaneously exhibits a swaggering, debunking stance, a subversive analogy-building characteristic of these sociologists: a questioning of the purity of ideals, by linking them to structurally similar, but morally opposite, claims.

Fred Davis's *Passage Through Crisis*

Fred Davis (1925–93) was born in New York City. He attended Brooklyn College and in 1943 joined the U.S. Army. Entering graduate school at the University of Chicago in 1946, he received his M.A. in 1951 and his Ph.D. in 1958. Like Goffman, Davis spent the middle 1950s in a series of applied settings, working for the Human Resources Research Institute of the United States Air Force in Montgomery, Alabama (1951–53), for the Research Office for Research Services, Limited, in London (1955–56), and as a research sociologist for the Polio Project at the Psychiatric Institute of the University of Maryland Medical School in Baltimore (1953–57). It was at the latter institution that he conducted the research for *Passage Through Crisis: Polio Victims and Their Families*.

Davis's *Passage Through Crisis,* published in book form in 1963,[17] dealt with techniques by which polio victims and their families coped with the challenges of the disease. This work represents, in part, an account of threats to the good life by external forces; he depicts how the happy family can be imperiled, and how it fights back. Unlike Goffman, Davis does not write with a sardonic pen, but this does not blunt the literary quality of the text. Its naturalistic style does not hide the metaphor of polio as the snake in the garden, the fifth column; implicitly polio serves as a critique of the American way.[18] We had to combat polio as a society, much as we had just overcome the Axis, through a just war (Davis 1991, p. xvi). Just as President Franklin Roosevelt led the fight against the Nazis, so, too, did he serve as the primary leader of the fight against polio, as a fellow sufferer who was able to triumph against the disease through personal effort (Davis 1963, p. 6).

Davis's account of polio victims and their families incorporates a consideration of crises, social systems, bureaucracy, and stigma in a manner that reveals and confronts American views of the individual's place in society. Davis describes the medical crisis thrust upon these families in a manner that is reminiscent of accounts of the broader economic crisis that blanketed the nation twenty years before: a structural social problem that masquerades and is treated as a personal trouble. Each of the fourteen families in Davis's research were victims of forces beyond its control, and yet all searched for explanations by scrutinizing their own individual actions, in an attempt to personalize their misfortune. Parents regularly blamed themselves for their child's disease, and, conversely, praised the willpower of the child for effecting his own recovery. Their sense of agency was undeniable; their questioning of externality was palpable. Davis sets these attitudes in the content of American cultural mythology, noting "our culture's ample storehouse of myths, tales, and 'known instances' of man's triumphing over seemingly impossible circumstances to prove that it is he and he alone who fashions his fate" (p. 92). Each child who recovered significantly from the illness was portrayed by the parents in the manner of a Horatio Alger figure. Recovery became the reenactment of the mythic American success story. Likewise, permanent disability was its inverse, as parents continued to reflect on their own lives for clues to past failings that were deserving of punishment: a sense of divine justice made palpable and medical. Polio, like AIDS later, was invested with a moral character (Sontag 1988).

Personal traumas were situated within a medical bureaucracy, producing confrontations between the individual and the institution. Here, as elsewhere within the occupational order, hospital employees refused to be bearers of bad news, and the families' perspectives on their children's recovery were deeply influenced by the hospital's desire to avoid unpleasantness and disorder. The hospital staff, like the manipulators that Goffman discusses, disdains uncomfortable truths. The physician becomes a public relations agent, hoping to avoid disruptive emotional displays in waiting rooms, manipulating patients and their families, while preserving the image of the establishment, allegedly for clients' own ends. The conflicting interests—the family seeking accurate and predictive information on their child's condition and the hospital's unwillingness and inability to provide more than vague responses—generate misunderstanding. The hospital, concerned for its own welfare, echoing Goffman's emphasis on institutional primacy, provided parents with little concrete information, and parents were left to formulate their own tentative prognoses for their child's recovery. The families passed through the crisis in constant indeterminacy, carving out a meaningful personal space as best they could. Like Goffman's mental patients, they constructed a more benign institution, an institution of the air. In families of children who were permanently impaired, the optimism induced by the hospital's intentionally vague responses led to further emotional trauma as the family was forced slowly and repeatedly to lower its expectations for recovery, producing continual disappointment.

Unlike Goffman, with his *sociology noir,* Davis produces a sunnier scene.[19] These families are able to cope with the institutional trauma (Goffman's patients do as well, but at a profound cost). Davis's families did not "lose it." He asks (1963, p. 11): "Why did they not become alienated, disorganized, or otherwise detached from their historic sense of who and what they were?" He holds (1963, p. 134) ultimately to a belief in a "fundamental stability in the family, enabling it with reasonable facility to absorb the impact of the polio experience while at the same time insulating it from both serious disorganization and creative reorganization." The experience with polio and the lack of disruptive change in the family reflected "an excessive contentment with the familiar and the known that inhibits the discovery of new meanings and purposes when important life circumstances change" (1963, p. 164). Davis's portrayal serves as a critique of the 1950s family from within.

If the AIDS epidemic represents a critique of sexual politics and a hedonistic lifestyle, as some suggest (Sontag 1988), the polio epidemic represents a dire threat to and critique of the lifestyle of the American nuclear family in the 1950s. Davis (1963, p. 6) writes in this vein:

> It is not surprising, therefore, that of the many critical diseases which afflict man, polio had come to occupy a pre-eminent— and, according to some, an exaggerated—place in the aware- ness, sympathy, and philanthropy of the American people. By the time of the development of the Salk vaccine it had emerged in popular thought as more than a sometimes crippling disease of children; it was regarded as a powerful symbol of blind, devastating, and uncontrollable misfortune whose victims were specially entitled to the support and good will of the com- munity.

That public swimming pools were taken as the symbolic vector for this threat is notable for what it suggests about the American dream, as repre- sented in an increasingly suburban population. Here is the beginning of the decentering of America: "it is a truism that the American image of the good life is predicated on the proposition that calamity may befall others but will not touch one's immediate family" (p. 40). "The child's contracting of the disease, therefore, loomed for the family as a kind of discriminatory barrier in the attainment of important social values; in short, it was 'un- American'" (p. 41).

The family's challenge was to make themselves whole in the face of the threat. Davis presents the metaphor of a ripped tapestry:

> Metaphorically, this phenomenon may be likened to a fleet- ingly glimpsed, occasionally distracting repair in an elaborate tapestry—enough of the fabric of family life remained intact to make what was new and different in the weave blend in (albeit incongruously, from certain angles and in certain lights) with the familiar design of the whole. (P. 177)

Davis closes by suggesting that the problem he presents is general, con- nected to the study of deviance. Normals may suddenly, cataclysmically be made deviant, and must then cope with the suddenness of the transfor- mation. Those not labelled are only provisionally normal.

Julius Roth's *Timetables*

Julius Roth received his M.A. (1950) and Ph.D. (1954) degrees from the Committee on Human Development at the University of Chicago, where he worked with Everett Hughes and David Riesman. Unlike the

others examined, Roth's degrees were in the Human Development program, but his orientation was distinctly sociological, and all his subsequent teaching was in sociology departments (at Boston University and
the University of California at Davis). Because Roth's writings are often
linked to those of Goffman, Davis, and Becker, and because of his connection to Hughes, we felt justified to include Roth in this quartet, despite his
different graduate home. Like the others, Roth did not receive a university
teaching job until the 1960s, remaining a research associate at the University of Chicago from 1954 until 1959, and then joining Becker and Hughes
at Community Studies, Inc., in Kansas City, Missouri, where he studied
tuberculosis treatment.

Timetables evolved from Roth's experiences shortly after leaving
Chicago. He describes his entry into the field with a deadpan seriousness:

> Just one half-year after getting my Ph.D. and a few months
> after starting my first full-time professional job, I was faced
> with a long and uncertain stretch in a tuberculosis hospital.
> My disease was not a complete surprise. I had been under ob-
> servation for tuberculosis, and my condition, although never
> serious up to this point, had apparently been somewhat un-
> stable. . . . Now with a more frankly active disease than I had
> had before, it looked as if my career were going to suffer an-
> other interruption. However, during the latter part of my grad-
> uate career, my main focus of interest had been the sociology
> and social psychology of institutions and occupations. Rather
> than an interruption of my career, a period of hospitalization
> might be viewed as a research opportunity. A hospital bed
> would make a good observation post. (Roth 1963, p. vii)

Turning adversity to account, Roth analyzed how patients adjust themselves to hospital demands, fighting institutional resistance to their needs
and desires for detailed information on their status and prognoses.

Tuberculosis, in the 1950s, required lengthy hospital stays—recovery
demanded that patients become clients of a total institution: the TB sani-
torium. Unfortunately for the patient, these stays are unpredictable in
length, and, thus, uncertainty is built into the relationship between doctor
and patient. Their relationship is inherently conflictual: the patient demands to know the exact length of his internment (his "sentence"), while
the doctor wishes to retain the maximum occupational autonomy to make
sequential decisions, without being second-guessed. (These physicians
surely envy the control of the psychiatrists, whose patients' questioning

can be taken as symptomatic.) The "game" for TB patients is to discover and develop timetables to chart their progress to discharge, just like the enlisted man, who uses rumor to ascertain his future deployment (Shibutani 1966). As Shibutani notes, most people (patients, soldiers, and the rest of us) feel uncomfortable dealing with ambiguity—perhaps a reaction more compelling for this generation because of the economic uncertainty of their childhood. The patients want normative timetables and physicians' promises, and they look for benchmarks that suggest them. As Roth observes (p. 11): "they grasp at anything that looks like it might be a benchmark in the progress of time," noting later (p. 93) that "people will not accept uncertainty. They will make an effort to structure it no matter how poor the materials they have to work with and no matter how much the experts try to discourage them." Roth and Davis present us with nicely paired analyses. Polio and TB—like economic cycles—are unpredictable events that their targets wish to tame.

Patients discern benchmarks along the timetable at which privileges are granted, and they take as promises any non-negative indications from the physicians concerning their progress along this trajectory. Once a "normative" timetable is discovered, patients see themselves as entitled to the privileges (e.g., exercise schedules) that come with their position on the time chart. Privileges are desired not only in and of themselves, but because of what they symbolize for the patient's self: each privilege reflects progress toward discharge from the hospital, a benchmark uncomfortably close to those rumors that military units have about their own discharge possibilities. Deviation from expected treatment is often "blamed" on the doctor, rather than on the disease. Like the parents of polio patients, TB patients have endless hope that doctors encourage, sometimes to their subsequent frustration. As Roth notes, these implicit promises can have a life of their own, influencing doctors' decisions, as patients expect and demand rewards for putting in time, for paying their dues. Like Goffman's mental patients, they learn to "work" the system. The implications of organizational structure recursively affect those who have constructed that structure. Like polio parents, TB patients find unintended and implied promises in the words and actions of doctors and staff. One difference, of course, is that the adult TB patients have a greater array of clues and conversations than do the polio parents, who are insulated from their child's treatment by institutional walls.

As is characteristic of the period, an assumption of conformity to group standards emerges as a primary, publicly stated concern of everyday life. Specifically, patients come to estimate their own personal timetables based on those they see operating for others "like them," along the lines of reference group theory. These patients are outer-directed. Opposed to the specific and technical classification schemes of physicians, the patients place themselves in categories of seemingly similar cases, and attach powerful symbolic meanings to these reference groups. The driving concern is not only one's personal timetable, but also that timetable in light of the pattern for the reference group: a model that fits well into systems of control such as the military. TB treatment becomes an exercise in conformity, with the patient working the system while maintaining his own identity in a self-proclaimed group.

Becker et al.'s Boys in White

Like many young scholars, the sociologists at the University of Chicago were not prone to coauthor works—few of the memorable works were team efforts.[20] Yet, notable exceptions are the collaborations of Howard Becker and his colleagues, Everett Hughes, Anselm Strauss, and Blanche Geer, which produced studies of medical school (*Boys in White*) and college (*Making the Grade*). *Boys in White: Student Culture in Medical School* (1961, reprinted in 1977)[21] is based on data collected by the authors at the University of Kansas Medical School during the mid-1950s. Three of the four authors (all except Blanche Geer)[22] had close affiliation with the Department of Sociology at the University of Chicago. Howard Becker (1928–), born in Chicago, received his B.A. (1946, at age eighteen), M.A. (1949), and Ph.D. (1951) from the University of Chicago. Although he served as an instructor at Chicago from 1951 to 1953, and as a postdoctoral research fellow at the University of Illinois from 1953 to 1955, Becker, like the other authors discussed in this chapter, spent much of the 1950s outside of the academy, serving as a project director at Community Studies, Inc. of Kansas City, Missouri, from 1955 to 1962. Everett Hughes had gotten Community Studies to support the beginning of the research at the Medical School of the University of Kansas. Hughes then hired Becker, who remained in Kansas City for seven years. Given our boundaries (1946–60), Becker was the only one of the authors of *Boys in White* who was a member of the "second school," and according to coauthor Anselm Strauss, "the book is really his" (personal communication, 1991). To the extent this claim is just, it can be seen as a second school product. Hughes was on the faculty as professor of sociology and was a major influence on each of these scholars, as he was on so many students at

Chicago during the period. Strauss received his Ph.D. degree in 1945 (just missing membership in this postwar group) and taught in the department as assistant professor from 1952 to 1958. Geer received a Ph.D. in education from Johns Hopkins in the early 1950s, and, according to Strauss, acquired much of her sociological training from Becker.

While Goffman's *Asylums* is littered with concrete examples from life in concentration camps, *Boys in White* is pruned of examples not drawn directly from observations at the University of Kansas medical school; it is a tightly focused ethnography. Despite the lack of examples explicitly linking the study to other aspects of contemporary American life, *Boys in White* analyzes organization loyalty and the dynamics of the mass processing of people—trainees and staff (and, dimly visible, patients). The study attempts to address how individuals protect themselves from the demands of the organizations in which they are embedded, and, thus, allows one to sketch similarities between medical school and other agencies of socialization. In a society in which the production of moral citizens is essential, in a world of perceived rapid change and in an era of large and demanding organizations, this point is crucial.

Boys in White has three major themes. First, the authors describe medical school as an agent of socialization, a medical "factory" producing physicians as products. But the end result is not always created through the means prescribed by the faculty. This marks the second theme, the conflicting demands and perspectives of faculty and students. The goal is to "get through" with as much interpersonal smoothness as is possible: to create space for personal comfort. Part of the mandate of these researchers was to learn how people shape their lives and institutions in the face of successes, obstacles, and other contingencies. While the faculty have (high) expectations of what and how students should learn, students collectively arrive at a strategic and economical perspective which allows them to survive medical school. Given time constraints, students develop strategies to "get by," and bypass the lofty demands of their instructors, while pursuing their goal. Yet, in escaping conformity to organizational demands, the students must answer collectively. They have carved out a space for themselves, and this space demands their allegiance.

The third theme is related to the notion of idealism. Students arrive at medical school with an idealistic purpose—a medical patriotism—that must soon be abandoned if they are to survive academically and if they are to recognize realistically the underside of medical practice. It is not too far-fetched to suggest that wanting to serve humanity becomes a luxury in a social system in which time is precious. The instrumental demands of medicine take priority over its moral demands; ideals of "serving humanity" are sacrificed to the mundane demands of practicing medicine. Idealism goes "underground," only to emerge at the end of the training period in a revised, more "realistic" form, which circumstances allow. Becker and his colleagues depict the cultural organization of social order. While the other three volumes examined here explicitly take the perspective of the patient, Becker and his colleagues focus on the "doctor." Yet, these doctors-to-be are in some sense as much "worked on" as those afflicted with psychoses, TB, or polio: the issue is what is done to them and how they cope with and struggle for control.

Interestingly, given the powerful images of the Second World War, we discern an implicit, if unintended, military metaphor in this analysis, with the organizational conformity implied by that the army. The homosocial quality of medical school resembles that of traditional military units. These predominantly male companies share a rough and ready camaraderie—the teasing, joking, and aggression characteristic of groups of male bodies. In addition, medical school maintains an emphasis like that of the military's basic training. Young men are trained to think and act as responsible adults—and are trained to think alike. Further, they are awash in blood, and must be trained, despite their best intentions, to take death in stride. Indeed, these young men are socialized into a profession in which death is a regular occurrence, and where even routine and relatively minor procedures can have grave consequences: "the students learn that a doctor's action can be mistaken and cause great damage, even death" (p. 229). In lectures and discussions with the hospital staff, the responsibility of the physician for the patient is stressed, and fatal mistakes are portrayed dramatically:

> there is almost always a reference to the possible death of a patient at a physician's hands; since this is an experience the students can easily envision themselves having when they become physicians, and since death is such an ultimate fact, such a [dramatic] presentation will be forceful. (P. 230)

Students not only learn that their best intentions may have fatal consequences, but that death is a routine feature of hospital life. Death, a traumatic event in everyday life, becomes a standard part of both the doctor's and the soldier's occupational terrain. The key to both medical and military training is the draining of emotion from routine tasks, so that these tasks do become routine; a key feature of dirty work is not to question or to "care."

The nature of the we-them relationship in medical school mirrors not only the military, but, more generally, images of postwar society. Students, in their collective redefinition of the means to the end, attempt to present a "united front" against the faculty, an illusion of sincerity. Their appearance (and actual reality) of preparedness and competence must be collectively constructed and maintained. The redefined social order presents the full embrace of idealism, because socialization demands a competent appearance. Indeed, we can see this same theme in the other volumes under discussion here as well, as each group—victims and controllers alike—collaborate interpersonally in the illusion of preserving legitimate authority. This illusion is most dramatically evident in Goffman's discussion of how patients must altruistically "help" their student nurses by acting appropriately crazed.

The militaristic and postwar metaphors are merely implicit; only at the end of *Boys in White* do the authors link their research to organizations, institutions, and general human conduct. The final paragraphs are perhaps most telling. In their summation, the authors note the broader implications of their findings, emphasizing the conditioning effects of the social situation on individuals. Institutions are often resistant to change, and attempts at alteration may be met with hostility from actors defending traditional ways. Those who seek to improve institutions may not always produce the desired changes. The authors close (1977, p. 443) by noting that:

> To attempt to change human conduct by manipulating institutional practices thus requires of the innovator the courage and strength to resist conservative pressure, the wisdom to foresee the consequences of his actions, and the resiliency to meet new problems generated by the ramified effects of his actions.

This final paragraph is telling in its recognition of the likelihood of a set of latent effects unplanned and undreamed of by those seeking change.[23] The unpredictability of effects and reverberations suggests that there will always be a need for adjustment and negotiation between individuals and the institutions in which they are embedded.

The Group

These four ethnographies, read together, focus on the microprocesses by which individuals attempt to limit the power of institutions. They reveal the uncertainties of life in institutions, and the attempts of inmates, trainees, and clients to manage the large blocks of time during which they are voluntarily or involuntarily confined. Becker et al. see medical students resisting the "unrealistic" demands of their instructors by making their own decisions about the necessary and sufficient direction and level of effort they must invest in their coursework. Davis and Roth see hospital patients (and their parents) actively searching for indicators of their condition and prognosis: indicators that are not always in the interest of the staff to provide. Goffman provides a model of how encapsulated, controlled individuals learn to work the system to realize, in some small measure, their own selfhood, apart from the tight limits of institutional control. "The disposition," according to Joseph Gusfield (personal communication, 1990), "was to see the social structure as more process than structure and also not to take it quite as established." The focus is on the processes by which individuals can survive from within, and realize freedom from, oppressive systems. Each of these authors describes processes by which the individual actively carves out a space within an institutional structure, a fundamental problem of postwar American society. Their sense of agency is apparent, as the individual is invested with, and actively uses, the power to resist. The problem is the danger of an institution that is too dominant, coupled with a drive for conformity among individuals.

Not only are these scholars interested in how individuals carve out personal space within an institution, but there is parallel emphasis on immediate action, rather than on long-term social placement. In these studies, the here-and-now actions of the individual are emphasized over the long-term results of institutional influence. Becker et al. find that medical students dispense with their long-term perspectives on careers and adopt a more "practical" perspective, one by which they decide what and how intently to study that evening. Similarly, Roth demonstrates how TB patients overcome the uncertainty surrounding their long-term prognoses by noting the implicit promises and symbolic privileges granted to them by the staff. For all of these groups, a focus on immediate needs and situations provides a coping mechanism within institutional constraints.

These four ethnographies uncover competing "definitions of the situation" within institutional walls. In addition to their focus on the here and now, they also ask about variations from "normality" and failures to conform: the microsociology of nonconformity to institutional expectations. Gusfield underlines his cohort's "disposition to see the society from outside in a way which led us perhaps to overstate the case for those who lived on the margins of the society." This is a concern with conformity on a micro, individual, interpersonal level. In each of these ethnographic analyses, the themes of agency, process, deviance, and resistance converge. Individuals confined in these institutions are actively engaged with each other—separate from their doctors, guards, or teachers, although occasionally in alliance with them—in the process of determining what is "normal," what the proper level of conformity to these norms should be, and how they can realize freedom from control by engaging in low-level negotiations.

Together, these themes reveal a concern with the self in relation to society and social structure. Perhaps this is best summarized by Goffman (1961, p. 320):

> Without something to belong to, we have no stable self, and yet total commitment and attachment to any social unit implies a kind of selflessness. Our sense of being a person can come from being drawn into a wider social unit; our sense of selfhood can arise through the little ways in which we resist the pull. Our status is backed by the solid buildings of the world, while our sense of personal identity often resides in the cracks.

The cracks, the loopholes in social structure, represent opportunities for individuals to realize freedom from total control; these are the points of emphasis for this group of ethnographies. The Chicago tradition oscillates between demands of freedom and constraint, challenge and restraint, with different emphases in different works and passages (Anselm Strauss, personal communication, 1991).

CHICAGO ETHNOGRAPHY OF THE "THIRD SCHOOL"

By the end of the 1950s the Department of Sociology at the University of Chicago was no longer known as a department that specialized in ethnographic research. Yet, despite this change in its reputation (if not its mission), it continued to attract outstanding graduate students. Several chose to conduct ethnographic research, despite the dominant quantitative tradition of the department. Some of the cohort of the 1940s and

1950s found it remarkable that there was any ethnography at all, given the changed emphasis of the department.[24] To examine what made our select group of Chicago sociologists of the 1950s special, we contrast their writings with four ethnographic writings published during a five-year period in the late 1970s and early 1980s by researchers who received their Ph.D.'s in 1975 and 1976. If the research of the second school represents America of the 1950s, these writings represent America of the 1970s, coming at the end of the radical years of the 1960s. Specifically, we discuss Elijah Anderson's *A Place on the Corner* (1978),[25] Charles Bosk's *Forgive and Remember* (1979), Michael Burawoy's *Manufacturing Consent* (1979), and Ruth Horowitz's *Honor and the American Dream* (1983). While we lack space to describe these works in depth, we hope to present enough to suggest a meaningful contrast.[26] The four early monographs were tightly focused on the medical terrain, but Bosk's is the only later work so situated. Burawoy presents an ethnography of a factory; the other two describe impoverished communities (African-American and Hispanic) in the tradition of *Street Corner Society* (Whyte 1943) and *Tally's Corner* (Liebow 1967).

Taken together, these ethnographers are more driven by macrolevel concerns than are the "second school" ethnographers, perhaps as a function of the radical critique of social order. In a sense, the later ethnographies can be read as the "flip-side" of the earlier ones, as some of the issues of the 1950s had been "worked through" in the following decades. Within the later ethnographies, the focus is on how the institution or society imposes itself on the individuals, and on the techniques of social control used to keep individuals in line. The emphasis is on the power of the institution to control, rather than the attempts of the individual to break free. The institution succeeds in these studies. The nature of conformity is seen differently, in that it is the institution that sets the normative structure, and any manipulation or attempts at negotiation by individuals may lead to increased institutional control.

Bosk's hospital is a fundamentally different place than Becker's. In Bosk's hospital, the staff exercises far greater power over the student physicians. While the students are held accountable for everything they do, the supervising attending physicians are not required to explain their decisions. On the contrary, they exercise absolute power in determining which student behaviors constitute unforgivable errors, and which constitute "blameless misfortune." In this sense, it is the agents of the institution, and not the students, who ultimately determine career paths. There are not the same cracks in the system to which Goffman refers. The normative structure is set by the institution and remains largely unchallenged. Indeed, Bosk argues that part of the controlling power of the institution is in the ability to hide the *outward appearance of control,* not the individual's hiding the *outward appearance of resistance,* as in the earlier studies. From this perspective, the attending physicians exercise a control in their routine surveillance of medical students that Becker's physicians could only envy. Bosk writes, for instance (p. 80): "Because clinical dialogue is so embedded in the environment, the testlike quality of rounds is sometimes lost on participants."

Burawoy, Anderson, and Horowitz each focus on the total control by institutions and communities, as revealed in capitalism, culture, and microsystems. (It is significant to realize that despite the important qualitative research of the 1950s, those scholars never produced a community study.)[27] These later scholars seem to see the individual as *lacking* the power to break free from institutional control, or even that the idea of breaking free is merely an illusion. Horowitz is concerned with the influence of cultural standards over Chicano youth, and the competing pressures of conforming to their ethnic roots while pursuing the American dream. They are tugged in two directions. These youths find themselves caught between conflicting cultural systems, feeling the need to conform to both sets of standards, and punished by each if they do not. The normative structure is set by the culture, and the concern is with individual conformity, not with the techniques of avoiding this conformity.

Anderson is concerned with the structure of status systems and competition for social esteem. But the individual is not the active agent in determining status; rather, others determine whether you can "be somebody," for, as in Horowitz's Chicano community, it is others who determine which claims to status an individual can make. Here, the self is a residual category: "a person knows who he is or to what 'crowd' he belongs in part by knowing about the subgroups, statuses, and identities to which he does not belong and which others will not allow him to claim" (Anderson, p. 53). Further, for the regulars at the corner liquor store, status is granted when one can demonstrate a connection to the wider society to which these individuals are generally considered *not* to belong. Horowitz finds a similar need to belong to the larger culture. Rather than carving out a private space, these actors crave a connection.

While Burawoy's argument is not as focused on conformity per se, he demonstrates that conformity to institutional pressure is the ultimate concern. In the factory, union and management devise a system that links workers and managers. His point nicely contrasts with that of Becker. Where Becker saw the individual pulling back from institutional control in the face of unreasonable demands, Burawoy sees factory workers drawn into the process, and increasing production in order to gain power. But in "playing the game" this way, the worker ends up doing just what the institution demands. What results is consent, not freedom or subversion.

Ultimately, rather than focusing on miniatures, the goal of these later studies is to examine the "big picture"—careers, communities, capitalism, culture, and status. They take for granted the individual's placement in an institution, and downplay the extent of challenges. The danger of conformity has lost its punch in the 1970s, when individual freedom in a personal sphere is taken for granted, as is institutional hegemony in the public arena.

CONCLUSION

Excavating implicit meanings and themes is dangerous. As a generation of literary critics have explained, we have little right to delegate such a task to ourselves. Yet, we argue that these researchers can plausibly be classed together. We hope that our contention that the ethnographic writings of the second school are different in tone from those four comparable works from two decades later is persuasive. An arrogance of critical purpose surrounds such claims.

Whether it is our reading or their intent, these "second school" texts demand our attention. They are each in their way (or ours) concerned about the position of the individual within a social system, and in this they raise questions about how individuals survive under that weight. Each study is slyly subversive of the established order. The choice of medicine for this subversion is symptomatic in that medicine is perhaps that area of social organization in which the public is most likely to accept the claims of these "professionals," or so the theory goes. Medical men are contemporary priests, our medicine men. These sociologists suggest, not that God is dead, but that we should be wary of accepting the message as gospel truth.

In the 1990s cynicism comes with the sociological turf, but during the late 1950s and early 1960s empirical suspicions were liberating and breathtaking. As children of the Depression, youngsters of the war, and professionals being trained in the age of consensus, their experience shaped what was to be said and the way that society was to be analyzed. Contemporary sociologists are their children.

NOTES

The authors wish to thank and acknowledge the comments of Andrew Abbott, Robert Faulkner, John Galliher, Joseph Gusfield, and Jennifer Platt, and the warm and generous help of Howard S. Becker, Fred Davis, Hans Mauksch, Julius Roth, and Anselm Strauss. In a chapter of this type, especially, the authors must assume responsibility for all interpretations and misinterpretations. While we do not agree, in all details, with the interpretations of these scholars, we do recognize that they were there.

1. In addition, most who examine the sociology of knowledge would agree that scholarship involves literary choices (Gusfield 1976; McCloskey 1990), drawing on metaphors (Brown 1977) from the cultural surround.
2. In analyzing a group, a number of approaches might be taken. One could (and some other chapters do) focus on the structural conditions of the department, for example, the extraordinary impact of Everett Hughes on these writers or the way in which these writers were "interacting" with those who had come (and written) before. Although this chapter does not focus on organizational, biographical, or network considerations in its attempt to suggest a thematic analysis, such a task is just as legitimate: another road to a more complete and complex understanding.
3. In this we consider Howard S. Becker as the representative of the second school, even though each of the authors played a role in the construction of the text.
4. Several students at Chicago during this period specifically commented on the importance of the perspective brought by returning servicemen (e.g., letters to Gary Fine by Eugene Wilkening, 1990; Bevode McCall, 1990; Leo Bogart, 1990).
5. Anselm Strauss (personal communication, 1991) also doubts the effects of conformity on these writers, noting that these "were children of the late 40ies [a time of cultural vitality], even if they did their actual writing in the [conformist] 50ies." Of course, as emerging scholars collecting data and writing reports in the 1950s, they surely should have had an impact. Strauss also notes, justly, that these men experienced the Depression differently: "Personally, I hardly knew there was one."
6. Davis notes (taped conversation, 1991): "When I was [at Chicago] one had a very palpable sense of living in the shadow of the Depression. It might reoccur at any moment, everyone might be out on their ass. The future really didn't look promising at all. . . . The depression was . . . a tremendous influence and I think it's what sustained much of the interest in social problems, race relations, and all of the critical concerns of American society."
7. This is not to suggest that other schools did not produce works that could

be likened to those produced at Chicago. Philip Selznick's *TVA and the Grass Roots* (1966) was written at Columbia, Alvin Gouldner's *Wildcat Strike* (1954) was another Columbia ethnography, Renee Fox's *Experiment Perilous* (1959) was a slightly later Harvard product. However, the ethnographic model is linked to Chicago, and probably more representative of that training (particularly through Everett Hughes) than elsewhere. Alvin Gouldner (1962, p. 207) specifically notes the differences between the "respectful" medical research conducted at Harvard and Columbia, with the more "secular" view found among Chicago sociologists. He contrasts the Columbia title, *The Student Physician* (Merton, Reader and Kendall 1957), with the more "irreverently labelled" *Boys in White*. The Harvard-Columbia researchers "buy into" the medical model, whereas the Chicagoans are more likely to be outsiders—hip and tongue in cheek (Gouldner 1962, p. 208; personal communication, Hans Mauksch, 1991). Hans Mauksch (personal communication, 1991) suggests that the division was between Columbia's emphasis on reliability and Chicago's on validity. However, when comparing such large and diverse cohorts, one might wish to be careful with such generalizations.

8. This selection posed some problems in that by emphasizing this setting, we have selected one work (Roth's) by a scholar whose degree is outside of the Department of Sociology, despite his sociological training, and a second (Becker et al.'s) by a team of scholars, only one of whom is from the cohort under study (although a second, Anselm Strauss with a 1945 Ph.D., nearly fits). These are not the only research projects that examine the calling of medicine from a Hughesian perspective; notable in this regard is the research of Oswald Hall, a 1944 Chicago Ph.D. (who, like Hughes, was a Canadian), on the stages and types of medical careers.

9. A more mundane, practical explanation for the choice of setting was that external funding existed for supporting these studies, perhaps less likely for observations and interviews in other sites (Jennifer Platt, personal communication, 1991).

10. Many things cannot be learned through this process—treating sociological works as literary confections. Here we find ourselves dangerously near the guesses of authorial intentionality, a mire we strive to avoid. More misleading is treating these scholars apart from the discipline of sociology. We cannot demonstrate whether there are systematic differences between Chicago Ph.D.'s of the period and scholars who graduated from Harvard or Columbia. Yet, we claim that the ethnographic monograph, found more frequently at Chicago than elsewhere, suggests a particular and lasting effect. (An exception to this generalization is Renee Fox's fine medical ethnography, *Experiment Perilous* [1959], prepared under the influence of Talcott Parsons at Harvard.) Further, by choosing a select group for examination, we cannot extend our analysis to all Chicago graduate students of the period, an enormously diverse group (see Platt, this volume). Finally, since these works were published in the early 1960s (although based on research conducted, and, in some cases, published in article form earlier), we cannot determine the specific events that gave rise to the images contained within.

11. The late 1940s and early 1950s represented a cultural attempt to deal

with the "text" of Nazism. The themes of the postwar decade are in part transfor-mations of concerns about fascism. The concern with conformity and the theme of individual versus the community are central and filled with ambivalence, as if we were in a debate with Germany of the 1930s. The discussion of the proper level of social and communal control appears in debates over political loyalty (the House Un-American Activities Committee) as well as in more general concerns of conformity (*The Man in the Gray Flannel Suit*) and cultural effects of suburbia. The dominant culture of postwar America reflected concerns with "Kinder, Kuche, and Kirche." The culture was marked by a fascination with things Ger-manic, and the Americanization of those things. We see in architecture the domi-nance of the Bauhaus International Style architecture (see Wolfe 1981); in paint-ing, Abstract Expressionism was a reinvigoration of the Germanic Expressionism of the 1920s; Freudian psychoanalysis was the dominant mode of therapy; Par-sonian grand theory became dominant in sociology, with its Germanic roots and style. This Germanic academic compulsion could even be seen in such massive works as the Kinsey reports on sexual behavior. Not least important, the themes of American culture were often set by a cohort of talented German refugees, as in the question of "The Authoritarian Personality," raised by Theodor Adorno and his colleagues. The power of the Nazi example was so great that it took America a generation to digest all that Germany "meant" symbolically.

12. We do not mean to suggest that conformity to group standards was not an issue at other times, or in other sociological treatments (e.g., *Middletown*); however, as noted, many commentators suggest that this emerged as a particular theme of this period.

13. Strauss (personal communication, 1991) notes that this tradition stemmed, in part, from the pragmatic tradition of Park and Thomas (and Mead) that had long addressed reform elites. There was a balance between addressing sociological issues and "doing good for the world."

14. Some felt that he was "too difficult and idiosyncratic to hold down an academic job at a first rate institution" (personal communication, Fred Davis, 1991).

15. *Asylums* is Goffman's only explicitly and extended published ethno-graphic analysis, and was selected for this reason. He never published a book-length monograph based on his ethnographies. Some argue that *Asylums* is not representative of Goffman's thematic interests; yet, we find the issue of social con-trol throughout his early works, and while *Asylums* represents a dramatic vision, it is not a unique one.

16. Many scholars of the period—including qualitative sociologists—had their own therapists (personal communication, Andrew Abbott, 1994).

17. Portions of the manuscript had been previously published in the *Ameri-can Journal of Sociology*, and, according to Davis, the manuscript was originally written in 1957 (Davis 1991, p. vii).

18. Ironically, polio was created as disease through technological improve-ments. In preindustrial times most people would develop antigens against polio as infants from a mild colic; improvements in the water supply prevented this illness

and the resulting immunity to polio (Andrew Abbott, personal communication, 1994).

19. All hospitals are not created equal. Hospitals specializing in organic diseases are likely to be more hopeful locales than state mental institutions, warehousing hopeless cases.

20. The text/reader, *Collective Behavior,* by Ralph Turner and Lewis Killian, although not an empirical study, is a notable exception to this rule. An empirical example is the research by Strauss, Schatzman, Bucher, Ehrlich, and Sabshin, *Psychiatric Ideologies and Institutions* (1964). Team research was beginning to enter sociology in the mid-century period. There were a few notable works of the earlier Chicago period, perhaps the most notable being Thomas and Znaniecki's *The Polish Peasant in Europe and America* (1918), and the Park and Burgess's *Introduction to the Science of Sociology* (1921).

21. The references to this volume come from the 1977 reprint.

22. Blanche Geer received a Ph.D. in Education from Johns Hopkins in the early 1950s. She later taught sociology at the University of Syracuse and at Northeastern University.

23. Howard Becker notes that this paragraph was almost certainly written by Hughes, and, in this sense, may not represent the attitudes of his younger colleagues, although presumably they did not disagree strongly.

24. Ethnographic training for later Chicago graduate students was provided by Gerald Suttles and to a lesser extent by Morris Janowitz, who hired Suttles to help reinvigorate the Chicago ethnographic tradition (Andrew Abbott, personal communication, 1994).

25. Elijah Anderson received his M.A. degree from the University of Chicago, working with Gerald Suttles, and received his Ph.D. degree from Northwestern University with Howard S. Becker. Strictly speaking, then, he is not a "Chicago" Ph.D.

26. Although three of the early books were published by commercial publishers (all except Becker et al.), all of the later books were published by university presses (all but Horowitz were published by the University of Chicago Press). Aside from intellectual changes, this suggests an organizational change in the structure of scholarship.

27. The great community study of the 1950s, *Small Town in Mass Society* (1957) was not written by Chicago Ph.D.'s, but by a Harvard-trained sociologist (Vidich) and a Columbia-trained one (Bensman).

REFERENCES

Anderson, E. 1978. *A Place on the Corner.* Chicago: University of Chicago Press.
Becker, H., B. Geer, E. Hughes and A. Strauss. 1961. *Boys in White.* Chicago: University of Chicago Press.
Becker, H., B. Geer and E. Hughes. 1968. *Making the Grade.* New York: Wiley.
Bell, D. 1960. The End of Ideology. Glencoe, Illinois: The Free Press.
Bosk, C. 1979. *Forgive and Remember.* Chicago: University of Chicago Press.

Brown, R. 1977. *A Poetics for Sociology.* Chicago: University of Chicago Press.
Burawoy, M. 1979. *Manufacturing Consent.* Chicago: University of Chicago Press.
Carter, P. A. 1983. *Another Part of the Fifties.* New York: Columbia University Press.
Davis, F. 1963. *Passage Through Crisis.* Indianapolis: Bobbs-Merrill.
———. 1979. *Yearning for Yesterday.* New York: The Free Press.
———. 1984. "Decade Labeling: The Play of Collective Memory and Narrative Plot." *Symbolic Interaction* 7: 15–24.
———. 1991. Introduction to the Transaction edition. Pp. vii-xx in F. Davis, *Passage Through Crisis.* New Brunswick: Transaction.
Diggins, J. P. 1988. *The Proud Decades: America in War and Peace, 1941–1960.* New York: Norton.
Elder, G. 1974. *Children of the Great Depression.* Chicago: University of Chicago Press.
Fine, G. A. and D. D. Martin. 1990. "A Partisan View: Sarcasm, Satire, and Irony as Voices in Erving Goffman's *Asylums.*" *Journal of Contemporary Ethnography* 19: 89–115.
Fox, R. 1959. *Experiment Perilous: Physicians and Patients Facing the Unknown.* Glencoe, Illinois: The Free Press.
Goffman, E. 1951. "Symbols of Class Status." *British Journal of Sociology* 2: 294–304.
———. 1959. *The Presentation of Self in Everyday Life.* New York: Anchor-Doubleday.
———. 1961. *Asylums.* Chicago: Aldine.
Gouldner, A. 1962. "Anti-Minotaur: The Myth of a Value-Free Sociology." *Social Problems* 9: 199–213.
———. 1954. *Wildcat Strike.* Yellow Springs, Ohio: Antioch Press.
Gusfield, J. 1976. "The Literary Rhetoric of Science." *American Sociological Review* 41: 16–34.
Halbwachs, M. 1992. *On Collective Memory.* Chicago: University of Chicago Press.
Harvey, L. 1987. *Myths of the Chicago School of Sociology.* Aldershot: Avebury.
Horowitz, R. 1983. *Honor and the American Dream.* New Brunswick: Rutgers University Press.
Liebow, E. 1967. *Tally's Corner.* Boston: Little, Brown.
Mannheim, K. 1952. "The Problem of Generations." In *Essays in the Sociology of Knowledge.* London: Routledge & Kegan Paul.
Manning, P. 1992. *Erving Goffman and Modern Sociology.* Cambridge: Polity Press.
McCloskey, D. 1990. *If You're So Smart.* Chicago: University of Chicago Press.
Merton, R. K., G. G. Reader, P. L. Kendall, eds. 1957. *The Student-Physician: Introductory Studies in the Sociology of Medical Education.* Cambridge: Harvard University Press.
Mills, C. W. 1956. *The Power Elite.* New York: Oxford University Press.
Morris, K. E. and B. Schwartz. 1993. "Why They Liked Ike: Tradition, Crisis, and Heroic Leadership." *The Sociological Quarterly* 34: 133–51.
Nisbet, R. 1976. *Sociology as an Art Form.* New York: Oxford University Press.

O'Neill, W. L. 1986. *American High: The Years of Confidence, 1945–1960.* New York: The Free Press.

Park, R. E. and E. W. Burgess. 1921. *Introduction to the Science of Sociology.* Chicago: University of Chicago Press.

Riesman, D. 1950. *The Lonely Crowd.* New Haven: Yale University Press.

Roth, J. 1963. *Timetables.* Indianapolis: Bobbs-Merrill.

Schuman, H. and J. Scott. 1989. "Generations and Collective Memories." *American Sociological Review* 54: 359–81.

Selznick, P. 1966. *TVA and the Grass Roots.* New York: Harper and Row.

Shibutani, T. 1966. *Improvised News.* Indianapolis: Bobbs-Merrill.

Sontag, S. 1988. *AIDS and Its Metaphors.* New York: Farrar, Straus, Giroux.

Strauss, A., L. Schatzman, R. Bucher, D. Erlich, and M. Sabshin. 1964. *Psychiatric Ideologies and Institutions.* New York: The Free Press.

Thomas, W. I. and F. Znaniecki. 1918. *The Polish Peasant in Europe and America.* 5 vols. Boston: Gohram.

Turner, R. and L. Killian. 1957. *Collective Behavior.* Englewood Cliffs: Prentice-Hall.

Vidich, A. and J. Bensman. 1958. *Small Town in Mass Society.* Princeton: Princeton University Press.

Whyte, W. F. 1943. *Street Corner Society.* Chicago: University of Chicago Press.

Whyte, W. H. 1956. *The Organization Man.* New York: Simon and Schuster.

Winkin, Y. 1988. *Erving Goffman: Les Moments et Leurs Hommes.* Paris: Seuil.

Wolfe, T. 1981. *From Bauhaus to Our House.* New York: Farrar, Straus, Giroux.

CHAPTER FOUR

THE SOCIOLOGY OF RACE AND ETHNICITY IN THE

SECOND CHICAGO SCHOOL

R. Fred Wacker

In the interwar years, the intellectual and social complex termed the "Chicago school" was at the center of sociological thought in the United States. Many key members of the intellectual and professional networks associated with the Chicago school were committed to the analysis of racial and ethnic processes. Indeed, this portion of the Chicago heritage can be traced back to the early scholarship of W. I. Thomas, Florian Znaniecki, and Robert Park.

These scholars and their students, along with scholars trained at Columbia University and heavily influenced by Franz Boas, were crucial to the establishment of an American social science of race and ethnicity. During the 1920s and up to his retirement in the early 1930s, Robert Park could be considered the dominant intellectual presence in this area at Chicago. Many students were drawn to Chicago in large part because of his tradition of scholarship. These include such notable figures as E. Franklin Frazier, Charles S. Johnson, Edgar T. Thompson, Andrew Lind, Donald Pierson, and John Dollard. A smaller number of students, influenced by Thomas, such as Emory Bogardus and Edward Reuter, completed their graduate work prior to World War I. Others, most notably Guy Johnson, left after taking an M.A. (Persons 1987; Wacker 1983).

By the end of the 1930s, there was in place not only an important network of scholars associated with Chicago scholarship but also a set of "outposts" where Chicago products and approaches to studying race and ethnicity dominated. These included the University of Hawaii, Fisk University, the University of Southern California, and the University of Washington. Since the history of sociology is, even compared to the history of other social sciences, so underdeveloped, the history of this network and the individual centers is virtually terra incognita.

During the late 1930s and 1940s Chicago sociology as a whole lost its institutional dominance. More important, for the purposes of this chapter, the style of research embodied in the Chicago perspective on race and ethnicity declined in popularity. There are many reasons for this relative decline including those examined by the historian Fred Matthews

136

(Matthews 1977, chap. 6; Matthews 1989). The causes carefully examined by Matthews' pathbreaking scholarship include "internal" forces at Chicago and "external" forces in the discipline as a whole. Matthews also argues that shifts in epistemology and the relative status of various methods and larger shifts in ontology played a role in the decline of Chicago's influence. Although his account is more detailed than that of Edward A. Shils, in many ways it tracks Shils's stimulating article on the "ecology" of sociological knowledge and institutionalization in the United States and abroad (Shils 1970).

In an essay of this scope it is impossible to do more than summarize the points made by Matthews and Shils, but several of them are important to understanding what happened in the postwar era. The aim of this chapter is to examine the work of Chicago scholars in the area of race and ethnicity in the postwar era, 1945 to the mid-1950s. The questions which I will explore are to what extent did the scholarship in the postwar era perpetuate the perspectives and methods of the interwar years and, second, to what extent did the postwar intellectual and professional environment encourage or allow for creative elaborations of those perspectives and methods?

This chapter has three major parts. In the first, I will summarize key elements of the Chicago school's approach to race and ethnicity. In the second, I will explore some of the work of three faculty members who were products of the 1920s, Everett Hughes, Louis Wirth, and Herbert Blumer. Each of these professors maintained a vital interest in racial and ethnic studies after World War II. The third and last portion of the chapter examines the scholarship of five members of the postwar cohort—Tamotsu Shibutani, Lewis Killian, Morris Janowitz, Joseph Gusfield, and Herbert Gans. Each of the five both perpetuated the traditions of scholarship transmitted by Hughes, Wirth, and Blumer and elaborated or deepened them.

ROBERT PARK AND SUBJECTIVIST AND PROCESSUAL SOCIOLOGY

Park's sociology and social psychology, as Matthews has described it, was a particularly "American" product. Like much Chicago sociology of the pre–World War II years, it was neither theoretically sophisticated or clear. When scholars such as Ralph Turner or Barbara Lal have taken the time to examine the complexity of his thought and judge it for its relevance to contemporary sociology, especially in the area of race and ethnicity, however, they note that it remains useful and stimulating. I would argue that much of Park's theoretical and methodological framework was developed precisely to examine change and persistence in the situations and life experiences of racial and ethnic groups. Park began with expertise in the situation of African Americans, but expanded his interest to immigrants and Asian Americans and to the situations of ethnic and racial groups around the globe. From early in his career, moreover, he was interested in the reactions of subordinated groups to their status and in the individual and collective manifestations of those reactions. The sociology and social psychology he developed was particularly attuned to "nationalistic" sentiments and movements (Turner 1967; Lal 1990).

Park worked out the framework of his social psychology of race and ethnicity during the 1920s. He was convinced that racial and cultural relations should be studied in situations of "contact." Historical accounts were valuable for understanding many early stages or forms of relations, but sociologists could also study contemporary forms in cities and on what he and his students termed "racial frontiers." Frontiers were where relations were in flux, usually due to challenges to the status relations structured by custom, but also due to mobility on the part of peoples.

There is not space here to deal with the various misconceptions and distortions of Park's thought that have often prevented social scientists from taking his scholarship and that of his students seriously. It is necessary, however, to discuss briefly the race-relations cycle. The cycle suggested that there was a "natural" or "inevitable" movement for groups from competition to conflict to accommodation to assimilation. Park did posit such a cycle and a small number of his students used it in their research. But it is a major distortion to claim that it dominated Chicago research, and this should be clear to those who examine Chicago scholarship or Park's work with open minds.

Another common distortion of the work of Park and his students is the interpretation of the concept of "marginality" and "marginal man." Although a few students may have later used it to connote racial or ethnic individuals who were prone to depression and personal disorganization, as originally conceived by Park, it was a much more complicated concept. The marginal person was likely to be more alert, critical, "intelligent," and often was a leader in cultural or nationalistic organizations. Park believed that racial and ethnic relations could be understood and perhaps eventually improved largely through mutual understandings between groups and between individuals from different groups. This process could be systematically observed by sociologists, and what they learned could eventually be communicated to wider publics. What was, in large part, exciting for Park about so-called marginals was they they were in effect in dialogue with themselves. Whatever directions or degrees of affiliation or alienation they may have expressed, their personal struggles and careers would be illuminating for the sociologist of race and ethnicity (Turner 1967, xxxix–xl).

Turning from Park's overall scheme to his "methodology" or modes of penetrating the psychology of subordinated and superordinate groups, it should be clear that Park was heavily influenced by Cooley, Thomas, and Znaniecki. So much has been written about the methodenstreit in sociology that I will be brief here. Park believed strongly that in their quest for precision and scientific status many sociologists were attracted to techniques and methods which could not adequately penetrate the reserve, defenses, or strangeness of subjects, especially in the area of racial and ethnic relations. Park believed that autobiographies, letters, fiction, and types of data which were not constructed by the social scientists were most revealing. Martin Bulmer, Lee Harvey, and other scholars have corrected to some degree the portrayal of Park and his students as dogmatic and softheaded and have argued that Chicago sociology, despite Park's scorn, was eclectic in its methodologies and approaches to the collection of data (Bulmer 1981; Harvey 1987).

Even if Chicago figures and Park were more eclectic and pragmatic than earlier stereotypes held them to be, the question of the social scientific status of human documents and life-history materials needs to be addressed. The resistance of many sociologists to relying heavily upon this type of data collection was in large part a judgment that its interpretation relied far too much upon the personal insight and empathic skills of the individual practitioner. Park sought an intersubjective understanding of groups and individuals, but he didn't bother himself much about the needs many sociologists may have felt for not merely more precise techniques but techniques which led to more agreement between sociologists themselves (Turner 1967). Today, of course, there is a renewed interest in qualitative methods and strong commitments to the sort of "subjectivist" sociology promoted and developed by Park, Znaniecki, and Thomas. This expresses itself, for example, in the renewed interest in figures such as Herbert Blumer and in reconstructions of Blumer as a "macro" as well as a "micro" sociologist (Lyman and Vidich 1988; Maines 1989; Lyman 1984).

In the postwar period, however, the trends in the discipline were running away from "subjectivist" sociology. With the decline of the subjective dimension, the favorite methods of figures such as Park were challenged and seen as outmoded. Fred Matthews argues that for several complicated reasons the fundamental view of society and culture of scholars such as Park, which stressed fluidity and process (a William Jamesian view) was undercut by structural views which stressed the power of norms and systemic needs. He locates this shift in the late 1930s and 1940s and suggests that it was a deep, if not paradigmatic, seachange in the outlook of American social scientists (Matthews 1989).

The interwar production of scholarship in the area of race and ethnicity at Chicago was linked to the momentum created by Robert Park's leadership and his inspirational impact upon many students. Edward Shils notes that when Park retired in the early 1930s there was no adequate replacement for him as a leader. The rise of new research centers at Harvard, with the inspirational leader Talcott Parsons, and at Columbia, led by the duo of Paul Lazarsfeld and Robert Merton, suggests that "schools" of sociology arise with an attractive articulation of a renewed sociology by charismatic figures. While these centers were ascending, the heritage of Park and others was handed on to "lieutenants" such as Louis Wirth, Everett Hughes, and Herbert Blumer (Tiryakian 1979).

HUGHES, WIRTH, AND BLUMER IN THE POSTWAR PERIOD

Everett Hughes was a friend and colleague of Robert Park. He returned to Chicago in the late 1930s after teaching at McGill University in the early 1930s. Hughes was a vital force in transmitting a "Parkian" approach to race and ethnicity in the postwar years. A large section of his collected papers of 1971 was titled "The Meeting of Races and Cultures." In 1952 he wrote, along with his wife, Helen MacGill Hughes, a text titled *Where Peoples Meet: Racial and Ethnic Frontiers.* In 1958, along with Edgar T. Thompson, he edited a comprehensive collective of articles and readings on ethnic processes around the world, *Race: Individual and Collective Behavior.* The latter two books dealt at length with the conditions under which ethnicity arose and with forms of racial, ethnic, and national consciousness and movements (Wacker, 1986).

Hughes, however, also was engaged in research in the areas of work and occupations. He encouraged a cohort of postwar students to take up topics in these areas and joined with them in influential research projects up into the 1960s. Hughes was also important for combining Park's interest in race and ethnicity with the interaction of individuals in new work settings. Exemplars of these studies were included in his book *Men and*

Their Work and some were included in *Where Peoples Meet.* "Dilemmas and Contradictions of Status" (originally published in 1945) and "The Knitting of Racial Groups in Industry" (1946) were articles combining emergent sociological interests in work, occupations, and status dilemmas with attention to "contacts" and "situations."

In his essay "Social Change and Status Protest: An Essay on the Marginal Man" (1949), Hughes not only returned to elaborate the concept of Park but expanded it to new status dilemmas of women:

> I have used the case of women to show that the phenomenon [of marginality] is not, in essence, one of racial and cultural mixing. . . . Migration and resulting cultural contact simply create the grand fields on which the battle of status is fought out among humans; a confusing and bloodier battle because its essence is that so many people are in doubt about which side they want to be on or may be allowed to be on.
>
> . . . In our own society the contact of cultures, races and religions, combines with social mobility to produce an extra-ordinary number of people who are marginal in some degree, who have some conflict of identity in their own minds, who find some parts of the social world which they would like to enter closed to them, or open only at the expense of some trea-son to things and people they hold dear. (Hughes and Hughes 1952, 196)

Hughes thus elaborated the concept of marginality and continued the comparative thrust initiated by Park in the 1930s. Along with gender, however, he also expressed his sensitivity to the "brutal bargain" which may accompany social and economic mobility.

Hughes's research productivity in the 1940s and 1950s contrasts sharply with that of Louis Wirth. Wirth was very important as an orga-nizer of social scientists and citizens interested in alleviating racial ten-sions and responding to racial conflicts. Wirth was a leader of the Ameri-can Council of Race Relations, an umbrella organization which coordinated civic action and some research during the postwar years. Some indication of the scope of attention to racial and intergroup rela-tions in the postwar period is given by the *Directory of Agencies in Race Relations: National, State and Local,* published by the council in 1945. Over one hundred city, regional, and national "interracial councils" were listed, along with many groups associated with religious organizations, labor unions, and school systems (Salerno 1987, 17–33).

Wirth's career as an activist intellectual in the 1940s, however, came at the expense of his scholarly productivity. He wanted to inspire and co-ordinate research and was excited by the concentration of attention among sociologists, social psychologists, and other social scientists on the alleviation of prejudices and what were termed "group tensions" (Wirth, in Allport, 1946; Matthews, in Rischin, 1987). Wirth began teaching a course in "Minorities" at Chicago in 1945 and continued to teach it until his death in 1952. Interestingly, no other faculty member took it up. Wirth did write a much-anthologized article on "The Problem of Minority Groups" in 1945. This article developed a typology of minorities, concentrating on ethnic rather than racial minorities, and took a "Parkian" and comparative approach (Gleason 1992, 91–122).

Hughes was critical of the direction Wirth took after the war. It was his opinion that the study of race and ethnicity at Chicago had been split apart by Wirth. Wirth had abandoned the detached and skeptical standpoint of authentic Chicago research. The postwar research which focused upon the problems of majority prejudice was running counter to the comparative thrust of Park. It also often assumed that the minority individual was a relatively passive victim of prejudice. Hughes criticized what he saw as the "ethnocentric" biases of social scientists. He, like Park, believed that the sociologist's attention should also be given to the struggles of the subordinated and to their attempts to achieve solidarity and build institutions (Hughes 1971, 167–91, 276–78).

According to the premises of Park, which Hughes would attempt to transmit faithfully, prejudice was an inevitable reaction to attempts by subordinated people to improve their status. Individuals and groups might be harmed by prejudice, but prejudice also had the potential to mobilize group members and even increase their morale. This view ran counter to the hopes underlying much postwar research on prejudice (Hughes interview, 1979; Rose 1983, 178–80; Gleason 1992, 97–100).

Herbert Blumer began writing on race contacts and racial ideologies in 1939, but the bulk of his writing in this area was accomplished in the 1950s and after he left Chicago to chair the newly formed Department of Sociology at the University of California at Berkeley. Blumer was often absent from the Chicago campus in the 1940s. He worked in industrial relations in the steel industry and traveled extensively. Although he had maintained a close relationship with Park, he did not teach race and ethnic courses at Chicago. He did teach and study racial and ethnic relations (along with industrial relations) within the context of collective behavior.

Blumer took over Park's course on "The Crowd and the Public" upon Park's retirement in 1933 and was an important figure in the later development of the fields of collective behavior and social movements.

Blumer approached racial and ethnic relations as complex and rooted in history and politics or power relations. He sought to elaborate and expand the framework which Park and other students at Chicago had worked with in the 1930s to enable it to cover the new nationalisms arising in the 1940s and 1950s as well as the various ideologies that emerged to counter movements towards civil rights and civic inclusion. Blumer demonstrated how dominant groups developed and used collective definitions in response to fears and to protect their status and power. This approach was an extension of Park's view of racial prejudice as a defensive reaction to status challenges and fear of strangers.

From Blumer's perspective, however, there was a deliberate movement to make subordinate groups into objects and, at times, scapegoats. Blumer added his own neologisms, moreover, since by the late 1950s and 1960s he was describing the process of definition of the subordinate racial group and the relationship between the dominant and subordinate groups as a "running process." This running process could lead to the redefinition and modification of images and of feelings. He also paid increasing attention in his later writing to the roles of leaders, elites, the media, legislatures, and new or revitalized interest groups.

Blumer's view of the running process meant that it was inaccurate and unscientific for scholars or others to seek the causes of race prejudice in the makeup of individuals. The process had many "different lines and degrees of formation." At the same time, he believed that it might be fruitful to alter the behavior of various "functionaries" who implement segregation in communities (school boards, real estate boards, hospital superintendents, etc.) (Blumer 1939, 1955, 1958a, 1958b, all included in Lyman and Vidich, 1988).

Blumer was asked in 1958 to compile a critique of race-relations research studies in the U.S. for UNESCO. He summarized and criticized 207 research reports made since 1945. This critique is illuminating for several reasons. It reveals the sort of research that Blumer believed would be most useful for policy-makers and the directions he believed social science ought to travel to make significant progress toward a comprehensive understanding of race relations. It also represents a side of Blumer that seldom was found in print. Although Hughes had criticized Wirth's path away from "Parkian" research, Blumer, even taking his audience and task into consideration, reveals how powerful the forces for a useful and pragmatic sociology had become. Blumer, at least briefly, wanted as much as Wirth to direct social scientists toward social betterment. In the UNESCO survey, Park and his suspicion of "do-gooders" is forgotten. Of course, by the 1950s, there were a large number of sociologists and social psychologists who had taken jobs and made research commitments to the study of prejudice and the alleviation of racial and group tensions. It was, in significant respects, a different world than that in which Robert Park had operated.

Moreover, Blumer's UNESCO piece is interesting insofar as it recognizes many of the postwar cohort for their contributions to what he saw as a "realistic" and, he hoped, a new, emerging paradigm of research. Blumer had known many of the Chicago graduates he cited and had perhaps directed many of their dissertations. The survey, in contrast to others such as that published in 1947 by Robin Williams, Jr., had a distinctive Chicago bias.

Blumer first praised those studies (such as E. Franklin Frazier's *Black Bourgeosie*) which give scholars insight into the internal organization and behavior of minority groups. Along with Frazier's highly critical analysis of the African-American middle class and its culture, he noted the works of other Chicago figures, such as Arnold Rose (Ph.D. 1946), Mozell Hill (1946), and Charles King (1951). He also noted the valuable work of pre-1945 graduates Oliver C. Cox on Negro leadership and Charles Parish on Negro communities. Here Blumer was reiterating Park's emphasis upon the need for social scientists to find ways to penetrate into the communities and, it was hoped, the mentalities of African Americans. Among the ironies of his praise, of course, is that no matter how valuable the early research of these scholars, with the exception of Rose they were hampered severely as African Americans from getting jobs in research universities (Jones 1974; Platt 1991; Wilmoth Carter to Fine, 1990; Charles King to Fine, 1990).

Second, he summarizes the many studies of discrimination made since the war, including that of members of the postwar cohort such as Otis Duncan (Ph.D. in 1949), and Beverley Duncan (1957) on housing segregation indices; G. Franklin Edwards (1952) on the attitudes of southern Negro teachers towards desegregation; Ralph Turner (1948) on Negro workers, and Lewis Killian (1949) on southern white workers in the north; Jack London (1952) on managers with policies against discrimination; and

William Kornhauser (1953) on the ambivalent position of Negro union leaders in largely white unions.

For Blumer, the importance of these studies was that they often explored sites of interracial contact and revealed the complexity and variety of "situations" where relations were in process. Since Blumer believed that most attitudinal studies, perhaps especially those of the "prejudiced" personality, were artificial and misleading, he had little praise for most social psychological studies of the late 1940s and early 1950s. He did praise Ralph Turner's study of the symbolic replacement of "Mexicans" with the image of "Zoot-suiters" and the studies of Negro stereotypes of whites by Tilman Cothran (1949), along with those by Olive Westbrooke Quinn (1950) of the transmission of racial attitudes among white Southerners.

Blumer's greatest praise was for those very few studies that he saw demonstrating the situational determination of behavior. The most encouraging were those of Joseph Lohman (a lecturer at Chicago) and Dietrich Reitzes (1952). He was encouraged by their innovative qualities and the fact that they "point to the marked discrepancy between 'prejudicial attitudes' and overt behavior." Lohman's work in Washington, D.C., and Reitzes' in Chicago led them to discover that whites behaved "entirely differently toward Negroes" in different situations—at work, in residential neighborhoods, and in shopping centers. Blumer, in a rare burst of optimism, suggested that these studies and some others (by Arnold Rose, Jessie Bernard, and Robin Williams) were the start of a very positive trend of research. Perhaps the "situation" was replacing "attitude" in the explanation of behavior and therefore "personality components of racial prejudice are coming increasingly to be regarded as mere individual variations inside a collectively defined orientation" (Blumer, 1958b, 112–13).

Blumer concluded his survey by criticizing those who were attempting to achieve exactitude in social science at the price of direct and naturalistic study. He reiterated his hope that the shift in interest among students of race relations to the "question of how situations may be structured to yield desired forms of race relations" would flourish. Students would have to study mobilized power groups and many "devices" for change including legislations, managerial arrangements, administrative regulations and power structures.

Blumer's (1958b) critique was the first lengthy discussion of research in race relations made by a Chicago scholar in the postwar period. Blumer by this time had been in Berkeley for over five years, but his critique still is of interest and perhaps indicates what was promoted as good research at Chicago in the postwar years. Because his task was to concentrate soley on research in the U.S., Blumer's own comparative interests and research, reminiscent of Park's in the 1930s, is not evident. But Blumer was continuing the earlier concentration upon situations of "contact." He was frustrated with studies which avoided complexity, history, and power as parts of the process of collective definition. In his most optimistic mood, he asks sociologists to turn away from a quest for exactitude and toward the creation of a democratic social intelligence that can direct public action (Lyman and Vidich 1988).

SHIBUTANI AND KILLIAN

Among the students Blumer was closest to was Tamotsu Shibutani. Among Shibutani's outstanding pieces of research was the most ambitious textbook on racial and ethnic processes to emerge from the postwar cohort. *Ethnic Stratification,* written with the assistance of Kian Kwan and the historian Robert H. Billigmeier, was published in 1964. Shibutani took his B.A. at Berkeley, where he met W. I. Thomas and Dorothy Thomas (Baldwin 1990; Deegan 1991). He came to Chicago after the war and was one of the few graduate students chosen to become an instructor. When Blumer was absent from the campus toward the end of the decade, Shibutani taught several of his courses and then co-taught the course "Crowd and Public" with Blumer. He joined Blumer in the Sociology Department in Berkeley in the early 1950s (Baldwin 1990; interview with Shibutani, 1988).

Ethnic Stratification adopted a processual perspective on intergroup relations. It fulfilled many of Blumer's guidelines and hopes as expressed in 1958, including examinations of collective image development and decline, the role of media and public institutions in the alteration and perpetuation of stereotypes and images, and the historical complexity of most racial and ethnic situations.

In Shibutani's conceptual scheme, all racial and ethnic relations were encompassed by four master processes termed differentiating, sustaining, disjunctive, and integrative. While these processes at time overlap with Park's four master processes of conflict, competition, accommodation, and assimilation, they are infinitely more detailed and comprehensive. Shibutani, with the aid of his colleagues, covered racial and ethnic groups around the world in a manner which fulfilled much of the promise of

Park's global vision. It also added, from the perspective of the 1960s, a discussion of integrative processes.

Differentiating processes occur when stable status relations and color lines come into being, often sustained by race ideologies. Sustaining processes are those which reinforce color lines when they are subject to pressure to change. Among the mechanisms for sustaining the color lines are modes of maintaining social distance, the control of education and communication channels, and the monopoly of the means of violence. When sustaining processes are operating, stable minorities live in their own social world, reconciled to their subordinate status and benefiting from cathartic outlets for frustrations. Conflict, however, occurs in disjunctive processes, including collective protest, formation of contrast conceptions, and movements of nationalism and succession. Shibutani, benefiting from the rich scholarship in many fields which analyzed nationalism in Asia and Africa, here elaborates and brilliantly summarizes the hints and suggestions of Robert Park and his early students. Integrative processes occur when new ethnic groups are formed and when peoples "come to regard themselves as alike." Shibutani here reconceptualizes the research on "factionalism" within changing minorities. Important subprocesses under the integrative schema include communications channels which facilitate acculturation, social disorganization in communities and families, and the redefinition of ethnic categories and the establishment of a new moral order.

Shibutani's book was a tour de force consolidating the Chicago interests in racial and ethnic relations with the burgeoning literature in postwar sociology in stratification phenomena. He recognized that ethnic peoples are usually stratified but argued for the heuristic value of viewing such stratification as an "on-going process rather than as a structure." He was also not sanguine about the elimination of stereotypes. While the popular view that people inherit different tendencies to act is incorrect, it is important, he noted, to recognize how deep and persistent are the barriers to interaction. This approach to prejudice was close to that of Park and Blumer and may explain in part why the book, for all its virtues, was not adopted as a textbook.

Shibutani's book was richly detailed and clear in its theoretical schema. However, despite its virtues, the work is seldom cited and has not proved popular. This neglect is probably due in part to the complexity of the book for most students and in part due to the "conservative" nature of its approach and conclusions about conflict, prejudice, and change. Recent work which seeks to revitalize other "macro" aspects of symbolic interactionism may eventually lead to a rediscovery of and renewed respect for Shibutani's work on race and ethnicity.

A contemporary of Shibutani's at Chicago was Lewis Killian. Killian was a G.I. Bill graduate student and completed his Ph.D. in 1949. He has written an autobiographical account of his days on the Midway, including his recollections of the creative cohort of graduate students he had as friends and acquaintances. Killian was encouraged to study white Southerners in their neighborhoods and in their workplaces and he produced a classic Chicago ethnography. However, his research was also closely linked to what Blumer was calling for in his 1958 article for UNESCO. It was the study of change and stability in Southern white attitudes, but it was based upon "situational" rather than experimental methodology.

Killian was drawn to the subject in part because racial disturbances and riots in Detroit and elsewhere had been portrayed as "caused" in large part by Southern whites and their Jim Crow traditions. He found that although the whites still harbored distrust of blacks and prejudices toward them, these prejudices did not have a great impact in plants where employers had been willing to hire blacks (Killian 1952).

When Killian went to Oklahoma to take his first teaching position, he continued his interest in race and ethnic relations, but it was supplemented and, more accurately, combined with an interest in collective behavior. He worked with a graduate school friend, Ralph Turner, to produce in 1952 the popular and pathbreaking textbook *Collective Behavior.* Killian, however, returned more fully to racial and ethnic studies in the 1950s and 1960s when he studied black leadership and other aspects of the civil rights struggles. He participated in the civil rights movement by working on the *amicus curiae* brief submitted by Florida in the crucial *Brown v. Board of Education* case in the early 1950s. He also published five books in the 1960s and 1970s on race and racial relations in America.

Killian also returned in the late 1960s to the study of white Southerners. Peter Rose, editor of the Random House series on minorities in American life, asked Killian to write a contribution on white Southerners. Killian took on this task with verve, placing Southerners not only in perspective as an ethnic group with a "minority psychology" and a set of traditions, but also exploring "marginal white Southerners," including Jews, Catholics, and transplanted Yankees (Killian, 1985/1970).

Killian wrote many important articles, several coauthored with his colleague Charles M. Grigg during his years at Florida State University. Of the postwar students, he was the most active in studying communities under the stress of racial and political change. He studied leadership, biracial committees, and agitators. Moreover, taking up a challenge and an opportunity, he did comparative work in Great Britain, studying school busing and what he termed the "race relations industry." The latter is the administrative institutional structures set up to enforce change in the area of racial discrimination.

Killian's career is important for the sustained attention he has given to the development of political and social movements among blacks and whites. He took up one of Blumer's chief themes, the collective definition of public problems, and he explored many of the situations Blumer thought might reveal how race relations in process actually worked. In his emphasis upon racial ideologies and their perpetuation by leaders and media, he took up issues which Park only hinted at in his last published articles. These were areas of research, however, which Blumer was emphasizing and were consistent with a creative elaboration of Chicago traditions in the postwar period.

Killian's most recent work, however, is often pessimistic about trends in race relations. His analyses of the race relations industry concludes that it is perpetuating racial consciousness in opposition to the original goals of the civil rights movement. The gains of the civil rights movement are being eroded, ironically in part because of government-legitimated revitalization of racial consciousness (Killian in Gordon 1981; Killian 1985). With this turn in his work, Killian takes an "ironic" turn, examining and criticizing what Robert Merton and others have examined as the unanticipated consequences of purposeful social action.

MACROSOCIAL AND CULTURAL ELABORATIONS

The scholarship of Shibutani and Killian exhibits how traditions of thought and research were reworked by those who took up the study of race and ethnicity in the postwar years. Several other figures from the postwar cohort had briefer careers as racial and ethnic scholars. Ralph Turner, Helen Z. Lopata, and Rose Hum Lee all produced interesting work on ethnic relations during portions of their careers (Turner and Surace 1956; Turner 1954; Turner to Wacker 1991; Deegan 1991, 257–72). The fact is, however, that Killian and Shibutani were rather the exceptions. There are at least two major factors for the decline in the production of scholars who made race and ethnicity their major research interests. First, the Chicago perspective flowing from Park was linked to a subjectivist and processual set of assumptions and techniques of research which were out of fashion in a more activist era and one in which forms of "structural-functionalism" dominated. Second, many of the students who committed themselves to racial and ethnic topics for their dissertations and early scholarship were simply, if tragically, not eligible for careers in research universities. Students were perhaps attracted to postwar Chicago in part (as during the 1920s and 1930s) because of its deserved reputation as a center of research in this area and because of the links of professors such as Hughes, Wirth and Blumer to the network of researchers and leaders in race and ethnic scholarship. But they, for many reasons, including the racism and sexism prevalent in most academic institutions, never had productive research careers. Brilliant scholars such as E. Franklin Frazier would chair Howard's department and Charles S. Johnson would chair Fisk's, but where would the other African-American scholars go after World War II? The situation of women and Asian American scholars were analogous (Deegan, this volume; Yu, in progress).

Henry Yu, in a Ph.D. in progress, examines the careers of many of the Asian-American students at Chicago before and after World War II. He notes their accomplishments and the importance of the "problem" of prejudice and discrimination toward Asian Americans for the development of Chicago sociology. Among his most creative suggestions is that the very status of the students as "marginal men" (and women) placed them in various binds. They were valued for their insights into their groups and as "middle-men" between the sociological community and their groups. However, this very status could and often did become a stereotype and limit their careers and reputations. Wu's points merge with the attitude of many African American scholars who were encouraged, if not subtly forced, into roles as experts on their own group. While realism pushed them toward taking advantage of their "insider" status, many thought of black studies and even a concentration upon race and ethnicity as a sort of career trap.

Several other scholars also took up portions of the Chicago heritage, those which emphasize elements that are "macrosociological" or "symbolic and cultural." The movement toward macrosociology and public enlightenment is exemplified by the scholarship of Morris Janowitz. The study of symbolic and cultural productions is examined in the scholarship of Joseph Gusfield and Herbert Gans.

Janowitz received his Ph.D. in 1948. After serving in the Army in World War II, he began working with Bruno Bettleheim in the late 1940s on studies of prejudice. These studies, like the more famous Authoritarian Personality Studies, were supported by the American Jewish Committee (Wiggershaus, 1994). Janowitz later returned to Chicago to chair the Department of Sociology.

Blumer had recognized the value of the Bettelheim-Janowitz studies in his 1958 review, especially their analysis of the linkages between social mobility and prejudicial attitudes. When the two scholars updated their work in 1964, they concluded that their analysis of prejudice revealed that most people were willing to comply with external forms of controls and that legal reform could increase the potential for social integration. This answered, in part, Blumer's call for studies of the impact of organized expression of norms upon prejudice and discrimination. It is another example, moreover, of studies of institutions, here legislation and legal reform, which Park and the interwar generation did not foresee.

James Burk has recently argued that Janowitz had a definite mode of theory construction, one which was clearly linked to three postulates of symbolic interaction (that reality is in a state of flux, that structure is an emergent process, and that sociological practice entails an ideological commitment to social reconstruction). Janowitz worked in the latter phases of his career on the articulation and demonstration of a macrosociology. Along with combining the analysis of various levels of institutional life (primary groups, communities, bureaucratic structures, and nation-states), Janowitz emphasized social control. His emphasis upon social organization and social control drew upon his own respect for and knowledge of W. I. Thomas and Robert Park (Burk, 1989).

Although Janowitz took up themes that are related to racial and ethnic studies, he did not study race relations in any consistent manner. He studied the urban riots of the 1960s and contrasted them with early twentieth-century riots. He also also pointed out that the growing ethnic diversity and immigration of the period after the mid-1960s in the United States raised serious problems for "maintaining a balance between ethnic diversity and a core of central values essential for citizenship" (Janowitz 1968; Janowitz 1983).

Although Janowitz's ambitious macrosociology focused upon major institutions of society, other postwar students took up very different approaches to modern society and institutions, looking at their symbolic aspects and to the construction of individual and collective identity. Two of the figures who adopted a more "constructivist" approach were Joseph Gusfield (Ph.D. 1955) and Herbert Gans (M.A. 1949). Both scholars were influenced by Hughes, Blumer, and W. Lloyd Warner. However, another of their mentors, one often neglected in the intellectual history of Chicago, was David Riesman. Riesman, coauthor of the influential study of American character, *The Lonely Crowd,* came to Chicago and played an important role in the college and its social science curriculum in the mid-1940s.

The autobiographical recollections of Gusfield, Gans, and Riesman are valuable evidence of the intellectual atmosphere and "ethos" of the postwar period. They describe tensions and animosities within the department but also opportunities for creative research. Insofar as students were able to make use of the dynamic ethos, including the variety of faculty approaches and the diversity of graduate students and graduate lecturers or assistants, they often produced extremely interesting and pathbreaking research. While this chapter focuses upon only Gusfield and Gans, it has implications for the research creativity of many others in the postwar cohort.

Riesman's autobiographical account of the late 1940s and early 1950s suggests that an old "debate" at Chicago between the advocates of quantitative methods and those committed to the prewar emphasis upon qualitative methods and field research methodologies intensified during the late 1940s. In this period, moreover, the definition of what was good sociology became even more important since the older faculty (with the exception of Hughes and Warner) retired, died, or left the university. This was the "watershed" period in the opinion of many, although perhaps Hughes and Blumer, wishing to maintain much of the prewar perspectives, felt beleaguered prior to mid-century. In any event, Riesman recalls that

> the emnity was a problem for graduate students who worked with Hughes and with me, as well as for nontenured colleagues, particularily with Nelson Foote and Anselm Strauss. . . . Unrealistically, if understandably, translating acidulous comments by faculty members into actual prescriptions of what would pass muster, some able graduate students feared to write a dissertation without tables in it. . . . I sometimes had the dismal experience of having as a doctoral candidate someone who had been a spirited undergraduate and watching that person become more timid and less original as time went by (Riesman, in Berger 1990, 63)

Among the students who resisted the pressures and confusions suggested by this account was Joseph Gusfield. Gusfield grew up in Chicago, entered the university as an undergraduate in 1941 and left for nearly three years in the Army in April of 1943. His experiences with the "cataclysmic destruction of belief in the special providence of America" in the Depression and the "sense of fate of the unknown, controllable forces surrounding us while serving in the war in Europe" were both formative experiences (Gusfield, in Berger 1990, 104–8).

Gusfield stresses the variety of social science perspectives available to graduate students. There was continuity with "the Park tradition and the Chicago School of Field Observations" as a model of what sociologists did best and a recent exemplar of this in William F. Whyte's study of *Street Corner Society*. But this tradition was also an intellectual framework for what Gusfield terms "marginalization."

> [This was] an orientation that brought us outside of our own cultures [which fit] in well with the impact or influence of the very idea of marginalization, which I think was crucial and important to our later contributions. By marginalization I mean the disposition to see the society from the outside in a way which led us perhaps to overstate the case for those who lived on the margins of the society, for the deviant. (Gusfield to Fine, 1990)

Gusfield points especially to the importance of Everett Hughes as a model of the emancipated marginal, an individual with "a strong identification with what one might call the less established parts of society." Assuming Gusfield's characterization of Hughes to be accurate, it is probable that Hughes was encouraged in his attitude by Robert Park, who also had an unusual empathy for the looser and less established parts of his own era. Then again, the meeting of Hughes and Park, like that of Park and Thomas, may be simply a crucial example of elective affinity (Matthews 1977, 84; Wacker 1983, 43).

Gusfield notes that his own cohort of graduate students (he lists Bill and Ruth Kornhauser, Howard Becker, Bob Habenstein, Bill Westley, Gladys Frisch, Kurt Lang, Fred Davis, Helena Lopata, Aliza Dworkin, Herman and Frances Piven, Hal Wilensky, Bernard Karsh, Erving Goffman, and Saul Medlovitz) was largely concerned with meaning and how meaning was developed. This diversity of students was apparently welcomed by the faculty and the students were encouraged to challenge accepted meanings in a creative manner by figures such as Hughes and Ries-man. At the same time, the cohort was a postwar cohort and perhaps should be compared with the post–World War I cohort. An unusually diverse (racially, regionally, ethnically, and in terms of gender) cohort of graduate students attended Chicago in the early 1920s as well. Perhaps the experience of upheaval during wartime makes aspects of sociology, at least the Chicago variety of sociology, attractive. On the other hand, the G.I. Bill and the delayed graduate education of masses of talented students led to an influx of graduate students at Harvard, Columbia, and many other centers of research.

Gusfield's dissertation was unique for the department insofar as it was both an ambitious historical analysis of the temperance movement and a study of status and cultural conflicts. The 1955 dissertation was published as *Symbolic Crusade: Status Politics and the American Temperance Movement* in 1963. It was a study of a social movement but also a study of the making of meaning and the role of moral reformers in the definition of deviance. In his later work, Gusfield has continued in this vein, studying the construction of "social problems" such as alcoholism and drunk driving.

Although *Symbolic Crusade* is sharply different from the more traditional Chicago work of Shibutani or Killian, it exhibits an innovative way of expropriating the processual traditions. For instance, the last chapter title of the book, "Dramatistic Theory of Status Politics," may serve as an indicator of the direction of his work and that of other "marginalized" social scientists. The Catholic and Protestant, "native" and immigrant groups involved in the long battle over temperance were examined at a more general level of analysis. Gusfield was among the first sociologists (although his work is similar in some respects to that of the Columbia scholar Richard Hofstadter) to look in this oblique and challenging way at American status politics.

Herbert Gans was an undergraduate student at Chicago at the same time as Gusfield. Like Gusfield, his recollections make use of the concept of marginality to explain themes in his sociology and his particular attention to cultural studies. Gans was born into a middle-class German Jewish family in Cologne and came to Chicago in 1940. His graduate training was unique in that he took a Master's degree in the social science divisional program and worked there with a sociologist, Earl Johnson (Gans, in Berger 1990, 439).

Gans was influenced at Chicago by several scholars, including W.

Lloyd Warner, who encouraged his interest in the relationship between class and mass media. Gans notes that his relationship with David Riesman had the greatest affect on his later career. Riesman was important as a mentor, and his research on *The Lonely Crowd* was a model for the study of popular culture. Gans was also influenced by the tradition in field observation noted by Gusfield. Although Gans left Chicago without taking a Ph.D., he completed one in city planning in 1957 at the University of Pennsylvania.

Gans later published many books and articles dealing with high and low culture, equality in America, and the fate of American individualism. His particular elaborations of the Chicago traditions, however, are found in the two field studies of communities, *The Urban Villagers* (1962/1982) and *The Levittowners* (1967). In his methodological appendices to the former book, he notes his debt to several Chicago figures, including Hughes and members of his cohort such as Howard S. Becker. His second edition of *The Urban Villagers* is among the most interesting self-reflexive accounts in Chicago sociology, as he amends his former work in an unflinching manner.

Gans also has written several important articles on ethnicity. In 1979, in a volume dedicated to David Riesman, he summarized much of his basic position on "modern" ethnicity in the article "Symbolic Ethnicity: The Future of Ethnic Groups and Culture in America." He here criticized those scholars who believed that ethnic groups were undergoing authentic revivals of primordial or intrinsic group consciousness. Rather, he argued, ethnics were becoming more visible as a result of their upward mobility. They might be adopting new forms of ethnic behavior or affiliation, but ethnic roles were, for current generations, largely voluntary rather than ascriptive. Moreover, the largely symbolic ethnicity of the present might be encouraged because in contemporary life the costs of ethnic identity were lower and benefits higher (Gans 1979, 202, 198).

In a more recent article, Gans takes on a similar task, arguing that many scholars have mistaken symbolic aspects of ethnic identity for the ascriptive and bounded identities of the past. While the "straight-line" assimilation theories of figures such as W. Lloyd Warner do not capture all ethnic experiences, he also notes that on many important measures of intermarriage, language use, and residential concentration, there is still a straight-line movement toward what most term "assimilation" (Gans 1992).

Gusfield and Gans are certainly among the most creative members of the postwar cohort of graduate students. It is interesting to note, however, that among the immediate postwar cohort there were no students save Killian who wrote influential works on African Americans. Perhaps the funding networks that helped produce a classic study like Horace Cayton and St. Clair Drake's *Black Metropolis* simply did not exist in the postwar years. It is just as important to reiterate that opportunities for African-American scholars were severely limited in the academic world and ambitious students may have entered other fields of endeavor (Stanfield, 1985; Platt, 1992).

Stanley Lieberson, who received his Ph.D. in 1960 and is at the far end of the postwar generation, of course, has become a major force in the study of ethnicity and race. Andrew Greeley, who received his Ph.D. later, has been one of the most prolific and innovative scholars in the area of ethnicity for many years.

The Chicago heritage has also been taken up by people outside the orbit of the Midway. The British scholar Michael Banton has explored the contemporary usefulness of the scholarship and conceptual apparatus of figures such as Park and Warner. A student of Blumer, Barbara Ballis Lal, has written the most lengthy and detailed book on the urban and racial sociology of Robert Park and demonstrated how many questions raised by contemporary racial, ethnic, and cultural movements needs to take account of his conceptual and theoretical leads. As noted earlier, Stanford Lyman and others have begun to reconstruct our image of Herbert Blumer in the context of the "micro" and "macro" sociology debate. Lyman has also produced a book and a series of articles which reexamine Park's theory in a generally positive fashion.

This attention to the Chicago traditions in race and ethnic studies may be much less than a revival, but it does suggest that the burial was at best premature. This chapter at least raises the possibility that in this area of scholarship and research earlier accounts of "outsiders" to Chicago sociology such as Fred Matthews and "insiders" such as Edward A. Shils, which portrayed the department as losing momentum after the late 1930s, appear to be overdrawn. And even if the interwar coherence was not maintained, it is possible that for some students the diversity of viewpoints and personnel, along with the more elusive emphasis upon personal and intellectual marginality, may have allowed for and encouraged creativity in scholarly models and in the use of the conceptual and theoretical heritage of the past. While three core faculty members, along with the important mentor and researcher Riesman, transmitted portions of the earlier heritage, it was probably Everett Hughes who was the most important. This was due to his personal qualities along with his ability to exemplify in his own research and collaboration with younger colleagues how concepts and methods might be adapted to new and old problems.

The postwar ethos is hard to recapture, but the autobiographical recollections of Gusfield and Gans, along with many of the letters sent to Gary Fine, suggest that the racial, ethnic, gender, and religious mix of students and the networks of friendship and collegiality established in the graduate program were important factors in the elaboration of Chicago sociology. The cohort also included several scholars whose careers and creative research are now being examined, including Anselm Strauss and Howard Becker (Maines, ed. 1991; Ben-Yehuda et al. 1989) Their elaboration of concepts and methods in the processual and interactionist tradition is similar to what happened in racial and ethnic research.

If the contributions in the area of race and ethnicity of many of these figures, especially Shibutani, have been largely ignored, forgotten, or resisted, it may be due in large part to a persistent if seldom discussed conflict between scholars who emphasize "structure" and "discrimination" and those who emphasize process and agency when studying race and ethnicity (Higham 1990; Matthews 1989; Wacker 1989). Among scholars of the first kind, Chicago processual perspectives have often been seen as undercutting structural explanations of racial subordination and ethnic persistence. In a rush to judgment, the aspects of the Thomas-Park heritage as transmitted through later generations have been distorted as "conservative" or "assimilationist" or "soft." Recent reevaluations of Chicago sociology and social psychology, especially with regard to racial, ethnic, and cultural identity and group and individual levels of analysis— and the complex interaction between each of these—suggest that major portions of this heritage will become part of the "usable past" for social scientists inside and outside the United States.

BIBLIOGRAPHY
Books and Articles

Allport, Gordon, ed. 1946. *Controlling Group Prejudice. Annals,* vol. 244. Philadelphia: American Academy of Political and Social Science.
Baldwin, John. 1990. "Advancing the Chicago School of Pragmatic Sociology: The Life and Work of Tamotsu Shibutani." *Sociological Inquiry* 60: 115–26.

158   R. Fred Wacker

Banton, Michael. 1983. *Racial and Ethnic Competition.* Cambridge: Cambridge University Press.
Ben-Yehuda, Nachman et al. 1989. "Howard S. Becker: A Portrait of an Intellectual's Sociological Imagination." *Sociological Inquiry* 59: 467–89.
Berger, Bennett M., ed. 1990. *Authors of Their Own Lives: Intellectual Autobiographies by Twenty American Sociologists.* Berkeley: University of California Press.
Blumer, Herbert. 1939. "The Nature of Racial Prejudice." *Social Process in Hawaii* 5: 11–21.
Blumer, Herbert. 1955. "Reflections on the Theory of Race Relations." In *Race Relations in World Perspective,* Andrew W. Lind, ed. Honolulu: University of Hawaii Press.
Blumer, Herbert. 1958a. "Race Prejudice as a Sense of Group Position." *Pacific Sociological Review* 1: 3–7.
Blumer, Herbert. 1958b. "Research on Racial Relations: The United States of America." *International Social Science Bulletin* 10: 403–47.
Blumer, Herbert and Troy Duster. 1980. "Theories of Race and Social Action." In *Sociological Theories: Race and Colonialism.* Paris: UNESCO.
Bulmer, Martin. 1981. "Charles S. Johnson, Robert E. Park and the Research Methods of the Chicago Commission on Race Relations, 1919–22: An Early Experiment in Applied Social Research." *Journal of the History of the Behavioral Sciences* 27: 312–31.
Bulmer, Martin. 1984. *The Chicago School of Sociology.* Chicago: University of Chicago Press.
Burk, James. 1989. "A Pragmatic Approach to Macrosocial Theory." *Sociological Inquiry* 59: 409–22.
Carey, James T. 1975. *Sociology and Public Affairs: The Chicago School.* Beverly Hills: Sage.
Deegan, Mary Jo, ed. 1991. *Women in Sociology.* Westport, Conn.: Greenwood.
Directory of Agencies in Race Relations: National, State and Local. 1945. Chicago: Julius Rosenwald Fund.
Drake, St. Clair and Horace R. Cayton. 1945. *Black Metropolis: A Study of Negro Life in a Northern City.* New York: Harcourt, Brace.
Faris, Robert E. L. 1970. *Chicago Sociology 1920–1932.* Chicago: University of Chicago Press.
Faught, Jim. 1980. "Presuppositions of the Chicago School in the Work of Everett C. Hughes." *The American Sociologist* 15: 72–82.
Fisher, Berenice M. and Anselm L. Strauss. 1980. "Interactionism." In *A History of Sociological Analysis,* Thomas Bottomore and Robert Nisbet, eds. New York: Basic Books.
Gans, Herbert. 1967. *The Levittowners: Ways of Life and Politics in a New Suburban Community.* New York: Pantheon.
Gans, Herbert J., et. al. 1979. *On the Making of Americans: Essays in Honor of David Riesman.* Philadelphia, University of Pennsylvania Press.
Gans, Herbert J. 1962/1982. *The Urban Villagers: Group and Class in the Life of Italian-Americans.* New York: The Free Press.

Gans, Herbert J. 1992. "Comment: Ethnic Invention and Acculturation, A Bumpy-Line Approach." *Journal of American Ethnic History* 12: 45–52.

Glazer, Nathan and Daniel P. Moynihan, eds. 1975. *Ethnicity: Theory and Experience.* Cambridge: Harvard University Press.

Gleason, Philip. 1992. *Speaking of Diversity: Language and Ethnicity in Twentieth-Century America.* Baltimore: Johns Hopkins Press.

Glick, Clarence. 1948. "Collective Behavior in Race Relations." *American Sociological Review* 13: 287–94.

Gordon, Milton, ed. 1981. *America As A Multicultural Society.* Annals, vol. 454. Philadelphia: American Academy of Political and Social Science.

Gusfield, Joseph. 1963/1986. *Symbolic Crusade: Status Politics and the American Temperance Movement.* Urbana: University of Illinois Press.

Gusfield, Joseph, ed. 1989. *Kenneth Burke: On Symbols and Society.* Chicago, University of Chicago Press.

Gusfield, Joseph R. and Jerzy Michalowicz. 1984. "Secular Symbolism: Studies of Ritual, Ceremony, and the Symbolic Order in Modern Life." *Annual Review of Sociology* 10: 417–35.

Halliday, Terence C. and Morris Janowitz. 1992. *Sociology and Its Publics: The Forms and Fates of Disciplinary Organization.* Chicago: University of Chicago Press.

Harvey, Lee. 1987. *Myths of the Chicago School of Sociology.* Aldershot, England: Avebury.

Higham, John. 1975. *Send These to Me: Jews and Other Immigrants.* New York: Atheneum.

Higham, John. 1990. "From Process to Structure: Formulations of American Immigration History." In Peter Kivisto and Dag Blanck, *American Immigrants and Their Generations.* Urbana: University of Illinois Press.

Hollinger, David. 1975. "Ethnic Diversity, Cosmopolitanism and the Emergence of the American Liberal Intelligentsia." *American Quarterly* 27: 133–51.

Hughes, Everett, C. 1971. *The Sociological Eye.* Chicago: Aldine-Atherton.

Hughes, Everett C. and Helen M. Hughes. 1952. *Where Peoples Meet: Racial and Ethnic Frontiers.* Glencoe: The Free Press.

Jackson, Walter. 1986. "Melville Herskovits and the Search for Afro-American Culture." In George W. Stocking, Jr., ed., *Malinowski, Rivers, Benedict and Others: Essays on Culture and Personality.* Madison: University of Wisconsin Press.

Janowitz, Morris. 1983. *The Reconstruction of Patriotism: Education for Civic Consciousness.* Chicago: University of Chicago Press.

Joas, Hans. 1993. *Pragmatism and Social Theory.* Chicago: University of Chicago Press.

Jones, Butler A. 1974. "The Tradition of Sociology Teaching in Black Colleges: The Unheralded Professionals." In James Blackwell and Morris Janowitz, eds. *Black Sociologists.* Chicago: University of Chicago Press.

Killian, Lewis. 1952. "The Effects of Southern White Workers on Race Relations in Northern Plants." *American Sociological Review* 17: 327–31.

Killian, Lewis. 1973. "Herbert Blumer's Contributions to Race Relations." In T.

Shibutani, ed., *Human Nature and Collective Behavior: Papers in Honor of Herbert Blumer*. New Brunswick: Transaction.

Killian, Lewis. 1985. "The Stigma of Race: Who Now Bears the Mark of Cain?" *Symbolic Interaction* 8: 1–14.

Killian, Lewis. 1985/1970. *White Southerners*. Amherst: University of Massachusetts Press.

Kivisto, Peter. 1990. "The Transplanted Then and Now: The Reorientation of Immigration Studies from the Chicago School to the New Social History." *Ethnic and Racial Studies* 13: 455–81.

Lal, Barbara. 1990. *The Romance of Culture in an Urban Civilization: Robert Park on Race and Ethnic Relations in Cities*. London: Routledge.

Lewin, Gertrud Weiss, ed. 1948. Kurt Lewin, *Resolving Social Conflicts*. New York: Harper and Row.

Lohman, Joseph and Dietrich Reitzes. 1952. "Note on Race Relations in Mass Society." *American Journal of Sociology* 58: 240–46.

Lohman, Joseph and Dietrich Reitzes. 1954. "Deliberately Organized Groups and Racial Behavior." *American Sociological Review* 19: 342–46.

Lopata, Helen Z. 1976. "Florian Znaniecki: Creative Evolution of a Sociologist." *Journal of the History of the Behavioral Sciences* 12: 203–15.

Lyman, Stanford M. 1972. *The Black American in Sociological Thought: A Failure of Perspective*. New York: Putnam.

Lyman, Stanford M. 1984. "Interactionism and Study of Race Relations at the Macro-Sociological Level: The Contribution of Herbert Blumer." *Symbolic Interactionism* 7: 107–20.

Lyman, Stanford M. and Arthur J. Vidich. 1988. *Social Order and The Public Philosophy: An Analysis and Interpretation of the Work of Herbert Blumer*. Fayetteville: University of Arkansas Press.

Lyman, Stanford M. 1990. "Robert E. Park Reconsidered: The Early Writings." *American Sociologist* 21: 342–51.

Maines, David R. 1989. "Repackaging Blumer: The Myth of Herbert Blumer's Astructural Bias." In *Studies in Symbolic Interactionism,* Norman K. Denzin, ed. Greenwich: JAI.

Maines, David R., ed. 1991. *Social Organization and Social Process: Essays in Honor of Anselm Strauss*. New York: Aldine De Gruyter.

Matthews, Fred. 1970. "The Revolt Against Americanism. Cultural Pluralism and Cultural Relativism as an Ideology of Liberation." *Canadian Review of American Studies* 1: 4–31.

Matthews, Fred. 1977. *Quest for an American Sociology: Robert Park and the Chicago School*. Toronto: McGill-Queen's University Press.

Matthews, Fred. 1987. "Louis Wirth and American Ethnic Studies." In Moses Rischin, ed., *The Jews of North America*. Detroit: Wayne State University Press.

Matthews, Fred. 1989. "Social Scientists and the Culture Concept, 1930–1950: The Conflict Between Processual and Structural Approaches." *Sociological Theory* 7: 87–101.

McKee, James B. 1993. *Sociology and the Race Problem, The Failure of Perspective.* Urbana: University of Illinois Press.

Meier, August. 1977. "Black Sociologists in White America." *Social Forces:* 259–70.

Merton, Robert and Matilda W. Riley, eds. 1980. *Sociological Traditions from Generation to Generation: Glimpses of the American Experience.* Norwood, N.J.: Ablex Publishing Corp.

Persons, Stow. 1987. *Ethnic Studies at Chicago, 1905–1945.* Urbana: University of Illinois Press.

Platt, Anthony. 1992. *E. Franklin Frazier Reconsidered.* New Brunswick: Rutgers University Press.

Rex, John and David Mason, eds. 1986. *Theories of Race and Ethnic Relations.* Cambridge: Cambridge University Press.

Reiss, Albert. 1964. *Louis Wirth on Cities and Social Life.* Chicago: University of Chicago Press.

Rose, Arnold, ed. 1961. *Human Behavior and Sociological Processes: An Interactionist Approach.* Boston: Houghton Mifflin.

Rose, Peter. 1983. *Mainstream and Margins: Jews, Blacks, and Other Americans.* New Brunswick: Transaction.

Rose, Peter. 1965. *The Subject is Race: Traditional Ideologies and the Teaching of Race Relations.* New York: Oxford University Press.

Salerno, Roger. 1987. *Louis Wirth: A Biobibliography.* Westport, Conn.: Greenwood Press.

Shibutani, Tamotsu. 1955. "Reference Groups as Perspectives." *American Journal of Sociology* 60: 562–69.

Shibutani, Tamotsu and Kian Kwan. 1964. *Ethnic Stratification.* New York: Macmillan.

Shibutani, Tamotsu, ed. 1973. *Human Nature and Collective Behavior: Papers in Honor of Herbert Blumer.* New Brunswick: Transaction.

Shils, Edward A. 1970. "Tradition, Ecology, and the Institution in the History of Sociology." *Daedalus* 99: 760–85.

Shils, Edward A. 1982. *The Constitution of Society.* Chicago: University of Chicago Press.

Shils, Edward A. 1948. *The Present State of American Sociology.* Glencoe: The Free Press.

Shils, Edward A. 1981. "Some Academics, Mainly in Chicago." *American Scholar* 50: 163–79.

Simpson, Christopher. 1994. *Science of Coercion, Communication Research and Psychological Warfare, 1945–1960.* New York: Oxford University Press.

Smith, Dennis. 1988. *The Chicago School: A Liberal Critique of Capitalism.* New York: St. Martin's Press.

Stanfield, John H., II, ed. 1993. *A History of Race Relations Research, First-Generation Recollections.* Newbury Park: Sage Publications.

Stanfield, John H., II. 1985. *Philanthropy and Jim Crow in American Social Science.* Westport, Conn.: Greenwood Press.

162   R. Fred Wacker

Strauss, Anselm. 1978. "A Social World Perspective." *Studies in Symbolic Inter-action* 1: 119–28.
Stocking, George W., Jr. 1968. *Race, Culture, and Evolution: Essays in the History of Anthropology.* New York: The Free Press.
Symbolic Interaction. 1988. "Special Issue on Herbert Blumer's Legacy." 11: 1–144.
Thompson, Edgar T. and Everett C. Hughes, eds. 1958. *Race: Individual and Collective Behavior.* New York. The Free Press.
Tiryakian, Edward. 1979. "The Significance of Schools in the Development of Sociology." In William E. Snizek et al., eds., *Contemporary Issues in Theory and Research: A Metasociological Perspective.* Westport, Conn.: Greenwood Press.
Turner, Ralph. 1954. "Occupational Patterns of Inequality." *American Journal of Sociology* 59: 437–47.
Turner, Ralph, ed. 1967. *Robert E. Park on Social Control and Collective Behavior.* Chicago: University of Chicago Press.
Turner, Ralph and Samuel J. Surace. 1956. "Zoot-suiters and Mexicans: Symbols in Crowd Behavior." *American Journal of Sociology* 62: 14–20.
Wacker, R. Fred. 1983. *Ethnicity, Pluralism and Race: Race Relations Theory in America before Myrdal.* Westport, Conn.: Greenwood Press.
Wacker, R. Fred. 1986. "The Chicago Research Program in Race and Ethnicity." In Richard C. Monk, ed., *Structures of Knowing.* Lantham, Md.: University Press of America.
Wacker, R. Fred. 1989. "Modern Ethnicity and Its Challenge to Social Theory." *Journal of American Ethnic History* 9: 120–26.
Wiggershaus, Rolf. 1994. *The Frankfurt School: Its History, Theories and Political Significance.* Cambridge, England: Polity Press.
Wiley, Norbert. 1979. "The Rise and Fall of Dominating Theories in American Sociology." In William E. Snizek et al., eds., *Contemporary Issues in Theory and Research: A Metasociological Perspective.* Westport, Conn.: Greenwood Press.
Wiley, Norbert. 1986. "Early American Sociology and the Polish Peasant." *Sociological Theory* 4: 20–40.
Wirth, Louis. 1946. "The Unfinished Business of American Democracy." In Gordon Allport, ed., *Controlling Group Prejudice. Annals,* vol. 244. Philadelphia: American Academy of Political and Social Science.

Letters

Carter, Wilmoth, to Gary Alan Fine, 1990.
Gusfield, Joseph, to Gary Alan Fine, 1990.
Killian, Lewis, to R. Fred Wacker, 1991.
King, Charles, to Gary Alan Fine, 1990.
Turner, Ralph, to R. Fred Wacker, 1991.

Interviews and Unpublished Materials

Herbert Blumer, interviews with R. Fred Wacker, 1970 and 1980.
Everett Hughes, interview with R. Fred Wacker, 1979.
Lewis Killian, autobiography
Bernard Meltzer, interview with R. Fred Wacker, 1991.
Tamotsu Shibutani, interview with R. Fred Wacker, 1988.
Henry Yu, "An America That Would Not Melt: The Oriental Problem in American Thought, 1920–1960." Ph. D. dissertation in process, Princeton University History Department.

CHAPTER FIVE

CHICAGO'S TWO WORLDS OF DEVIANCE

RESEARCH: WHOSE SIDE ARE THEY ON?

John F. Galliher

INTRODUCTION

During the years immediately following World War II the University of Chicago's sociology department continued to be one of the most eminent in the country. At most, only Harvard, Columbia, and Wisconsin matched the prestige of Chicago. This essay deals with the contributions of Chicago graduates from this period to the study of crime and other deviant behavior. The influence on the discipline of this one department clearly extended to this substantive area. The graduates of the department reflected an unexpected diversity and thereby largely set the agenda for research in what was at the time of their graduation becoming an ever-widening field of sociology. The diversity was unexpected because Chicago sociology of the time is usually associated with a relatively distinct tradition of fieldwork and qualitative, interactionist analysis. In fact, there have been at least two distinct methodological and theoretical orientations among these Chicago graduates. As will be argued below, these differences are largely, but not totally, contingent on the degree to which each researcher was suspicious of government authority.

FACULTY AND GRADUATE STUDENTS

Those making the most significant contributions to the literature on criminology and deviant behavior, together with their years of graduation, include: Albert Reiss, 1949; James Short, 1951; Howard Becker, 1951; William Westley, 1951; Erving Goffman, 1953; Lloyd Ohlin, 1954; Joseph Gusfield, 1954; Kai Erikson, 1963; Harold Finestone, 1964. This survey excludes five others: Daniel Glaser, who graduated in 1954, but whose primary contact with the department was approximately a decade prior to that of most in this cohort; Guy E. Swanson, who finished a dissertation on juvenile delinquency in 1948 but wrote thereafter primarily in other areas; Nathan Goldman, who also wrote little in the area after his 1950 dissertation on juvenile courts; and Andrew F. Henry, who received a Ph.D. in 1950 and coauthored a significant book—*Suicide and Homicide*

(1954)—with James Short, but whose career was cut short by an early death in 1957.

Howard Becker recalled in an interview that during this postwar period, while he was a graduate student at Chicago, there was a "tiny faculty of approximately ten, but with around 200 graduate students who were formed into a tight community" in spite of their large numbers. Robert Dentler (1987) recalled that graduate student housing provided by the university was filthy, crime-ridden, and surrounded by violence, but that the atmosphere was always intellectually stimulating. Becker noted that many graduate students were older W.W.II veterans and would not have been in school except for having the G.I. Bill, which distinguished them from most other students. Certainly many were from lower social-class backgrounds than would otherwise have been the case. The social-class backgrounds of many of these students may help explain the unusual direction of their work. Dentler has noted (1987) of himself and his fellow graduate students: "Together we were cynical and arrogant toward civil servants, foundation officers, and agency representatives. It was the kind of cynicism that masks an excess of idealism, I think, because we believed earnestly that our science would steadily create a higher quality of social policy and social practice. Our arrogance was technocratic, not totalitarian." This cynicism or suspicion of political power undoubtedly was a product of the times. In the image of the Third Reich these budding social scientists had ample evidence of political power used for tyranny, at home they could witness, close up, the oppression of the McCarthy era, and as veterans these students could have been expected to have developed a jaded view of authority.

Robert Habenstein was a graduate student at Chicago during this period, having arrived in time for the first quarter of 1946. He (1990) recalled that "at that time the department was in the process of expanding terrifically with respect to students. But slowly with respect to faculty." Habenstein also recalled (1990):

> The department did not have a big block of granite like Blumer to develop criminology. Burgess was interested in criminology and was bitten, or smitten, with the notion that sociology which is the most useful would be sociology that could provide prediction. In his eyes the end result was that if you could predict behavior you could control behavior. Hopefully you would be guided by the best of all possible morality so that when you controlled behavior you controlled it the right way.

But of course, as Habenstein's comments imply, there are no built-in guarantees. As will be demonstrated below, it is precisely such ethical and moral issues that have provided the focus of some lively debates and divisions in the contemporary study of crime and deviant behavior.

Unlike in many other universities, the Chicago department did not approach criminology as a separate subfield. And while among the faculty there was no organized interest group in criminology, there was a tradition of concern with social disorganization and personal disorganization, as found in the work on the Polish peasant by W. I. Thomas and Florian Znaniecki. According to Habenstein (1990):

> It was not that Chicago did not have any concern with criminal behavior, it was that criminal behavior was seen as another word for a social outcome, and if one wanted to understand criminal behavior one had to understand what went into the social mix in order to produce this outcome. And the best way to get at the elements of the social mix would be to put people into the actual areas where these problems were arising, whether they were murders or dumping garbage on the street.

Even without a star such as Blumer, criminology did have a genuine criminological presence, according to Habenstein, in the person of Joseph Lohman. Lohman seems to be an unlikely figure to have left his imprint on the department. He first came to Chicago as a graduate student to study with Blumer. For his dissertation research he made contact with a gang of killers who agreed to let him study them on condition of total secrecy. Habenstein's version has it that some member of Lohman's committee, however, leaked some of the details of Lohman's research and the gang members were apparently so angry that they even considered killing Lohman in reprisal. In exchange for his life he had to drop the study. In any case, for whatever reason Lohman never finished his dissertation. Without his dissertation completed and without publications he eventually became a permanent instructor at the University of Chicago. Yet even in this marginal role he had a profound impact on a number of graduate students, although he could not direct their dissertations. For example, it was through Lohman that William Westley became interested in studying the police. Later Lohman became sheriff of Cook County, and ultimately, when Blumer left for the University of California at Berkeley, Joseph Lohman also left to become the director of the new school of criminology there. Becker (1991) recalls:

Joe was quite influential for some of us, certainly for me. He was a model of someone who had done real fieldwork with criminals, and he was contemptuous of a lot of criminological research that was going on, on the grounds that it was innocent and naive about how things worked, especially about the role of corrupt local politics in crime.

As will be shown below, the "tight community" of graduate students described by Becker was nonetheless the spawning ground for some profound differences among those studying crime and deviant behavior. This lack of consensus may be explained by the fact that there was no "big block of granite" in criminology to lead the way for graduate students, Edwin Sutherland having departed a decade earlier during the 1930s (Gaylord and Galliher, 1988). I will show that among this small group of faculty an even smaller minority apparently had a direct influence on the research careers of these young scholars destined to study criminology and deviant behavior. Most of these writers were significantly influenced in their study of deviant or criminal behavior by Everett Hughes (especially Hughes's interest in occupations as seen from the perspective of those actors actually involved), and this determined the perspective from which his students have viewed the world of crime and conducted their research. But also they were all significantly influenced by Herbert Blumer. According to Becker (1988, 19):

> He gave students (and the field) a basic approach, an approach I eventually concluded (for myself) was (despite all the controversy in our field) the basic set of ideas that underlay (that *had* to underlay) almost any theoretical position a sociologist might take. . . . Students in the department at Chicago, in the 1950s thought of themselves as Hughes students *or* Blumer students, but not both. Most people learned, some sooner than others, that we were almost always both.

By contrast with Blumer, Hughes "was too scattered to give us a basic theoretical framework to work from" (Becker 1991). Along with the influence of Hughes and Blumer, another influence on the thinking of this cohort of graduate students was William Foote Whyte, the author of *Street Corner Society* with its "intimate observation of criminal activity and of its connection to corrupt political activity" (Becker 1991).

It was this combined influence that led this cohort of graduate students to the study of deviance of all types on the vibrant streets of the city of Chicago. The city itself did not preordain this orientation; New York

City offered equally exciting prospects for fieldwork to Columbia University sociologists, yet that department never took advantage of the opportunity. At Chicago, if fieldwork was emphasized, other types of information used by other deviance researchers, such as census data and survey research, were ignored. And with rare exceptions any analysis of the macro-structures of society was eschewed in favor of more intensive analysis of human interaction at the street level.[1]

CITATIONS AND PROFESSIONAL RECOGNITION

Clearly, this cohort has had a remarkable impact on the study of crime and deviant behavior. In a study (Galliher and McCartney 1973) of frequency of citations in juvenile delinquency research, 1940–69, Short was 1st, Ohlin was 6th, and Reiss was 9th. In all deviance literature (Cole 1975) 1960–64, Ohlin was 3rd, Short was 8th; in 1965–69 Short was 4th, Becker 9th, Goffman 11th, Reiss 13th, Erikson 21st; in 1970–73 Becker was 1st, Reiss 5th, Goffman 10th, Short 11th, Erikson 12th, Ohlin 15th. The impact of Becker and Goffman on the field of criminology and deviance is all the more remarkable since their work is primarily in other areas.

Among these scholars there are three former American Sociological Association (ASA) presidents (Goffman, 1981; Short, 1983; Erikson, 1984), four former presidents of the Society for the Study of Social Problems (SSSP) (Becker, 1966; Reiss, 1969; Erikson, 1970; Gusfield, 1988), and two presidents of the American Society of Criminology (Reiss, 1983; Ohlin, 1986). Becker has served as a *Social Problems* editor and Short as editor of the *American Sociological Review* (ASR). For their books and careers this group has received many awards. From the American Sociological Association, Erikson received the MacIver book award in 1967 and the Sorokin book award in 1977. Reiss was elected a Fellow of the American Academy of Arts and Sciences in 1983, and in 1981 received the Sutherland career award from the American Society of Criminology; Short received the Sutherland Award in 1979. Goffman received the MacIver Award in 1961 and was elected a Fellow of the American Academy of Arts and Sciences in 1969. Gusfield received the Cooley Award for his research from the Society for the Study of Symbolic Interaction (SSSI) in 1983 and the Mead career award from the SSSI in 1991. And Becker was given the Common Wealth career award in 1981, as well as the Mead career award in 1985 and the Cooley Award in 1987.

Prior to the 1960s there existed no field referred to as deviant behavior, as opposed to criminology. Yet studies of deviance were quickly accepted as a logical extension of the study of criminology, for the field is now often referred to as criminology and deviant behavior. I will demonstrate below how these nine scholars contributed to criminology and deviant behavior. I will also demonstrate that criminology is more likely to have an applied focus with direct policy implications than is the study of deviant behavior. Moreover, criminology typically relies on a different set of methodological and political assumptions than does the study of deviant behavior. I will also demonstrate that the two schools are typically mutually exclusive with practitioners contributing to one but not both. By its contributions to this deviant behavior tradition, which is different than that of mainline criminology, Chicago has had an impact on the study of crime, delinquency, and deviance that could not have been greater.

WHOSE SIDE ARE WE ON? TAKING SIDES *AGAINST* POLICY-MAKERS

While Becker was the president of the Society for the Study of Social Problems in 1966 he delivered his famous presidential address, "Whose Side are We On?" where he argued that since some type of bias is inevitable in all research on human subjects, to gain a full understanding of the world it is essential that we consciously take the perspective of the oppressed rather than the oppressor (1967). The primary reason for this choice, according to Becker, is that since the latter's views are typically given greater credibility we have more to learn from the powerless. In support of this position Becker has studied both oppressors and the oppressed, as in his discussion of powerful moral entrepreneurs who lobby for prohibitionist laws, for imposition on the less powerful. "[The crusader] operates with an absolute ethic; what he sees is truly and totally evil with no qualification. Any means is justified to do away with it. The crusader is fervent and righteous, often self-righteous" (Becker 1963, 148). Becker is quoted as follows (Bennett 1981, 229–30):

> by making moral entrepreneurs objects of study as well as those they seek to control, violate[s] society's hierarchy of credibility. They [deviance researchers] question the monopoly on the truth and the "whole story" claimed by those in positions of power and authority. They suggest that we need to discover the truth about allegedly deviant phenomena for ourselves, instead of relying on the officially certified accounts which ought to be enough for any good citizen. . . . They make it impossible to ignore the moral implications of our work.

Becker's labeling theory of deviant behavior is consistent with his admitted political bias. In *Outsiders* he reported on careers in deviant behavior which included the process of being publicly labeled as a deviant. He noted that the meaning and significance of an act are not inherent in the behavior itself but rather are a consequence of audience reactions. Moral entrepreneurs are a significant part of the process of defining behavior as *deviant* behavior.

> From this point of view, deviance is not a quality of the act the person commits, but rather a consequence of the application by others of rules and sanctions to an offender. The deviant is one to whom that label has successfully been applied; deviant behavior is behavior that people so label. (Becker 1963, 9)

Mental illness can be subjected to analysis from this labeling perspective, as can the behavior of Jesus and carnival freaks, prostitutes, strippers, and transvestites, to mention just a few. As Cole (1975, 207) has observed: "Researchers studying so-called crimes without victims may find the labeling perspective more useful." Becker's fieldwork reported in *Outsiders* includes studies of dance-band musicians and marihuana users.

The study of drug use and the sociology of law all show the influence of Alfred Lindesmith, a long-time student and critic of American narcotics prohibitions and himself a graduate of Chicago in the 1930s. Lindesmith's criticism of drug prohibitions, together with Becker's own experience working as a musician led Becker to a similar disrespect for laws and legal authority. Becker often recalled that many of the musicians with whom he worked had frequently used marihuana with none of the ill effects the government claimed as the basis for the drug's prohibition. Becker said: "I got my idea for studying marihuana users from Lindesmith's *Opiate Addiction* [1947], but I knew the method would have to be altered because marihuana is not addictive."

Habenstein (1990) recalls that when he was a graduate student at Chicago "deviance was not central to the language of people who dealt with crime. When I was there, and that's 1946 through most of 1950, I don't recall that deviance was the unity word of the day." Rather it was "disorganization." By the 1960s, however, things had changed. In 1963 Howard Becker had published *Outsiders,* which became the flagship of labeling theory and deviance studies. Moreover, this perspective was given a special push when Becker was editor of *Social Problems* during the early 1960s (Spector 1976). With these twin assists deviance soon became the

focus of books, college courses, and even sessions at the American Sociological Association.

THE SOCIOLOGY OF DEVIANT BEHAVIOR: FIELDWORK
AMONG THE POWERFUL AND NOT SO POWERFUL

Most of this cohort of Chicago graduate students wrote in the style
of Becker and Hughes. Along with Becker the most obvious impact on
the study of deviant behavior, as distinct from criminology, is from Erikson and Goffman, but also from Gusfield, Westley, and Finestone. Indeed,
it is the interactionist approach to data collection and theory that is often
seen as synonymous with the "Chicago school." What is probably responsible for making their contributions so innovative is that they were not
originally intended to be a part of criminology. At the suggestion of Everett Hughes, Becker, Goffman, and Finestone studied a variety of roles
including those of dance-band musicians, mental patients, and drug-users,
as careers much as Hughes would have studied any occupation. A critical
point in such studies was the analysis of the occupation from the point of
view of those in it. These scholars have also studied the oppression of the
poor, blacks, and the sick at the hands of religious and secular authorities.

A famous study of the permanent black male underclass by Harold
Finestone, "Cats, Kicks and Color" (1957, 4–5), describes the tastes and
preferences of black male drug-users including the value they place on
their "kicks" and "hustle."[2] Both are described as a cultural preference, as
are tastes for expensive clothing and the use of personal charm, together
with a "large, colorful, and discriminating vocabulary." All are described
from the drug-users' point of view as a "gracious work of art." The description of the lives of chronic drug-users diverges sharply from the contempt of law enforcement or the pity of political liberals. In Finestone's
analysis one finds no hint of either pity or contempt, but rather careful
description based on respect for what he found to be unique cultural practices. This study of drug-users shows respect for those lower in the stratification system, as does Becker's work on musicians and marihuana users.
Indeed, it could be argued that such respect is essential for the careful and
undistorted description of the cultural or subcultural practices in question. Thus, users of illegal drugs can be studied in the same fashion as
physicians or engineers.

Other evidence of oppression of African Americans comes from
William Westley, who was a Hughes student who wrote a dissertation on
police at the suggestion of Lohman, using interviews and direct observa-

tion, and published a book (1970) and articles (1953, 1956) from this research. Westley found great differences in police treatment of the wealthy and the poor due to the greater political power of the former. One police officer was quoted by Westley as saying that "in the better districts the purpose is to make friends out of people and get them to like you" (1970, 98). On the other hand, it seemed just as obvious to the police that they could only elicit respect and obedience from the slum dwellers by resorting to force. Police officers felt superior to the poor and expected them to recognize this superiority. Westley found police were afraid to brutalize the wealthy because of their political influence, but that it was both permissible and necessary to use force on those who were poor or black. One officer observed (Westley 1970, 103): "The high crime rate among the colored is due to the fact that they still have one foot in Africa. They go savage when they get mad and they want to kill. When they are mad you can't handle them." Another officer: "The colored. . . . Just as soon as they get a few drinks under their belt the savage comes out and they want to do bodily harm to the other party." Another reserved special scorn for black females: "The nigger women are all whores. When the old man goes on the night shift they try to pick up a few bucks to supplement the family income. They just love crime, they're natural criminals." Westley studied the police as an occupation, not as a part of criminology, which has had difficulty using the idea of social structure to understand police behavior. At the time of Westley's research criminologists relied largely on individualistic personality explanations of police behavior (Galliher 1971). Both Westley and Goffman offer severe criticism of caretaking institutions responsible for processing deviant actors.

Erving Goffman ended his American Sociological Association presidential address by noting: "If one must have a warrant addressed to social needs, let it be for unsponsored analyses of the social arrangements enjoyed by those with institutional authority—priests, psychiatrists, school teachers, police, generals, government leaders, parents, males, whites, nationals, media operators, and all the other well-placed persons who are in a position to give official imprint to versions of reality" (1983, 17). The power and influence of his ideas are such that although only a small portion of his work involved deviant behavior and social control it is still prominent in the field.

Goffman found systematic oppression in "total institutions" (1961), which can run the gamut from prisons and mental hospitals, on the one hand, to convents and ships at sea, on the other. Whatever their differ-ences, total institutions are places of work and residence where individuals are cut off from the wider society for a long period of time and lead a life of strictly controlled routine. When a resident first enters a total institu-tion, the staff begins a process of degradation and humiliation that serves to strip newcomers of their personal identity. The new arrival must submit to the staff or be engaged in a "will-breaking contest" of escalating pun-ishments until they do. If the individual complains about such harsh treat-ment the staff will use such complaints as grounds for further punish-ment—the "looping process." The reaction of the resident to the original situation is looped back into the situation itself. This process can be seen when complaints by mental patients about electroshock therapy often re-sult in hospital staff deciding the patient requires even more of this therapy because of the complaints.

In his analysis of these organizations of social control Goffman used sarcasm, satire, and irony to attack and discredit those in positions of power, along with cutting metaphors for the total institution as a "storage dump for inmates" and a "finishing school" (Fine and Martin 1990, 99). Goffman studied "careers" of mental patients, including how they became socialized by the staff of such institutions, concluding (1961, 379):

> I am suggesting that the patient's nature is redefined so that, in effect if not by intention, the patient becomes the kind of ob-ject upon which a psychiatric service can be performed. To be made a patient is to be remade into a serviceable object, the irony being that so little service is available once this is done.

This research had a major impact on the sociological study of prisons because it was a theoretical study in a largely atheoretical field. Goffman's later book, *Stigma* (1963), provides new theoretical tools for understand-ing soiled identities of all varieties, including merely "covering" one's devi-ance and "passing" as nondeviant. An example of the former is when a sightless person wears sunglasses to cover distorted eyes while still being easily recognized as visually impaired. A well-known example of the latter is a black passing as white.

If blacks and psychiatric patients have been oppressed, the same is also true of America's Irish and German immigrants. The only major con-tributor to the criminology-deviance literature from Chicago to study pri-marily with Herbert Blumer is Joseph Gusfield. Undoubtedly influenced

by Blumer's interests in collective behavior, Gusfield's dissertation focused
on the Woman's Christian Temperance Union (WCTU), and the national
prohibition of alcohol, as a social movement (1955, 1963, and 1967). Gusfield studied the rise and eventual decline of the WCTU. This movement
became relevant for criminology and deviance as a study of the making of
criminal law, a substance prohibition, by moral entrepreneurs much as
described by Becker. Gusfield developed the distinction between instrumental and symbolic law, which has become essential for investigations of
the origins of criminal laws. The prohibition legislation, even if not en-
forced, served to distinguish rural Protestant prohibitionists from alcohol-
drinking immigrants from Ireland and Germany.

> The significance of abstinence as a symbol of respectability
> was enhanced when large numbers of Irish and German immi-
> grants entered the United States and made up the unskilled
> labor forces of the growing urban centers during the 1840s and
> 1850s. In the culture of the Irish and Germans, use of whiskey
> and beer was customary and often a staple part of the diet.
> Both groups were at the bottom of the class and status struc-
> ture in American society. . . . If the lowly Irish and Germans
> were the drinkers and drunkards of the community, it was
> more necessary than ever that the aspirant to middle-class
> membership not risk the possibility that he might be classed
> with the immigrants. (Gusfield 1955, 50–51)

It is clear that Gusfield is on the side of the immigrants and tacitly opposed to the irrational and puritanical demands of the native-born rural
Protestants.

In Kai Erikson's study of the Puritans of the Massachusetts Bay colony the apparent irrationality of oppressors is replaced by an analysis of
the positive role oppression can play in the social organization and collective survival of a culture. Kai Erikson is the author of the widely cited
Wayward Puritans, based on his Ph.D. dissertation. In the book's preface
he (1966: xii) acknowledges the help of his father, Erik Erikson: "It happens that I have had the rare good fortune throughout the writing of this
book to review its contents with Erik H. Erikson: the finished work has
profited greatly from the counsel he gave and the discussions we shared."
The elder Erikson (1958) was a Pulitzer Prize–winning psychoanalyst at
Harvard University who is most well known for the notion that a cultural
upheaval can be associated with an identity crisis in powerful and zealous

reformers, as in the case of Martin Luther and the Protestant Reformation. Perhaps not by coincidence, Kai Erikson argues that witches were found and punished in the Massachusetts Bay colony due to a *collective* crisis of identity as the colony and its environment continued to change. Punishment of the witches gave renewed meaning to the group by establishing its moral boundaries. Thus seemingly irrational and arbitrary behavior takes on new meaning in the junior Erikson's hands. Prior to writing a dissertation, Kai Erikson coauthored with fellow graduate student Robert Dentler the well-known *Social Problems* article "The Functions of Deviance in Groups" (1959). Dentler recalls that the senior Erikson demonstrated a "fury over his son's presumption in theorizing about pathologies as a by-product of interpersonal relations" (Dentler 1987, 165).

With *Wayward Puritans* Kai Erikson distances himself from Becker. He is distinct from the other Chicago sociologists discussed above in the theoretical level of his analysis as well as the political implications of his conclusions. *Wayward Puritans* emphasizes macrostructural changes based on an emerging collective consensus as the basis for crime and punishment—diametrically opposed to labeling theory and analysis of moral crusades that emphasized the irrational and destructive use of political power. Soon Kai Erikson published a *Social Problems* article (1967) criticizing the use of disguised participant observation, directly challenging Becker's inclusion of covert observation as one of several legitimate sociological methods. Included in Erikson's litany of reasons for proscribing such techniques is that they will give the profession a bad reputation, serving to "close off promising areas of research for future investigators" (1967, 369). Perhaps deception is most acceptable in dealing with abuses of power such as that described by Becker in the case of H. J. Anslinger, the long-time director of the Federal Bureau of Narcotics, who Becker says manipulated the nation to insure the passage of federal prohibition of marihuana in 1937. Correspondingly, in his SSSP presidential address Erikson challenged Becker's notion of explicitly taking a moral and political position, concluding (Erikson 1972, 436): "When self-evaluation threatens to become a *morality* rather than a *method,* an invitation to scoff rather than a source of intellectual discipline, we run the risk of dissipating whatever advantages a scholarly community can furnish its members."

Whatever their differences, Matza (1969, 37) has referred to such students of deviance as:

neoChicagoans because they have revived the Chicago school's
stress on direct observation and field work, have maintained
and extended the relevance of the subject's view, and in a variety of ways have indicated their appreciation of deviant phenomena and their connected enterprises. A theme that has
more or less unified the neoChicagoans has been their emphasis on the *process of becoming deviant* and the part played by
the official registrars of deviation in that process.

WHOSE SIDE ARE WE ON? THE CONCERNED CITIZEN-SCHOLAR ADVISING POLICY-MAKERS

Lloyd Ohlin, very different from Becker, was interested in correctional policy. Prior to receiving his Ph.D. degree he worked as a sociolo-
gist-actuary for the Illinois Parole and Pardon Board at the Joliet peniten-
tiary from 1947 to 1950, and then from 1950 to 1953 worked as a research
sociologist for the Chicago parole office (Laub 1983). Ohlin has been
quoted as saying: "The prison experience had a profound effect on me and
I have drawn on it ever since. I think that is one reason I have always
stayed close to practice" (Laub 1983, 207). While employed by the Illinois
Division of Corrections in 1951, Ohlin published *Selection for Parole: A
Manual of Parole Prediction.* In 1952 he published an article, "A Comparison of Alternative Methods of Parole Prediction." Later, in 1956, he published *Sociology and the Field of Corrections.* Regarding parole prediction
studies, he recalled that "it seemed to me at the time that the methodology
of the statistical analysis had already outrun the data" (Laub 1983, 208).
Future generations of sociologists would largely ignore this warning. In
Theoretical Studies in Social Organization of the Prison (1960), Ohlin's
chapter "Conflicting Interests in Correctional Objectives" discusses various correctional interest groups, such as custodial, therapeutic, administrative, and educational interests. In 1956 Ohlin moved to Columbia University's Department of Social Work. During his first semester there,
"Ohlin visited classes and read extensively in the literature of social work
to prepare for his teaching responsibilities" (Moritz 1963, 306–7). In 1967
he moved to Harvard Law School, where he retired in 1982. All of his
positions have been outside sociology departments and in some way have
dealt with applied social science. In 1986 he served as president of the
American Society of Criminology.

Ohlin's famous monograph *Delinquency and Opportunity* (1960),
with Richard Cloward, became the officially approved theoretical policy

model for the 1960s War on Poverty. It was politically attractive because the theory claimed that delinquents have the same success goals as other Americans. This was an attempt to use sociological theory in the formation of more intelligent and humane social policy. Moynihan describes Cloward and Ohlin's argument:

> Delinquency, they argued, arises when socially approved goals—owning a car, dressing well—are made impossible to achieve through legitimate methods, because of motor vehicle licensing requirements, lack of part-time jobs for juveniles, and so on. The delinquent is a normal youth with normal expectations that society does not permit him to achieve through normal channels. Whereupon he turns to alternate channels, which typically are illegal. Lacking opportunity to earn money to buy clothes, he steals it (Moynihan 1969, 50).

Moynihan explains that the policy failed because it was "a plan devised by a group of middle-class intellectuals to bring about changes in the behavior of a group of lower class youth who differed from them in ethnicity and religion, in social class and attitudes, in life styles, and above all, in life prospects" (Moynihan 1969, 51).

Whatever the merits of the theory, it clearly had an immense impact on the total federal welfare expenditures during the 1960s. But surely it is unfair to lay all the blame for the program's failures on the theory, however significant it was in formulating social policy. While Richard Cloward was radicalized by the experience of the 1960s, Ohlin was not. "I have always been more optimistic than Cloward about the possibilities for affecting change within the system through the political process and technical developments" (Laub 1983, 215). "The whole emphasis on evaluation and on creating models for system-oriented research represents new technical and theoretical competence that ensures the future of the field. I don't think funds will dry up. The field is established" (Laub 1983, 223). This fiscal optimism undoubtedly colored his view of radical criminology. "Radical criminology has rediscovered power, class structure, and relationships. But I don't feel it has yet added much to our understanding" (Laub 1983, 221–22). In *Prisoners in America* (1973), Ohlin's introduction to the collection deals with policy issues facing American corrections systems. In *Juvenile Correctional Reform in Massachusetts: A Preliminary Report of the Center for Criminal Justice of Harvard Law School* (Ohlin et al. 1977), he evaluates Massachusett's policy of deinstitutionalization of juvenile delinquents. In *Understanding and Controlling Crime: Toward a New Research Strategy* (1986) the policy implications for law enforcement of existing research are reviewed. From the beginning of his career, Ohlin sought to have sociology accepted as a legitimate source upon which to base social policy.

This same attempt to address correctional policy-makers is found in the work of Burgess. Since 1928 Burgess had been interested in parole prediction, and he obviously influenced Ohlin, as well as Reiss and Short. Ohlin's 1954 dissertation, "The Stability and Validity of Parole Prediction Tables" predictably shows the influence of Burgess, who served as Ohlin's Ph.D. advisor. The 1949 dissertation of Albert Reiss, "The Accuracy, Efficiency, and Validity of a Prediction Instrument," also shows the influence of Burgess. Short completed his dissertation in 1951 and claims that Burgess and Ogburn were his mentors (Short 1969).

ALBERT REISS: A FOOT IN BOTH WORLDS

Albert Reiss reflects both the concerns of traditional criminology and the perspectives of the students of deviant behavior, and thus demonstrates an unusual breadth in scope and methodology. His SSSP presidential address, "Putting Sociology into Policy" (1970), discusses the need for sociology to aid in informing government policy-makers. Seemingly distant from such practical policy concerns, however, he also published a *Social Problems* article in 1961 in which he found that teenage males do not consider themselves to be homosexual even if they engage in homosexual acts, provided it is done for financial gain. This is much the same genre as the Finestone study, and Reiss uses qualitative data and acknowledges the help of Hughes. Later Reiss studied police behavior and used covert direct observation somewhat like Westley before him, and came to conclusions much like Westley's (1968, 1971). Merely to conduct such a study shows a certain disrespect for authority, or at least questions the integrity of the representatives of government authority, as do Westley, Becker, and Goffman. Even so, Reiss earlier (1951) published a study entitled "The Accuracy, Efficiency and Validity of a Prediction Instrument" and also "Social Correlates of Psychological Types of Delinquency" (1952) and "Delinquency as the Failure of Personal and Social Controls" (1951). Reiss bridges the gap between Becker, Goffman, and Finestone on the one hand, and Lloyd Ohlin on the other. This stretch by Reiss within the study of criminology and deviant behavior is remarkable in and of itself, but Reiss is also well known for his research in community, urban sociology, and occupational mobility. The writing of few scholars has covered such a range of substantive and methodological issues. As of 1989 Reiss had published 16 books and 125 journal articles and book chapters.

ODD MAN OUT: JAMES SHORT AND THE SEARCH FOR A VALUE-FREE SOCIOLOGY

Unlike the other University of Chicago graduates of this postwar period, James Short has not explicitly aligned himself with the oppressed in most of his work, nor has he attempted to provide direct advice to government policy-makers. Thus, in this sense Short is aligned with neither of the two worlds of Chicago's study of crime and deviant behavior. Instead he has sided with the interests of academic social scientists. While Short's position is undoubtedly a common one among contemporary sociologists, among this cohort of Chicago-trained sociologists it is the exception rather than the rule. Short is well known as the leading expert on the measurement and testing of deviance theory. The publications of this former ASA president and ASR editor include a 1957 article on "Scaling Delinquent Behavior" (on the basis of seriousness); a 1958 article on the "Extent of Unrecorded Juvenile Delinquency"; a 1963 piece, "Values and Gang Delinquency: A Study of Street Corner Groups," testing various sociological theories of delinquency with the semantic differential; and a 1965 article, "Perceived Opportunities, Gang Membership and Delinquency," which is a statistical analysis of Cloward and Ohlin's theory. Two articles attempt an empirical test of Edwin Sutherland's famous Differential Association Theory of Criminal Behavior: "Differential Association as a Hypothesis: Problems of Empirical Testing" (1960) and "Differential Association and Delinquency" (1957). A methodological study, "Reported Behavior as a Criterion of Deviant Behavior," was published in 1957.

In an autobiographical sketch Short has written "While measurement problems have long fascinated me, I have been guided in my work primarily by the hope that I might contribute to the testing and refinement of statements of theoretical significance" (1969, 126). In a later personal profile Short wrote (1988: 6): "Study of delinquent and criminal behavior by means of self-reports is now highly developed and widely accepted. I am happy to have been among the 'pioneers' in developing the method, and happier still to acknowledge that others have carried it to a state of technical excellence and acceptance that I never envisioned." Robert Meier (1988, 231–39) concludes that Short's research firmly established the use of self-reports in measuring delinquency and in the process demonstrated the consistent biases of official statistics. Short's 1989 vita shows 17 books and 95 articles and book chapters that are at the heart of modern sociology, concerned as it has been with problems of scientific measurement. If Becker, Goffman, Finestone, Westley, Gusfield, and Reiss can be seen as consciously adopting the perspective of the underdog, and if Ohlin used sociology in an effort to humanize social policy, Short is very much a person of the discipline. He explained (1991):

> My personal sympathies are nearly always with "underdogs," though I have tried to hew to the scientific approach, rather than urging advocacy. . . . Ogburn was my chief influence in this regard. . . . I suppose that is what makes me a person of the discipline, despite some misgivings and doubts that what we do either does or can make a difference.

CONCLUSION

The perspectives and methods used by these University of Chicago products were very diverse. They run the gamut from the fieldwork and analytic induction in Becker's study of marihuana users to the statistical analysis where Short did not so much attempt to develop new theory as to test existing theory. Becker, Finestone, and Goffman take the perspective of deviants themselves, as does Reiss in his study of adolescent homosexual prostitution. Ohlin, on the other hand, attempted to communicate with policy-makers. In the preceding paragraphs are found studies of deviants, such as drug-users and mental patients, as well as those who successfully lobbied for new legal prohibitions and the major institutions that process deviants, such as mental hospitals and the police. As noted earlier, what gave such work the potential to be so innovative for criminology was that it was influenced and informed by the study of occupations and social movements, rather than criminology per se. Hughes and Blumer seem ultimately responsible for the most dramatic impact on the study of deviant behavior. Their students were not only sensitized to social structure but were skeptical of authority and of a sociology serving this authority. This is not surprising since Hughes was unusually sensitive to the hidden political agenda inherent in all social science research. He referred to this hidden meaning of research (1971) as the major premise of any investigation.

Recall that Becker explicitly enjoins the social scientist to take what is sometimes aptly referred to as the perspective of the underdog. Some of Becker's attitudes concerning such issues are reflected in the following quotation: "Unfortunately, the study of deviance lost its connection with the mainstream of sociological theory and research. It became a practical pursuit, devoted to helping society deal with those it found troublesome. Students of deviance devoted themselves to answering the questions posed by laymen and their elected and appointed officials, [such as] predicting who would violate parole . . . [with possible reference to the influence of Burgess and the dissertations of Ohlin and Reiss]" (Becker 1964, 1). The underdog perspective is clearly the view of Finestone, who showed such respect for law-violating drug addicts. Goffman also demonstrates this perspective in attempting to understand both social stigma and confinement from the point of view of those oppressed in these ways. One also learns a considerable amount about the oppression of the powerless from the work of Westley on police hatred and violence directed against poor and black citizens. The same is true of Gusfield's view of the underlying motivations of the WCTU. He found there was much more to this social movement than Christian charity. The main purpose of the law was that it served to proclaim the superiority of the Protestant way of life and thus distinguished the Protestants as morally superior to the newly arrived Roman Catholic Irish and German whiskey-drinking immigrants.

All of these underdog studies violated society's "hierarchy of credibility" (Becker 1967, 242). Clearly a value-free orientation would not suffice. Following Hughes's lead in going out into the field and understanding an occupation from the worker's point of view required that the researcher take the deviants' perspective. According to such reasoning the researcher always adopts some perspective, and therefore it is best to do so consciously. In this sense the work of these Chicago sociologists, by their "appreciation" of deviant behavior, distanced itself from mainstream scientific criminology which avoided any explicit ethical stance (Matza 1969). Mainstream criminology simply assumed that crime and criminals were pathological and that it was the business of criminology to learn how the costs of crime could be minimized and how criminals could be corrected or controlled.

Yet as Matza has noted, the differences between this distinctly Chicago style of the sociological study of deviance and other approaches "can be easily exaggerated" (1969, 18). The blurred distinctions are in turn to a great extent a consequence of the diversity of the Chicago contributions to the study of crime and deviance. While the quantitative work of Ohlin and Short is less concerned with legal authority illegitimately exercised, the research of Reiss is generally quantitative but with a clear suspicion of police abuse of power (see especially Reiss 1968). On the other hand,

among those sociologists more oriented to the study of deviance through
the use of fieldwork and qualitative methods, only Erikson's work directly
implies a legal authority based on community consensus, while the
works of Becker, Goffman, Westley, and Gusfield examine power illegitimately exercised. These patterns show that the type of data selected
does not completely restrict the type of theory utilized but apparently does
exercise considerable influence. Notice also that Becker, Gusfield, and Erikson each deal with the development and consequences of moral crusades. Becker and Gusfield emphasize moral entrepreneurs whose interests
are often imposed on those who are less powerful. Erikson, on the other
hand, looks to a simple society where there appears to be less conflict in
values and where the weight of public opinion can be given greater credibility, based, as it may be, on an emerging collective consensus required in
building community solidarity.

Although the distinctly "Chicago" sociology is typically associated
only with those using qualitative data, the other quantitatively oriented
graduates have had a considerable impact on the study of crime and delinquency. In any case it is clear that the Chicago sociology department encouraged variety in its graduates, unlike many contemporary graduate sociology programs. In the Chicago department there was no need for
doctrinaire acceptance of departmental dogma. Because the Chicago sociology department did not insist on a local orthodoxy there was a great
hiatus between the interests and pursuits of these two groups of students.

Chicago-trained students of criminology and deviant behavior were
at the center of the developing literature until the emergence in the 1970s
of an American radical criminology, whose main proponents were trained
elsewhere. Even so, Becker's original research provided the conceptual
tools that made a radical criminology possible, questioning the methodological, theoretical, and substantive perspectives of social science research. Labeling theory set the stage for the development of a sociology of
the origins of criminal law and ultimately an indigenous American radical
criminology, due to the emphasis of the theory on powerful moral entrepreneurs who can determine the course of cultural and legal definitions.
As Schumann (1976, 288) has noted, a central question for a critical or
radical criminology is "Why are some conflicts regulated by criminal law
while many others are not?" While Becker's work provided the basis upon
which a radical criminology could be built, in itself it is not a radical critique of American society. As Gouldner (1968) notes, labeling theory represents a critique only of middle-level officials such as police executives

and psychiatric hospital administrators (or middle-class moral interests such as the WCTU), and leaves oppressive social institutions, supporting racism, sexism and capitalism, to go unchallenged. Perhaps it is too much to expect that a truly radical criminology would be produced in such a department. It was programs that insisted on a technocratic orthodoxy, as at Indiana University and the University of Wisconsin, that produced radical academics such as William Chambliss and Richard Quinney.

It is well to remember that both Robert Park and Louis Wirth were interested in ethnography. Short (1990) concludes: "It does seem to me that the Second Chicago School was not much interested in grand theory." Gusfield agrees (1982) that the Chicago department was empirical and atheoretical:

> We used to say that a thesis about drinking written by a Harvard student might well be entitled "Modes of Cultural Release in Western Social Systems"; by a Columbia student it would be entitled, "Latent Functions of Alcohol Use in a National Sample"; and by a Chicago graduate student as, "Social Interaction at Jimmy's: A 55th St. Bar." It was a methodology that held the student firmly to what he/she could see, hear, and experience at first-hand. . . . Abstractions and concepts ungrounded by the experience with concrete observations were suspect. . . . I remember first hearing Talcott Parsons present his theoretical perspective at a lecture in Mandel Hall [on campus] at which he was introduced by Louis Wirth who then sat in the front row and proceeded to read his mail during Professor Parsons' presentation!

This episode shows the low priority of theory at Chicago.

Clearly, there are no grand theorists among these scholars. All rely on theoretical generalizations very close to empirical observations, very much a part of the Chicago fieldwork tradition. Moreover, this cohort includes neither a conservative apologist for American racism and poverty, nor a radical critic of the entire system. And there are no biological positivists among these writers, even though this is a continuing temptation for American students of criminal behavior. These scholars have avoided the extremes of both the right and the left. In the final analysis the true impact of this University of Chicago cohort is that it had a significant impact upon government policy, on criminology from the 1950s through the 1980s, and on the development of new ways to study deviant behavior in its various forms.

NOTES

Thanks are due Howard Becker, James Short, Kai Erikson, Joseph Gusfield, and Robert Habenstein for help with various phases of this research. The participants in the "Second Chicago School" symposium offered many helpful suggestions. They remain unnamed, but not unthanked.

1. Working in the University of Chicago's Institute for Juvenile Research, Clifford Shaw and Henry McKay published a series of books and articles from the 1920s to the 1940s. Their work emphasized the relationship of crime and delinquency to the social situation in which they occur as well as the actors' definition of their own behavior (Gaylord and Galliher 1988). By the 1940s they had become institutions in the sociological study of crime and thus were undoubtedly a presence in Chicago's sociology department in legitimating the study of crime, delinquency, and other deviant behavior.

2. During an interview, Becker recalled that "Finestone was a Canadian, like Goffman, who came to Chicago because of Hughes, who was a major figure in Canada."

REFERENCES

Becker, Howard S. 1963. *Outsiders: Studies in the Sociology of Deviance.* New York: The Free Press.
———, ed. 1964. Introduction, pp. 1–6, *The Other Side: Perspectives on Deviance.* New York: The Free Press.
———. 1967. "Whose Side Are We On?" *Social Problems* 14: 239–47.
———. 1988. "Herbert Blumer's Conceptual Impact," *Symbolic Interaction* 11: 13–21.
———. 1991. Letter in possession of the author, April 20.
Bennett, James. 1981. *Oral History and Delinquency: The Rhetoric of Criminology.* Chicago: University of Chicago Press.
Cloward, Richard A. and Lloyd E. Ohlin. 1960. *Delinquency and Opportunity: A Theory of Delinquent Gangs.* Glencoe: The Free Press.
Cole, Stephen. 1975. "The Growth of Scientific Knowledge: Theories of Deviance as a Case Study," pp. 175–220 in Lewis A. Coser, ed., *The Idea of Social Structure: Papers in Honor of Robert K. Merton.* New York: Harcourt Brace Jovanovich.
Dentler, Robert A. 1987. Secrets of a Sociologist. Manuscript, draft copy.
Dentler, Robert A. and Kai T. Erikson. 1959. "The Functions of Deviance in Groups." *Social Problems* 7: 98–107.
Erikson, Erik H. 1958. *Young Man Luther: A Study in Psychoanalysis and History.* New York: W. W. Norton.
Erikson, Kai T. 1966. *Wayward Puritans: A Study in the Sociology of Deviance.* New York: John Wiley.
———. 1967. "A Comment on Disguised Observation in Sociology." *Social Problems* 14: 366–73.
———. 1972. "Sociology: That Awkward Age," *Social Problems* 19: 431–36.

Fine, Gary Alan and Daniel D. Martin. 1990. "A Partisan View: Sarcasm, Satire, and Irony as Voices in Erving Goffman's Asylums." *Journal of Contemporary Ethnography* 19 (April): 89–115.

Finestone, Harold. 1957. "Cats, Kicks, and Color." *Social Problems* 5: 3–13.

Galliher, John F. 1971. "Explanations of Police Behavior: A Critical Review and Analysis." *Sociological Quarterly* 12: 308–18.

Galliher, John F. and James L. McCartney. 1973. "The Influence of Funding Agencies on Juvenile Delinquency Research." *Social Problems* 21: 77–90.

Gaylord, Mark S. and John F. Galliher. 1988. *The Criminology of Edwin Sutherland.* New Brunswick: Transaction Books.

Goffman, Erving. 1961. *Asylums: Essays on the Social Situation of Mental Patients and other Inmates.* Garden City: Doubleday.

———. 1963. *Stigma: Notes on the Management of Spoiled Identity.* Englewood Cliffs: Prentice-Hall.

———. 1983. "The Interaction Order." *American Sociological Review* 48: 1–17.

Gouldner, Alvin W. 1968. "The Sociologist as Partisan: Sociology and the Welfare State." *American Sociologist* 3: 103–16.

Gusfield, Joseph R. 1955. "Social Structure and Moral Reform: A Study of the Woman's Christian Temperance Union." *American Journal of Sociology* 61: 221–32.

———. 1963. *Symbolic Crusade: Status Politics and the American Temperance Movement.* Urbana: University of Illinois Press.

———. 1967. "Moral Passage: The Symbolic Process in Public Designations of Deviance." *Social Problems* 15: 175–88.

———. 1982. "The Scholarly Tension: Graduate Craft and Undergraduate Imagination." Presented at the 40th Anniversary of Social Sciences II, University of Chicago, November.

Habenstein, Robert W. 1990. Tape recording.

Henry, Andrew F. and James F. Short, Jr. 1954. *Suicide and Homicide; Some Economic, Sociological and Psychological Aspects of Aggression.* Glencoe: The Free Press.

Hughes, Everett C. 1971. "Principle and Rationalization in Race Relations," pp. 212–19 in *The Sociological Eye: Selected Papers.* Chicago: Aldine-Atherton.

Laub, John H. 1983. *Criminology in the Making.* Boston: Northeastern University Press.

Lindesmith, Alfred R. 1947. *Opiate Addiction.* Bloomington, Ind.: Principia Press.

Matza, David. 1969. Becoming Deviant. Englewood Cliffs: Prentice-Hall.

Meier, Robert F. 1988. "Special Essay: Discovering Delinquency." *Sociological Inquiry* 58: 231–39.

Moritz, Charles, ed. 1963. *Current Biography,* pp. 306–8. New York: H. W. Wilson.

Moynihan, Daniel P. 1969. *Maximum Feasible Misunderstanding: Community Action in the War on Poverty.* New York: The Free Press.

Ohlin, Lloyd E. 1951. *Selection for Parole: A Manual of Parole Prediction.* New York: Russell Sage Foundation.

———. 1952. "A Comparison of Alternative Methods of Parole Prediction." *American Sociological Review* 17: 268–74 (with Richard A. Lawrence).

————. 1956. *Sociology and the Field of Corrections.* New York: Russell Sage Foundation.

————. 1960. "Conflicting Interests in Correctional Objectives," pp. 111–29 in Cloward, Richard A., Donald R. Cressey, George H. Grosser, Richard McCleery, Lloyd E. Ohlin, Gresham M. Sykes, and Sheldon L. Messinger, eds., *Theoretical Studies in Social Organization of the Prison.* New York: Social Science Research Council.

————, ed. 1973. *Prisoners in America.* Englewood Cliffs: Prentice-Hall.

————. 1977. *Juvenile Correctional Reform in Massachusetts: A Preliminary Report of the Center for Criminal Justice of Harvard Law School.* Washington, D.C.: National Institute for Juvenile Justice and Delinquency Prevention, Law Enforcement Assistance Administration, United States Department of Justice (with Alden D. Miller and Robert B. Coates).

————. 1986. *Understanding and Controlling Crime: Toward A New Research Strategy.* New York: Springer-Verlag (with David P. Farrington, Lloyd E. Ohlin, and James Q. Wilson).

Reiss, Albert J., Jr. 1951. "Delinquency as the Failure of Personal and Social Controls." *American Sociological Review* 16: 196–207.

————. 1951. "The Accuracy, Efficiency and Validity of a Prediction Instrument." *American Journal of Sociology* 56: 552–61.

————. 1952. "Social Correlates of Psychological Types of Delinquency." *American Sociological Review* 17: 710–18.

————. 1961. "The Social Integration of Queers and Peers." *Social Problems* 9: 102–20.

————. 1968. "Police Brutality—Answers to Key Questions." *Trans-action* 5: 10–19.

————. 1970. "Putting Sociology into Policy." *Social Problems* 17: 289–94.

————. 1971. The Police and the Public. New Haven: Yale University Press.

Schumann, Karl F. 1976. "Theoretical Presuppositions for Criminology as a Critical Enterprise." *International Journal of Criminology and Penology* 4: 285–94.

Short, James F., Jr. 1957. "Differential Association and Delinquency." *Social Problems* 4: 233–39.

————. 1957. "Scaling Delinquent Behavior." *American Sociological Review* 22: 326–31 (with F. Ivan Nye and James F. Short).

————. 1957–58. "Reported Behavior as a Criterion of Deviant Behavior." *Social Problems* 5: 207–13 (with F. Ivan Nye).

————. 1958. "Extent of Unrecorded Juvenile Delinquency: Tentative Conclusions." *Journal of Criminal Law, Criminology and Police Science* 49: 296–302 (with F. Ivan Nye).

————. 1960. "Differential Association as a Hypothesis: Problems of Empirical Testing." *Social Problems* 8: 14–25.

————. 1963. "Values and Gang Delinquency: A Study of Street Corner Groups." *American Journal of Sociology* 69: 109–28 (with Robert A. Gordon, James Short, Desmond S. Cartwright and Fred L. Strodtbeck).

————. 1965. "Perceived Opportunities, Gang Membership and Delinquency."

American Sociological Review 30: 56–67 (with Ramon Riveria, Ray A. Tennyson).

———. 1969. "A Natural History of One Sociological Career," pp. 117–32 in *Sociological Self-Images: A Collective Portrait.* Irving Louis Horowitz, ed. Beverly Hills: Sage Publications.

———. 1988. "Aleatory Elements in a Criminologist's Career." *The Criminologist* 13: 1, 3, 6, and 7.

———. 1990. Letter to Gary Alan Fine, May 31.

———. 1991. Letter in possession of the author, April 24.

Spector, Malcolm. 1976. "Labeling Theory in Social Problems: A Young Journal Launches a New Theory." *Social Problems* 24: 69–75.

Westley, William A. 1953. "Violence and the Police." *American Journal of Sociology* 59: 34–41.

———. 1956. "Secrecy and the Police." *Social Forces* 34: 254–57.

———. 1970. *Violence and the Police: A Sociological Study of Law, Custom, and Morality.* Cambridge: The MIT Press.

CHAPTER SIX

THE CHICAGO APPROACH TO

COLLECTIVE BEHAVIOR

David A. Snow and Phillip W. Davis

Collective behavior is one of the oldest areas of inquiry within sociology (Lang and Lang 1961, 545; Strauss 1947, 352), with its American roots easily traced to a University of Chicago seedbed. Among earlier Chicago scholars, concerns about the topic were intertwined with conceptualizations of the very discipline itself, as seen in Robert Park and Ernest Burgess's (1921) definition of sociology as the "science of collective behavior." In a more restrictive sense, they viewed collective behavior as a subarea limited to "the processes by which societies are disintegrated into their constituent elements and the processes by which these elements are brought together again into new relations to form new organizations and new societies" (Park and Burgess 1921, 924–25).

Collective behavior was always part of the Chicago tradition, but interest in the area reached a low point by the end of World War II, with relatively few sociologists' names associated with it (Strauss 1947; Turner 1988).[1] The graduate cohort starting their careers at the time, however, took up the topic with amazing intensity. Our thesis is that a dozen or so of them, matriculating in the decade following W.W. II, formulated an approach to collective behavior and social movements that can be read as distinctive and seminal within that substantive area of inquiry. We refer specifically to the work of Joseph Gusfield, Morris Janowitz, Lewis Killian, Orrin Klapp, William Kornhauser, Gladys and Kurt Lang, E. L. Quarantelli, Tamotsu Shibutani, and Ralph Turner.[2] Building on the work of Park, Burgess, and Herbert Blumer, and influenced by other members of the "first" generation of Chicago sociologists and anthropologists, such as Louis Wirth, William Ogburn, Everett Hughes, and Lloyd Warner,[3] these scholars comprise a significant portion of what this book has identified as the "second Chicago school of sociology."

When characterizing strands of theory and schools of thought, there is always the danger of reconstructing original themes, neglecting important differences, and overstating thin similarities. As Turner (1988, 319) notes in a discussion of various characterizations of the earlier period at Chicago, "We often make the mistake of reading into early writings the meanings that have entered and suffused our thinking at a later date." In characterizing later Chicago scholars, we recognize there are significant differences reflected in their work. Yet, for the most part, the differences are more topical or substantive than differences in focal concerns and processes. Indeed, it is our argument that a close reading of the work of these second-generation scholars reveals a set of anchoring concerns and processes that together point to a distinctive perspective on collective behavior.

The existence of a Chicago school of collective behavior is not a novel observation. There are references to its "marriage" of crowd analysis and the study of social movements (McCarthy 1991, xii; Morris and Herring 1988, 146–50), its theoretical affiliation with symbolic interaction (Turner 1981), its focus on the emergent nature of social order (Turner and Killian 1987, 7; Morris and Herring 1988, 146–50), and, in its early days, a keen interest in circular reaction and social contagion (McPhail 1991). But there are no statements specifically identifying the theoretical and empirical contributions of the group coming after Park, Burgess, and Blumer. Our primary aim in this chapter is to identify and elaborate the focal concerns and processes making up the second generation's contributions in a fashion suggestive of a reasonably coherent and distinctive perspective. At the same time, we hope to avoid what Killian (1980, 276) cites as a problem in discussing the Chicago collective behavior tradition, that is, the creation of grotesque, polemical, caricatures.[4] In keeping with the pragmatist roots of the "Chicago approach," we will also assess the utility of this perspective by addressing the question of how and to what extent it advances understanding of collective behavior and social movement phenomena vis-à-vis other perspectives.

SCHOOLS OF COLLECTIVE BEHAVIOR

It is useful to begin by identifying the key perspectives on collective behavior and social movements in American sociology. Most of this thinking flows from three schools or communities of thought, each of which is characterized by a different focal concern and each of which can be associated intellectually with a particular university. We might think of each of these schools as functioning much like a geological "mother lode." Each constitutes a seminal concentration of much of the theorizing and research on collective behavior and social movements over the last two to three decades, and each is associated with far-reaching veins of related conceptualizations and affiliations.[5] Our purpose in denoting the schools, and the kinds of theorizing they reflect, is not to pit one against the other and evaluate each for its coherence, falsifiability, and degree of empirical support. Rather, we discuss them in order to draw the backdrop against which the thrust and tradition of the Chicago school takes on meaning and significance. Since we are primarily interested in the Chicago approach, we will not attempt a detailed elaboration of the other schools of thought. Our thumbnail discussions are meant to be helpful for purposes of contrast.

The three schools or mother lodes include, in addition to Chicago, what can be referred to as the Harvard and Michigan perspectives. The main concern of the Harvard school, as reflected in the work of Parsons (1954, 1963), Smelser (1963, 1972), Bell (1960, 1963), and Johnson (1966), is with the beginnings of collective behavior and movements, and with their *underlying strains*. Parsons (1954, 1963), for example, attributed McCarthyism to international and domestic strains creating high levels of anxiety, aggression, and "wishful patterns of beliefs" (Parsons 1963, 218). He likened it to a financial panic in which the scapegoating of officials is widespread. For Bell, status strains are the basis of right-wing political participation. For Johnson, a "disequilibrated social system" creates demands for change that are associated with revolutionary situations.

Perhaps the role of underlying structural strains is best illustrated in Smelser's *Theory of Collective Behavior* (1963). Smelser views the several forms of collective behavior as disruptions of the social system in response to structural strain. His model tends to dichotomize institutional from collective lines of action, dissociating the rationality of institutional processes from the emotionality, or irrationality, attributed to actors within collectivities. His reliance on some of the assumptions of Parsons's structural-functionalism regarding social action and integration have been discussed elsewhere and need not be repeated (Brown and Goldin 1973; Currie and Skolnick 1970; Killian 1980; Marx and Wood 1975; Oberschall 1973).

In the case of the Michigan school, associated initially with the work of Zald and McCarthy (1987), Tilly and his associates (1975, 1978), and Gamson (1990), among others, the focal concern has been with *resource mobilization* and its constituent elements, and the consequences of collective action. The school would have us ask about movements, for example: How do they appropriate and allocate resources? What accounts for changes in the availability of discretionary resources, and how do such changes affect social movement activity? What difference do movements make? What kinds of changes do they achieve? Connected with such questions are five central concerns that have animated most research associated with the perspective. They include the structure of political opportunities and the factors that account for its expansion and contraction (McAdam 1982; Tilly 1978); the organizational context of and basis for social movement activity (Morris, 1984; Oberschall 1973; Zald and McCarthy 1987); the processes of resource acquisition and deployment (Jenkins and Perrow 1977; Zald and McCarthy 1987); the rational character of collective action at both the individual and organizational levels (Oberschall 1973; Zald and McCarthy 1987); and the outcomes or consequences of social movements and kindred collective action (Gamson 1990).

Because of its assumption that decisions regarding collective action are predicated on the rational assessment of the anticipated costs and rewards of alternative lines of action, the perspective has been called the "rational calculation approach" (Wood and Jackson 1982) and the "super-rationalistic approach" (Killian 1980). Although the merits of such labels are open to debate, it is clear that research associated with the perspective is driven by more than the rationality theme. It is also arguable that the Michigan school and its resource mobilization perspective gained hegemonic status in the 1970s and early 1980s (Snow and Oliver 1995, 573). As one of its chief proponents argued in a retrospective in the early 1990s, "It had become so dominant that its assumptions have often been assimilated as the routine and unstated grounds of much contemporary work" (Zald 1992, 327).[6]

Because of its central concerns and its influence, the perspective has been routinely contrasted to the so-called "collective behavior tradition," which has come to function as a cover term for all work on crowds and social movements that preceded the 1970s and the ascendence of the resource mobilization perspective. This proved to be an unfortunate appellation, since it lumped together under the same umbrella work emanating from both the Harvard and Chicago mother lodes, as well as disparate psychologically oriented works ranging from LeBon's *The Crowd* (1960) to Hoffer's *The True Believer* (1951), works that have little, if any, resonance with the collective behavior processes of interest to the scholars associated with the Chicago mother lode.

For the Chicago school, the focal concern is with neither underlying strains nor resources or outcomes, but with *processual development and dynamics*. The themes that together make it a distinctive approach include:

(1) emergence, (2) symbolization, (3) cognitive and affective transformation, (4) interactive determination, and (5) fluidity. The following schematic summarizes the essence of each school, indicating their respective central concerns and constituent themes. With this schematic as backdrop, we turn to an elaboration of the themes that define the Chicago school or perspective.

TABLE 6.1. SUMMARY OF THREE MAJOR SCHOOLS OF COLLECTIVE BEHAVIOR

	Harvard	Chicago	Michigan
Focal Concern	Strains	Process	Resource mobilization
Constituent Themes	Structural disequilibrium or strains resulting in systemic breakdowns	Emergence	Political opportunities
		Symbolization	Organization
		Cognitive & affective transformation	Resource Accumulation
	Consequential psychological tensions	Interactive determination	Rational calculation
		Fluidity	Outcomes
Exemplars	Parsons	Turner/Killian	Zald/McCarthy
	Smelser	Shibutani	Tilly
	Bell	Gusfield	Gamson

CONSTITUENT THEMES OF THE CHICAGO SCHOOL

For Park (1927, 735), collective behavior bears the stamp of normalcy to the extent that "institutions and social structures of every sort" are the products of collective action. Social forms, he believed, have a natural history of development, a typical sequence shaped by natural forces in which each stage triggers the next (Turner 1967, xxiii). Behavior becomes collective behavior when the behavior, thought, and sentiments of everyone in an assemblage is directed by a shared mood (*stimmung*) or impulse resulting from interaction. Aggregates on the street become true crowds under the heightened influence of such a mood. Lacking tradition and loyalties, crowds generate and intensify mood and impulse through circular reaction.

Like Park, Blumer saw the study of collective behavior as a way of examining new social orders.[7] He developed Park's ideas about crowds and collective behavior, creating a typology of crowds and developing the concepts of social unrest and circular reaction. His early text chapter (Blumer 1939) did much to establish collective behavior as a subarea within sociology, locating a vast array of phenomena under the rubric, including movements, crowds, mobs, panics, manias, mass behavior, fads, and fashions. Reprinted several times, the chapter may be the most influential writing on the topic in this century, at least within sociology (Gusfield 1978).

The second generation of Chicago collective behaviorists furthered the ideas of Park, Burgess, and Blumer but also differed, to some degree, with their mentors. They tended to demystify the concept of impulse, reject the mechanical nature of circular reaction, and abandon the pathological connotations of contagion. They emphasized the continuity of collective and institutional action, rejecting or qualifying the classical assertion of LeBon (1960) and Tarde (1890) that crowds are characterized by spontaneity, suggestibility, and mental unity. This is clear, for example, in a careful statement by Lang and Lang (1968) about the limited importance and relative nature of spontaneity:

> Although normative standards continue to have some influence on the direction in which activities unfold, the interaction is characterized by relatively greater *spontaneity, volatility, and transitoriness* than it would be if the behavior of the participants were more securely anchored in recognized norms. (Emphasis in the original, Lang and Lang 1968, 56)[8]

In the discussion that follows, we document and illustrate the five constituent themes we have identified as running through the work of the second generation. We begin with the theme of emergence.

Emergence

This term refers to the process out of which distinct social products arise that constitute fractures of, or departures from, everyday routines and practices. As crowds form, objectives emerge and action develops in the relative absence of applicable or relevant standards, and new conventions and guidelines for conduct arise to shape and legitimate what is taking place. Communication in the form of rumor contributes new meanings to relatively unstructured situations.

These emergent phenomena may differ in several ways. First, they vary in form such that the products may be normative, ideational, social relational, organizational, or patterns of activity. On a normative level, the new understandings may take the form of emerging guidelines for conduct, new meanings of objects, redefinitions of the situation, reconstructions of reality, or new standards against which the legitimacy of everyday action is measured. On an ideational level, new or formerly popular styles of thought may now characterize the way people approach problematic situations, conceptualize issues, and interpret events. Relationally, new associations, roles, or groups may emerge in the face of relatively unstructured situations. Organizationally, movements or crowd activity may lead to the development of relatively formal, durable structures. And, in terms of activity, emergent patterns may be highly instrumental and expressive.

Second, emergent phenomena may vary in function, serving alternatively as means or ends. For example, in his study of rumor, Shibutani notes that the rumor (spread by planted rumormongers) that Genghis Khan had a "horde" of soldiers enabled him to take control of village after village, while at the same time it met the local demand for information about villagers' level of risk (Shibutani 1966). Similarly, Lang and Lang (1978) view public opinion as the result of specific deliberations, and as a form of social control, as was the case during Watergate. They have continued to emphasize the importance of studying the formation and dynamics of public opinion (Lang and Lang 1987).

Third, emergent phenomena may vary temporally, such that some may be highly transitory and ephemeral, as in the case of rioting crowds and mass panic, whereas other products may be quite enduring, as in the case of social movements. Groups sometimes drop emergent lines of action rather abruptly in order to resume former patterns; in other situations, emergent patterns persist and become routinized. Some forms, like fads and fashion, are short-lived by definition in particular instances, although persistent and recurring as a collective phenomena.

Fourth, emergent phenomena may vary in scope or breadth, such that some may be situationally specific and relatively narrow in scope and effects, while others may be quite pervasive with far-reaching consequences for large numbers of people. Many social movements, for example, appear to pass through "incipience" (Jackson et al. 1960) towards extinction, perhaps barely getting off the ground and exerting only local consequences. Others are responsible for new cultural themes that permeate a society and affect millions of lives.

The centrality of the process of emergence in the Chicago approach clearly stems from Mead's (1934) emphasis upon the novel and emergent nature of the act, and is reflected in Blumer's (1939) contention that the various forms of collective action are not only emergent phenomena in and of themselves, but frequently constitute the basis for the emergence of yet newer forms of social life. For Blumer, following Park and Burgess, the emergence of new aspects of the social order was equivalent to the emergence of new forms of collective behavior.[9]

Most collective behavior scholars trained in the Park-Blumer tradition at Chicago make emergence a key theme in their explanations of collective behavior. Kurt and Gladys Engel Lang (1961) focus at one point on the emergence of social objects for collectivities, paying special attention to people as objects in the forms of victim, villain, martyr, idol, hero, and fool. They stress the importance of examining how collectivities select victims and scapegoats in the community, and the conditions under which rallying points emerge. For an understanding of riots, and all crowd behavior, action must be studied for its problem-solving aspects, as small incidents precipitate large disturbances (1970, 110). Finally, in their study of the "battle for public opinion," they examine the qualities of media coverage that are conducive to the emergence of public issues. Watergate emerged as a public issue, for example, only after the media gave prominence and continuity to the story (Lang and Lang 1983).

Park and Blumer's concern for the emergence of collective behavior was refined and concretized by Turner and Killian (1957), who made it the central aspect of their conceptualization of collective behavior, defined "as the process through which coordinated behavior arises and changes under the guidance of emergent normative definitions" (Turner and Killian 1972).[10] This idea of emergent norms reflects Park's close linkage of social control and collective behavior, and stresses the development of common understandings of what is expected of people in collectivities. In their view, the concept of emergence complements a continuity with preexisting structures (see Killian 1984, 780). Their conceptualization of norms goes beyond just a concern for behavioral prescriptions and proscriptions, however. Emergent norms include collective definitions of the situation; indications of appropriate and inappropriate actions within the situation; justifications of reality constructions; and evaluations of potential actors in relation to defined situations (Killian 1980, 284).

Turner and Killian (1972) specify conditions associated with the emergence of collective behavior, among them spatial arrangements and systems of control that increase the possibility of communication; the homogeneity of the aggregate; a shared sense of hope that action can better the group's plight; unanticipated events that set off rumors; and the presence of cues which might meaningfully explain events. More recently, they

note the importance of perceived changes occurring in the normative order, social structure, and the flow of communication (Turner and Killian
1987).

To differentiate among types of collectivities, Weller and Quarantelli
(1973) added the idea of emergent social relationships, arguing that collective behavior is constituted by any form of collective action that is based
on emergent norms, emergent relationships, or both. This partially reflects
Quarantelli's interest in what he calls emergent accommodation groups
in crisis situations like disasters, emergencies, and riots (1970). Emergent
accommodation groups include ad hoc rescue units and grass-roots crowd
control groups.[11] Such groups are likely to emerge in the face of precrisis
interaction, keynoting, and legitimation of the group's activities as necessary. He notes the emergence of such groups in other societies during,
for example, the Florence floods of 1966, the student occupation of the
Sorbonne in 1968, and the Chilean earthquake of 1965.

Conceptualizations of collective behavior within the Chicago school
have evolved to the point where they hinge largely on the process of emergence. But it is not viewed as a process that is activated solely by structural
dislocations or strains. Nor are the resultant forms of collective behavior
determined solely by exogenous social factors. Rather, both the process of
emergence and the character and course of the collective behavior that
evolves are part and parcel of ongoing interaction and communication,
the most important aspect being the process of symbolization, which constitutes the second cornerstone of the Chicago approach.

Symbolization

This theme refers to objectification, a process through which events
and conditions, artifacts and edifices, people and aggregations (e.g.,
classes, ethnic groups, status groups) and other features of the ambient
environment take on particular meanings, becoming objects of cognitive
orientation that elicit specifiable feelings and reactions. More concretely,
it is through processes of symbolization that appropriate objects and targets for action are constructed and defined, and actions with respect to
those targets are legitimated.

The importance and centrality of this process in the theorizing and
research associated with the Chicago school are clearly reflected in several
works. Symbols, for example, are seen as a powerful influence, a "unifying
force," on movement activity by Lang and Lang (1961, 639). Crowd symbols can vary in their favorable or unfavorable connotations, and in degree

of ambiguity, as seen in Turner and Surace's (1956) study of the 1943 zoot-suit riots in Los Angeles. They concluded that the "zooter" symbol, less complex than a "Mexican" symbol, effectively neutralized norms inhibiting hostile crowd action, thus functioning as an effective coordinating symbol.

The research of Quarantelli and his associates (Quarantelli and Dynes 1968; 1970) on patterns of looting in riots and disasters also reflects this constituent theme. Their work points to the stages in civil disturbances that mark a cumulative shift in the redefinition of objects, with plundering finally becoming normative within a segment of the population for which property symbolizes white exploitation (Quarantelli and Dynes 1968, 135). Elsewhere, Drabek and Quarantelli (1967) point to the importance of individual officials as public scapegoats constituting accessible and punishable symbols of responsibility in the wake of disasters.

In Shibutani's (1966) classic work on rumors, *Improvised News,* we find yet another theoretical and empirical statement with a clear emphasis upon the emerging cognitive orientation of actors participating in collective behavior. Rumors are conceived as collective transactions made up of cognitive and communicative activities with a low degree of formalization, and they are said to originate in ambiguous situations as institutional news channels are absent or discredited. The extent to which their construction is deliberate or extemporaneous and the associated collective excitement is mild or intense, depends on whether the unsatisfied demand for news is moderate or great (Shibutani 1966, 57). The content and form of rumor symbolization are linked to the group's demand for news and ongoing presuppositions (plausibility). The rumor that General MacArthur was of Japanese ancestry, for example, was plausible in light of unexpectedly benign American military occupation practices like food distribution and social reforms. Shibutani's work is especially significant for its rejection of the idea that rumor is a false report, the distortion of once accurate information (Baldwin 1990).

Orrin Klapp's (1964, 1972) research on symbolic leaders and his text on collective behavior, *Currents of Unrest,* reveal a view of collective behavior as symbolic transactions and public dramas. For Klapp, people are the *animal symbolicum* (1972, 94), making their own worlds by constructing images, symbols, and stereotypes. Outside of institutional contexts, constructions of reality in public dramas in mass settings are free-flowing and improvisatory as people compete for status symbols, emerge as symbolic leaders, and define situations. Symbolic leaders are an emergent phenomenon (Klapp 1964, 32), usually coming as an unpredictable, surprising discovery for the leaders and the publics that select them. Leaders' symbols emerge in a dialectic between their actions and style on the one hand, and the public demand for function on the other. Emerging leaders can seize the moment, attend to cues about how they are perceived, and try to capitalize on the situation. The eventual symbol associated with them, however, depends on many things beyond their control.

More than other members of the second generation of Chicago scholars, Klapp emphasizes circular interaction as a key process and contagions as a key phenomenon. But he does not retain these classical emphases uncritically. For Klapp (1972, 44), Park and Blumer's notion that crowd members experience escalating interstimulation is best seen as a symbolic transaction, "not just an intensification of feeling but a change in the terms of reference, conceptions of things about which emotion is felt." Even as he cites an elaborate typology of contagions, he notes the problems in positing mechanical explanatory triggers. Contagions necessarily involve interpretation and symbolic negotiations of meaning that are contingent on the development and communication of symbols. Hence, "contagions of rebellion" like "ghetto riots" represent attacks on the authority symbols of one's own group (Klapp 1972, 125). Movement participation reflects a collective search for identity in the face of society's loss of rituals and meaningful symbols (Klapp 1969).

The Chicago school's concern for symbolization is also clearly seen in Joseph Gusfield's analysis of alcohol and drinking as symbols in American society. These symbols helped shape the emergence, development, and consequences of the temperance and drunk-driving movements. For Gusfield, the study of movements is, in part, the study of attachment to new symbols and beliefs (Gusfield 1970, 8). In everyday life, for example, drinking alcohol symbolizes the passage from day to night, and weekdays to weekends (Gusfield 1984). In the context of a national movement, since temperance and prohibition symbolized the status gains and losses of conflicting groups in American life, the significance of the movement and the legislation it championed cannot be understood solely in terms of its instrumental effects on drinking behavior (Gusfield 1963). More recently, the "killer drunk" symbol infuses ceremonies conducted by legislatures, courts, and police. These public dramas villainizing the drinking driver are "acts undertaken in the name of and in the sight of the collectivity, visible and observable" (Gusfield 1981a, 175). The three aspects of the "killer-drunk" as a symbol of villainy are the antisocial character of drinking-driving, the drinking drivers' presumed responsibility for their actions, and their morally and factually deviant status. Theirs is the deviance of valuing play over work.

The constituent theme of symbolization is perhaps nowhere more clear than in the collective behavior text by Turner and Killian (1957, 1972, 1987), now in its third edition. For Turner and Killian, the central process in collective behavior is the collective reconstruction of a dominant definition of the situation. Crowds and other collectivities act on the basis of emerging and shared images of an object, and mood and behavior can shift with changes in the symbolic value of the object. Crowd action partially reflects the symbolization of their own activities and the external environment. Even expressive crowds that are often thought to have no direct object of orientation, as in the case of a Billy Graham rally or a pentecostal religious service, may act on the basis of their definition that actors' excitement is evidence that the Lord is present (Turner and Killian 1987, 92). Symbolization is also related to movement development in Killian's (1964) review essay where he describes emerging movement norms that often require people to act in ways that symbolize their loyalty to the movement. Particular events which symbolize unsatisfactory conditions may "be crucial in bringing social unrest to a head" (Killian 1964, 447).

Claims about the importance of symbolization frequently provoke responses of the "So what?" genre. What difference does symbolization or signification make in the end? So what if the temperance movement symbolized the anguish of Protestant, native, rural groups vis-à-vis Catholic, immigrant, urban groups? Isn't the important point the fact that the movement realized its primary goal, at least temporarily, with the establishment of prohibition? More generally, one might ask what else matters other than whether a movement achieved its objective(s) by forcing the enactment of legislation or by exacting concessions through organized and persistent protest and perhaps even obstructionism.

A great deal matters, from the standpoint of the Chicago school. As the writings of Gusfield, Killian, the Langs, Quarantelli, Shibutani, and Turner have shown, not only is the form or character of collective behavior and its targets determined in part by the process of symbolization, but so is the incentive and commitment to act in ways that enhance the prospect of goal attainment. The implication is that we do not always act on utilitarian grounds alone or solely in terms of some kind of rational calculus, and that even when we do, the weighing of the costs and benefits of lines of action is undergirded by processes of symbolization. One of the crucial consequences of the symbolization process is the frequently emergent set of conceptions that adherents and constituents have not only of themselves and their own activities, but also of other actors and their activities. Symbolization is thus inextricably connected to the third constituent theme: cognitive and affective transformation.

Cognitive and Affective Transformation

The importance of this third cornerstone to understanding the Chicago school's approach to collective behavior and social movements is premised on the assumption that whether and how people act towards an object depends on whether they see it, what it is that they see, and how they feel about what it is that they see. The central refrain in "Amazing Grace" clearly reminds us of the importance of these considerations:

> Amazing Grace, how sweet the sound
> That saved a wretch like me.
> I once was lost, but now am found,
> Was blind but now I see.

As people communicate, reflect, and act towards objects of mutual concern in both institutional and noninstitutional contexts, some change their way of seeing and doing things, and experience different feelings for those things. Such changes in thought and feeling need not be deep and all-encompassing, but when they attach to a wide sphere of the person's roles, identities, and everyday activity, we can speak of fundamental cognitive and affective transformations.[12]

Such transformations, as well as less dramatic and far-reaching changes in cognition and affect, can be linked to collective action, goals, and effects in two ways. First, on one level, it is often a necessary condition for readying and mobilizing some individuals to act in support of a particular campaign or more general goals and activities. Its function, so to speak, is to gather and rally the troops to "staff the barricades." This may involve some degree of change in the way targets of action are viewed, or in the way potential constituents view themselves in relation to the targets. Shibutani's (1970) essay on the "personification of adversaries" is illustrative. Shibutani argues that interpretations of an act are limited by the perceived plausibility of the actor's motives. In conflict situations, a double standard of morality often emerges that legitimates one's own violence as necessary or heroic, while the opponent is seen as engaging in brutal atrocities:

> Tales of mutilation of prisoners and the violation of women reinforce the belief that the enemy is a fiendish perpetrator of dark deeds and a violator of all rules of decency. . . . if a bitter conflict is prolonged, the major objective is transformed. What had started as the quest for a limited aim becomes a crusade for the total obliteration of the adversary. (1970, 229)

Such transformations are not limited to conflict situations. It may be that the "consciousness-raising" process, for example, routinely involves the recasting of self and target so that group members identify with a new category of people and translate the ideology of what is defined as their enlightened position into practical action vis-à-vis designated targets.

Second, on another level, cognitive and affective transformations have to do with a deeper and perhaps more pervasive change in hearts and minds, such that behavior patterns are changed, thus resulting in the realization of primary goals at the everyday, interactional level. Whereas changes at the first level may help prompt activists to press more assertively for legislative and political concessions, they may be fleeting in the absence of changes of the second type. Clearly, the success of the women's movement continues to be dependent not only on what happens in Washington, D.C., and in statehouses across the country, but also on what transpires between men and women on a daily basis at home, work, and school. If students of collective behavior and social movements have learned anything from presidential politics, it is that hard-won legislative and political concessions can be quite tenuous without corresponding change in the hearts and minds of people at the grass-roots level.

Such cognitive and affective changes, then, are not only means to the realization of other goals but important consequences or products of collective action as well. As Turner noted in an essay that makes this issue a central theme: "altered ways of viewing both self and larger systems of social relationships are often more important products of social movements than any specific organizational or political accomplishment" (1981, 6). Elsewhere he notes that these individual changes in lifestyle and values have been mistakenly taken as the ground against which seemingly more important, easily identified, movement-effects are the figure (Turner 1983a).

Transformation is a theme within many movements in the second half of this century, and self-concepts can be rediscovered or reconstructed as they become anchored to, and rectified by, movement participation (Turner 1969a; Turner and Killian 1987). For Lang and Lang (1961, vi),

"These processes of transformation can be observed in many contexts, in organized groups no less than in unorganized multitudes." Similar ideas are reflected in Gusfield's (1980) views on the privatization of social movements, and Klapp's (1969) examination of modern movement participation as a collective search for identity.[13]

Interactive Determination

This fourth cornerstone process refers to a generally dialectical view of the character and operation of collective behavior and movements. Decoded, this theme suggests that the character and course of a social movement is shaped externally through continuous interaction between the movement, outside institutions, the community, countermovements, and interest groups that make up its environment of operation; and internally through the dynamic interplay of ideology, power, and participation considerations. This means, even more concretely, that a movement's character is the product of "the visible actions of the movement, the public response to those actions, and movement adaptations to this response" (Turner 1964b, 124).

This highly interactive, dialectic position can be contrasted to three other classification schemes. The first involves a life cycle or *natural history* model that views collective behavior and, more specifically, social movements as unfolding in a series of steps or phases.[14] Most statements are similar to Mauss's (1975, 61) ideal-typic model that identifies the path cut by movements through incipiency, coalescence, institutionalization, fragmentation, and demise. The second set of schemes is based on a *value-added* model, where a set of necessary conditions are specified as sufficient, in combination, for a particular form of collective behavior to occur. Smelser's (1963) theory of collective behavior, and Lofland and Stark's (1965) model of conversion, are two well-developed examples of this approach. Third are those schemes which emphasize *immanent determination* in the sense that the course and character of movements are viewed in terms of qualities that are presumed to be intrinsic to them, such as goals, ideology, and class foundations (Turner 1964b, 124). Social movements, for example, are classified as inherently reformist or revolutionary because of their ideologies, stated objectives, leadership styles, or values.

In contrast, the Chicago approach, as it has evolved, argues that movements should be classified according to the way in which they are defined or responded to in their environment of operation. This logic is probably most clearly reflected in Turner and Killian's text when they note that movements are characteristically in a state of flux. Immediately outside the movement, the responses and definitions of mediating publics affect the course and character of movement development (Turner 1964a, 1969b; Turner and Killian 1987). Others associated with the Chicago mother lode point to the importance of outside responses, including the reactions of spectator components in neutralizing arbitrary coercion by partisans (Shibutani 1986, 271), and the reactions of publics to a movement's presentational dimensions as dramatic objects (Gusfield 1980; also see Zygmunt 1970).

Movements and their presentations are characteristically filtered and interpreted in modern societies, often with what Lang and Lang (1953) call television's "unique perspective." In their classic pilot study, they positioned observers at several strategic points along the Chicago parade route followed by General Douglas MacArthur's motorcade in 1951 as he was welcomed home after President Truman relieved him of military command in Korea. Compared with television portrayals of the crowd's continuous enthusiasm, observers saw more lulls in the excitement and a more calm, overall crowd response.

In his discussion of mediating publics, Turner (1964a) notes that public definitions of collective behavior can curtail or facilitate recruitment. The effects of mediating publics are seen in the ways they see incidents of collective action as precipitating an issue, committing groups to a stand, exemplifying action perhaps only previously contemplated, and identifying the character of participants on either side of an issue. In this vein, bystander publics (Turner 1970), not concerned with the goals of a particular movement, may become involved due to the inconvenience posed by movement tactics that might figuratively and literally bring social traffic to a halt. Because of such considerations, movement leaders, or at least the strategically smart ones, are likely to keep bystander publics in mind, attempting to size up their possible reactions to various movement tactics.

The importance of interactive determination is also explicit in Klapp's (1972) collective behavior text when he discusses the "seeding" of meaning-seeking movements as a dialectic between collectivities and the problematic reactions of mass audiences. As movements develop and organize, collectivities and mass audiences make "offers and deals, sorties and retreats, coalitions and betrayals, thrusts and counterthrusts, the outcome of which is highly contingent—that is, depend [sic] on circumstances of the moment and what the other just did" (Klapp 1972, 370). Ritualizing forces in the surrounding culture, such as the mass media, threaten to "buy-off" counterculture heroes and turn religious leaders into celebrities, so meaning-seeking movements must constantly work against those forces.

Even in Kornhauser's (1959, 1962, 1968) largely structural analysis of mass political movements, the theme of interactive determination between participation and outside institutions is apparent. The absence of mediating structures between masses and the state tends to create accessible elites and available masses. In contrast to class and reform movements, mass movements lack internal group structure and stable leadership. While numerous investigators have found little empirical support for this thesis (see Snow and Oliver 1995, 573–75), Kornhauser's theory is not one in which all social movements spring from the availability of socially isolated and unattached people. It is a theory of mass movements in which the availability of people hinges on the absence of effective linkages between their membership groups and decision-making bodies, and it is this part of the theory that, according to other scholars in the Chicago tradition, deserves further attention (Turner and Killian 1987, 389–90).

Two further examples of the constituent theme of interactive determination are found in works of Killian (1968, 1984) and Lang and Lang (1960). Killian's (1968) analysis of the civil rights and black power movements posits the linkage of internal and external dynamics as critical in explaining their development, and his examination of the Tallahassee bus boycott in 1956 points to the interplay between spontaneous action, emergent groups, and preexisting organizations (Killian 1984). While the boycott was precipitated by the unplanned actions of two Florida A. & M. students, preexisting organizations and networks, such as the university student body, churches, and the local NAACP, played a part. One important contingency occurred when, during the initial confrontation between the bus driver and the students, the driver told them they couldn't sit in the front seats. One of the students told him she would get off if he would give her back her dime. He told her he "couldn't," and then drove to a gas station where he phoned the police. Soon, a new organization, the Inter-Civic Council, was born at one mass meeting. It was a merger of the NAACP, a ministerial alliance, and the Civic League. Killian notes, "The movement was launched more on faith than on the basis of an inventory of resources in reserve, internal or external" (Killian 1984, 781).

Lang and Lang's (1960) analysis of how and why people made "decisions for Christ" at Billy Graham rallies in 1957 in Madison Square Garden also reflects the theme of interactive determination. They note the importance of organizational planning by the Graham staff and established churches in the community, on the one hand, and the meaning of "stepping forward" for audience members, on the other. People did not "convert" in the sense of being born again. Instead, they confessed nominal sins and made limited commitments with a minimum of affect after experiencing a buildup resembling a conventional Sunday church service.

Fluidity

The fifth and final theme is an overarching and summary one that can be captured by the term "fluidity." Gusfield (1981b) uses the term to suggest an alternative to the more standard linear conception of social movements.[15] "Linear" conceptualizations tend to share the following foci: the beginnings of movements; organizations and associations; dissidence, protest, rebellion, and deviance; success as measured by stated goals; and the public arena. In general, they emphasize the conscious, deliberate pursuit of change by an association of partisans (Gusfield 1981b, 322). The unit of analysis is the association organized to achieve the desired change. Linear models focus on movements as associations with ideologies, goals, memberships, and activities. They tend to employ an overpoliticized view of movement life, and neglect private and local implications and meanings in microsocial arenas (Gusfield 1980, 296–301).

In contrast, a "fluid" conception of collective action is characterized by a number of alternative considerations. First, it is not limited to organizational action, and is "more alive to the larger contexts of change" in which movements are embedded. Second, it is concerned with the consequences of movements in a wider variety of areas, such as the construction of movement awareness throughout a culture. Third, it places more emphasis on the cultural side of movements, such as the transformation of meanings, vocabularies, and structures of discourse. And fourth, the focus of attention is on long-term movement developments in the "less political parts of human life."

Other members of the Chicago school have noted these themes as well. Killian (1964), for example, points to the emergence of "special languages" within movements as reflections of the emergence of distinctive norms. Familiar terms are redefined and neologisms (e.g., "temperance" and "drys") arise. Turner (1981) also stresses the importance of looking beyond formal movement boundaries.

Since movement boundaries are more nebulous under the fluidity construct, Gusfield (1981b) leaves it to the sociological observer to identify the existence, parameters, and effects of a movement on general and specific levels, and to identify how changes in meaning on one level may reflect changes in meaning on another. At the same time, those observations will inevitably be shaped by external, historical forces, like those that led sociologists to focus on religious movements in the first half of the century and political movements in the second (Gusfield 1978). Whatever the character of these overarching external, historical forces, however, a fluid conceptualization of movements will draw greater attention to diversification within movements, the spread of movement values and symbols throughout a culture, and the incorporation of movement themes into individual and interpersonal everyday rituals in social encounters, religious experience, and styles of work and leisure (Gusfield 1980, 305).[16]

VARIATIONS AND RELATIVE UTILITY

The research and writing associated with specifiable schools of thought rarely constitute a consensual or homogeneous corpus. Rather, there are typically discernible departures from the constituent themes, as well as attempts to extend or refine one or more of the basic themes. Such is the case with the second Chicago school of collective behavior. Thus, having identified and elaborated the themes that define this perspective on collective behavior, we now identify a few important variations within the school, and then assess the relative utility of the school's processual emphasis and constituent themes.

Lateral Divergence

The key differences within the school are best described as lateral divergence, reflecting departures from the core of the mother lode in varying degrees rather than as leaps to other models altogether. These differences go beyond topical considerations such as an interest in rumors and disasters or crowds and riots. There are at least three points of lateral divergence within the second Chicago school. First, authors differ in the extent to which they retain an emphasis upon anonymity, spontaneity, and suggestibility in conceptualizing collective behavior phenomena. There are significant differences, for example, between Turner and Killian

(1972), Klapp (1972), and Lang and Lang (1961). All mention these terms at one point or another, but Turner and Killian "challenge the myth" (McPhail 1991) more head-on than the others, especially in successive editions of their text.

Second, there are differences in the relative emphasis given to social structural factors in explaining collective phenomena. For example, Kornhauser's (1959) mass society theory is closely attuned at points to the constituent themes of the Harvard school. At other points, however, he is attuned to Chicago's concern with processual development and dynamics, showing an appreciation of the interactive basis of radical and liberal political commitment. His focus lies not only on the presence or absence of personal ties to the community, but also on the locus of radicals' and liberals' "personal world," and the selective recruitment and socialization of leaders (Kornhauser 1962).

Third, Klapp's work is difficult to classify (Gusfield and Michalowicz 1984), not only because his typologies continue to give a high profile to collective contagions, but also because of his efforts to integrate symbolic interaction with systems and communications theory. According to Klapp's synthesis (1972), collective action is a function of homeodynamics and information feedback. Some of the contagions of the 1970s were reflections of entropic communication (when the message flow has worse consequences than silence). For example, Rachel Carson's exposé of the dangers of pesticides led to a nutritional puritanism. The resurgence of satanism and the furor over William Peter Blatty's novel and the movie made from it, *The Exorcist,* show how popular information confuses norms and "damages the order of a system" (Klapp 1972, 96). In his most recent statement, *Inflation of Symbols* (1991), Klapp examines how mass contagions, fads, and fashions are affected when associated symbols lose value with their overabundant supply throughout a culture.

Lateral Entry

Although the work of Erving Goffman does not exhibit strong interest in crowd and movement activities, several scholars have woven his conceptual schemes into the fabric of collective behavior analysis over the past decade. This represents the most notable lateral entry (or importation) of a second-generation Chicago scholar to the field. We have already noted Gusfield's (1980) observation that the presentational behavior of movements reflects sensitivity to a diversity of public audiences. Snow, Zurcher, and Peters (1981) have also drawn on this dramaturgical theme that permeates a portion of Goffman's work (1959), applying it to victory celebrations and crowds more generally. Goffman's (1961) model of the social organization of face-to-face encounters and his work on frame analysis (1974) have been applied by Gamson and his associates to the analysis of how small groups mobilize to resist unjust situations (Gamson et al. 1982). And Snow and Benford have drawn on and extended Goffman's framing concepts to examine and theorize about the relevance of interpretive processes to movement mobilization (see Benford 1993; Snow et al. 1986; Snow and Benford 1988, 1992).

Utility

Although the influence of what we have dubbed the Chicago approach to the study of crowds and social movements is fairly pervasive within the field, there are several ongoing contributions that are particularly noteworthy. Here we note a few of the more concrete and specific contributions. First, the Chicago school's approach to collective behavior was instrumental in the shift away from crowd conceptualizations based on assumptions of homogeneous participation and irrational actors. In describing crowd unanimity as an illusion, and arguing that emotion and reason are both operative in the context of collective behavior, Turner and Killian (1972) advanced the field by insisting that classical images of the crowd and crowd participants be held up to closer empirical scrutiny (McCarthy 1991, xvi; McPhail 1991).

Second, the writings of Chicago scholars on the seemingly newsworthy varieties of collective behavior that occur in crisis situations, such as panic, disasters, and looting, have similarly brought empirical and conceptual clarity to our understanding of these phenomena. For example, their investigations of emergence, symbolization, and interactive determination as they pertain to these collective phenomena have effectively refuted the folklore and media-inspired myths about how individuals and groups behave during crisis situations (see Dynes and Quarantelli 1968a, 1968b; Lang and Lang 1976; Quarantelli 1989; Quarantelli and Dynes 1968, 1970; Turner 1983b). In his classic statement on the nature and conditions of panic, for example, Quarantelli (1954) emphasized how reactions of acute fear occur in the context of individual and group definitions of the situation as dangerous, beliefs of possible entrapment, and a "social or group predefinition of a crisis as one that is likely to eventuate in panic flight" (Quarantelli 1954, 275).[17]

Third, the recent entry of Goffman's dramaturgical and framing analyses onto the collective behavior stage has clearly functioned to temper and broaden over the past decade what some scholars have perceived as the "supperrationalism" (Killian 1980) of the initial writings of the Michigan school.

Fourth, the current thrust within the social movement field in particular is to integrate social psychological perspectives and issues with mobilization processes that operate at the macro-, meso-, and micro-levels of social life and analysis (see McAdam, McCarthy, and Zald 1988; Snow and Oliver 1995). The five constituent themes that define the Chicago perspective clearly provide analytic leverage for such integrative work, as well as inform recent interest in specific substantive issues, such as the relationship between meaning and mobilization (Ferree and Miller 1985; Snow et al. 1986), rational choice processes and participation in collective action (Klandermans 1984, Snow and Oliver 1995), strategic interaction and tactical innovation (McAdam 1983), and the conceptualization and assessment of collective identity (Melucci 1990; Taylor and Whittier 1992). These specific concerns, along with the overarching integrative efforts, are certainly consistent with and can be informed by the thematic concerns of the Chicago school, particularly in its insistence that a thoroughgoing understanding of crowds and social movements are not possible without attention to processual development and dynamics.

SUMMARY

In this chapter we have identified and elaborated what we take to be the central themes that are constitutive of the second Chicago school of collective behavior. We have argued that although the scholars associated with the second Chicago school build on the earlier work of Park, Burgess, and Blumer, among others, they do so in a manner that yields a distinctive perspective on, or approach to, the study of collective behavior. We have also suggested, for the purposes of heuristic clarification and perspective, that the Chicago school can be contrasted to two other major schools of collective action, the Harvard and Michigan schools. Each of these schools, we contend, has functioned in a manner akin to a geological "mother lode," providing the seminal impetus for much of the theorizing and research on collective behavior and social movements over the past several decades. Although these three schools ask somewhat different questions and provide different conceptualizations and empirical foci, we do not see them as being mutually exclusive. Instead, they overlap at various points, each casting light on questions and issues to which the others do not fully attend.

In the case of the second Chicago school of collective behavior, we have argued that what makes it both seminal and salient as a perspective is the light it sheds on the generic collective behavior processes of emergence, symbolization, cognitive and affective transformation, interactive determination, and fluidity. Additionally, we suspect that these constituent thematic processes will appear at pivotal points in new and continuing orientations seeking to explain crowd and social movement phenomena. For one thing, attention to the five constituent themes may help us to understand and account for the development of movements beyond the condition of emergence, an area of inquiry that some contend is underdeveloped in the sociology of social movements (see McAdam, McCarthy, and Zald 1988). The contributions of the second Chicago school to the process of symbolization should also be of assistance in gaining leverage on the construction of heroes and villains for target groups, for constituents and beneficiaries, and for the movement itself; on the long-term cultural effects of symbols; on the emotional, even nostalgic, meanings of movement symbols; and, as Turner (1958) noted over three decades ago, on the emergence and transformation of symbols in collective behavior in general.

The process of cognitive and affective transformation also suggests research directives by turning our attention away from the putative transformative effects of mere membership in a collectivity to the process, form, and functions of change in the hearts and minds of collective behavior participants across a wider array of social contexts. While this kind of transformation is most apparent when we look at religious movements, questions remain as to its relevance to the political arena and the conditions under which it is operative.

Finally, the process of interactive determination poses perhaps the greatest challenge to researchers and theorists in explaining collective behavior. This is because it requires the close examination of processual development of collective behavior in response to both exogenous and endogenous conditions, and the continuous interaction between the movement and elements within its environment.

NOTES

We wish to thank Joe Gusfield, Henry Quarantelli, and Ralph Turner for their helpful comments on an earlier draft of this chapter.

1. Shibutani (1988) notes that many of Blumer's students regarded his course on "Folkways and Fashions" as his finest during the 1930s, but at the end of the war Blumer was occasionally away, involved with labor relations research and consulting (Turner 1988).

2. Other members of this post–W.W. II Chicago cohort also made contributions to the study of collective behavior, although it was not their main area of interest or the area to which they made their most significant contributions. Anselm Strauss (1944, 1947), for example, had an early interest in the area, publishing an article on panic in 1944, two years before receiving his Ph.D., and writing a review of research needs in collective behavior a few years later. Rue Bucher and Strauss (1961) applied the Chicago collective behavior approach to the development of professions, and Bucher (1957) wrote on blaming and scapegoating in disasters. Fred Davis, who entertained the possibility of doing his master's thesis on fashion until Herbert Blumer dissuaded him from doing so in the late 1940s (Davis 1991, 2–3), later wrote a number of important works on the topic (1991, 1992). Also, Joseph Zygmunt wrote his 1953 master's thesis on the Jehovah's Witnesses movement. Titled "Social Estrangement and the Recruitment Process in a Chiliastic Sectarian Movement," the thesis was a useful source of information on the midcentury Jehovah's Witnesses, coming quick on the heels of the persecution of Witness children for refusing to salute the flag in school during the early years of World War II. It also apparently functioned as the springboard for the publication seventeen years later of a historical account of the resilience of the movement's belief system in the face of a succession of prophetic failures between 1878 and 1925 (Zygmunt 1970). Zygmunt (1972) also wrote, with more insight than most movement scholars in the early 1970s, about the complicated and dynamic relationship between psychological predispositions and actual movement participation. Finally, while Kai T. Erikson's (1976) study of a community's response to disaster is not a collective behavior study in the traditional sense, it can be taken as a further reflection of the widespread interest in collective behavior phenomena among sociologists who matriculated at Chicago during the decade following W.W. II (also see Erikson 1994).

3. Faculty in other departments or centers at the university, such as Edward Shils and Bruno Bettelheim, were also influential, especially for Janowitz (Suttles 1985).

4. Killian is referring specifically to characterizations of Chicago scholars as making the assumption that collective behavior is inherently less rational than institutional behavior. The second generation of authors vary in their assumptions and analyses, but we agree with Turner and Killian (1987, 5) that a careful reading of most Chicago collective behaviorists does not support this blanket generalization.

5. Examining the institutional bases of theoretical diversity has its problems

212   David A. Snow and Phillip W. Davis

(Reynolds and McCart 1972). In response to Meltzer and Petras (1970), and Meltzer, Petras, and Reynolds (1978), who discuss the Chicago and Iowa schools of symbolic interaction, Stryker (1988) notes the problem of scholasticism when schools are defined in a polemical atmosphere (his reaction at the mention of an Indiana school of symbolic interactionism: "God forbid that any such should exist!" [Stryker 1988, 41]).

6. We should note that the Michigan school can be traced to Vanderbilt, where Zald and McCarthy were on the faculty in sociology in the early 1970s. But it was not until Zald moved to Michigan, where he worked in association with Gamson and Tilly, that the resource mobilization perspective took root and flowered. For an overview of the perspective and related work through the early 1980s, see Jenkins (1983). For a later assessment and stock-taking, see Zald (1992). For critiques of the perspective by scholars associated with the second Chicago school, see Killian (1980) and Turner (1981).

7. Turner and Killian (1987, 6) identify Blumer as a student of Park's, while Bulmer (1984, 113) states he was not. Perhaps at issue here is the meaning of "student." Whether Blumer was formally a student of Park's may be open to question, but there is little doubt that Park's work had a considerable influence on Blumer's thinking as regards collective behavior.

8. Elsner (1972) notes that the Langs' (1961) text is more closely linked to the classical position, and reflects a psychoanalytic view that sets them apart from other Chicago writers. This may be the case for their text (Lang and Lang 1961), but much less so, or not at all, for their other writings.

9. See McPhail (1991) for criticisms of what he regards as partial tautologies in these statements. As for Mead's influence, Ellsworth Faris (a philosophy and psychology graduate student under Mead and Dewey) brought much of Mead's philosophy to the sociology department when he was hired to fill W. I. Thomas's position and became chair in 1925 (Faris 1970, 158). Faris had an interest in sects as a form of "rising institutions." His article, "The Sect and the Sectarian" was not published until 1955, in *The American Journal of Sociology,* but his idea that sect members act in terms of their image of the outside world with which they are in conflict played a part in Lang and Lang's (1961) thinking about the "crystallization" process in collective behavior.

10. As a graduate student in Burgess's seminar on prediction, Turner wrote a paper on the effects of keynoting by legitimate authorities in race riots. For a seminar taught by Hans Gerth, he wrote a paper on the ideological justifications of European pogroms. These interests and activities were fundamental in shaping the development of the emergent norm perspective (Turner 1988).

11. Anderson, Dynes, and Quarantelli's analysis of "counter-rioters" provides a nice illustrative discussion of such groups (1974). Quarantelli was also interested in the emergence of new forms of social organization such as a college Ouija board cult in which eight students met nightly for over two months to "work the board." The emergence of the cult was shaped by the macro trend of increased occult interest in the early 1970s, and by a chance gathering of people in a dormitory who were already familiar with the board (Quarantelli and Wenger 1973). Other influences on the new group's emergence were a milling process in which

people tried to resolve an ambiguous situation (one night during a session with the Ouija board the lights in the room went out and a cigarette "flew" from a woman's hand) through consensual validation. The presence of role models (two of the women were heavily involved in seances and other occult activities) was also influential.

12. Our use of the term "transformation" should not be confused with McPhail's (1991) recent critique of the classical and (early) Chicago school's "transformation hypothesis." He traces LeBon's thesis of the mental unity of the crowd through Park and Blumer's model of the effects of interstimulation on the intensification of feeling, suggestibility, and acting on impulse. He finds a closer link between LeBon and Tarde, and Park and Blumer, than others such as Turner (1964a) and Turner and Killian (1972, 1987).

13. Turner (1975) questions whether a modern "quest" for identity is the driving force behind most modern social movements, finding in a sample of Los Angeles adults that most were not generally conscious of such a quest. While most students in his college sample were conscious of a personal quest, they relied primarily on institutional routes of discovery for answers to questions about who they were. Hence, the "quest" may be most pronounced among students within the university culture.

14. Chicago scholars do not necessarily reject natural history and life-cycle models of movement development. Blumer's (1939) classic statement, for example, draws upon Dawson and Gettys' (1935) movement stages of social unrest, popular excitement, formalization, and institutionalization. Turner and Killian (1987, 253) recognize the importance of timing in explaining the conditions that contribute to a revised sense of injustice. And Janowitz (1968, 1979) was very much concerned with the phases within the natural history of "commodity riots" that reached a high point between 1964 and 1967. Chicago scholars, however, tend to view the matter of timing and progression as problematic, rather than natural, aspects of collective behavior.

15. Klapp (1972) also invokes the liquid metaphor in discussing the flow of collective action, likening symbolic transactions to a stream that flows through institutional structures but flows more freely outside them.

16. The constituent theme of fluidity should not be confused with the overstated claim that collective behavior is characteristically transitory and therefore cannot be studied as effectively with traditional research methods as more long-lasting phenomena. See Aguirre and Quarantelli (1983) for a response to this claim.

17. This was the topic of his master's thesis at Chicago in 1953, "A Study of Panic: Its Nature, Types, and Conditions." For his appraisal of contemporary disaster research, and needs for new direction, see Quarantelli (1989).

REFERENCES

Aguirre, Benigno and E. L. Quarantelli. 1983. "Methodological, Ideological and Conceptual-Theoretical Criticisms of the Field of Collective Behavior." *Sociological Focus* 16: 195–216.

Anderson, William, Russell Dynes, and E. L. Quarantelli. 1974. "Urban Counter-rioters." *Transaction* 11: 50–55.

Baldwin, John D. 1990. "Advancing the Chicago School of Pragmatic Sociology: The Life and Work of Tamotsu Shibutani." *Sociological Inquiry* 60: 115–26.

Bell, Daniel. 1960. *The End of Ideology: On the Exhaustion of Political Ideas in the Fifties.* Revised edition. New York: The Free Press.

———, ed. 1963. *The Radical Right.* Garden City: Doubleday-Anchor Books.

Benford, Robert D. 1993. "Frame Disputes within the Nuclear Disarmament Movement." *Social Forces* 71: 677–701.

Blumer, Herbert. 1939. "Collective Behavior." Pp. 219–88 in *Principles of Sociology,* edited by R. Park. New York: Barnes and Noble. Also appears in *New Outlines of the Principles of Sociology,* edited by Alfred McClung Lee, 1951, pp. 167–224. New York: Barnes and Noble.

Brown, Michael and Amy Goldin. 1973. *Collective Behavior: A Review and Reinterpretation of the Literature.* Pacific Palisades: Goodyear.

Bucher, Rue. 1957. "Blame and Hostility in Disaster." *American Journal of Sociology* 62: 467–75.

Bucher, Rue and Anselm Strauss. 1961. "Professions in Process." *American Journal of Sociology* 66: 325–54.

Bulmer, Martin. 1984. *The Chicago School of Sociology: Institutionalization, Diversity, and the Rise of Sociological Research.* Chicago: University of Chicago Press.

Currie, Elliott, and Jerome H. Skolnick. 1970. "A Critical Note on Conceptions of Collective Behavior." *The Annals of the American Academy of Political and Social Science* 391: 34–45.

Davis, Fred. 1991. "Herbert Blumer and the Study of Fashion: A Reminiscence and A Critique." *Symbolic Interaction* 14: 1–21.

———. 1992. *Fashion, Culture, and Identity.* Chicago: University of Chicago Press.

Dawson, C. A. and W. E. Gettys. 1935. *Introduction to Sociology.* Revised edition. New York: Ronald Press.

Drabek, Thomas and E. L. Quarantelli. 1967. "Scapegoats, Villains, and Disasters." *Transaction* 4: 12–17.

Dynes, Russell R. and E. L. Quarantelli. 1968a. "Group Behavior Under Stress: A Required Convergence of Organizational and Collective Behavior Perspectives." *Sociology and Social Research* 52: 416–26.

———. 1968b. "What Looting in Civil Disturbances Really Means." *Transaction* 5: 9–14.

Elsner, Henry, Jr. 1972. Introduction to *The Crowd and the Public,* by R. Park. Pp. vii–xxvi. Chicago: University of Chicago Press, edited by H. Elsner, Jr.

Erikson, Kai T. 1976. *Everything in Its Path: Destruction of Community in the Buffalo Creek Flood.* New York: Simon and Schuster.

———. 1994. *New Species of Troubles.* New York: Norton.

Faris, Robert E. L. 1970. *Chicago Sociology, 1920–1932.* Chicago: University of Chicago Press.

Ferree, Myra Marx and Frederick D. Miller. 1985. "Mobilization and Meaning:

Toward an Integration of Social Movements." *Sociological Inquiry* 55: 38–51.

Gamson, William A. (1975) 1990. *The Strategy of Social Protest.* Homewood, Ill.: Dorsey.

Gamson, William A., Bruce Fireman, and Steven Rytina. 1982. *Encounters with Unjust Authority.* Homewood Ill.: Dorsey.

Goffman, Erving. 1959. *The Presentation of Self in Everyday Life.* New York: Anchor/Doubleday.

———. 1961. *Encounters.* Indianapolis: Bobbs-Merrill.

———. 1974. *Frame Analysis.* New York: Harper Colophon.

Gusfield, Joseph R. 1963. *Symbolic Crusade: Status Politics and the American Temperance Movement.* Urbana: University of Illinois Press.

———. 1966. "Functional Areas of Leadership in Social Movements." *Sociological Quarterly* 7: 137–56.

———. 1968. "The Study of Social Movements." Pp. 438–52 in *The International Encyclopedia of the Social Sciences.* New York: Crowell, Collier, and Macmillan.

———. 1970. "Introduction: A Definition of the Subject." Pp. 1–8 in *Protest, Reform, and Revolt: A Reader in Social Movements,* edited by J. Gusfield. New York: Wiley.

———. 1978. "Historical Problematics and Sociological Fields: American Liberalism and the Study of Social Movements." *Research in Sociology of Knowledge, Science and Art* 1: 121–49.

———. 1980. "The Modernity of Social Movements: Public Roles and Private Parts." Pp. 290–307 in *Societal Growth,* edited by A. Hawley. New York: The Free Press.

———. 1981a. *The Culture of Public Problems: Drinking-Driving and the Symbolic Order.* University of Chicago Press.

———. 1981b. "Social Movements and Social Change: Perspectives of Linearity and Fluidity." *Social Movements, Conflict and Change* 4: 317–39.

———. 1984. "Passage to Play: The Ritual of Drink in Industrial Society." In *The Anthropology of Drink, Hospitality and Competition,* edited by M. Douglas. Cambridge: Cambridge University Press.

Gusfield, Joseph R. and Jerzy Michalowicz. 1984. "Secular Symbolism: Studies of Ritual, Ceremony, and the Symbolic Order in Modern Life." *Annual Review of Sociology* 10: 417–35.

Hoffer, Eric. 1951. *The True Believer: Thoughts on the Nature of Mass Movements.* New York: New American Library.

Jackson, Maurice, Eleanora Petersen, James Bull, Sverre Monsen, and Patricia Richmond. 1960. "The Failure of an Incipient Social Movement." *Pacific Sociological Review* 3: 35–40.

Janowitz, Morris. 1968. *Social Control of Escalated Riots.* Chicago: University of Chicago Press.

———. 1979. "Collective Racial Violence: A Contemporary History." Pp. 261–86 in *Violence in America: Historical and Comparative Perspectives,* edited by

H. Davis Graham and T. Gurr. Revised Edition. Beverly Hills: Sage Publications.

Jenkins, Craig. 1983. "Resource Mobilization Theory and the Study of Social Movements." *Annual Review of Sociology* 9: 527–53.

Jenkins, Craig and Charles Perrow. 1977. "Insurgency of the Powerless: Farm Workers' Movement." *American Sociological Review* 42: 249–68.

Johnson, Chalmers. 1966. *Revolutionary Change.* Boston: Little, Brown.

Killian, Lewis. 1964. "Social Movements." Pp. 426–55 in *Handbook of Modern Sociology,* edited by R. E. L. Faris. Chicago: Rand McNally.

———. 1968. *The Impossible Revolution?* New York: Random House.

———. 1980. "Theory of Collective Behavior: The Mainstream Revisited." Pp. 275–89 in *Sociological Theory and Research: A Critical Appraisal,* edited by H. M. Blalock, Jr. New York: The Free Press.

———. 1984. "Organization, Rationality and Spontaneity in the Civil Rights Movement." *American Sociological Review* 49: 770–83.

Klandermans, Bert. 1984. "Mobilization and Participation: Social-Psychological Expansions of Resource Mobilization Theory." *American Sociological Review* 49: 583–600.

Klapp, Orrin. 1964. *Symbolic Leaders.* Chicago: Aldine.

———. 1969. *Collective Search for Identity.* New York: Holt, Rinehart and Winston.

———. 1972. *Currents of Unrest: An Introduction to Collective Behavior.* New York: Holt, Rinehart, and Winston.

———. 1991. *Inflation of Symbols: Loss of Values in American Culture.* Rutgers: Transaction Press.

Kornhauser, William. 1959. *The Politics of Mass Society.* New York: The Free Press.

———. 1968. "Mass Society." Pp. 58–64 in *International Encyclopedia of the Social Sciences,* volume 10, edited by D. Sills. New York: Macmillan and The Free Press.

———. 1962. "Social Bases of Political Commitment." Pp. 321–39 in *Human Behavior and Social Processes,* edited by A. M. Rose. Boston: Houghton Mifflin.

Lang, Kurt and Gladys Engel Lang. 1953. "The Unique Perspective of Television and Its Effect: A Pilot Study." *American Sociological Review* 18: 3–12.

———. 1960. "Decision for Christ: Billy Graham in New York City." Pp. 415–27 in *Identity and Anxiety,* edited by M. R. Stein, A. Vidich and D. White. Glencoe: The Free Press.

———. 1961. *Collective Dynamics.* New York: Thomas Y. Crowell.

———. 1968. "Collective Behavior." Pp. 556–64 in *International Encyclopedia of the Social Sciences,* volume 10, edited by D. Sills. New York: Macmillan and The Free Press.

———. 1976. "Planning for Emergency Operations." *Mass Emergencies* 1: 107–17.

———. 1978. "Polling on Watergate: The Battle for Public Opinion." *Public Opinion Quarterly* 44: 530–47.

————. 1983. *The Battle for Public Opinion: The President, the Press, and the Polls During Watergate.* New York: Columbia University Press.

————. 1987. "The Future Study of Public Opinion: A Symposium." *Public Opinion Quarterly* 51, 4:S173-S191.

LeBon, Gustave [1895] 1960. *The Crowd: A Study of the Popular Mind.* New York: Viking.

Lofland, John and Rodney Stark. 1965. "Becoming a World-Saver: A Theory of Conversion to a Deviant Perspective." *American Sociological Review* 30: 862–74.

Mauss, Armand. 1975. *Social Problems as Social Movements.* New York: Lippincott.

McAdam, Doug, John McCarthy and Mayer Zald. 1988. "Social Movements." Pp. 695–737 in *Handbook of Sociology,* edited by N. Smelser. Beverly Hills: Sage.

McAdam, Doug. 1982. *Political Process and the Development of Black Insurgency, 1930–1970.* Chicago: University of Chicago Press.

————. 1983. "Tactical Innovation and the Pace of Insurgency." *American Sociological Review* 48: 735–54.

————. 1988. *Freedom Summer: The Idealists Revisited.* New York: Oxford University Press.

McCarthy, John D. 1991. Foreword. Pp. xi-xviii in *The Myth of the Madding Crowd* by Clark McPhail. New York: Aldine de Gruyter.

McPhail, Clark. 1991. *The Myth of the Madding Crowd.* New York: Aldine de Gruyter.

Marx, Gary T. and James L. Wood. 1975. "Strands of Theory and Research in Collective Behavior." Pp. 363–428 in *Annual Review of Sociology,* vol. 1, edited by A. Inkeles, J. Coleman, and N. Smelser. Palo Alto: Annual Reviews.

Mead, George Herbert. 1934. *Mind, Self, and Society.* Chicago: University of Chicago Press.

————. 1938. *The Philosophy of the Act,* edited by Merritt H. Moore. Chicago: University of Chicago Press.

Meltzer, Bernard N. and John W. Petras. 1970. "The Chicago and Iowa Schools of Symbolic Interactionism." Pp. 3–17 in *Human Nature and Collective Behavior: Papers in Honor of Herbert Blumer,* edited by T. Shibutani. Englewood Cliffs: Prentice-Hall.

Meltzer, Bernard N., John W. Petras, and Larry T. Reynolds. 1978. "Varieties of Symbolic Interactionism." Pp. 41–57 in *Symbolic Interaction: A Reader in Social Psychology.* Third edition, edited by J. Manis and B. Meltzer. Boston: Allyn and Bacon.

Melucci, Alberto. 1990. *Nomads of the Present: Social Movements and Individual Needs in Modern Society.* Philadelphia: Temple University Press.

Morris, Aldon D. 1984. *The Origins of the Civil Rights Movement: Black Communities Organizing for Change.* New York: The Free Press.

Morris, Aldon D. and Cedric Herring. 1988. "Theory and Research in Social Movements: A Critical Review." Pp. 137–98 in *Annual Review of Political Behavior,* volume 2, edited by Samuel Long. Boulder: Westview Press.

Oberschall, Anthony. 1973. *Social Conflict and Social Movements*. Englewood Cliffs: Prentice-Hall.

Park, Robert. 1927. "Human Nature and Collective Behavior." *American Journal of Sociology* 32: 733–41.

Park, Robert E. and Ernest W. Burgess. 1921. *Introduction to the Science of Sociology*. Chicago: University of Chicago Press.

Parsons, Talcott. 1954. *Toward a General Theory of Action*. Cambridge: Harvard University Press.

———. 1963. "Social Strains in America: A Postscript." Pp. 193–99 in *The Radical Right*, edited by D. Bell. Garden City: Doubleday.

Quarantelli, E. L. 1954. "The Nature and Conditions of Panic." *American Journal of Sociology* 60: 267–75.

———. 1970. "Emergent Accommodation Groups: Beyond Current Collective Behavior Typologies." Pp. 111–23 in *Human Nature and Collective Behavior: Papers in Honor of Herbert Blumer*, edited by T. Shibutani. Englewood Cliffs: Prentice-Hall.

———. 1989. "The Social Science Study of Disasters and Mass Communication." Pp. 1–19 in *Bad Tidings: Communication and Catastrophe*, edited by L. Walters, L. Wilkins, and T. Walters. Hillsdale, N.J.: Lawrence Erlbaum.

Quarantelli, E. L. and Russell Dynes. 1968. "Looting in Civil Disorders: An Index of Social Change." Pp. 131–41 in *Riots and Rebellion*, edited by Louis Masotti and Don R. Bowen. Beverly Hills: Sage.

———. 1970. "Property Norms and Looting." *Phylon* 31: 168–82.

Quarantelli, E. L. and Dennis Wenger. 1973. "A Voice from the Thirteenth Century: The Characteristics and Conditions for the Emergence of A Ouija Board Cult." *Urban Life and Culture* 1: 379–400.

Reynolds, Larry T. and C. McCart. 1972. "The Institutional Basis of Theoretical Diversity." *Sociological Focus* 5:16–39.

Shibutani, Tamotsu. 1966. *Improvised News: A Sociological Study of Rumor*. Indianapolis: Bobbs-Merrill.

———. 1970. "On the Personification of Adversaries." Pp. 223–33 in *Human Nature and Collective Behavior: Papers in Honor of Herbert Blumer*, edited by T. Shibutani. Englewood Cliffs: Prentice-Hall.

———. 1986. *Social Process: An Introduction to Sociology*. Berkeley: University of California Press.

———. 1988. "Herbert Blumer's Contributions to Twentieth-century Sociology." *Symbolic Interaction* 11: 23–31.

Smelser, Neil J. 1963. *Theory of Collective Behavior*. New York: The Free Press of Glencoe.

———. 1972. "Some Additional Thoughts on Collective Behavior." *Sociological Inquiry* 42: 97–101.

Snow, David A. and Robert D. Benford. 1988. "Ideology, Frame Resonance, and Participant Mobilization." *International Social Movement Research* 1: 197–217.

———. 1992. "Master Frames and Cycles of Protest." Pp. 133–55 in *Frontiers in*

Social Movement Theory, edited by A. Morris and C. Mueller. New Haven: Yale University Press.

Snow, David A. and Pamela E. Oliver. 1995. "Social Movements and Collective Behavior: Social Psychological Dimensions and Considerations." Pp. 571–99 in *Sociological Perspectives on Social Psychology,* edited by Karen Cook, Gary Alan Fine, and James S. House. New York: Allyn and Bacon.

Snow, David A., E. Burke Rochford, Jr., Steven K. Worden, and Robert D. Benford. 1986. "Frame Alignment Processes, Micromobilization, and Movement Participation." *American Sociological Review* 51: 464–81.

Snow, David, Louis Zurcher and Robert Peters. 1981. "Victory Celebrations as Theater: A Dramaturgical Approach to Crowd Behavior." *Symbolic Interaction* 4: 21–42.

Strauss, Anselm. 1944. "The Literature on Panic." *Journal of Abnormal Social Psychology* 39: 317–28.

———. 1947. "Research in Collective Behavior: Neglect and Need." *American Sociological Review* 12:352–54.

Stryker, Sheldon. 1988. "Substance and Style: An Appraisal of the Sociological Legacy of Herbert Blumer." *Symbolic Interaction* 11:33–42.

Suttles, Gerald D. 1985. "A Tribute to Morris Janowitz." Pp. 3–12 in *The Challenge of Social Control: Citizenship and Institution Building in Modern Society, Essays in Honor of Morris Janowitz,* edited by G. Suttles and M. Zald. Norwood, N.J.: Ablex Publishing Corporation.

Tarde, Gabriel. 1890. *The Laws of Imitation.* New York: Holt.

Taylor, Verta and Nancy Whittier. 1992. "Collective Identity in Social Movement Communities: Lesbian Feminist Mobilization." Pp. 104–29 in *Frontiers in Social Movement Theory,* edited by A. Morris and C. Mueller. New Haven: Yale University Press.

Tilly, Charles. 1978. *From Mobilization to Revolution.* Reading, Mass.: Addison-Wesley.

Tilly, Charles, Louise Tilly, and Richard Tilly. 1975. *The Rebellious Century.* Cambridge: Harvard University Press.

Turner, Ralph H. 1958. "Needed Research in Collective Behavior." *Sociology and Social Research* 42: 461–65.

———. 1964a. "Collective Behavior." Pp. 382–425 in *Handbook of Modern Sociology,* edited by Robert E. L. Faris. Chicago: Rand McNally.

———. 1964b. "New Theoretical Frameworks." *Sociological Quarterly* 5:122–32.

———. 1967. Introduction. Pp. ix-xlvi in *Robert Park on Social Control and Collective Behavior,* edited by R. Turner. Chicago: University of Chicago Press.

———. 1969a. "The Theme of Contemporary Social Movements." *British Journal of Sociology* 20:390–405.

———. 1969b. "The Public Perception of Protest." *American Sociological Review* 34: 815–31.

———. 1970. "Determinants of Social Movement Strategies." Pp. 145–64 in *Human Nature and Collective Behavior: Papers in Honor of Herbert Blumer,* edited by T. Shibutani. Englewood Cliffs: Prentice-Hall.

220   David A. Snow and Phillip W. Davis

————. 1975. "Is There a Quest for Identity?" *Sociological Quarterly* 16:148–61.
————. 1981. "Collective Behavior and Resource Mobilization as Approaches to Social Movements: Issues and Continuities." *Research in Social Movements, Conflict and Change* 4:1–24.
————. 1983a. "Figure and Ground in the Analysis of Social Movements." *Symbolic Interaction* 6: 175–82.
————. 1983b. "Waiting for Disaster: Changing Reactions to Earthquake Forecasts in Southern California." *International Journal of Mass Emergencies and Disasters* 1:307–34.
————. 1988. "Collective Behavior without Guile: Chicago in the Late 1940s." *Sociological Perspectives* 31:315–24.
Turner, Ralph and Lewis Killian. 1957. *Collective Behavior.* Englewood-Cliffs: Prentice-Hall.
————. 1972. *Collective Behavior.* Second edition. Englewood-Cliffs: Prentice-Hall.
————. 1987. *Collective Behavior.* Third edition. Englewood-Cliffs: Prentice-Hall.
Turner, Ralph H. and Samuel Surace. 1956 . "Zoot-Suiters and Mexicans: Symbols in Crowd Behavior." *American Journal of Sociology* 62:14–20.
Weller, Jack and E. L. Quarantelli. 1973. "Neglected Characteristics of Collective Behavior." *American Journal of Sociology* 79:665–85.
Wenger, Dennis E. 1987. "Collective Behavior and Disaster Research." Pp. 213–38 in *Sociology of Disasters,* edited by R. Dynes, B. DeMarchi, and C. Pelanda. Milan: Franco Angeli.
Wood, James L. and Maurice Jackson. 1982. *Social Movements: Development, Participation and Dynamics.* Belmont: Wadsworth.
Zald, Mayer N. 1992. "Looking Backward to Look Forward: Reflections on the Past and Future of the Resource Mobilization Program." Pp. 326–48 in *Frontiers in Social Movement Theory,* edited by A. Morris and C. Mueller. New Haven: Yale University Press.
Zald, Mayer N. and John D. McCarthy. 1987. *Social Movements in an Organizational Society.* New Brunswick: Transaction Books.
Zurcher, Louis A. and David A. Snow. 1981. "Collective Behavior: Social Movements." Pp. 447–82 in *Social Psychology,* edited by R. Turner and M. Rosenberg. New York: Basic Books.
Zygmunt, Joseph F. 1970. "Prophetic Failure and Chiliastic Identity: The Case of the Jehovah's Witnesses." *American Journal of Sociology* 75: 926–48.
————. 1972. "Movements and Motives: Some Unresolved Issues in the Psychology of Social Movements." *Human Relations* 25: 449–67.

CHAPTER SEVEN

Transition and Tradition:

Departmental Faculty in the Era of the

Second Chicago School

Andrew Abbott and Emanuel Gaziano

To graduate students, faculty are a familiar yet distant group. Students sometimes know the parties and the factions, the friendships and the hostilities. They may know individual faculty well. But they do not know the enduring memories—the bitter votes, the near-miss hires, the aggrandizements—that honeycomb an academic department. A mass of collective memory removes the world of faculty from that of students.

To the students in the University of Chicago's Department of Sociology in the years 1945–60, the department's collective being must indeed have seemed both immediate and remote. It was immediate because the department was small while students were many: because the faculty, then as now, engaged students directly in its research. At the same time it was remote because the principal faculty had known each other so well for so long. Burgess had been on the faculty since 1916, Ogburn since 1927, Wirth and Blumer since 1931, Warner since 1935, Hughes since 1938. Four of these—Burgess, Blumer, Wirth, and Hughes—had been Chicago students before becoming faculty. Some of the "new faculty" were old faces, too. Although Hauser had been in Washington for a decade before his own return in 1947, he too had been an instructor and a graduate student in the 1930s.[1]

In 1951–52, the core of this tight group disappeared. Ogburn and Burgess retired (although circumstances forced Burgess to remain another year).[2] Blumer went to Berkeley. Wirth died. Only Hughes, Warner, and Hauser remained. There were some new faculty. In 1950 Leo Goodman had been recruited by Wirth and Hauser from Princeton. Demographer Donald Bogue moved onto the regular faculty from his replacement teaching job midway through the 1950s. (These two were the only faculty members recruited in the period who would end up seeing long Chicago service.) Other than these few, however, the working faculty throughout the postwar period comprised mainly assistant professors. Often these were locals who stayed briefly before departing: Edward Shils (1945–47, returning [as professor] in 1957), William Foote Whyte (1945–48), Harold Wilensky (1952–53).[3] A few remained longer: Herbert Goldhamer (1947–51), Albert Reiss (1948–52), Otis Dudley Duncan (1951–57), D. G. Moore (1951–55), and Anselm Strauss (1952–58). And a few short-service professors came from outside the Chicago orbit: Assistant (later Associate) Professor Donald Horton (1951–57) and Assistant Professor Nelson Foote (1952–56).[4] David Riesman came into the department from the university's college faculty in 1954, but left in 1958. Associate Professor William Bradbury (1952–58) was another college-related appointment. There also began in 1954 a string of recruitments of recent Columbia Ph.D.'s; Peter Blau (1954–63), Elihu Katz (1955–70), Peter Rossi (1956–67), Allan Barton (1957), and James Coleman (1957–59, returning in 1973).

In terms of faculty present, then, the years 1945–60 included the last five years of the old faculty regime and a somewhat longer period of transition. In discussing the faculty who taught the students who were to become the "second Chicago school," this chapter aims to understand that faculty's experience of a turning point in sociology. We begin with an analysis of the department in its university context. We then focus our intellectual discussion on a Ford-Foundation-funded self-study of 1951–52. For a year, the department argued with itself about the nature and future of sociology and about its own role in that nature and future. The discussion, the position papers, and the documents all survive, thanks to Ernest Burgess. Here we can see in detail the mind of the department in which the second Chicago school took shape.

The common understanding of Chicago's history in the postwar period is that after the last of old department faded in the early 1950s, the department turned remorselessly towards quantification. Some understood this change as the twilight of Parkian sociology fading into the night of mindless empiricism. For others it was the rising of true science out of the midnight shackles of opinion and error. Fortunately, one needn't choose between these interpretations. What happened was far more complex than a sun rising or setting. And it tells us much more about quantification, observation, science, and theory than can any one-directional story.

Throughout, we have worked at a very detailed level. We have two aims in so doing. The first is historical. We wish to present conclusive evidence on aspects of the department's history that are presently the subject of much published and unpublished speculation. But there is also a theoretical reason for the detail. We wish to make the history of the faculty in this period so immediate as to de-objectify it, bringing the reader below the level of the "there was a steady move towards quantitative work" narrative. If we can make readers see this faculty as a group much like themselves, fighting all the usual academic battles with all the usual bizarre alliances, we can reopen the issue of what it means to speak of "a school." Once it is clear that no one faculty member stood for any absolutely consistent and unified position, we can begin to reflect on how coherent positions exist as collective relationships and emergent symbols above the bricolage of the individuals. That reflection then transforms the question of "how does a school or tradition get created" into the question of how a group of bricoleurs can through interaction produce and maintain an apparently coherent set of traditions. We take this last to be the central issue of analyzing a first or a second Chicago school.

THE DEPARTMENT'S ENVIRONMENTS

In the immediate postwar years, the University of Chicago was best known not for its graduate schools but for its charismatic chancellor, Robert Maynard Hutchins, and the revolutionary College he had created. By this time, the "Hutchins College" had a curriculum of four years of required courses. It allowed few electives, and those only in the last two years. It admitted students directly from the tenth grade on the basis of examination. Its education was largely aimed at great books and great ideas.

This extraordinary experimental college had its own faculty. Hutchins had abolished the university-wide Faculty of Arts and Sciences and assembled departments into Humanities, and Social, Physical, and Biological Sciences Divisions. The College faculty were themselves such a separate division, and thus many faculty pursuing what was elsewhere called sociology were located not in the department but in the College. David Riesman was best known of these, but in the late 1940s his co-instructors in "Soc 2" (the second of the three year-long, required, social science sequences) included Daniel Bell, Lewis Coser, Murray Wax, Howard Becker, Joel Seidman, Mark Benney, Phillip Rieff, Benjamin Nelson, Joseph Gusfield, and Reuel Denney (MacAloon 1992). Other sociologists, both faculty (Wirth) and students (Janowitz), taught in other Social Science Core courses. Hiring in the College had little to do with academic credentials; most of these people had no degree, although some—like Gusfield, Wax, Becker, and Janowitz, for example—were local graduate students. (Of the departmental faculty only three, Shils, Bradbury, and Riesman, had actual joint appointments in the College.)

The College "sociologists" shared with their College colleagues an intense but general intellectual commitment, something that for Hutchins was explicitly opposed to routine academic work. Hutchins's love of high thoughts and classic texts made him distinctly hostile to empirical science. His repugnance for empirical social science in particular was unconcealed. As a result, the Division of Social Sciences, and with it the Department of Sociology, did not fare well during the Hutchins years (Bulmer 1984, 202ff.).

In January 1951, Hutchins, then only fifty-one, unexpectedly resigned. His replacement was Lawrence Kimpton, a philosopher who had become a career administrator (Ashmore 1989). Although Kimpton did not immediately destroy the Hutchins College, by 1955 it was clear that he would ultimately do so (McNeill 1991). Free-floating intellectuals who had been purely college faculty began needing homes elsewhere. Such considerations brought David Riesman into the sociology department, with the support of Hughes (then chair) and social science dean Morton Grodzins, but in the face of sustained opposition from Philip Hauser (Riesman 1990).

The animus between department and College that developed in the Hutchins years had a long-standing effect on the department; it guaranteed that the department would not make a distinguished record in general sociological theory, precisely the kind of work represented by Riesman, Shils, and Bell in the Hutchins College. Although department members disagreed about many things, the various factions united in their antipathy to Hutchins's views. Even the diplomatic Ernest Burgess resented Hutchins's attitudes, as did Lloyd Warner and Philip Hauser (Farber 1988, 349–50).

Shils's career illustrates the results of this feud. Originally appointed jointly in sociology and the College, Shils moved out of both into the Committee on Social Thought in 1947. Social Thought was one of Hutchins's pet creations: a collection of great intellectuals free to browse at will in social knowledge but aimed against "narrow specialism." To Hutchins, theoretical and empirical work on society were intellectually and departmentally separate affairs. To be sure, Shils eventually reentered the Department of Sociology (in 1957) and Donald Levine, another theorist, was hired in 1962 (after a period of fieldwork that made him acceptably empirical). But both were marginalized. (At a graduate-student party in 1955,

Hauser had publicly announced his opposition to Levine's thesis proposal.) Yet in these very years, Riesman and Bell (inter alia) built the "theoretical" careers that eventually made them central members of the Harvard Social Relations pantheon. At the same time, Shils was collaborating with Parsons at Harvard in the Carnegie Foundation–sponsored work on the "general theory of action." "Theory" was thus an active area in sociology. But most of the department wanted none of it. Nor was this anti-theory prejudice a matter of quantitative researchers only; Warner and Hughes also opposed the concept of dissertations in theory.[5]

The College was not the only external university force shaping the department during this era. The university's small size and interdisciplinary character meant that faculty had important extradepartmental commitments. The National Opinion Research Center (NORC), a nonprofit survey house founded in 1941, was one of these. NORC moved to Chicago from Colorado in 1947, a move required by sociologist Clyde Hart as a condition of his taking the job as NORC director. Hart, who like Warner had only a B.A., became a full professor of sociology. Under the Hart regime (till 1960), NORC principally housed researchers funding themselves on external grants. (The contract survey arm, which was to dominate NORC's funding in later years, matured only under Peter Rossi in the early 1960s.) All study directors at NORC during the Hart era were either recruited from, graduates of, or courtesy faculty in the sociology department, including Hart himself, Josephine Williams, Shirley Star, Eli Marks, Jack Elinson, Ethel Shanas, and Louis Kriesberg. At one point, late in the 1950s, sociology faculty feared block voting by the NORC contingent and moved to lessen the NORC presence.[6]

But other units drew faculty attention and commitment as well. The Committee on Human Development (HD), for example, was another of Hutchins's interdisciplinary centers for reflective, qualitative social science, dating from the early 1940s. Burgess, Hughes, and above all Warner put much of their time and effort into HD, whose offices were then in Judd Hall, two blocks from the sociology department. The central figure in HD was Ralph Tyler, professor of education, who became dean of the Division in 1946 and remained so until 1953. Tyler, an aggressive power-broker centrally located in university politics, played a determining role in sociology during this period.[7]

Another external tie was with the Industrial Relations Center, whose affiliates included Wilensky, Moore, and Blumer, the latter capitalizing on his experience in mediation. There was also the Committee on Education,

Teaching, and Research in Race Relations, an interdisciplinary study center of which Wirth was chair. (And over which he had fought with Hughes [R. Turner 1988, 317].) There was the Family Studies Center, for which Burgess had raised the money and of which Foote was the first director.[8]

Yet another research center was the Chicago Community Inventory, a mile away in NORC's building at 4901 S. Ellis. Run by Hauser, the CCI was a center for his students and protégés. The money for CCI had originally been raised by Wirth and Burgess, but the whole operation was gladly given to Hauser on his return. As director of studies of Chicago communities, Hauser was quite explicitly the heir of the Chicago school in the eyes of Burgess and Wirth, whatever retrospective judgment makes of the matter.[9]

The research centers were the centers of department activity, particularly for the younger faculty. Daily life was spent less in the Social Science building itself than in whatever quarters one's research center occupied. (Hence the invisibility of any particular faculty member to students not located in that member's center. Recall that most faculty did not teach undergraduates.) Moreover, much time was spent hustling for research money, and much effort spent eking out what money was found. A fundamental faculty schism emerged in this period to divide the hustlers—both the wealthy and the would-be wealthy—from the nonhustlers. Paralleling this was a distinction between bureaucratic and artisanal research. Only a few—Hughes is a conspicuous example—had feet in both camps. Wirth and Blumer tended to work alone, while Duncan and others were collaborators, and Hauser, increasingly, was a large-scale bureaucrat.

DEPARTMENT AND ADMINISTRATION

But the College and the external centers played less of a role in shaping the department than did the administration. For the documents leave little doubt that in the eyes of the university administration the department was more or less "in receivership" from 1950 to 1957. If we take as a working definition of receivership the breaching of a department's control over its appointments, the receivership period probably runs from 1950 to 1953. The only way to understand the detailed history of the faculty in the period 1945–60 is to work carefully through the department's relation to the administrations: chancellors Hutchins (to 1951) and Kimpton (after 1951) and deans Ralph Tyler (1946–53), Morton Grodzins (1954), and Chauncy Harris (1954–60).

The central theme of administrative discontent was insularity. In a letter to Hutchins, Tyler contemptuously described Ogburn's research proposals of 1950 as hopelessly out of date. Seven years later, Hauser would still be justifying his personnel policies to a new dean by crowing about how few Chicago graduates the department was now hiring.[10]

The sources of this attitude are obscure. It is possible that Tyler was influenced by Hutchins's own long-standing dislike of Louis Wirth, one of the department's central figures. And certainly concerns about insularity would not have been allayed by the recruitment of old Chicagoan Hauser from the Census in 1946–47. But overall, it seems more likely that worries about Chicago insularity reflected the realities of disciplinary change. Harvard was emerging as a prime force in theory, as Columbia was in empirical research. As the administration heard about these fads—and administrations do hear about them whether departments like it or not— it may have begun to worry that the middle generation of Wirth, Hauser, Hughes, Warner, and Blumer (four of the five being local Ph.D.'s) was not of the same disciplinary eminence as the senior generation of Burgess and Ogburn.

In a curious way, this result was inevitable. Nationwide, university enrollments soared after the war, never to stop soaring until the late 1970s. The consequent seller's market for academic talent put the department in an unexpectedly weak position precisely when it needed to rebuild for a coming generation. One can read the changes here discussed as simply the department's desperate response to this changed structural condition.

The administration's already antagonistic attitude toward sociology began to worsen in the immediate postwar period. Shils, one of Hutchins's favorites, left the department for the Committee on Social Thought in 1947, giving as his reason a Hutchinsonian desire to think broadly about society. At the same time, Hauser was returning as heir apparent to the Burgess/Wirth wing of empirical sociology. It undoubtedly did not help that Hauser and Wirth were close friends (Wirth found Hauser his Chicago house) nor that Hauser, who had taken a substantial pay cut to come to Chicago, immediately became active in the faculty's attempt to overturn the "4E regulations" that effectively forbade faculty consulting.[11]

It was clear to all that the department was about to face a major turning point. The retirements of Ogburn and Burgess were expected, and the university did not continue even the most eminent of faculty beyond the age of sixty-five. Moreover, the administration's fears of departmental insularity were not unfounded. In thinking about replacement, Burgess thought first of locals: "In considering personnel for the department, it seems to me that we should take account of our own PhD's." The department did do just that, for Dudley Duncan was recruited to return to Chicago, after brief sojourns at Penn State and Wisconsin, in the spring of 1951.[12]

But the first clear indication that the transition would be problematic was the department's curious inability to replace Herbert Goldhamer. When he found out that Goldhamer would not return from his year's leave in Washington, Ogburn (acting chair for Burgess) considered continuing Shibutani (a recent Blumer Ph.D. then teaching on a three-year appointment), getting Ellsworth Faris to come back and teach with Shibutani (Faris was seventy-six at this point), or "bring[ing] Robert Faris here for a quarter or so from Seattle if his father isn't considered a possibility." That the latter two expedients were considered suggests both insularity and a kind of desperation. Meanwhile, the department tried, and failed, to secure a substantial teaching commitment from Josephine Williams, a recent Chicago Ph.D. who turned them down to go full-time at NORC.[13]

Yet the list of candidates for positions in late 1950 suggests either that the department was in fact looking outside or that it had already succumbed to administration pressure to do so. In a letter of 30 October (to Blumer EWB 3:1), Burgess lists those under consideration for tenured appointments in social psychology: Newcomb, Dollard, and Goldhamer (i.e., to be reprieved and promoted). Outside social psychology, the potential hires were Frederick Stephan, Conrad Taeuber, and Hans Speier. Potential untenured hires, seen by Burgess as fallbacks, included Jack Seeley, Herbert Hyman, Arnold Rose, Philip Selznick, and Otis Dudley Duncan. Some of these were Chicago graduates, but some were not.

But matters were moving above the department level as well. In 1950, there was a concerted attempt, unmentioned in Burgess's letter, to entice Robert Merton and Paul Lazarsfeld to Chicago. Merton was impressed. He had always admired both university and department. Lazarsfeld was less interested, perhaps because of his market-research client base in New York, perhaps for family reasons. The two had agreed to act together, so Lazarsfeld's ultimate unwillingness meant that they remained in New York. The administration was to attempt to hire Merton and Lazarsfeld (separately) later in the decade.[14]

Another departmental strategy for handling the transition was seeking long-run active status for the retiring Burgess and Ogburn. Both refused. In Ogburn's case, the refusal was quite heartfelt. "For four or five years I have been taking less and less interest in University affairs, its committees, in thinking and planning for the Department of Sociology and the University. It might indeed be said that I have, in view of my impending retirement, been neglecting this phase of my work." By contrast, Burgess was still advising the occasional student in the mid-1950s. It may have been very consequential for the department that Ogburn gave so little help in the transition.[15]

At this very time, late in 1950, the department sent forward to Dean Tyler the name of Louis Wirth as chair to succeed the retiring Burgess. Wirth had certainly waited his turn; he had been on the faculty for twenty years. He was without question the central figure in the department. Close to Burgess, he was also best friend in the department of both Hauser and Blumer, as well as a long-standing acquaintance of Clyde Hart. To be sure, his relations with Hughes were less close (although they collaborated on the Chicago school desegregation study) and he got along badly with Warner (but Warner was to some extent marginalized in Human Development). But overall Wirth was probably the central actor in the active department at this point. Unfortunately, he was detested by the administration, largely because his outspoken criticism of the university's position in the community. Tyler turned Wirth down, requiring the department to think again. Meanwhile, Burgess remained chair, a situation that persisted off and on for nearly two years after his retirement.[16]

By 1951 the department was forced to heed the administration message a little more effectively. The department agreed to meet and discuss "the likely trends in the different fields of sociology and what the department of sociology at the University of Chicago could do in regard to this development." Burgess's annual report of 1951 shows that the department's one (failed) senior recruitment was external, and of the junior recruitments one was internal (Duncan), one mixed (Horton had worked with Ogburn for four years), and one external (Foote, who nonetheless was directly tied to Chicago through his mentor, Leonard Cottrell.) Burgess viewed the planned "faculty seminar" (the Ford Foundation self-study discussed below) as an attempt to fight off the administration's claim that the department lacked intellectual depth. The annual report itself was the first such document, part of a planned effort to increase information to both administration and faculty.[17]

Burgess's drafts for an undated "departmental aims" document of 1951 show what the various faculty then had in mind. He recorded his conversations with each faculty member. Duncan talked at length about his mentor William Sewell.[18] Hart, not surprisingly, wanted better integration with NORC. Wirth told Burgess to play to departmental strengths and to avoid the new grand theory. "The Problems we wish to deal with are actual problems existing in the world and not conjured up problems. There is a clamor for theory with contemplation; we should study social life and not abstract from it." Hughes, too, toed the Chicago line; he told Burgess of the tradition of sending students into the city, of following problems where they lead, and of making use of the city.

The outsiders gave slightly different advice. Goodman told Burgess to get as many top-notch people as he could. He emphasized divergence of views. Horton, like Wirth, emphasized playing to strengths, but insisted that the new systematized theory had to be taken seriously. Warner's lengthy comments mainly concerned his own area of social organization.

The document that came from these conversations was entitled "Objectives and Program of the Department of Sociology." Like the discussions, it shows that the drift toward eclecticism was coupled with a very firm sense of and confidence in the Chicago tradition. The department's objectives were to be:

1. The development of a sound body of sociological theory inter-related with social life and empirical research.
2. Cooperation with the other social sciences.
3. The all-around training of our students.
4. The selection of those areas for research in which we can make the most significant contributions.
5. Emphasis on ideas rather than organization.
6. Revival of the publication program of the department.
7. A research program in:
   urban problems—CCI, Planning Department, NORC
   stratification/mass society—Duncan, Foote, Hauser, Horton, Hughes, Warner, Wirth
   intellectual life of the city—[what would now be called urban culture]
   social trends[19]

This was in fact a profoundly conservative document. In its own eyes, at least, the department saw the stratification area as the only seriously new area for departmental research, and Warner had already given that area a strong Chicago accent. Thus, while faculty were willing to think somewhat eclectically in terms of hiring strategy, most still had a pretty clear idea that Chicago stood, and should stand, for a particular approach to social science, enshrined in the justification for objective 1, a sound body of sociological theory interrelated with social life and empirical research:

> This contribution is timely in view of the present trends in sociology and would counteract certain existing tendencies to develop sociological theory out of abstractions with little or no relation to social phenomena. By making this contribution, the Department would exercise a balancing and steadying influence in the sociological field.

There is little question who is the enemy.

Throughout the late 1940s and early 1950s, a crucial factor exacerbating internal problems and relations with students and with the administration was the lengthy absence of key department members. Blumer spent much of 1946 as full-time chair of the arbitration board solving a Pittsburgh steel strike. Hughes spent much of 1948 in Frankfurt, helping to get the university there going after the war. Wirth spent time on leave in Stanford, Paris, and Beirut. Perpetually on the move, Hauser had returned to Washington in 1949 as acting director of the Census, failing to get the permanent directorship because he attempted to defend the Census against the Democratic patronage machine and was then faced with trumped-up loyalty charges. His return to Chicago was brief, for he immediately left on a fifteen-month sojourn in Burma as census advisor. Blumer, too, was absent on a long leave (at the University of Hawaii) in 1950. Hughes spent time at Columbia.[20]

The year 1951 did bring one piece of good news. This was the unexpected departure of departmental bugbear Hutchins at mid-year. But still, few issues were resolved.

By the winter of 1952, the department was proposing two unacceptable candidates for chair instead of just one. There is no documentary evidence who these were. But it seems overwhelmingly likely that the two were Blumer and Hauser.[21] Neither was acceptable to the administration, a fact communicated by Dean Ralph Tyler in late February. The department was bluntly ordered to think again. Nine months later, an administration press release announced Hughes as chair. A complex history intervened.[22]

A preliminary event was the disappearance of two crucial players from the scene. Wirth died quite unexpectedly in early May and Blumer announced his resignation, equally unexpectedly, around the same time.[23] With these disgruntled locals off their hands, the new administration began looking outside for a chair. Chancellor Kimpton talked to senior sociologists around the country, both getting advice and trying to recruit. In the summer of 1952, he sought to bring Samuel Stouffer back, apparently without bothering to notify the department. At the same time, William Sewell (of Wisconsin, a Minnesota Ph.D.) was recruited as a potential chair. Sewell got the full treatment. Kimpton promised massive resources. His longtime acquaintance Ralph Tyler pressured him strongly. But Sewell didn't move to Chicago, for reasons that were plaguing the administration's general plan of overcoming insularity. Hyde Park had become "nearly unlivable." Moreover, as in the Merton/Lazarsfeld recruitment, the university's financial situation created difficulties, despite Kimpton's promises. Meanwhile, on its own the department was trying to get Kingsley Davis, although not as chair.[24]

When it became clear that an internal chair was necessary, around midsummer, Donald Horton was acting chair. Horton himself had no desire for the office; it was early in his career and he needed more time for research. At a faculty meeting he listed the various people who had refused to become chair, including Hughes. The only remaining possibility, he said, was Duncan. Shortly thereafter, Hughes, who disliked Duncan intensely, changed his mind and announced himself available.[25]

Hughes was acceptable to the administration for a number of reasons. There was a link through HD, in which both Tyler and Hughes were active. Indeed, it was in this year that Hughes (and Foote) moved onto the HD executive committee (Warner had already been on it for a decade). Perhaps, too, the administration may have felt that Hughes would be weak enough to allow them to dictate departmental policy. Or they may have simply been buying time while other expedients were tried.

Once Hughes became chair, the department quickly polarized. Coming after the expected losses of Burgess and Ogburn, the unexpected losses of Wirth and Blumer had turned a worrisome transition into an openly recognized rout. Therefore pressure for an instant solution was great. But the loss of Burgess and Wirth—probably the most central people in the department despite the latter's acerbity—meant an empty middle. Moreover, Blumer's and Wirth's departure removed the important constraints that these friends had placed on Hauser's often domineering behavior. Taken together, these various forces divided the department sharply.

Other forces reinforced that separation. Less visible now, but central at the time, were long-standing political differences. The Burgess/Wirth wing of the department was politically active and reformist. As a result, both Burgess and Hauser had been the target of national-level loyalty investigations, Burgess in connection with work for the Public Health Service and Hauser in connection with the census directorship. Burgess, like Ogburn, had long-standing memberships in various American-Soviet friendship organizations, and the two of them, together with Wirth and other university faculty attached to various organizations on the attorney general's list, had been investigated in the Illinois "Red-ucators" hearings in 1949. Blumer's politics were aligned with his friends' activism and reformism, although he was not investigated. By contrast, Hughes and, particularly, his close friend Riesman to some extent felt themselves victims of a left backlash against McCarthyism. Similarly, neither Hughes nor Warner was a reformer in the manner of Thomas or Wirth. As one commenter put it, "more than sociology divided Hughes and Warner from the rest." [26]

There was, too, a difference of style. Hughes was an aristocratic gentleman. Distant, witty, and gracious, he was forebearing to his enemies and quiet, even timid, in public meetings. (He could be hard on students, however.) His friend Riesman, although less retiring in public settings, was equally the gentleman, scion of an old Philadelphia Jewish family and proud of its heritage of learning and professionalism. The Riesman/Hughes correspondence often concerns private schools, English and Continental traditions, and detailed markings of social class. By contrast, Hauser was a brash, self-made child of poverty from Chicago's Jewish far West Side. Duncan was a plain-spoken second-generation sociologist from Oklahoma. While Wirth and Blumer remained, this gap of style was not so great, for both of them, although brilliant and caustic, were longtime acquaintances of Hughes. But with them gone, and Riesman arrived, the gap became an abyss. [27]

Over the three years of Hughes's chairmanship, these various forces worked themselves into an open war. To some extent, this war worked itself out on the turf of quantitative and qualitative, but, as we shall see, these and many other intellectual issues were merely symbolic units manipulated in a competition driven by other things.

From the start, things were difficult. Blumer's first act on going to Berkeley was to recruit Hauser at a formidable salary. Kimpton himself had to intervene to retain Hauser. Indeed, the administration had little confidence in the department's own efforts. Kimpton admitted to alumni of the department that it was not as good as it ought to be, even while emeritus chair Ellsworth Faris, one of his important advisors, was telling him that Hughes's judgment could not be trusted and that there was serious doubt around the discipline about recent appointments.[28]

In the early stages, it was not clear which departmental faction the administration wanted to support. Kimpton seemed genuinely to regret the loss of Blumer yet found himself "in complete agreement with" the retiring Ogburn over Ogburn's anti-Blumer memorandum on "Some Criteria for Appointment to the Department of Sociology." In part, this administrative confusion simply reflected the mixed signals coming from the department itself: Burgess's last official message to the chancellor strongly praises the very appointments that emeritus chair Faris had attacked six months before. More important, however, the whole axis of departmental struggles was shifting. The division was no longer Hughes/Warner versus Blumer/Wirth, but had not yet settled into the new alignment of Hughes/Riesman versus Hauser.[29]

No secret was made of the department's troubles. Hauser spoke with characteristic gusto of "our present position of mediocrity among the Departments of Sociology in the United States." Gradually, strategies emerged to deal with the situation. All of these aimed at an eclectic department. A cohesive core remained in the graduate curriculum areas and the prelim examination, which dates in its modern form from the self-study later discussed. But the goal of eclecticism, originally the heart of administration policy, became by 1953 accepted by the department.[30]

Most faculty urged a variety of approaches to eclecticism. For example, Hauser urged three strategies: hiring major outsiders (like Kingsley Davis), hiring the best of recently departed Chicago students (Janowitz, Reiss), and making better use of locals (Shils, the NORC staff, Lloyd Ohlin). Hauser also condemned Goldhamer's rejection and urged his re-recruitment at the level the department had refused him three years before. Duncan, Hauser's strongest protégé, urged many of the same things. But Nelson Foote answered (junior staff took big risks in those days) with a ringing denunciation of Davis's reputation as a teacher and resolute opposition to the "great man" strategy he felt was implicit in Hauser's memo. Great departments, he argued, were built from within and, moreover, were founded on great teaching. And Foote spoke for a large group in the department when he attacked certain versions of theory:

> Some of the opposition to theory as such is well-grounded. When theorizers see themselves as taxonomisers, catalogers, chroniclers or glorified book-reviewers, they are not worth a

damn and I am for excluding them from this department. The theorists who can innovate and inspire and create new syntheses out of a fertility in fresh insight, on the other hand, are pearls without price.[31]

In responding to these blasts, new chair Everett Hughes belittled the great-man strategy. "Our experience of the last two years clearly indicates that the "big name" policy is not feasible." He was talking about Lazarsfeld, Merton, Davis, and Sewell (he probably did not know about Stouffer). Hughes emphasized the "use the locals" strategy. He had already gotten Shils to cross-list courses, and was taking aim at NORC and Ohlin. What he did not mention, but was about to do, was to engineer his friend David Riesman into the department. Hughes also pushed eclecticism by starting in 1954 the steady parade of junior hires from Columbia, a move that reflected the administration's insistence on external hiring, although the name of Peter Blau (the first such hire) was originally suggested by Nelson Foote, who had known Blau at Cornell.[32] The administration, however, went right on with the big names. Merton was tried again in 1954.

In late 1953, however, there was a glimmer of hope that department and administration might get together. Kimpton tried to recruit Hans Speier, a close Hauser friend, eminent sociologist, and director of social science at the Rand Corporation, as dean of the division. As it happened, Speier did not come, and the department continued in its caretaker status through the deanship of Morton Grodzins. Grodzins, with Hughes, now arranged for the move of Riesman into the department, although, on the quantitative side, Donald Bogue also came onto faculty status. At the untenured level, the department tried various people, getting some (Strauss and Katz) and losing others (Lipset and Smelser.) It is striking that Grodzins often discussed senior recruitment as if the department itself had no relevance.[33]

The move of Riesman into the department cemented the new lines of departmental faction. Riesman was a long-standing personal intimate of Hughes's, as close to Hughes as Hauser had been to Wirth. Riesman had privately supported Hughes's claims during the years when, in Hughes's words, "I felt very much under pressure and under fire from some of my colleagues." (The colleagues involved were the other claimants to Park's throne, Blumer and Wirth.) Riesman was strongly hostile to Blumer and Wirth, indeed even to Burgess.[34]

Once Hughes became chair, Riesman's role became more open, although he did not officially enter the department until fall 1954. Already in late 1952, just as Hughes's ascension was announced, Riesman was "scouting" for new faculty, in this case Lipset. In an early letter, he wrote that Hughes was the only true heir of Park, that he ought to break with Hauser and his party, and that he needed strong allies in the department (Riesman, clearly, would be one of these).[35]

Riesman, however, was equally aware of attacks on his and Hughes's version of social science from the humanistic side. He had a low opinion of Hutchins's old favorite Richard McKeon and worried that the good (i.e., broad vision) social science of the Social Relations Department at Harvard was beleaguered by antiscientific humanists like Arthur Schlesinger, Jr. Once in the department Riesman played a central role in recruiting, largely because he spent so much of his time on leave at other universities, traveling the lecture circuit, and vacationing in the East. He more than anyone else was the source of the connection with Columbia, for he was a great admirer of Lipset and the Bureau of Applied Sociological Research and a friend of the Lynds. Rossi and Katz both came to Chicago's attention through Riesman.[36]

Riesman's practical aims in these recruitments were twofold. First, he wanted young people to supervise the immense projects he and Hughes had begun, like the multifaceted Kansas City project. The pair had lost a major grant through Chicago's lack of such young project directors, and Riesman made their potential as study directors a central part of his judgments of St. Clair Drake and of Janowitz. Wide-vision social science need not be small-scale social science; bureaucratic ethnography has a long pedigree reaching back through Middletown to the Pittsburgh Survey and General Booth.[37]

But Riesman also wanted votes. His ratings of prospective senior recruits were more in terms of their prospective departmental politics than in terms of their work, even after one makes due allowance for the intimacy of the letters. His attitude towards tenure candidates clarifies this feeling. When Riesman admired a candidate's work, he discussed the work in the letters. When he did not, he discussed the candidate's personal style and voting potential.[38]

Hughes clearly tried to keep Riesman at arm's length. His letters are learned and affectionate, but when Riesman needed reigning in—he occasionally led people to think he was offering them jobs—Hughes was diplomatic but firm. More important, Hughes refused to become the grand leader Riesman wanted, opting to take a leave and return to full-time scholarship rather than continue his labors as chair.[39]

By 1955 departmental polarization was complete. The addition of Riesman, together with his close association with Hughes, Warner, Horton, and Foote in the new Center for Leisure Studies, meant a coherent focus for the "qualitative" party, centered on the close friendship of Hughes and Riesman. Nearly all of the Riesman party were also on the executive committee of HD. Moreover, Riesman had made a great impression on Marshall Field, a key member of the university's Visiting Committee, and had thus become an administration darling. He had also been on the cover of *Time*. Meanwhile, Hauser was increasingly identified with NORC. He had arranged, with new Dean Chauncy Harris and NORC's Clyde Hart, a new relation between the department and NORC. His personal power bases—the Population Research Center and the Chicago Community Inventory—were successful and well integrated with NORC. And Bogue was now tenured regular faculty, as was the meteoric Goodman.[40]

The first major issue that clarified the polarization was Foote's tenure. Foote was by this time securely within the Hughes/Riesman party. He had underlined that position, and lost Hauser's original good will, by besting him in a public debate over "cumulation" in sociology sponsored by the Society for Social Research. An exponent of participant observation and an active researcher, Foote had, however, also offended Warner by siding with Duncan on the latter's critique of Warner's work. As a result, he had little chance for success. He moved to the private sector, where he became a major figure in applied sociology.

Matters came to open conflict in 1956, by which time local opinion agreed that Everett Hughes would not have a second term, which, in any case, he did not seem to want. Hauser and Riesman were the candidates. (Apparently looking for an external chair had been stopped.) The faculty was still about evenly split between quantitative and qualitative work, although the balance inclined toward the qualitative. Warner, Hughes, Riesman, Foote, Horton, Blau, and Strauss were all qualitative in one way or another, although only Hughes and Strauss really represented old Chicago. Hauser, Goodman, Duncan, Bogue, and Katz were quantitative, although themselves divided between survey work and demography. Candidates Hauser and Riesman disliked each other intensely. Hauser was publicly contemptuous of Riesman's work, and Riesman, for his part, had made it clear that he would leave the university if Hauser became chair.[41]

The affair was undecidable in the department and the Riesman party approached Leo Goodman as a compromise candidate. Goodman was a methodologist's methodologist, and hence necessarily acceptable to the quantitative faction. Goodman was willing, but Dean Harris wouldn't accept him. After interviewing each tenured department member individually, Harris decided to ask Hauser to chair the department for one year, at the end of which the situation would be reviewed. But the chancellor overruled him. Kimpton felt the department ought to have a firm decision and made Hauser chair for three years. Kimpton's feelings for Hauser seem always to have been strong, and it seems likely that he saw in Hauser the strong hand necessary to rebuild the department. After all, for Kimpton, this particular academic headache was now six years old.[42]

Yet his motives in this choice were by no means unmixed. In responding to media-star Riesman, who at once moved ahead on an offer from Harvard, Kimpton seems affectionate, deeply regretful. "You would desolate the University if you accepted the Harvard offer. . . . I do hope you remain and hope I could help to make your life about here a happier one." On the other hand, his enthusiasm for Hauser was great, and they were sufficiently close that Hauser apparently raised with Kimpton the delicate issue of the department's tenure vote on Duncan. It seems clear that Kimpton, like Tyler and Harris, regarded the "youngsters" with their "techniques of modern social research" as the future of the department.[43]

The immediate effects of polarization continued to be felt largely by the junior faculty. In 1955 it had been Foote's turn. Now came Duncan's. Like Foote, Duncan had another job waiting, an open tenure offer from Blumer at Berkeley. Like Foote, Duncan got the easily predicted mixed vote. Unlike Foote, however, Duncan stayed, entering full-time research status after 1957. (He reentered the department briefly, 1960–62, before eventually leaving for Michigan.) Some thought him happy with the result—his research flourished—but others were not sure.[44]

In 1957, the last victim became Anselm Strauss, who like Duncan was on his way to a career shaping whole subfields of the discipline. Although there were some new faces (Rossi had been promoted and Strodtbeck brought in from the law school), the result was the same.[45]

Thus, the brief Hughes epoch closed with the reduction and isolation of the qualitative wing of the department. True to his promise, Riesman left within a year. Foote was gone, Strauss going. Warner and Hughes held on, although Warner left four years before retirement when the administration refused him a distinguished service professorship in 1959. Unlike

Riesman, Hughes was not bitter, indeed cautioning Riesman against bitter talk in public.[46]

Even after Hauser assumed control, the Kimpton administration never seems to have lost its sense that the department was in crisis. In mid-1957, Vice President R. W. Harrison wrote Kimpton that "Hauser is not through with building of tenure-covered aspects of Sociology and is thinking of three or four more spots" and made clear, apropos of the potential tenuring of Peter Rossi, that the administration might regard that tenure as foreclosing other perhaps more desirable possibilities. This was clearly still a department on probation.[47]

In his chair's report of 1958 Hauser noted "a sharp break from adherence to identification with the 'Chicago School' of Sociology." He proudly lists the origins of current teaching faculty, notes that only four of thirteen are Chicago graduates, and speaks of "some grumbling on the part of some Chicago graduates that we have gone too far in the avoidance of placing Chicago men on the faculty." He speaks of "the complete disappearance of the earlier bipolar division of departmental interests." (Riesman was gone by this point.) But at the same time, he is worried about managing the transition impending through Warner's and Hughes's departures. There is an immense amount of material about NORC in the report, indicating that NORC's relation to the department had become a major problem. Finally, Hauser regrets the "serious loss" of James Coleman.[48]

A year later, Hauser was less sure. "I would say we are still in a state of transition." He mentioned Warner's loss, about which he in fact cared little, but began to worry about the potential loss of Goodman, who was planning to take a leave at Columbia in his hometown of New York. Hauser rated the department as well-rounded, which he clearly now viewed as a virtue. He saw social psychology as rescued by Strodtbeck, who could draw in Katz, Rossi, and Jim Davis. Rossi and Duncan MacRae (a joint appointment with political science) would make up a program in political sociology. On the weakness side, he noted the social disorganization field, but hoped the appointment of James Short would at least shore it up. And he was pleased with the strength of theory (Shils was jointly appointed in the department and Vernon Dibble had been appointed), which sounds surprising given his widely publicized views.[49]

That Hauser was publicly pleased to be stronger in theory indicates the degree to which Chicago's distrust of "theory"—and it was strong in both the quantitative and parts of the qualitative camps as we have seen—

had finally bowed to administration pressure for eclecticism. Also, it is noteworthy that joint appointments were crucial to the new department. That much of the Hughes strategy Hauser continued with verve.

A number of things contributed to Hauser's ability to create a stable moment for the department. The most obvious was the removal of his adversary, Riesman. The second was administration cooperation, extended for the first time in six years. But the third was Hauser's own ability as a judge of academic horseflesh. His ratings of his staff (present in the sources but unquoted here) were nearly unerring, both at the time and in terms of later careers. But that judgment extended only within those realms he himself knew and liked. It may be true that Hauser recognized at once the extraordinary potentialities of Harrison White, then a postdoc two years past his physics Ph.D. and only one year past his sociology Ph.D. But on the other hand, he worked hard to get rid of Foote and Strauss, and in his insistence on ignoring locals he ignored department graduates who were achieving disciplinary eminence—Goffman, Becker, and others.[50]

Despite Hauser's apparent hostility, after 1957, to the old Chicago tradition, he eventually helped rebuild it. Since the early 1950s, he had been pushing Morris Janowitz on the department, and in 1961 Janowitz was finally secured. Once in Chicago, Janowitz energetically rebuilt the tradition, insisting that the University of Chicago Press reissue the old departmental classics, inserting those classics on the preliminary examination list, sending students into the field, backing appointments of scholars like Gerald Suttles and David Street. This was essentially the program of the "Departmental Objectives" document of ten years before. A generation of students flooded back to the field, from William Kornblum to Ruth Horowitz, Charles Bosk, and Michael Burawoy.[51]

* * *

Thus the postwar department did not, as is commonly assumed, move inexorably toward a quantitative stance. And to the extent that such a stance emerged, it was not the department but rather the chancellor who made the final decision. In the department most evidence controverts a strict quantitative-qualitative interpretation for this period. Hauser and Wirth were intimate friends, but Wirth disliked Warner. Blumer did not have a very high opinion of Hughes but thought enough of Hauser to try to lure him to Berkeley, and, in return, was highly regarded by Hauser himself. Riesman took the lead in the recruitment of Alice and Peter

Rossi. Goodman was willing to be a qualitative party's candidate for chair.[52]

Rather, the department in this period rotated around a number of strong relationships. During the years 1945–51 the whole group was held together both by the immense weight of their common memories and by two central figures, Burgess in the older generation and Wirth in the younger. All this was changed by Burgess's retirement, Wirth's death, and the departure of Blumer. With their disappearance and Hughes's attempt to strengthen his hand through absorption of Riesman, the rifts opened wider. The disappearance of Wirth and Blumer also removed the strong personal forces wedding Hauser to Chicago-style thinking; as his vita shows, he became more of a demographer in the strict sense. (He also became, in many ways, more an impressario than a researcher.)

As this rift opened, younger people without the depth of memories allied themselves with the powerful personalities of the middle generation, and squabbling became more open. Tyler's opposition to the abrasive, dominant Hauser left the department in the hands of Hughes, who had been something of a departmental outsider for a long time. It was this, and the presence of Riesman with his strong views, that produced the relatively brief period of open factional conflict that cost the department, in Foote, Duncan, and Strauss, three figures who would be central to the discipline over the next three decades.

Kimpton's decision for one side had the effect of destroying the other, at least temporarily, but did not bring the department lasting peace. But the Kimpton decision did establish the turf upon which peace would be made. For if Riesman had become chair, Hauser might very easily have given in to Berkeley's continuing blandishments, and Riesman could have led the department towards the combination of grand theory and qualitative empirical work that had come to mark the Ivy League departments other than Columbia's. For the department itself, then, the crucial transition years were from the administration's refusal of Wirth in 1950 to their designation of Hauser in 1956.[53]

The Department That Viewed Itself

The faculty's history from 1945 to 1960 thus falls into three periods: the gradual emergence of the split between Wirth/Blumer and Hughes/Warner, the polarization between Hauser and Riesman, and the Hauser hegemony. These periods are separated by two turning points: the seminar debates of 1951–52 and the chairmanship battle of 1956.

As one watches the web of alliances and battles unfold, it becomes clear that no one individual maintained a constant position throughout. Hauser could attack theory in one breath and pursue Smelser in the next. Hughes could feel unappreciated at one point and defend the department that had rejected him at another. The Riesman party could damn Hauser's work as "industrial" and yet mount projects that dwarfed most of the quantitative research. As we said earlier, we cannot find the "Chicago school" at the level of individuals. Enmeshed in the constant ebb and flow of interaction—the deals over hiring, the proposals for grants, the challenges of students—individual faculty make use of ideas at hand, imposing on them a style that, while perhaps modeled on a tradition, is uniquely personal.

It is rather in those interactions themselves that the tradition emerges. Fortunately, we can see this emergence in detail in the faculty seminar of 1951–52.[54] This year-long wrangle about who really wore the mantle of Robert Park shows how the loose tangle of maxims and practices that had sustained the department in its glory years could come to be molded, in the minds of those who argued about it, into an independent object, a thing capable of reproducing itself through their later work. Not that those maxims and practices weren't taught in various graduate programs throughout the country, nor that they wouldn't have lasted without the seminar. But rather that this kind of argument forced the participants to bundle together all the various strands, to objectify them in the person and the heritage of Park, and to thereby make in their own minds a cultural object that would attract to itself, and claim parentage of, many sorts of activities throughout diverse areas of sociology.[55] The very looseness of the seminar reflected this task of assemblage. Every time one more thing was crammed into the concept of "sociology" (which here meant "Chicago sociology") something else would fall out on the other side. The sticks piled on the heap wouldn't stay there until they began to be woven together enough to provide a restraining framework.

The seminar debates are thus about the creation not of the second Chicago school but of the first. As its era closed, the survivors tried to define it for themselves. In so doing, they (and others having similar conversations) transformed the dying subject into a living object. That object survived the partisan squabbles of the 1950s and was available for Janowitz to husband, as it was available to Hughes for transplantation to Brandeis.

* * *

The seminar ended in a moment of despair. It was late May 1952. Louis Wirth was dead. The department had just been suddenly told that an "objectives" document was immediately needed by the chancellor. Yet before they finalized the objectives, Nelson Foote proposed that they should "hear a few 'last words' and ask a few questions of those who won't be here next year. . . ." Reiss, Blumer, Williams, Burgess, and Ogburn (who wasn't there) were leaving.

Blumer led off with a ringing valediction:

> MR. BLUMER: . . . . I have the belief that much of the emi-
> nence of this department for over half a century has
> stemmed from the fact that the leaders in the Depart-
> ment have been quite concerned with trying to develop,
> not an assemblage of discrete facts, but something in the
> nature of a coherent body of knowledge of human group
> life as such. We can certainly note that in the case of Dr.
> Small; we see it most forcefully in the instance of Dr.
> Park, who combined with his very vigorous research inter-
> ests a very pronounced and steady concern with trying to
> weld together a picture of human group life as such. I
> think, from my own point of view, based on my familiar-
> ity with the work of Dr. Thomas, that he likewise was
> concerned with the effort to develop something in the
> form of a coherent scheme for the study of human group
> life. I think the loss of that sort of interest would be most
> unfortunate in the Department. . . .

After Blumer finished, Burgess turned to Reiss:

> MR. BURGESS: Mr Reiss, you're leaving us—a fact which qual-
> ifies you for the status of wise man.
> MR. REISS: I think that I agree thoroughly with Mr. Blumer,
> when one looks at what is happening to sociology today.
> I find myself in the position, very often, of kind of going
> along with the stream. It doesn't quite square up with the
> views of society which characterize what has come to be
> known as the Chicago school of sociology and which I
> learned as a student in the Department.
> MR. BURGESS: Why did you deviate?
> MR. BLUMER (to Burgess): Why did *you*?

Here, in Social Science 116 on the evening of 28 May 1952, was the end of the road: the young generation gently confessing a loss of faith, the middle generation accusing even its elders of forgetting. Was Blumer right that only he had the true relics of Chicago? Or did the discussion rather signify that the relics taken separately were so much worthless wood? Or was it rather that in squabbling over their inheritance, the children of the 1920s manufactured the relics within themselves?[56]

The twelve seminar sessions covered a variety of topics. They began with two full sessions on agenda-setting. These led to a decision to consider the "syllabi," or annotated reading lists, on which the new foundational exams were based.[57] There were then three sessions each in the syllabi for social psychology and social organization respectively, with one brief interpolated meeting on the shortened *Announcements* texts for all six syllabi. The last three sessions included two about very particular matters: Nelson Foote's report of a project on participant observation and a psychology department proposal to found an "Institute of Behavioral Sciences" at Chicago. The final session, although designed to help Dudley Duncan redraft the department's "objectives" document, in fact turned into a wake for the Chicago school.[58]

The seminar began with a murky discussion about what to do and how to do it. Burgess asked Wirth to set out "what ideas have occurred to him." In Wirth's elaborate scheme, there are three main topics—the discipline's subject, its relation to other social sciences, and its subfields—from which four subsidiary topics flowed. (The subsidiaries were the actual content of teaching, the discipline's presuppositions, understudied topics, and actual research problems.) In the discussion, Blumer strongly urged consideration of "the fundamental logical problems of our discipline." Against him, Foote urged empirical study of work in other departments, particularly those at Harvard and Columbia, more successful because of their study of the "more timely" problems of large organizations as opposed to Chicago's studies of "social problems." Warner too urged an empirical approach, suggesting that they proceed at once by studying the subject syllabi themselves. When Burgess agreed with him, a clear opposition emerged between Warner and Burgess on the one hand and Wirth and Blumer on the other. Hughes and Hart then reconciled the two, suggesting that at the next meeting the department continue with general issues, but thereafter turn to consideration of the syllabi. Both also raised the issue of methods, which they felt Wirth had obscured.

In this first meeting arise a number of themes that recur continuously: the contrast between Blumer's insistent abstraction and others' desire for an empirical understanding of the discipline, the multicornered worry about the justification of method, the comparison with Harvard and Columbia. But this first meeting also shows the amorphousness of the major participants' positions before the exigencies of discussion formalized them into place. Here, Hughes was the broker between Blumer and Burgess. Never again.

At the end of this meeting, each department member pledged to write "a statement of what he would like to see done," as Hart put it. Most wrote a short paragraph or page. Hughes and Warner each wrote a few pages. But Wirth wrote 4,000 words on his own three central questions: the field, its interrelations, and its subdivisions. For him the seminar was an apologia pro vita sua, a chance to set forth verbally and in print the credo of the Chicago school as he understood it.

No such aim or urgency informs the writing of Hughes or Warner. For them, the day of unity is past. There is no one Chicago school, there is rather a department of "several smaller nuclei of interest and enterprise, consisting each of one or more individuals" in Hughes's kind phrase. Warner was more blunt. "For purposes of maintaining outward peace among us, each and all of us pretend to ourselves that our relations are such that we are inwardly as well as outwardly harmonious and that there is general consensus among us. I do not believe that [this] is true in fact." Both Warner and Hughes favor an archipelagic definition of sociology. It is a "way of viewing problems of social behavior and organization that arise in all areas of life" (Hughes) or "the study of the organization of human behavior, in its persistence" (Warner).

Wirth, by contrast, thinks that sociology really is something. He starts with what it is not: study of society, of group life, of social institutions, even of social interaction. Nor is it simply what sociologists do, by which judgment he denies Foote, Hughes, and Warner. He settles on "sociology is concerned with what is true about man by virtue of the fact that he leads a group life." He recognizes the ill-definedness of "group," but says that

> the group factor refers to the universal fact that men live in association with others, that they interact with others, or are affected by and affect others.

After noting the difference of groups of humans from groups of other things, he moves on to state that sociology should be a science: public, verificationist, predictive, cumulative. He then emphasizes that

> our data are the real-life situations in which human beings find themselves and not some artificial problems we might concoct

246 Andrew Abbott and Emanuel Gaziano

in our imagination. We will have a science of sociology to the extent that we address ourselves to the actual life situations in which people are involved.

Finally, he urges a very cautious approach to universal propositions.

We should, I believe, not attempt to arrive at universality for the sake of universality, if as a result we distort our picture of social reality to a point where it is no longer recognizable or meaningful and if the abstractions at which we arrive are so abstract that they can no longer be referred back to concrete instances or empirical situations.

Wirth never improved this statement, which was in fact a staple part of all his courses. Although he was an inspired polemicist and a leader of his colleagues, he was not a systematic thinker. No more than Park, his predecessor as leader of the Chicago school, could he articulate the core of the school as other than a series of maxims. But here they were. Find the groupness of groups, which lies in how people and groups affect other people and groups. Aim at science, but not so much that you lose the reality. Talk about real people and real problems. Beyond that, Wirth's position was simply a list of vague axioms.[59]

The second session (25 October 1951) settled on the procedure of considering the two existing syllabi (social psychology and social organization) in terms of the questions Wirth had set forth at the first meeting. The group unanimously rejected the idea of spending the Ford money on planning an actual training program, as had been done at several other departments; it was premature to train people if you could not specify what you were training them for. (There was an overt condemnation of Harvard and Columbia here.) But again, Warner intervened to make clear that for him, not doing what Harvard was doing meant precisely "learning how to disagree." "It could be assumed that, just as Harvard has in effect tried to work out a basic, over-all doctrine, we ought to develop our 'line.' We all know that we aren't the kind to do that." This position, which made the extraordinary research freedom of the university into a general model for intellectual life, explicitly forbade the search for a Chicago core that was central for Wirth, and, in his own way, for Blumer.

The agenda-setting meetings thus pushed the major departmental figures into two groups. On one level, this was surprising, for Blumer, Wirth, and Hughes each believed themselves individually to be the heir of Robert Park. But there were deep differences between the pairs. Hughes and Warner were productive scholars with numerous large projects under way or in planning. Blumer was a perfectionist who refused to publish manuscripts others would have long since regarded as finished. Wirth had actually published very little in the past decade, although he too was sitting on a book-length study. As this contrast implies, Warner and Hughes were far more enmeshed in empirical social investigation than were Blumer and Wirth. There was a contrast in students, too. By this time Hughes was beginning to attract many of the best students in the department, as he previously had not. Blumer and Wirth, with their extraordinary verbal performances, often frightened students away.

The first two meetings thus established a chiasmic irony. Wirth, representing the party of abstraction, codified the Parkian practices. Yet his codification denied itself; don't abstract, it said, don't lose sight of real people and problems. And Hughes, despite his appearance of concreteness and laxity, knew exactly what he meant when he called sociology "a way of viewing problems of social behavior and organization." Although his archipelago model seemed to imply live-and-let-live, his later seminar performance shows him to have a very clear conception of Parkian research; its core was precisely that militant openness to experience that Wirth here urges in abstract terms.

* * *

Charged with the social psychology syllabus, Blumer held that field against all comers for the next three meetings. Throughout, the same ironic connections began to establish themselves between his and the others' positions.

Blumer begins by saying that unknown to itself social psychology is more confused now than it was when he wrote his own thesis twenty years ago. For there is a delusion of nonconfusion, induced by mistaking techniques and methodological standards (those of then-current survey-based attitude research) for answers to basic problems. He then throws the floor open. Hughes poses some harmless questions ("Why do you consider social psychology a field?" "Do you like the term 'social psychology?'") to which Blumer responds with a basic position:

> if one is going to study [the things that happen to the child in
> interaction] the important thing is to study them through the
> use of orientations, schemes of approach, and bodies of ideas,
> the content of which is congruent with what one can observe.
> This might seem to be a very simple statement not worth mak-

ing. I make it because—and I could defend this—the overwhelming majority of the approaches today ignore this point.

Hart disagrees bluntly with the latter assertion and they spar for a
few minutes about stimulus and response theory, which Blumer condemns
out of hand. He claims that "field investigators" (survey workers) fail to
use the knowledge that a person always "acts on the basis of how things
appear to *him*." But Hart retorts that survey workers are continuously
rethinking the interview situation from the interviewee's standpoint.

Hughes begins to gently chide Blumer for demanding so much.
"Maybe the number of people should be very small, and social psychology
an exceedingly select field. . . ." Blumer rejects him with anger. "I would
be the first to disown any allegation that before people could make observations [all] theoretical confusion has to be eliminated. That would be
idiotic." He then specifically attacks Hughesian research: "Students sent
out on field investigations may go astray at a number of points by virtue
of the fact that they have a schema of objects which derives either from
the culture of their group or from a particular doctrine." Foote replies for
the empiricists: "you seem to advocate a lingering intellectual hypochon-
dria in which we dwell upon all the dire things which may go wrong if we
do attempt research." [60]

The fact, however, is that they all believe in the same thing. Hart
thinks he is being interpretive enough by wondering what respondents
make of interviews. Hughes couldn't possibly live with NORC-type interviews but thinks he is being interpretive enough by sending students directly into the field. But for Blumer, that too fails adequately to reach the
realm of the "other." All three agree on the nature of the Parkian standard
itself: be reflective and stay close to reality. They simply disagree about its
empirical content. Thus, tradition begins to emerge in the form of a
maxim that can mean radically different but "similarly shaped" things,
under the same words, to different people.

Burgess then reset Blumer the task of stating the foundations of social psychology. After holding that social psychology must embrace universal propositions on the one hand and historical interpretations (e.g.,
accounts) on the other, Blumer lists five problem fields calling for universal
propositions: "the nature of original nature, the nature of group life, of
interaction, of the formative process of the individual, and of the kinds
of association that the individual may develop." Thus, for Blumer social
psychology was the master social science; the last item embraced all of

social organization, as the first did all of pure psychology. In between, lay group life, interaction, and the formation of individuals. A quick glance verifies that this is, in more or less the same order but with slightly different emphases, the outline of the Park and Burgess textbook of 1921. Blumer is claiming, as he was always to claim, that social psychology—under its later label of symbolic interactionism—was the proper name for the entire Chicago tradition.[61]

Indeed, in these contradictory claims and counterclaims the central themes of the Chicago tradition begin to be heaped into a coherent wood-pile. Blumer and Wirth want to set forth a Chicago vision of social life, while Warner and Hughes think one can not and should not do so. Blumer believes that the heart of sociology is the intellectual problem of how individual and group reciprocally affect one another. Wirth believes that the heart of sociology is a set of maxims: theory grows out of research, and so on. Neither Warner nor Hughes cares what the heart of sociology is. They just want to get on with doing it, which for them takes the form of research following Wirth's maxims and animated by Blumer's problem. One side practices what the other preaches, while attacking the preaching because it doesn't practice and itself being attacked because its practice doesn't quite live up to the preaching. Of such bound-up contradictions are symbols made. For either side would defend the other against any outside conception of preaching or practice, be it Parsons or Lazarsfeld. The argument is all about what Chicago sociological practice really meant.

The later meetings on social psychology fill out many of these same topics. Blumer is unwilling to admit any research to be good, yet unwilling to openly deny the possibility of good research. Indeed, the second social psychology meeting—in which others propose dozens of research strategies and Blumer rejects them all—persuades one that Blumer's real fear is of seeing Mead's insights become simply a "model" to be tested, on the same level as stimulus-response, or psychoanalysis, or (his new bane) cybernetics. He fears lest the Chicago heritage be mangled by the cogs of Ogburnian verification.

Blumer was right that the fate of subtle ideas in routine minds is often brutal, but in his fear for his ideas he hid them. His dilemma captures precisely the problem of willed transmission of tradition. He feared to write his ideas out lest they become mere objects; indeed his most influential single work—the article collection of 1969—was dragged out of him against his will. But by keeping them within he objectified his ideas

in another way; he was scandalized when (outside the seminar) Becker
told him that students memorized a set of eight student-generated "Blumerian theorems" in order to pass the social psychology section of the prelim (Becker, personal communication.) Yet only by letting his ideas out
into use, by handing them over to others as subjects, could he avoid this
dreaded routinism.

The same issue arose in the third meeting, in which there was a long
discussion of motivation. Blumer says motivation "represents one of the
most confused and ill-understood conceptions that you can find in the
literature." The whole literature can be condensed to "you have motive and
then behavior." (For Blumer, of course, interpretation and construction of
behavior came in between.) But Foote catches him out: "That is only one
scheme." "Do you agree with me that that is the most common one? State
another one," retorts Blumer. Foote calmly lists three, then tells Blumer
he has just written a review of motivational theories placing forty of them
under six heads. Here again is the problem of being one among many. For
Blumer, social psychology is not just another model, a way of figuring out
a problem. It is a whole approach to thinking about social life, a framework, a stance. He backs off, in real confusion for once, and Burgess saves
him by changing the topic to the relation of social psychology to psychology more broadly.

This is the exact moment of transmission. For every learner makes
of his elder's theories an object, objectifying even the most subjective and
intentional aspects of a master's approach. But then in the work itself, if
the student is up to it, the subjective transformation occurs. In Blumer's
case, the clearest and oddest example of this was Duncan, who had gotten
A's in all of Blumer's courses. Here in the seminar, Blumer's position of
high and absolutist scientism was shared throughout by Duncan alone,
who also advertised his Blumerism by circulating to everyone, just before
the second meeting, a highly constructivist document entitled "Confes-
sions of a Confused Young Sociologist and Aphorisms for a Proper Rela-
tivist Sociology." Duncan went on to a distinguished career of what many
took for the epitome of empiricist, objectivist positivism. Yet late in his
career Duncan began to show his true colors, colors that many of his later
admirers found appalling indeed. *Notes on Social Measurement* (1984) be-
trays a disappointment in empirical sociology as great as Blumer's in 1951.
Duncan had broken some of Blumer's eggs, to be sure, but he was still
trying to make a Blumerian omelet.[62]

This third meeting touched another aspect of the Chicago tradition—ecology. Here too was the curious phenomenon of denial by Blumer's abstractions of something that in fact was central to his own ideas. Reiss raises the issue of how social psychology relates to ecology, defining ecology as "the study of human aggregates in time and space." Blumer attacks at once, saying that time and space are just part of the setting for interaction, the latter being what really matters. And others belittle time and space as simply two among many facts conditioning a certain social relation. Duncan tries to defend his colleague, unsuccessfully. So in a quick few minutes a central aspect of the Chicago tradition seems to be set aside. But in fact to Wirth, as to Burgess, and, in the last analysis to Blumer, it was location in time and space, certainly social time and social space, that was the heart of what they had tried to defend for two decades against Ogburn. Exactly what the new sociology of variables did was take social facts out of their contexts. Context was what Wirth had in mind when he spoke of not losing touch with social reality. Thus, we can only conclude that Blumer belittles Reiss's position because, once again, of his pathological fear of objectification (see Abbott 1992).

In summary, Blumer and Wirth throughout these discussions effectively make of "sociology" a pure form of subjectivity. Every attempt to assign it a content is denied. Every attempt to pin it down to a given practice is throttled. This issue came to a head at the close of the third social psychology meeting, in a brilliant analysis by Nelson Foote of what we would now call paradigms. He argues against

> slicing up the field of social science into a series of orderly pastures, with such-and-such interrelations. I feel that there is something terribly unreal about discussing the relationship between social psychology and other fields of knowledge, as if you were negotiating a cartel arrangement.

No, he says, the relation between fields is actually different. They are all imperialists. They all claim all of social life. He, as it happens, is an adherent of one of these views, social psychology. Social psychology, he says:

> is a very elaborate world-view and is quite self-consistent. . . . As a world view it contains or provides its own conceptions of history, of causation, of institutions and human nature. A comprehensive philosophy regulates the types of problems it presents itself, the way in which these problems are formulated, and even the nature of the evidence regarded as proof.

Blumer—who has been nothing if not imperialistic throughout the last three meetings—is scandalized by this relativism (which he calls "vitalism with a vengeance") and wants no part of it. For him, social psychology is simply the right view. It makes the appeal to real data. When Foote chides him that "real" is just what he, Blumer, thinks is real, he puffs up:

> I just can't understand what your thinking is, in suggesting that this area of test has no status other than to answer to my personal whims. To the contrary, it is the area of common human experience—open to anyone who is willing to view it with discernment. It doesn't require a lot of queer and, accordingly, discardable instruments.

When Blumer finally figures out what Foote means, that even the "area of common human experience" is simply Blumer's own assertion, he is scandalized and at once raises the extreme example of Nazi social psychology. Would force make that true? "I don't care to have truth determined by power," he says.[63]

Both men are right. On the one hand, Chicago sociology was a profound, existential commitment, as Blumer argued, not just another "perspective" or model to be tested. On the other, to avow such a commitment was to stand above the rhetoric of science Blumer so admired, and ultimately above the world of empirical reality toward which that commitment was in fact made. It is in the unstatable gap between these two positions that the Chicago position lived, just as it was in having the argument about the two sides that that unstatable gap could be stated and transmitted to another generation.

* * *

The meetings on social organization have little of this fire. From the start, things are different. For one thing, there is a group—Hughes and Warner, with their assistants Horton and Junker—who have already discussed how they are going to present the social organization syllabus. The presentation (by Hughes) sets forth a basic theme for the next two meetings, which is that the social organization group has essentially become one with the anthropology department. Robert Redfield of that department was involved in writing the syllabus. There are joint courses. There are joint researches.

The existence of a group, with external allies, is not the only difference. Unlike Blumer, the social organization group has a body of routine research practices—field methods. It has worked out its own answers to a group of difficult questions distilled (by the ever-rigorous Duncan) out of prior discussions: questions about reflexivity, about universal statements, about models, about fidelity to reality. And the group has a basic concept—"the interacting man, the man who is in varying degrees sensitive to the actions and gestures of others"—that is straight out of the Chicago lexicon.

The first social organization meeting sees Blumer in a characteristic mode. Warner takes a pragmatic stand, saying that ideas in social organization are tested by how much further insight they produce. Blumer asks how that judgment can be made. Again, he plays the scientific absolutist. (The attack is indeed reminiscent of Duncan's published attack on Warner.) Here again, while believing deeply in the Chicago-style unity of theory and research, Blumer derives such high standards from his theoretical rules that research becomes, in practice, impossible. This result was precisely the reverse from that of Duncan, who believed in the same unity but founded his equally impossible standards on methodological rigor and, later, on the substantive validity of measurement. Again it was a case of understanding the same pile of sticks from different sides.

The second social organization meeting questioned the real relation of the social organization field to anthropology. There was long and fierce argument. Wirth regarded the two fields as fundamentally different. Anthropology was focused on small, self-contained, preliterate societies. It knew nothing of sampling or method. It emphasized different institutions. Its master concept was culture. Sociology studied large, differentiated, modern societies. It had sophisticated methods of various kinds. Its master concept was society. Hughes patiently pointed out a hundred evidences against differentiation: borrowing of concepts, trespassing on each other's types of societies, the use of "society" and "culture" in both fields. But Wirth was not convinced, and went on to point to what he felt were serious holes in the social organization syllabus—lack of material on politics and power, on conflicting groups, on change and dynamics. Hughes gently conceded all of this, even going along with a discussion suggesting that separating the social organization and social change syllabi conduced to the appearance of stasis in the social organization syllabus. His handling of his group's syllabus has all the quiet confidence that Blumer's lacks. Whether this reflected the actual coherence of his own views or simply a willingness to admit incoherence in a way that Blumer would not is not really clear.[64]

But the emotional commitment of Hughes to his position becomes clear in his "Morning-After Fantasy on Night-Before Reality, with Counterpoint on Two Themes, 'Sociology begins at home' and 'let us not be static in our view,'" which was sent to seminar members the next day. This is a satirical retelling of the history of the department in which Hughes shows that his views had just as fine a Chicago pedigree as did anyone else's and that credentials as "sociologists" matter little, the great figures of the department having been a Baptist economist (Small), an English professor (Thomas), a philosopher turned newspaperman (Park), and a psychologist (Faris). All had gone far beyond the bounds set by Wirth and Blumer in their discussion of sociology, as Hughes shows again and again. The document is written as a hilarious parody ("any sociologist who leaves the country except to attend conventions or to advise the lesser breeds is obviously a traitor who wears an anthropology pin on his undershirt") and is filled with insider jokes ("And when Thomas had to go elsewhere to pursue his new experiences he left behind to Mr. Faris, a psychologist by training . . ."). It must have been a real slap in the face indeed to Wirth and Blumer. For underneath its satire is the bold assertion that Hughes himself was the real inheritor of Robert Park.

The story of the seminar is, then, the story of social psychology and social organization, of Blumer versus Hughes, more broadly of Wirth and Blumer versus Warner and Hughes. It is a story in which the pragmatists became romantics. Nothing would satisfy Blumer but that he vanquish whatever failed to meet his perfect standards. Yet he had not himself the heart, nor the wit, nor in reality the inclination, to create the synthetic social psychology that would have met his own standards. And it is a story in which the romantics became pragmatists and thereby built practical foundations for the survival of the insights they all valued so much. Hughes indeed had Park's "romantic temper," a love of the new and interesting social fact, but he organized routine research practices to find such facts.

In the context of these great debates, the later meetings of the seminar, discussing the Behavioral Sciences Institute and Foote's "Participant Experimentation" document, add little. And so we come again to the final meeting of 28 May 52.

After the wonderful byplay about deviation quoted above, Reiss confesses his fall from Chicago standards and leaves with a valediction: "It seems to me that the Department ought to try to implement what has come to be known as the 'Chicago point of view'—the emphasis upon the group as an interactive system, viewed in terms of change and process." He predicts, with unerring accuracy, that structural-functionalism will last about fifteen years. He fears the loss of the middle of the discipline, a manifold tieing together real theory and real research. "While I have these reservations about the way the science is going, I have equal, if not greater, reservations about another trend in sociology, which is in the direction of a sort of literary sociology. . . . I'm thinking of a kind of literary treatise of which I think you find quite a number in the field." True to his origins, Reiss was saying no to Parsons, and to much of survey research, and perhaps even to David Riesman.

While the older generation battled over Park's inheritance, the younger generation had gotten the point. Reiss knew well what was in the gap between Wirth's maxims, Blumer's abstractions, and Hughes's research practices. In that gap was the intense subjectivity that was to animate himself, Duncan, Strauss, and dozens of their peer students of this period, a desire to follow all three imperatives with a certain neurotic intensity. This was what he meant by "the Chicago point of view." Surrounding that intense subjectivity was the heap of maxims and abstractions and practices—the object now defined as the first Chicago school. But Reiss, like all the rest, knew that the heart of the matter was not the ideas and the techniques, but the attitude and the emotion.

It is Blumer who turns the discussion toward closure. "Mr. Burgess, we certainly want to hear what you have got to say." Burgess replies: "I heard Mr. Blumer remark that he regarded me as a deviationist. I don't think I am." There is laughter and joking. The group encourages Burgess to redo the Park and Burgess textbook. (In fact he did not. Morris Janowitz got it reissued in 1970.) Then a few of them return to the issue of the great "sociologists" who weren't sociologists. Foote, who admires them profusely, lists E. H. Carr, Peter Drucker, David Riesman, Daniel Bell, William H. Whyte. There is much discussion and debate about whether any academic could play such a role—are Veblen and Schumpeter examples? The discussion flickers toward Durkheim (did he study the big picture or just little things, like most sociologists?) and gradually extinguishes itself on the issue of the memorandum for the chancellor. "What of this document? Are we ready for it to go to the Administration?" asks Burgess. There are some comments, some caveats. Closing the seminar, Duncan speaks for them all in denying this one last request to trap the

Chicago subjectivity in an object: "I would feel rather ill-equipped to write a statement of what sociology is all about and how it stacks up with other disciplines." Thus ended and thus was born the original Chicago school.

ENVOI: THE DISCIPLINE

The death and life of the Chicago school came in a period marked by distinct changes for sociology as a discipline. These have been well-studied by Turner and Turner in *The Impossible Science* (1990). The maturing of market research and the demonstrated efficacy of social research in the war combined to create a substantial market for applied social survey work. Continuous opinion polling dates from this period, as does serious government funding for empirical social research. Market power was thus one force strengthening the hand of the quantitative researchers at Chicago, for now in addition to the demographers' long-standing grip on the U.S. Census (through Hauser), there emerged a powerful foundation in survey work. NORC was of course central to this.

Intellectually, the period brought not only the rise of survey research but also the grand theory of Talcott Parsons and his colleagues at Harvard. Parsons's lengthy dominance of the ASA, together with his position at a prominent university, gave him ideal resources for intellectual empire. A string of fine students spread the gospel from Cambridge. The Carnegie Foundation funded his project on "a general theory of action." However, Parsons's relation to the emerging empiricist tradition was largely arbitrary. He and Samuel Stouffer, a Chicago product (and former faculty member) who directed quantitative work at Harvard from 1944 to 1955, talked much together, but with little real effect. They were much further apart than Merton and Lazarsfeld at Columbia.

But there was an inevitable reaction to the rise of what C. Wright Mills was soon to call "grand theory" and "abstracted empiricism." It came first in the movement to found the Society for the Study of Social Problems, in which those who made up the "second Chicago School" were to play so strong a role. The SSSP emerged in exactly the period of the faculty seminar. It reflected a number of emerging splits in the discipline: Midwest versus East, radical versus establishment, activist versus scientist. The success of the SSSP proved that the revolution of the ASA against its Chicago tutelage—the movement that founded the ASR in 1936—was in fact a revolution from above, despite the use it made of discontent among the plebs (Lengermann 1979). Its result had not been a "more open" journal and society, but rather one dominated by Harvard and Columbia instead of by Chicago. Not surprisingly, Chicago became the leader of the opposition.[65]

Although the original impetus for the SSSP came from Brooklyn College and Alfred C. Lee, it was not for symbolism and political alliance alone that Lee and the others turned to Chicago figures for three of its first four presidents (Burgess, Blumer, and Arnold Rose). For people from the old Chicago tradition figured prominently in the movement to found SSSP. Of twenty-one people at the SSSP organizational meeting, nine were Chicago Ph.D.'s and two (Burgess and Wirth) were current Chicago faculty. And the graduate students discussed in this book became a large part of the organization's backbone. Of fifty-three people who have been either president, vice-president, or editor of *Social Problems* (and whose Ph.D. department we can identify), fifteen have been Chicago Ph.D.'s. From the period here studied come Rose, Lopata, Gold, Kriesberg, Gusfield, Becker, Reiss, Rainwater, Joan Moore, and Murray Wax.

In the 1950s, the SSSP was in fact the organizational home for old Chicago-style, empirical research on social problems. It was odd that of those remaining at Chicago, only outsider Donald Bogue really carried on the tradition of applied research on major social problems. As for the rest, they gradually scattered through the discipline. Blumer and Hughes left Chicago and in leaving flourished at other places as never before. Foote, Duncan, and Strauss, casualties of polarization, went elsewhere to transform the discipline. Riesman came and—never having really figured out the Chicago tradition—left. The Columbia group, too, came and went, although Coleman eventually defined Chicago as a worthy successor to Columbia, and returned.

As for the idea of the Chicago school, it became an animating force in some people's minds, an obnoxious fiction in the eyes of others. It matters little what its history actually is. The maxims and insights and practices that make up the objective face of the school were available in many other places as well. And the burning subjective experience of sociology as a commitment was felt in Cambridge and Morningside Heights and Bloomington as in Hyde Park. What has made Chicago unique is merely the ritual rehearsal of these things through an obsession with the tradition itself. Foolishly exclusive as that ritual often seems to be, it has the value of preserving a high ideal of what sociology—and more broadly, social science—can and should be.

Sources and Acknowledgments

There are two nonpublished sources for this chapter, personal communications and manuscript collections in the Joseph Regenstein Library at the University of Chicago. The personal communications vary from written documents to informal conversations. They are as follows:

Charles Bidwell, Professor of Sociology, 20 June 1994

Donald Bogue, Emeritus Professor of Sociology, 30 June 1994

Leo A. Goodman, Emeritus Professor of Sociology, 16 April 1994

Joseph Gusfield, Emeritus Professor of Sociology, University of California, San Diego, 5 August 1994

Chauncy Harris, Emeritus Dean of the Social Science Division, 6 May 1994

Philip Hauser, Emeritus Professor of Sociology, (Abbott talked to Hauser 7 January 1993 mainly about AJS matters, before the issue of this paper arose. Unfortunately Mr. Hauser was too ill to talk by the time this draft was in preparation.)

Donald N. Levine, Professor of Sociology, 23 June 1994

Robert K. Merton, Emeritus Professor of Sociology, Columbia University, 15 April 1994

William Sewell, Sr., Emeritus Professor of Sociology, University of Wisconsin, 27 June 1994.

Ethel Shanas, Emerita Professor of Sociology, University of Illinois, Chicago, 13 July 1994.

The following manuscript series were consulted for this paper, all located at the Joseph Regenstein Library of the University of Chicago.

EWB	Ernest Watson Burgess Papers
LW	Louis Wirth Papers
PMH	Philip M. Hauser Papers
ECH	Everett C. Hughes Papers
MJ	Morris Janowitz Papers
WFO	William F. Ogburn Papers
RMT	Ralph M. Tyler Papers
PP45	Presidential Papers, 1945–1950
PP52	Presidential Papers, 1952–1960

Citations to these are all given in notes. Since all these collections are organized in folders within boxes, they are cited as follows: EWB 33:2–4 means Burgess Papers, box 33, folders 2–4. (These are the minutes of the faculty seminar.) Certain materials were located in the Social Science Division vault. These are cited as SSV. We saw them with the kind permission of Dean Colin Lucas.

It is important to realize, when one is considering the department in this period, that source availability affects our reconstruction of the past. In particular, the absence of any personal papers of Blumer and Warner and the relative paucity of Hughes's personal material (most of his extensive materials cover his career at Brandeis) mean that we must judge these men through others' eyes. Also, we have found no central collection of department minutes from 1939 to 1956. What we have is what faculty (mostly Wirth) happen to have kept.

We should also indicate that our interpretations are influenced in part by participation in current departmental and administrative life. The senior author is Professor of Sociology and Deputy Dean of the Division of Social Sciences.

A final source deserves much thanks. We sent copies of the first draft to six sociologists who had been on the Chicago faculty in this period: Howard Becker, Otis Dudley Duncan, Nelson Foote, Leo Goodman, Alfred Reiss, Jr., and Anselm Strauss. All were kind enough to read the document on short notice and provide copious comments. These comments sometimes sent us to new sources, sometimes sent us back to old sources. They often challenged our interpretations. Although problems and differences undoubtedly remain, the chapter is much the better for the help these six gave us. We thank them deeply for their time and concern.

In general, the documentary sources provide the backbone for our account. We have used personal recollection—both from the list above and from our six commenters—largely to corroborate documentary materials. In no case have we presented as fact any information resting on one personal recollection and nothing else. Because of that, we have in general omitted direct citation of personal communications.

We would also like to thank the Department of Special Collections of the Regenstein Library and Assistant Dean Mary Brandon of the Social Science Dean's Office for help with sources. We dedicate this essay to the memory of Louis Wirth.

NOTES

1. Dates of faculty service are notoriously difficult to specify, partly because the long-standing practice of hiring internally meant that many people oozed into faculty status by degrees. Also, positions were often retrospectively redefined (because someone completed a Ph.D., for example). There is therefore room for reasonable disagreement. These dates cannot be exactly specified without reading the faculty personnel files for the period, which remain sealed (if they remain at all— we are not sure where they are). The reader should, however, be aware that the lists given by Harvey (1987) in his book on Chicago, while roughly accurate about dates of service, are often mistaken about rank. David Riesman, for example, was tenured throughout his official service in the department in the 1950s, Donald Bogue was tenured before Harvey thinks he was, D. G. Moore was never a full professor, etc.

2. Much pressure was put on Ogburn to stay, pressure that he respected but withstood. "I think I had better withdraw from the university. I am writing now so that you can be making other plans and cease your efforts to have me stay. I do appreciate more than I can say the wish that the department would have me stay on." Ogburn to Wirth, 21 March 1950, LW 62:7. Both Burgess and Ogburn spent an extra year in the department, ostensibly to reap the benefits of certain social security provisions. (Burgess to Blumer, 13 November 1950, EWB 3:1, Wirth to

Blumer, 14 December 1950, LW 1:8.) In fact, Burgess remained to chair the department while the administration made up its own mind who should be chair in the long run.

It should be noted that relations among the tight core group were extremely close. Burgess's many letters to Wirth and Blumer are clearly affectionate, while his letters to Ogburn are warmly collegial (e.g., Burgess to Ogburn, 17 April 1947, EWB 16:10). The Wirth-Blumer correspondence (in LW 1:8) makes it clear that Wirth was Blumer's best friend in the department, both of them sharing a coolness towards Hughes, about which Blumer was the more outspoken. The only negative relationship in this core of four was the apparently intense dislike between Blumer and Ogburn, about which considerable ink has been spilled. Even Blumer and Hauser had a past. Blumer had been Hauser's M.A. advisor, and they had published, in 1934, a book on the results (*Movies, Delinquency, and Crime*). Subsequent events were to prove them intellectually closer than anyone might imagine, as we note below. For the material on Hauser's M.A., see Hauser to Gideonse 26 March 32 and also Hauser's warm letter to Blumer of 14 February 1934, both in PMH 14:6. Hauser did not correspond with Blumer during his recruitment after the war, perhaps because the latter was in Pittsburgh much of the time. Their relation may also have cooled somewhat.

3. There were many more locals who held the rank of instructor for a few years in the late 1940s—Tomatsu Shibutani, Buford Junker, Donald Roy, for example. After 1951, the rank of instructor seems to have disappeared. The practice of extensive local hiring was a source of friction with the administration, as we note below.

4. Some of these are less familiar names in the Chicago roster. Goldhamer was a social psychologist hired in 1946 to participate in "our new general course in the social sciences at the divisional level . . . it was a general intro to the social sciences, run at the third year for the move into 'majors', which of course don't yet exist." Wirth to Harry Gideonse, 2 September 46, LW 4:2. (The remark about majors reflects the lack of electives in the Hutchins college.) Goldhamer left in 1950 because he was refused promotion and had better offers elsewhere (Ogburn to Goldhamer, 6 February 1950, 20 March 1950, Ogburn to Burgess, 10 March 1950, all in EWB 16:10). Horton was a Yale anthropology Ph.D. (1943) and collaborator of Ogburn's. He would later attach himself to Warner. He moved into regular faculty status from research associate status in 1951–52.

5. On Social Thought, see Nef's founding memo, "The Committee on Social Thought of the University of Chicago" (n.d.), PP52 150:6. Shils's trajectory can be traced in official university publications. The Levine story is from Levine himself (personal communication).

6. A useful source on the history of NORC in this period, and the source of our information about money and work flows, is Rebecca Adams (1977). The coalition supporting NORC was an interesting one. Wirth, for example, saw great prospects for it (Wirth memo appended to memo of Burgess to the faculty, 24 August 1949, LW 62:6). This vision was hardly disinterested; Hart had been a graduate student of Wirth's in the early 1930s. Wirth undoubtedly played a central role in NORC's choice of Chicago.

7. Another central figure in HD was Robert Havighurst, a specialist in education. Although HD was particularly the home of Lloyd Warner, Warner also had a contract survey research firm downtown (Survey Research Incorporated) in which students like Lee Rainwater were active. The firm specialized in a kind of qualitative market research tied to Warner's class analysis.

8. The Industrial Relations Center drew students like Donald Roy. Inside and outside the race relations committee, the relation of Wirth and Hughes was very complex. The two collaborated on a large research project on racial discrimination in the Chicago public schools, Wirth working on gerrymandering of districts and Hughes on issues with teachers. But Hughes tended to define race relations more broadly than did Wirth, focusing less on American issues.

9. For the NORC location, see R. Likert to Hart, 25 March 1948, PMH 14:10. CCI was at this location until 1955, when it moved to 935 E. 60th. NORC moved to 5711 Woodlawn in 1954. On the funding of CCI and the Burgess/Wirth view of it, see Burgess to Hauser, 27 September 46, Wirth to Hauser, 12 February 1947 both PMH 14:9. Hauser collaborated widely, at one point seeking Warner's aid in interesting St. Clair Drake in a CCI project on Chicago's black population. (Hughes to Riesman, 18 March 54, ECH 45:16).

10. Tyler to Hutchins, 6 December 50, PP52 148:1. Hauser to Harris (8 December 58, SSV) One commenter noted that when Tyler later went to the Palo Alto center, he showed the same taste.

11. The Hauser and Wirth houses were connected by a private electronic telephone arrangement (Hauser to Glass, 11 January 57, PMH 4:2) On the Hauser recruitment, see the extensive correspondence between Hauser, Wirth, and Burgess in PMH 14:9. Hauser's initial strong status was shown by Wirth's ability to install him as secretary of the SSRC, the internal grant-giving agency that oversaw university research funding (Tyler to Wirth, 21 October 47, PMH 14:10). Hauser's worries about money are evident in his negotiations (in the same files) and the 4E episode is evident both in the draft protest document (18 May 50, PMH 14:10) and in letters to Hughes and Horton (then acting chair) of 18 May 53 during the affair of his Berkeley offer (PMH 14:11).

12. See Burgess to Department, 25 November 49, PMH 14:10, with a list of 115 graduates!

13. Ogburn's diaries indicate that, unlike Burgess, he had folded his tents in anticipation of retirement (WFO 46:4). Therefore the futility of these expedients may be more a reflection of Ogburn's state of mind than anything else. In any event, Ogburn wrote Burgess (who was on leave in California, leaving Ogburn as acting chair) on 10 March 1950 (EWB 16:10) saying that Goldhamer was probably leaving (he had already been on leave in Washington for a year.) That the various expedients were raised with Blumer still on the faculty might be thought to suggest strongly that his departure was expected even at this point, two years before his actual resignation, although the stated reason for hiring was the end of Shibutani's appointment as an instructor (Burgess to Blumer 19 December 1950, EWB 3:1). But in fact, Blumer's was the primary voice against Goldhamer's promotion, and that it was taken seriously enough to deny promotion implies that Blumer was expected to stay. Moreover, Ogburn's letter to Burgess four days later (14 March

50, EWB 16:10) clearly takes Blumer's continued presence for granted. And Burgess himself, writing to Blumer later that year, (30 October 1950, EWB 3:1), while Blumer was on a leave in Hawaii, discusses social psychology hires at length in a way that suggests that he, at least, had no inkling of Blumer's (possible) intentions.

14. Professor Merton was kind enough to tell Abbott this story from his point of view. For the U. of C. side, see Wirth to Blumer, 27 October 1950, LW 1:8. A central problem was that salaries were frozen, part of the financial debacle left by Hutchins and cleaned up, over the course of a decade, by his successor, Lawrence Kimpton (McNeill 1991). The administration was also trying to cut down on tenured appointments; see Burgess to Blumer, 30 October 1950, EWB 3:1. Wirth's opinion was that the offer was *not* joint, and that Lazarsfeld was making it look as if he were the real target. According to Wirth, the offers were not turned down at once, but seriatim (Wirth to Blumer, 14 December 1950, LW 1:8). Incidentally, Wirth's bitterness may have reflected a feeling of friendship spurned: Wirth had maintained cordial professional relations with Lazarsfeld since the mid-1930s, when he had invited Lazarsfeld to Chicago to meet the Seminar on Racial and Cultural Contacts. The later offers were separate—Merton in 1954 and Lazarsfeld in 1958. (Hauser to Harris, 10 September 58, SSV). It is noteworthy that the administration conducted the 1954 negotiations with Merton itself, although with the department's authorization: "If the situation warrants [we will] have Everett Hughes join us at one stage or another of our discussion" (Grodzins to Merton, 15 February 54, PP52 148:2).

15. The correspondence on retirement is Wirth to Burgess, 28 February 50, Burgess to Wirth, 5 March 50, Ogburn to Wirth, 21 March 50, all LW 62.7. The quote from Ogburn is from the diaries, WFO 46:4, entry for 20 March 51. This attitude explains, by the way, why Ogburn absented himself from the faculty seminar of 1951–52 and why he played so little role in the struggles of the department to survive.

16. We are very lucky that Blumer was on leave in Hawaii during this episode, for other department members—particularly Burgess and Wirth—wrote him long letters about it. For Wirth's private views of the administration, see Wirth to Harry Gideonse, a close friend who had left the Chicago faculty, (2 September 1946, LW 4:2): "I read the clipping about the new world constitution with great interest. The boys are certainly hiding their light under a bushel. I am afraid if the world is going to be dependent on their solution to its problems, it is going to have to wait for a millennium or two." His own version of the administration turndown was "I was informed by [Dean Ralph] Tyler that I was not acceptable because I had for twenty-five years consistently disagreed with the Administration accept [*sic*] on the issue of academic freedom. I do not regret having done so and have no passion to be Chairman as you well know, but it leaves us in the air for the time being." (Wirth to Blumer, 14 December 1950, LW 1:8).

Blumer wrote to Wirth (21 December 1950, LW 1:8) saying "I am sorry the Administration would not accept the recommendation of the Department concerning your appointment as chairman. The Administration is running true to form. I fear that the compromise result of the impasse will be the ultimate selection of Everett as Chairman, something very unfortunate in my judgment, since he is not qualified by ability, scholarship, or student respect to fill the position" (LW 1:8). This and other letters show Blumer's extremely close relation to Wirth. For Burgess's view of the chair fiasco of 1950, see Burgess to Blumer, 19 December 1950, EWB 3:1. Many other faculty, of course, shared Wirth's dislike of Hutchins. Hauser wrote Blumer about a conference during his stint in Washington with the FERA: "I hope [the conference] will be more interesting than listening to Mortimer Adler. St. Thomas does seem so far away" (14 February 34, PMH 14:6).

Although or perhaps because Hutchins had largely ignored the problem of the community, it had become a matter of burning importance. Hyde Park had been gradually declining for years, and the sudden changes following from the Supreme Court's 1947 decision on restrictive covenants had rapidly brought the situation to a crisis level. Wirth spoke to this issue often and incurred Hutchins's implacable opposition for doing so. One commenter said that the true reason for Hutchins's detestation of Wirth was that Wirth had uncovered information that the university had bankrolled supposed "community" organizations that were supporting restrictive covenants and that Wirth provided extensive information to the lawyers arguing to strike those covenants down. We have not found documentary confirmation of this story, but it would account for the heat of Hutchins's relationship with Wirth.

A characteristic Wirth/Hutchins encounter is a memo from Wirth to Hutchins (25 January 46, PP45–50 35:4): "Some of my friends here tell me that at a recent dinner party on the North Side they heard you say that the IQ of the Sociology Department was very low. It is interesting to know what you think of us, but I doubt whether you will improve the Department or advance the interests of the University by such public proclamations." Hutchins replied: "Sorry—I have no recollection of this alleged conversation."

17. The minutes quote is from 5 March 51, LW 62:8. Burgess's annual report is 27 August 51, EWB 33:2. The projected annual report is discussed in "Steps in Achieving Objectives," n.d., EWB 33:2. Other "steps" were strengthening faculty at senior and junior levels, getting more fellowships, and funding student research. Also listed in steps are two pages of "interdisciplinary efforts," which translate into leveraging the faculty with outsiders in order to extend instruction and research.

18. On the back of the Duncan notes is yet another list of candidates: Robin Williams, Franklin Edwards, Morris Janowitz, Ed Swanson, Natalie Rogoff, Josephine Williams, Kingsley Davis, Robert Merton, Paul Hatt, Samuel Stouffer, Fred Strodtbeck; although Burgess was looking somewhat to the non-Chicago outside world by this point, the list is about 50 percent old grads.

19. Apparently other faculty were asked to contribute their own documents, so we have "On a Program for the Department of Sociology" by Reiss, also in EWB 33:2. The "Objectives" document is unsigned and unfinished. Internal evidence assures that Burgess either wrote it or rewrote it—there are near verbatim quotes from the discussions just referred to—but the document's organization and arguments exactly resemble those of Duncan's draft of department aims discussed

in the last faculty seminar meeting. Probably Burgess asked Duncan to rewrite his draft, since Duncan and Foote were the most active of seminar participants.

20. For Blumer's various trips, see the Wirth/Blumer correspondence, in LW 1:8. For Hughes, see Hughes to Burgess, 22 March 1948, EWB 9:3. Hughes went to Germany at the behest of the (university) administration and was quite worried that the resultant slowing of his research would impede his promotion. Hauser's trips are quite evident in his correspondence both within (14:6–11) and beyond (3:1–13, 4:1–5) the university. On the Census affair, see Hauser to Stuart Rice, 8 October 54, PMH 3:12. For Wirth, see correspondence with Burgess in EWB 23:3. It is curious that in the department's great spread over the world landscape the administration could not see evidence of its continuing eminence.

21. Hughes was acceptable as chair nine months later, and so is ruled out. Warner was at this time inactive in sociology and hence an unlikely candidate on internal grounds. That leaves Wirth, Hauser, and Blumer. We know Wirth was both an internal candidate and unacceptable, but he had just been unequivocally refused a year before. We know that Tyler found Hauser unacceptable (Sewell, personal communication) and that Hauser had the ambition to want, indeed to expect, to be director of the U.S. Census, a much bigger job than department chair. About Blumer, much less is known, although his ambition to be chair is evident in his acceptance of the chair at Berkeley on his resignation in July 1952. He, too, was a longtime local, and we know that Hauser, for one, considered him one of the ten most eminent sociologists in the country (Hauser to C. Mady, 2 March 54 PMH 14:8).

22. Tyler made his views clear in his letter to full professors (Burgess, Blumer, Hart, Hauser, Hughes, Warner; for some reason Wirth's name was left off. EWB 33:5, 13 February 1952.) The issue of chair was still open at this point, well over a year after Wirth was found unacceptable to the administration (which now meant Kimpton, Hutchins having resigned in the meantime.) The announcement of Hughes's chairmanship was by press release, 17 November 52, PP52 151:1. Tyler, like Kimpton, was deeply worried about factions and personal disagreements in the department, although at the same time he worried that the great continuity of the department over the past twenty years meant that "new ideas and new directions are necessary." He chose to ignore that the department was already conducting the faculty seminar on the future of sociology.

23. In general, Blumer's departure is hard to understand. His nemesis, Ogburn, was retiring. With his friends Wirth and Hauser, he was about to acquire dominance in the department. His dissatisfactions, although of long duration, had not prevented his remaining before. But there were crucial forces driving him out. Some were professional. An ambitious man—as his subsequent Berkeley chairmanship shows—he was (probably) denied the chair at Chicago and probably foresaw the ascension to that office of Hughes, of whom he thought little. But the crucial reason was personal. Blumer's wife's health required a milder climate. This was undoubtedly the principal motivation for the move, as for the great local secrecy with which it was carried out. We do not know when Blumer began negotiating with Berkeley. He resigned 22 July 52 [PP52 151:1], quite late in the year by

contemporary standards, although the department knew he was leaving at least by 28 May 52.

24. The "unlivable" quote is from Professor Sewell (personal communication). There is some unclarity about the date of the Sewell offer in Professor Sewell's mind and no documentary information on it. Summer 1952 best squares his own recollections with material for which we have documentary evidence. It is noteworthy that in Professor Sewell's recollection Everett Hughes wrote the original offer letter to him, not Burgess. This may mean the offer was later (summer of 1953), but Sewell also recalled that Blumer was not yet gone. Most likely, Hughes was acting for Burgess during one of his quarters out of residence. There is absolutely no indication in any department correspondence about the Sewell offer, and so we may take it as administration-induced. Oddly, Sewell's only close connection in the department was Duncan, whom he had known as a student when he was teaching at Oklahoma and mentored closely since. Sewell had arranged Duncan's appointments at Penn State and Wisconsin, and indeed urged him to go to Chicago rather than stay at Wisconsin in 1950–51.

On Davis, see Foote to Department, 20 February 53 and Duncan to Hauser, 15 July 52, both in PMH 14:11). The Kimpton-Stouffer letter, 10 July 1952, is in PP52 151:1.

25. Although we lack documentary evidence for this story, several personal sources told conforming versions of it.

26. Burgess was investigated in 1949 (by Broyles in Illinois), in 1951 (by the FBI for the USPHS) and in 1953 by the Jenner Subcommittee. Ogburn and Wirth were cotargets with Burgess (and nearly fifty other faculty) in the Broyles affair, in which Hutchins used his talent for ridicule so effectively against the politicians. (Ashmore 1989, 276) See materials in PP52 2:7 and PP45 4:1. On Riesman and Hughes, see particularly Riesman to Hughes, 22 Jun 53, ECH 45:16. The left group was carrying on the strong reformist heritage of the earlier Chicago school.

27. Hughes's style is evident in his correspondence with Riesman, warm but without Riesman's exuberant affection. His caution under fire was proverbial, and is shown in the seminar examined later. Riesman's style is equally proverbial and equally clear in his correspondence with Hughes. For the depth of the abyss, see Riesman (to Hughes 1 June 55) on Duncan. Undoubtedly the special heat between Riesman and Hauser had to do with their very different styles of Jewishness, on which see Riesman to Hughes, 15 May 57, ECH 46:4.

28. Blumer also tried to hire Goodman and Duncan in the years immediately after leaving Chicago. So much for his image as purely qualitative. Faris retained a strong interest in the department. "I am, you can well imagine, greatly interested in the department and hope that its strength and preeminence will not be diminished." Faris to Burgess, 12 July 1951, EWB 7:10. The Faris-Kimpton letter is 5 December 52, PP52:151:1. Of department members, Faris had been probably closest to Wirth; see the letters in LW 3:7. (Wirth was of course dead by this point. Faris seems to have disliked Hauser intensely.) Blumer's recruitment of Hauser lasted over two heavy years. For the first offer, see Hauser to Hughes and Hauser to Horton, both 18 May 53, PMH 14:11. That the first offer was turned

down we know from Burgess's letter to Kimpton (30 June 53, PP52 151:1) thanking him for his intervention. Kimpton was having trouble keeping Tyler himself at this point, and so Tyler's opposition to Hauser may have mattered less. Blumer kept at it: Blumer to Hauser, 10 November 53, PMH 3:6, Hauser to Hughes, 4 June 54, PMH 3:11, Blumer to Hauser, 10 June 54, PMH 3:11, Hauser to Hughes, 17 July 54, PMH 14:11. Hauser finally said no in summer 1954. Blumer was also trying to hire Goodman (personal communication) and Duncan. He kept after Duncan for years (see department minutes, 4 October 56.) For Kimpton's public position on the department, see T. K. Noss to Kimpton, 25 April 52, PP52 151:1: "You may recall that last Thursday night, you told me with a frankness I appreciated that the University of Chicago Department of Sociology is not quite what it used to be. Somewhat sadly I had to agree with you but with some reservations."

29. Kimpton to Blumer, 28 July 52, PP52 151:1, Kimpton to Ogburn, 18 August 52, PP52 151:1. The Ogburn memorandum is in fact an obvious attack on Blumer, with its glorification of quantity of academic production, its attack on public service (Blumer's arbitration work), its explicit valuing of "IQ, imagination, and insight" over "brilliance, debating qualities, skill in dialectics, verbalism and exhibitionism," and its argument that "the role of theory as formerly held is due for some deflation." It is the third characteristic—verbal brilliance—that clearly concerns Blumer, for the faculty seminar transcripts make it very clear that Blumer firmly enjoyed—and very much succeeded in—holding his own against all comers.

30. Hauser's quote is in a memo of 17 February 53, PMH 14:11.

31. Duncan's memo of 2 March 53 and Foote's of 20 February 53 are both in PMH 14:11.

32. Hughes's response is 14 March 53 in PMH 14:11. Shils's move may have been prompted by a fear that the Social Thought party was over. Kimpton was not enamored of the committee. In a memo (1 February 54, PP148:2) Morton Grodzins had said "The Committee on Social Thought performs a number of important and interesting functions." Beside it, Kimpton had penciled, "like what?" Hughes's negotiations with Shils were protracted, being still under way in the summer of 1956 (Hughes to Riesman, 12 August 56, ECH 46:2). That Blau was suggested by Foote is another piece of evidence that the "Columbification" of the department was not a Hauser plot, as is usually assumed. Katz and Rossi were both suggested by Riesman, as was Lipset, whom repeated tries failed to secure.

33. On the second Merton offer, see various letters in PP52 142:2. On outside advice, see Kimpton to John Gardner, 28 July 53, PP 148:2. On Speier, see Hauser to Speier, 10 November 52, PMH 14:11. On Lipset and Katz, see Hauser to Grodzins, 12 July 54, PMH 14:11. Blumer at Berkeley beat his former colleagues in the race for Parsons's star student, Smelser. Berkeley would successfully defend Smelser against Chicago a few years later. Riesman tells his version of his hiring in Berger 1990; Hughes's role was no secret, see, e.g., Hughes to Lipset, 11 February 58, ECH 46:1. The Riesman case tells us how reliable "student memories" are. Kimball Young's taped recollections of Chicago include the comment that Riesman was put into the department by Hutchins, with the result that Louis Wirth "just about had kittens." Wirth had been dead for two years by the time of Riesman's entry, and Hutchins had been gone for nearly three (cf Lindstrom and Hard-

ert, 1988, 305) On Bogue, see Bogue to Hughes, 4 February 53, PMH 14:11. (We also have Mr. Bogue's personal account.) However, Bogue's move into full faculty status was gradual. As late as 3 August 1955, Riesman was writing Hughes that he and Lloyd Warner had considered making a deal with the Hauser faction where the Riesman party would accept Bogue's full status if the Hauser party would agree not to promote Duncan (Riesman to Hughes, ECH 46:2).

34. The Hughes quote is in Hughes to Riesman, 11 February 58, ECH 46:1. That the Hughes/Riesman correspondence is the only major series of letters Hughes preserved from his Chicago years indicates something of the closeness on Hughes's side. On Riesman's side, the many surviving letters are intimate indeed. Both were much closer to each other than to Warner. The correspondence is mostly letters from Riesman to Hughes, since Hughes did not keep copies of many of his own letters. The letters are completely informal, filled with the throwaway thoughts characteristic of conversation—intimate family details, prejudices, and judgments kept carefully out of all more public settings. The letters' emotional force, coupled with Riesman's characteristic style of overstatement, can lead one to overrate the vehemence of Riesman's opinions. But nonetheless the overall pattern and tenor are unmistakable; despite his active recruiting of interesting young people, Riesman played a largely destructive role in departmental politics in the four years of his department membership. The correspondence is all located in ECH 45:15, 16 and 46:1–4, ordered more or less chronologically. We cite it simply by date. On Riesman's reaction to Hughes's chairmanship, and to Burgess, Wirth, and Blumer, see Riesman to Hughes, 22 August 52 and 27 August 52. In particular, Riesman believed that he had been stabbed in the back by Wirth for a job possibility at Haverford; see Riesman to Hughes, 9 March 53.

35. On Lipset, see Hughes to Riesman (n.d., ca. October 52). The cited letter of Hughes is 21 March 53.

36. On McKeon (Riesman also disparaged Fermi and Sewall Wright in the same phrase) see 23 June 53. On Harvard, see 31 August 54. On BASR, see, among many others, 29 June 54 and on the Lynds, 22 August 52. All letters in this note are Riesman to Hughes.

37. On the lost grant, 5 May 54, and on Drake and Janowitz, 22 July 54, both Riesman to Hughes.

38. Votes were a perpetual concern to Riesman, see, e.g., Riesman to Hughes, 1 June 55.

39. On the job issue, see Hughes to Riesman, 30 April 54 and 8 May 54. On Hughes's relief at quitting, see Hughes to Riesman, 3 August 56.

40. Various letters through the PP52 series (151:1,2,2.1) show that Hauser in fact cultivated Kimpton considerably, sending him reprints, notices of his activities, and the like. On the Leisure Center, see Riesman to Hauser, 26 September 55, PMH 14:11. On the Field affair, see W. B. Cannon to Riesman, 19 January 55, PP52 148:4. On the new NORC, see Norton Ginsburg to Hauser, 23 July 55, PMH 14:11. Interestingly, it was Hauser, not chair Everett Hughes, who at this time made a major presentation to the trustees on the department. See the Riesman memo above. Riesman was on the *Time* cover 27 September 54.

41. The men were also absolutely different as people, as we have noted

above. Riesman's position paper on the future of the department survives, 8 March 56, in ECH 46:2. It contains various olive branches to the other side but is not really a centrist document. In it, Riesman discusses in cold-war metaphors Hauser's attack on a Hughes/Riesman student at a dissertation hearing and goes on to discuss the two camps in considerable detail. His statement makes it clear that Warner was the only person who really tried to reconcile the two sides. On the public nature of Riesman's position, see Riesman to Hughes, 19 May 57, which tells of Grodzins' warnings to Kimpton about Riesman's probable departure.

42. Hauser had extensive prior administrative experience both in Washington and in Chicago. He had been associate dean of social sciences under Ralph Tyler in the late 1940s before he burned his bridges in the 4E episode. Sources for the Goodman twist of the "chair affair" are Leo Goodman and then-dean Chauncy Harris. Harris is our only source on Kimpton's role. Kimpton left no personal records about it.

43. Kimpton to Riesman, 1 May 57, PP52 151:2.1. Hauser to Kimpton, 16 January 59, same location. The "youngsters" quote is from Harris to Board of Trustees, 13 November 59, SSV.

44. The Duncan decision, like the chair debacle, was simply an outcome of prior politics, although Duncan had mortally offended Warner, one of the swing voters, before he arrived. In 1950 the ASR had published Duncan's characteristically sharp and effective attack on Warner's entire oeuvre in social stratification (Pfautz and Duncan 1950). Interestingly enough, it was a Chicago attack; the theoretical justifications invoked the names of Park, Burgess, Wirth, and Simmel. Warner, Duncan said, was being misled by the anthropologists. (Duncan himself attributes the theoretical parts of the paper to his coauthor, Harold Pfautz.) In hindsight, it is easy to read Duncan's article as a white paper for the *American Occupational Structure* (Blau and Duncan 1967). The University finally admitted its error on this particular decision. In 1979, Duncan was given an honorary degree.

45. On the Strauss tenure decision, see Riesman to Hughes, 24 October 57. Riesman accused the other side of favoring sociology with large divisions of labor, rather curious given his and Hughes's Kansas City project.

46. On the Warner affair, see Hauser to Kimpton, 16 January 59. In keeping with a "take-no-prisoners" attitude, Hauser opposed this. Warner had of course been a central force against Duncan, Hauser's most important protégé. On Hughes's cautions to Riesman, see Hughes to Riesman, 15 May 57.

47. Harrison to Kimpton, 24 June 57, PP52 151:1.

48. Hauser to Harris, 8 December 58, SSV.

49. Hauser to Harris, 3 November 59, SSV.

50. On White, see Hauser to Harris, 3 November 59, SSV.

51. Janowitz was actually someone on whom Hauser and Riesman agreed, although Riesman found Janowitz's personal style distasteful in the extreme. See Riesman to Hughes, 22 July 54. In studying this history one cannot avoid a conclusion that Hauser's take-no-prisoners attitude grew, like Riesman's, out of the almost visceral dislike of the two for each other. Whether a third party of sufficient

force could have controlled the two is matter for speculation; certainly Hughes did not have the fortitude.

52. On Wirth and Warner, see Farber 1988, 342. Riesman's claims about Alice and Peter Rossi are in Riesman 1990.

53. Riesman saw Parsons's social relations department as a social science ideal, but under threat. That he felt this at a time when Parsons's flow of turgid tomes was well under way—*The Social System, Economy and Society,* and *Towards a General Theory of Action* were all in print by this point—indicates his complete failure to grasp what the Chicago tradition was about. Hughes had profound insight into Riesman, who, he saw, was actually much more interested in undergraduate teaching than anything else. See Hughes to Riesman, 15 May 57, on the latter's resignation.

54. In 1950, the Ford Foundation gave grants of $300,000 apiece to seven institutions for the expansion of social science (Foote to Seminar, 12 May 52, EWB 33:4). At Chicago, the funds were auctioned by the Social Science Research Council, a divisional committee of which Wirth was the chair. The department used its funds to support and transcribe a seminar. It seems likely that the seminar was Wirth's idea. He made the application for the money (Minutes 11 October), he set the agenda with a long fall memorandum (undated, but eventually distributed 10 December 51), and he often dominated discussion. Moreover, Wirth's opening presentation makes it clear that his interlocutors had only hazy ideas of what was planned. In his annual report to Dean Tyler (27 August 51, EWB 33:2), Burgess platitudinizes on the seminar as dealing with research and training. But in opening the seminar on 11 October, he simply turned it over to Wirth. All documents relevant to this seminar are located, in roughly chronological order, in EWB 33:2–4. All primary material referenced in these sections is in those folders, and so we have provided no direct citation, only dates. We have dated some of the undated documents by inspecting the vouchers for reproducing them, which are in SSV.

55. The historians may deny that there is a Chicago approach to sociology, but for long periods most Chicago graduates thought there was. They disagreed about *what* it was. But that it existed, they had little doubt.

56. The group that sat down to this discussion in October included Burgess, but not Ogburn, who had dropped out of departmental affairs by this point. Of the next generation, Hauser was out of town for the entire year, but Wirth, Blumer, Hughes, and Warner were present. All were in their early fifties. Nearly all the rest of the group were thirty or less. Duncan, Goodman, Reiss, Williams, and Star were all very recent Ph.D.'s. Foote, Wilensky, and Moore were graduate students. Only Donald Horton, an anthropologist collaborating with Warner, and Buford Junker, a graduate student who was Warner's chief field worker, were between these two groups in age. Neither was very active, so the meetings took the interactional form of senior professors arguing with themselves or with much younger people.

The discussions were, as the administration would have predicted, untainted by knowledge of non-Chicago sociology. Of ten Ph.D.'s in regular attendance, eight were from Chicago. Of four graduate students, three were at Chicago. Nelson Foote, a Cornell graduate student, was the only voice persistently representing "other versions" of sociology in the discussion. Attendance at the seminars was very regular, with 11 of 16 attendees making at least 9 of 12 sessions. The irregulars included Warner, who made only five meetings, and the NORC group of Hart, Star, and Williams.

57. There were syllabi for each of the six major areas (Social Organization, Social Disorganization and Change, Social Psychology and Collective Behavior, Population and Human Ecology, Theory, and Methods.) These were large documents (typically thirty pages) of citations and notes, to be mastered for specialization in the field by the graduate student. The current form of the documents was new, but the areas (other than theory and methods) were over twenty years old at Chicago. Short versions of the syllabi were published in the *Announcements* and formed the basis of discussion at session #8. At the time of the seminar, only two of the syllabi were complete, as a remark of Foote's at the second meeting makes clear. That is why only two were discussed.

58. There may have been meetings whose minutes somehow did not make it into Burgess's files. But internal evidence suggests strongly that these twelve were the only ones held. Thus, the only lengthy conversations concerned social psychology, which was Blumer's chief responsibility, and social organization, which was that of Warner and Hughes. We thus have searching examinations of two major strands of the Chicago school, Blumerian symbolic interactionism and Hughesian anthropological study of social organization. Missing is the third leg of the stool, human ecology. Its syllabus unfinished, it was present only in its comments on the others.

59. Wirth does in fact note the specific connection of sociology with certain particular areas of inquiry—family, criminality, community. He knows that these give rise to the archipelagic impression. But for him the other quality, of "sociology as a general social science," is more important. Unlike Hughes and Warner, for whom recognition of sociology's general character allows one to get ahead with the business of discussing its local subdivisions, Wirth feels we must define the heart of sociology itself as a general point of view. He and Parsons agreed on that, although on nothing else. Joseph Gusfield tells a story of Parsons coming to give an important lecture at Chicago. Wirth sat in the front row, opening and reading his mail.

60. It is painfully clear from this discussion that, as his letters suggest, Blumer thought Hughes a very second-rate mind. On the other hand, they agreed that both had had the experience of finding their work and their students confined over the last decade. Blumer raised the point specifically, late in this meeting, and Burgess demurred. (Ogburn was obviously the culprit; all faculty voted on M.A. and Ph.D. proposals, and he clearly had carried out his prejudices.) But Hughes jumped in to defend Blumer.

61. The meeting closed with a discussion on particulars and universals that got Blumer, and everyone else, into a complete mess. It is relieved only by Blumer's hilarious travesty of Merton's then-recent phrase "middle-range theory" as "middle-class generalizations," of which, of course, Blumer disapproves as being illegitimate hybrids of the universal and the particular.

62. This episode suggests a two-stage loss model for a tradition. Blumer had

the central commitments, but did little research. To the Duncan generation, he and others passed on those commitments. But in their teaching, that next generation somehow trained a lot of people who mistook the methods for the commitments that animated them. In their hands, the methods became the dead machinery Duncan rails against in *Notes*.

63. The reader will note that the shape of this argument is exactly the current one. Foote's statements might have been copied verbatim by Kuhn ten years later, although Foote himself says his position was inspired by J. B. Conant. Blumer's position, oddly enough, is the position of contemporary empirical sociology, defending itself against the extreme positions of postmodernism. And the final argument for the existence of "real truth," as always, is the fact that most relativists agree with Blumer's desire to have truth determined by something other than power.

64. The syllabi tended to be identified with the old major courses. The social change syllabus derived from Ogburn's course of the same name. Duncan was particularly concerned, both in discussion and in a special memo of 4 February, that the Ogburnian perspective on overall social change in complex societies not be lost. "The Department is losing, by retirement, a man who was able to make a distinctive synthesis of views and approaches of sufficient cogency and appeal to render his name virtually synonymous—in American sociology, not only at the University of Chicago—with the idea of 'social change'."

It is hard, in retrospect, to imagine the emotions riding on the Park lineage. In this respect, too, the anthropology issue was an emotionally charged one, for anthropologist Robert Redfield—who had so much influenced Hughes and Warner and had collaborated with them on the social organization syllabus—was not only another Park student but also Park's son-in-law. The Redfield and Hughes families were close. Other aspects of the Park heritage, however, had gone elsewhere; Blumer, for example, got Park's office. One should recall that Wirth, Blumer, and Hughes all received degrees from the department when it still included the university's anthropologists (in their time, Fay Cooper-Cole and Edward Sapir).

65. On the history of the SSSP, see the various papers in the twenty-fifth anniversary volume of *Social Problems,* particular Skura (1976) and Lauer (1976).

REFERENCES

Abbott, A. 1992. "Of Time and Space." Sorokin Lecture. Southern Sociological Society, New Orleans, 10 April 1992.

Adams, R. 1977. "An Organization and Its Uncertain Environment." M.A. Thesis, University of Chicago.

Ashmore, H. S. 1989. *Unseasonable Truths.* Boston: Little, Brown.

Berger, B., ed. 1990. *Authors of Their Own Lives.* Berkeley: University of California Press.

Blau, P. M., and O. D. Duncan. 1967. *The American Occupational Structure.* New York: Wiley.

Bulmer, M. 1984. *The Chicago School of Sociology.* Chicago: University of Chicago Press.
Duncan, O. D. 1984. *Notes on Social Measurement.* New York: Russell Sage.
Farber, B. 1988. "The Human Element." *Sociological Perspectives* 31:339–59.
Gusfield, J. R. 1992. "The Scholarly Tension." Pp. 167–77 in J. MacAloon, ed., *General Education in the Social Sciences.* Chicago: University of Chicago Press.
Harvey, L. 1987. *Myths of the Chicago School of Sociology.* Aldershot: Avebury.
Lauer, R. H. 1976. "Defining Social Problems." *Social Problems* 24:122–30.
Lengermann, P. M. 1979. "The Founding of the American Sociological Review." *American Sociological Review* 44:185–98.
Lindstrom, F. B., and R. A. Hardert, eds. 1988. "Kimball Young on the Chicago School." *Sociological Perspectives* 31:298–314.
MacAloon, J. J., ed. 1992. *General Education in the Social Sciences.* Chicago: University of Chicago Press.
McNeill, W. H. 1991. *Hutchins' University.* Chicago: University of Chicago Press.
Park, R. E., and E. W. Burgess. [1921]1970. *Introduction to the Science of Sociology.* Chicago: University of Chicago Press.
Pfautz, H. W., and O. D. Duncan. 1950. "A Critical Evaluation of Warner's Work in Community Stratification." *American Sociological Review* 15:205–15.
Riesman, D. 1990. "Becoming an Academic Man." Pp. 33–74 in B. M. Berger, ed., *Authors of Their Own Lives.* Berkeley: University of California Press.
Riesman, D. 1992. "My Education in Soc 2 and My Efforts to Adapt It in the Harvard Setting." Pp. 178–216 in J. J. MacAloon, ed., *General Education in the Social Sciences.* Chicago: University of Chicago Press.
Skura, B. 1976. "Constraints on a Reform Movement." *Social Problems* 24:15–36.
Time. 1954. "Social Scientist David Riesman." Vol. 64, 16 September, pp. 22–25.
Turner, R. H. 1988. "Collective Behavior without Guile." *Sociological Perspectives.* 31:315–24.
Turner, S. P., and J. H. Turner. 1990. *The Impossible Science.*" Newbury Park Calif.: Sage.

CHAPTER EIGHT

THE CHICAGO SCHOOL OF SOCIOLOGY AND THE FOUNDING OF THE GRADUATE PROGRAM IN SOCIOLOGY AT BRANDEIS UNIVERSITY: A CASE STUDY IN CULTURAL DIFFUSION

Shulamit Reinharz

This volume asks whether or not a "second Chicago school" emerged in the Department of Sociology at the University of Chicago in mid-century. And if so, did that intellectual school have an impact analogous to the profound influence of the original Chicago school? This chapter, by contrast, poses a different, yet related question. It asks about the legacy of the first Chicago school. Specifically, did mid-century Chicago sociologists remain wedded to the earlier approaches or did the ideas of the first school leave Chicago and take root elsewhere? To examine these questions I draw on a single case—a graduate program created elsewhere in mid-century. The methods used to develop the argument are drawn from the Chicago school itself: life history and retrospective ethnography.

THE FOUNDING OF THE UNIVERSITY OF CHICAGO AND BRANDEIS UNIVERSITY

In 1890 a Baptist foundation, endowed with oil stocks donated by John D. Rockefeller, Sr., established the University of Chicago and helped to transform the Midwest.[1] In 1948 a Jewish group followed in this tradition, founded its own university, and helped to transform the composition of American higher education. In addition to contributing to the broad array of institutions of higher learning created by other denominations, this group's purpose was to counteract discrimination against Jewish students and faculty in the United States. This new, nonsectarian university took the name of Supreme Court Justice Louis Brandeis and chose the location of Waltham, Massachusetts, a working-class Boston suburb.

At the time of the founding of the University of Chicago, its president, William Rainey Harper, had a clear educational philosophy focusing on basic research and graduate training.[2] Although it would have an undergraduate college and an extension branch devoted to teaching, the university's central mission would be research. To achieve this atypical goal, Harper hired "the best available men in the country," senior professors with national reputations.[3] The founders of Brandeis University similarly aimed for national prominence. Eschewing "a pedestrian undertaking, shaming the American Jewish community," they wanted to establish "a high-quality institution that would meet the hopes of generations who had so long waited for fulfillment."[4]

Whereas Harper stressed research over teaching, the founders of Brandeis University stressed smallness of scale. Their idea was to begin as an undergraduate college with a favorable faculty-student ratio that would hasten accreditation. In time Brandeis would add graduate programs, "never unduly expanding enrollment so as to lose the character of intimacy,"[5] in the words of founding president Abram Sachar. This plan was geared to producing "a university with the very best graduate programs,"[6] capable of the same excellence in research that Harper had advocated. To achieve this goal Sachar, like Harper, was deliberate about the people he would hire. Basically, he recruited two types:

> young and feisty faculty who had the courage to join our experiment early in their careers. . . . and sagacious men and women whose scholarship had ripened, whose stature was national and international, and whose wisdom and experience would give us balance.[7]

Many faculty in the latter group were retirees "in their late sixties and even in their seventies, in excellent health and at the peak of their reputation and effectiveness."[8] The prestige of these scholars quickly put Brandeis on the academic map.

One of Harper's notable recruits in 1892 was Albion Small, president of Colby College, a small Baptist school in Maine. It was Small's idea to establish a sociology department (at first combined with anthropology), in part because none existed in the United States at the time.[9] The University of Chicago was able to implement Small's idea because as a new, midwestern university it was "relatively free from the constraints of older American academic traditions."[10] Soon the department became the home of a distinctive form of sociology known as "the Chicago school."[11] This chapter suggests that "the Chicago school" later diffused, in part, to Brandeis University's graduate program in sociology.

Innovation was part of the founding of Brandeis University in the late 1940s just as it was of the University of Chicago in the 1890s. For example, the post–World War II arrival in the United States of many academic refugees who then faced McCarthy-fueled antagonism offered Sachar an opportunity to provide a haven, even with little funds, for scholars unwelcome in other U.S. academic institutions.[12] A noted example is the political scientist Herbert Marcuse, who was recruited at a time when most universities were hostile to Marxists.[13] Others found in Brandeis a haven from mandatory retirement. By 1954 Brandeis University was a fully accredited college that began establishing one or two graduate programs each year, just as planned.

In the early 1960s the sociology department was ready to develop its graduate program. It was into this set of circumstances that Everett Cherrington Hughes was recruited from the sociology department at the University of Chicago in 1961 at the age of sixty-four to inaugurate graduate sociological study at Brandeis University. Hughes's move thus connected the oldest department of sociology in the United States with the youngest. This connection can be interpreted as a case study in the sociology of knowledge with three dimensions: (1) for Brandeis, Hughes provided the new graduate program with instant legitimacy; (2) for "the Chicago school," Brandeis provided a needed home;[14] and (3) for Hughes personally, the opportunity to create a new graduate program became a chance to flourish in a welcoming environment.[15] In addition, for sociology as a discipline, this transfer helped sustain an alternative research method.

Although there were intellectual connections between Brandeis and other universities, particularly Columbia and Harvard, the ties with the University of Chicago were unusual because of their relatively large number, their role in the formative period of the graduate program, and the fact that the individuals involved ranged from graduate students to senior faculty. The remainder of this chapter explains these processes by drawing on (1) interviews and written statements I solicited from the earliest recipients of Brandeis sociology Ph.D.'s; (2) interviews I conducted with current and former Brandeis faculty; (3) primary documents such as course materials, training grant applications and catalogues; (4) correspondence between the editor of this volume (Gary Alan Fine) and graduates of the University of Chicago; and (5) secondary literature. My extensive use of interviews reflects my intention of conveying *perceptions* of the Chicago-Brandeis connection and their *meaning* in sustaining "the Chicago school." Interview data reveal the "origin tales" people tell to construct a coherent understanding of the past.[16] Interview data allowed me to identify socialization practices that characterize this particular component of the larger cultural diffusion process. In order to understand the more general pattern of diffusion of a particular school of sociology, comparative case studies of other institutions are needed.

THE ROLE OF EVERETT HUGHES IN THE CHICAGO-BRANDEIS CONNECTION

At first glance Everett Hughes may seem an unlikely candidate for the position of creating a new graduate program at Brandeis. Hughes was the son of a Protestant minister—"the quintessential WASP"[17]—and Brandeis was a Jewish-sponsored university with a largely Jewish faculty and student body. On the other hand, Hughes had been an early critic of German fascism, had been surrounded by Jewish students at Chicago, and like many of the senior scholars recruited to Brandeis, he was a refugee of sorts. Not a survivor of war-torn Europe or hounded by McCarthyism, Hughes was a refugee from the prospect of mandatory retirement at Chicago. Gradually he had become an outsider in his own department in part because, ironically, as the department chair he had hired people whose definition of sociology clashed with his own.

A graduate of the University of Chicago in 1928, Everett Hughes represented the strength of qualitative Chicago sociology in its heyday. There is little disagreement that this tradition was declining as the century progressed. The question is simply when the decline began. Some scholars focus on the 1930s,[18] after William Ogburn was invited from Barnard College–Columbia University in 1927 to bring "scientific" sociology based on statistics.[19] Ogburn stayed at the University of Chicago until his retirement twenty-four years later in 1951. He had been recruited "in order to strengthen the quantitative side of the department's work and ensure that Chicago retained its strength as the leading department of sociology in the country."[20] The earlier tradition that was identified with W. I. Thomas and Robert Park conflicted with this positivist definition.

Everett Hughes had been Robert Park's student and the editor of his works[21] (as was Helen Hughes),[22] advocating the kind of empirical research inspired by W. I. Thomas and later by Park.[23] When Hughes returned to Chicago as a faculty member in 1938 after having taught at McGill and having been away for ten years, the older tradition was being contested both at the University of Chicago and around the country. Lines of antagonism had developed between rival methodological camps.[24] According to Patricia and Peter Adler,[25] two current analysts of field methods:

> In the 1930s, the Department of Sociology at Chicago lost its national position of preeminence. Park had retired early in the decade[26] and Burgess ceased to mentor many students. . . . Departments on the East and West Coasts began to rise in predominance. . . . By the 1940s and 1950s, with the advent of Parsons' rise at Harvard and Columbia's growing dominance in the field of public opinion polling and survey research, sociology in America had shifted to a more quantitative paradigm.[27]

Roger Salerno, the biographer of Louis Wirth who had studied at Chicago from 1916–1926 and taught there from 1930 on, agrees with this assessment:

> The Chicago school began to lose its position of prominence. . . . Blumer wrote very little; Faris and Ogburn were not outstandingly prolific nor creative scholars. Neither was as personally dynamic as Wirth. Burgess' contributions were minimal. By the time of the Second World War, Everett Hughes had joined the faculty, but it was too late. Sociology had taken a new direction. Columbia and Harvard had new and groundbreaking programs. Sociology was becoming more abstract and metaphysical, and . . . people such as Talcott Parsons were gaining prominence by viewing society from an extremely detached intellectual perspective.[28]

Whereas some scholars date the decline as early as 1927 or the 1930s, Brandeis sociology professor emeritus Kurt Wolff sees the major change as occurring in 1952:

> Blumer went to California; Wirth and Ogburn died.[29] Burgess died either that same year or the next year.[30] The major senior people disappeared. And in fact, I do remember that Everett talked about the total change in the department, which alienated him. Philip Hauser ran the [department] and his sort of sociology was demography.[31]

Reiterating the significance of these events, Chicago graduate James Short writes that Hughes alone remained from the old tradition.[32] Fred

Davis, a Chicago graduate, agrees, but like several insiders, Davis sees Hughes as having *caused* the change:

> The one sense I had from my contact with the place following my departure in the fall of 1951 was that there had been a tremendous transformation. Everett Hughes ironically enough in his attempts to bring Chicago more of what was then passing for contemporary sociology, managed to bring in quite a few people from the Bureau of Applied Social Research at Columbia, and this, it was my sense, profoundly changed the complexion of the place. By the time Everett left . . . there was almost no feeling for the Chicago we knew in the immediate post-war years.[33]

Former Brandeis faculty member Robert Weiss, an admirer of Hughes, describes the situation at Chicago in 1957:

> Everett was a little out of favor already. Hauser was the chairman of the department. He brought the Columbia people in like Pete Rossi, Jim Coleman, Elihu Katz. And they were heavy quantitative types. So the old Chicago was on the way out. Hughes was already becoming a relic.[34]

Morris S. Schwartz, a student at Chicago and a subsequent colleague of Hughes at Brandeis, found "Hughes to be very unhappy at Chicago. . . . And he was quite different here. . . . He knew this was going to be a good place. It was a new young school."[35] Many others who earned their Ph.D.'s at Chicago, from 1945 on, support this contention: the Chicago faculty retired,[36] died,[37] or went to Berkeley[38] and Michigan,[39] and the Chicago tradition was disappearing.

Some hallmarks of Hughes's views were indifference to academic boundaries; insistence that "empirical research . . . use a long temporal perspective," and that abstract and general categories be used to analyze social reality.[40] He defined social research broadly: the study of contemporary social reality with eclectic research methods.[41] The key element was a commitment to learn about the social world through active engagement in fieldwork rather than reliance on survey techniques or demographic data. The development of sociological concepts from observation of everyday life and discussion with key informants had characterized the Chicago school of sociology and Hughes's own work. As its prestige diminished, however, it was renamed "soft," anecdotal, unscientific, and journalistic. Hughes gradually became a remnant of a displaced tradition, a monument to the past in a neighborhood that had changed.

While sociology was shifting its focus in the country and in his own department, Hughes sustained the fieldwork tradition by urging students to observe in situ, as anthropologists did. He transmitted to his students the importance of studying communities, forms of work, and institutions, particularly medical and psychiatric settings. Although the tradition was waning, his influence can be seen in the work of many prominent Chicago graduates of the 1940s and 1950s, including Howard Becker,[42] Herbert Gans,[43] Erving Goffman,[44] and Anselm Strauss.[45] In Fred Davis's words:

> The other person (in addition to Blumer) who seemed to in-
> fluence a great many of us was Everett Hughes. And being in
> his classes . . . was tremendously exciting and refreshing. Ev-
> erything was grist for Everett's mill! You could look at . . . any
> situation. . . . He sort of made things congenial for a very in-
> ductive method in sociology.[46]

This influence was transferred to Brandeis even by Chicago graduates who were not Hughes's direct students, such as John Seeley and Morris Schwartz.[47]

As a faculty member in the Chicago sociology department from 1938 to 1961,[48] Hughes initiated a course in methods of field observation for students of sociology, anthropology, and social science. One study concludes that Everett Hughes "was perhaps the strongest driving force behind the development of participant observation as a distinct methodology," in part because he and his students had to "explain and justify their research procedures" in the face of criticism by statisticians.[49] Many of the students whom Hughes later taught at Brandeis similarly took up the mantle of defending and defining fieldwork techniques.[50] For example, the anthology on field research edited by Robert Emerson ('68)[51] is dedicated to Everett Hughes, "whose teaching and sensitivities link generations of fieldworkers."[52]

At Brandeis, Everett Hughes found fertile soil for the transplantation of his version of the Chicago school of sociology.[53] Like all transplanted phenomena, however, the Chicago school was transformed at Brandeis in response to existing conditions and new forces in the society at large (e.g. the antiwar, civil rights, and feminist movements). The Chicago tradition was not rigid and gradually became one of several forces, including more overtly and leftist political frameworks, Marxist theory, political economy, comparative historical and critical theories.[54] Because the Brandeis program did not establish a strong positivist or quantitative component, however, the Chicago tradition remained pronounced.

Hughes came to Brandeis with a five-year contract. When it expired in 1968, Sachar offered one-year renewable contracts until Hughes reached seventy. At the same time, Hughes received and accepted an open-ended contract from Boston College. Hughes's ties to Brandeis were not severed when he moved his office a few miles away to Boston College. Brandeis faculty encouraged graduate students to take his courses there; he continued to serve on numerous Brandeis Ph.D. committees; faculty consulted with him about their work;[55] and the Brandeis department sponsored his seventy-fifth birthday celebration. In 1987, four years after Hughes died and nearly twenty years after he had left Brandeis, the department held a contest to name its newly created graduate student lounge. Tellingly, the name with most votes was "The Helen and Everett Hughes Lounge."

LAYING THE GROUND FOR THE
CHICAGO-BRANDEIS CONNECTION

Although Everett Hughes's arrival at Brandeis was crucial in creating the perception that Brandeis was the home of the old Chicago school, one must understand the fledgling program which accepted it. As Robert Heine-Goldern wrote in an essay on cultural diffusion: "Whether a particular trait is accepted depends not only on its utility to the borrowers but even more on whether or not it can be integrated into the receiving culture."[56] One characteristic of this period was rapid expansion. In Brandeis's earliest years, sociology was taught in a social science department. Later, an anthropology-sociology department was formed, chaired by anthropologist Paul Radin. Sociologist Lewis Coser joined that department in 1951 (he stayed at Brandeis until 1969), and Maurice Stein joined in 1955 (he is still on the faculty).[57] The sociologists who made up the faculty that eventually brought in Hughes were Coser, Stein, Schwartz, Weiss, and Wolff. Each contributed to Brandeis's becoming a receptive host for Hughes's cultural diffusion.

Even though they were not Chicago graduates, Lewis Coser and Maurice Stein prepared the ground for the future Chicago-shaped graduate sociology program at Brandeis. Coser had had some personal contact with Chicago personnel. Specifically, at David Riesman's invitation, he had taught social science in the college at the University of Chicago before becoming a graduate student at Columbia. Later, Robert K. Merton suggested that Coser return briefly to Chicago to study with Hughes. Although Coser was not a field-worker, neither was he a survey researcher. After receiving his Columbia Ph.D., Coser accepted the offer from Brandeis, which he saw as a haven for liberal and radical ideas.[58]

Maurice Stein's connection was more substantive. He had been trained in fieldwork as an undergraduate by Alvin Gouldner at the University of Buffalo,[59] and in his first year at Brandeis he taught two courses, "American Communities—Theoretical Framework" and "American Communities—Field Research." Later he offered "Advanced Field Studies." In the catalogue Stein described the first course using concepts and authorities of the Chicago school:

> Field studies of American cities of diverse sizes, economies and regional locations . . . leading to a general theory of community growth, structures and functioning. . . . Community responses to urbanization, industrialization and bureaucratization as described by Park, Lynd and Warner.[60]

Similarly, Stein's field research course offered "training in techniques of community research including the use of ecological maps, demographic data, documentary materials, life-histories, questionnaires, participant-observation and depth interviewing."[61] In 1960 Stein published *Eclipse of Community,* a book that Everett Hughes noticed and praised. In addition Stein began writing critical analyses of survey research, structural functionalism, and positivist sociology,[62] the dominant trends at Columbia where he had been a graduate student with Coser.

In 1960 Coser and Stein hired Morris S. Schwartz, the first Chicago Ph.D. to join the Brandeis faculty. A field-worker and analyst of participant observation methods,[63] Schwartz entered as a full professor while Coser and Stein were junior faculty. Schwartz remembers the bifurcation of the Chicago faculty during his graduate-student days (1944–47) and the significance of fieldwork training:

> *Schwartz:* I was a Blumer student. There was this division between the more quantitative, "scientific" people which Ogburn represented [he was chair most of the time I was there], and the Blumerites, who were social psychologists and symbolic interactionists. In between was good old Ernie Burgess who tried to bridge both camps.
> *Reinharz:* Who represented fieldwork?

Schwartz: Hughes. And Warner a little bit too.[64] He was involved in fieldwork as an anthropologist. But Hughes primarily represented it. We had a seminar the first year. That's when the Gunnar Myrdal book came out and he had that part in the introduction about biases, and the best you can do is just state what they are rather than try to get rid of them. So we had a discussion about that as part of the fieldwork curriculum. Wirth was very much involved with fieldwork although he wasn't much of a fieldworker. But he was very interested in having people go into the field. He did a study of the Jewish community and did a book on the ghetto. Hughes was the primary one.[65]

In 1959 sociology separated from anthropology and became a free-standing department consisting of Coser (chair), Stein and Schwartz. This group hired Kurt Wolff and Robert Weiss.[66] Although Wolff came as a full professor from Ohio State University, he too had some personal and substantive Chicago connections. In 1943–44 he had been affiliated with the University of Chicago on a Social Science Research Council fellowship supervised first by Robert Redfield and then by Louis Wirth.[67] In Wolff's words:

> Louis Wirth was a fellow immigrant, you know, of considerably older vintage, via Hitler. He was nice. I sat in on his course on the sociology of knowledge. He could talk for two hours without notes, and usually quite interesting, totally without structure. He had translated Mannheim, who had been my most influential teacher.

Wolff used his fellowship to study the New Mexico town of "Loma":

> The other course I took was Redfield on methodology. . . . I'm not a Chicago sociologist, except in the sense that I'm very sympathetic to the way they went about studying the Jack Roller, the Gold Coast, the Slum, or whatever they studied.[68]

While in Chicago, Wolff met Everett Hughes, Ernest Burgess, William Ogburn and Sol Tax. Later, Wolff published an article about the ordering of fieldnotes and began work on "surrender and catch" as elements of fieldwork.[69]

As mentioned above, the second person hired by the faculty of the separate department of sociology was assistant professor Robert Weiss, a quantitative methodologist and researcher who had taught at the college of the University of Chicago after being brought there from the University of Michigan by David Riesman in the mid-1950s. Despite Weiss's background in mathematics, he was drawn to fieldwork and to the kind of sociology that Hughes represented. In his words:

> One of the attractions of Chicago was that I would be able to work with Everett Hughes. I don't know how I knew about Hughes but my image of him was that he was the grand guru of qualitative work and I knew that I wanted to apprentice myself.[70]

After a few years of teaching at the two-year college component of the University of Chicago, Weiss was ready to move to a university where he could have a different kind of faculty position. He found this opportunity in the new department at Brandeis:

> What Brandeis wanted was somebody who would be a quantitative person who would nevertheless be in sympathy with the generally anti-quantitative climate of the department. And the funny thing about that was that they found someone—me. It was an EXTRAORDINARY match.[71]

Hughes subsequently influenced Weiss profoundly, suggesting that faculty may influence their colleagues as much as they do students. Looking back, Weiss says that "it really was an extraordinary educational opportunity. If I know any sociology, I'm sure I learned it in that context from Everett."[72]

In 1959 and 1960, the Brandeis sociology faculty, then consisting of Coser, Stein, Schwartz, Wolff, and Weiss began to plan a graduate program. Weiss remembers the situation as follows:

> It was the end of the first year that the idea came by of Everett taking his sabbatical year with us. I think it was Dave Riesman who came up with the idea. I thought that was wonderful. I introduced it at one of the department meetings . . . and we got a positive response from Everett. And somewhere along here I must have seen Dave [Riesman] again, and . . . Dave said, 'Why invite him for a sabbatical? Why not invite him for an appointment?' It was evident that Dave had talked to Everett about that.[73]

Riesman had a high opinion of the sociologists at Brandeis[74] and knew it would be a suitable home for a man of Hughes's stature. At the same time, Hughes was increasingly uncomfortable in Chicago.

What turned out to have been happening [was that] Everett was being treated as an honored fossil at Chicago by the Young Turks who were, of course, highly machined. To them this was someone from prehistoric times. And even though they were nice to him, even deferential, they also wanted to get rid of him. And Everett was finding it intolerable. They wanted him to move to an honorable retirement and to bring him out for special occasions. So the notion to come to Brandeis was like a refuge, a haven. . . . So I came back to the department and said there's a possibility that Everett might join us full-time. Everett came on something like a 5-year appointment without tenure, without commitment for a raise, and without an extraordinary salary.[75]

Maurice Stein shares the view that hiring Everett Hughes fit exactly into the emerging department's needs at Brandeis:

Lew [Coser] thought that bringing in Everett would be a marvellous thing. I think he felt it would be wonderful to start a [graduate] department with someone as prestigious as Everett. Lew appreciated Everett's kind of sociology.[76] He had a sense of Everett as a key person. So we had this whole deal worked out where we were going to bring Morrie and Kurt and then Everett.[77]

Department chair Wolff knew that Hughes had to retire from Chicago in 1962 and proposed his name to Brandeis president Sachar as the person to launch the graduate program. According to Schwartz:

I think he was hired directly by Sachar because he had that big a name. He was or was close to being president of the ASA (1963). That may have been one of the reasons he was hired. They wanted some big names.[78]

According to Wolff, after Sachar gave Hughes the contract,

We waited for him to start the program, and we discussed the various aspects of the graduate program and how to start it and what the requirements would be and so forth. We had our first graduate students, and I think even then we had a very large number of applicants. For a number of years, we had an average of 200 applicants. . . . We were very popular and we took as many as 15.
    Reinharz: Why were we popular?

Wolff: Our courses sounded interesting; Coser and Hughes were very well known, illustrious; Schwartz had many connections in the social psychological area; and people were interested in the sociology of knowledge, which wasn't taught in many places.

Reinharz: Did you hire Everett to do something Chicago-like?

Wolff: A great majority of us liked Chicago sociology and we liked him. In my judgment he was one of the best, if not *the* best, of the Chicago sociologists. He had a major influence in the shaping of the graduate program. One aspect, of course, was fieldwork which he pushed, and for which, thanks above all to his connections and fame and status, we got two training fellowships . . . from government agencies. That was also an attractive feature of the graduate program because they paid quite well and they lasted quite a number of years. He and Weiss did those.

Reinharz: Did the department have a mission?

Wolff: The mission was qualitative sociology—it was the major focus and was recognized as such, "understanding sociology" in contrast to quantitative.[79] There was no pooh-poohing of quantitative aspects, as long as they didn't become the aim, but rather the means, to do work that made sense, not just following a cookbook. Part of that mission was to perpetuate the Chicago tradition of getting at people, trying to find out what people thought, how they think, why they think the way they do.[80]

Maurice Stein agrees:

Our mission was to not be Columbia.[81] We were not going to be structural functionalists or survey people. We weren't going to be parochial sociologists. I think our sense of our mission, MY sense of our mission, was to represent in American sociology, ethnography, fieldwork and critical social theory. . . . I think with Everett we were clearly defined visibly as the *old* Chicago, rather than the *new* Chicago which had been taken over by Bogue and Rossi whom Everett disliked.[82]

All of these early faculty members now see Hughes as representing more than himself—he represented the importation to Boston of Chicago sociology. In Schwartz's view this sociology had three components: fieldwork, symbolic interactionism, and "being different"; and as this definition became entrenched, the department hired people who fit rather than deviated.

> *Reinharz:* So you were the first Chicago person here?
>
> *Schwartz:* Absolutely. . . . But later on, Jack Seeley came in. He was from Chicago. I was the one who invited Jack Seeley. Hughes came in. He was from Chicago. So we started to develop that Chicago tradition. Then even later came Larry Rosenberg [Chicago '64] and Charlie Derber [Chicago '71]. They were also Chicagoans. So we started to build up. There was a great deal of appreciation for and tolerance of each other's orientation, because it was all anti-quantitative. We saw ourselves as distinctly being against the tide, representing a perspective that we thought was very little represented in the field. We became pretty important in this "against" way. Remember, quantitative sociology was all-powerful, so to be deviant required a certain amount of courage. So from my point of view it was the only place I probably could be.[83]

An additional Chicago school connection at the time, absent from Schwartz's list, was Blanche Geer[84] who spent a year as a research associate of Everett Hughes at Brandeis from 1962 to 1963,[85] and anthropologist Hanna Papanek, who did the same.

FACULTY HIRED AFTER EVERETT HUGHES'S ARRIVAL

After Hughes joined the department, John Seeley was hired.[86] Seeley had been a graduate student in Chicago with Schwartz and in 1956 had published *Crestwood Heights,* a community field study.[87] At Brandeis he taught the fieldwork course with many others. Seeley came as a visiting professor in 1964 and in his third year became chair of the department. He resigned the next year after presenting the university with ultimatums that were not accepted concerning political action, such as having the university take a stand of noncooperation with the Selective Service by not releasing student grades.[88] Hughes participated in some of these political activities, such as drafting a public statement supporting the bussing of minority students into Boston city schools located in white neighborhoods to assure them of an equivalent education.[89] During this period, a member of the Brandeis politics department (E. V. Walter) moved his tenure to sociology and conducted participant observation studies of poverty.[90] The transition of Seeley from visiting professor to chair represented more than the perpetuation of the fieldwork tradition. It also represented a radical philosophy of education that came to be another hallmark of the graduate program. In a sense, this component continued the influence of Herbert Marcuse, who earlier had functioned as an informal member of the department.[91] An esprit de corps around fieldwork and political opposition to mainstream politics had taken root.

To complement the core group of senior faculty, new assistant professors were hired.[92] Hughes's philosophy of hiring was "get the best person, not a person for a particular slot." While he was at Brandeis, seventeen people were hired or invited to be visitors; not all seventeen stayed. As the oldest man among several younger people, and as a president of the American Sociological Association, Hughes was the departmental member to whom other faculty were likely to defer. Among the assistant professors hired who remained for substantial periods were Philip Slater (1961–71), Irving Zola (1963–94), and Gordon Fellman (1964–), all of whom had degrees from Harvard University's social relations department, where their training was interdisciplinary. Hughes was also instrumental in securing a joint appointment for Steve Miller in the Department of Sociology and the Heller School for Social Welfare at Brandeis.[93] A committed field-worker, Miller had conducted community studies in Kansas City and continued the Chicago tradition of studies of medical settings, particularly of interns and residents at Boston City Hospital.[94]

Hughes wanted to hire people with broad interests and backgrounds, regardless of the field in which they had earned a degree or their experience as field-workers. For example, although Zola had done some fieldwork as a graduate student, he thought of himself as a survey researcher.[95] Hughes convinced Zola that "he was a fieldworker although he didn't know it."

> *Zola:* Hughes called me in before I was hired, and said, "I just got a grant funded by NIMH, field studies, and that's why I came to Brandeis. I've come to Brandeis to rejuvenate it. Chicago wasn't me anymore." And he said, "I'd like you to become supervisor of fieldwork." I looked at him and said, "I don't know what fieldwork is." He said, "You may not know what it is, but you're doing it." He took out my article on gambling and told me it was very good. So I said, "What exactly do you want me to teach?" It turns out the actual job was to teach with him. He floored me. I knew who the hell he was. Very eminent. He saw something in me and I was willing to do it. He offered me a possibility, I thought, of another piece of

graduate education. What he said to me, and I thought it was crazy, was "You'll watch me, and we'll talk." And he was absolutely right. Osmosis.[96]

At the same time, an unusual event occurred in the department at Chicago, according to Donald Light, a student there at the time:

> In the winter of 1966, the students had one choice of a guest speaker whom the department would support. We chose Maurie Stein which was a pretty uppity or iconoclastic thing to do. So Maurie Stein, with his terrible beard and golden tongue, came out and twinkled and glowered as he spoke, and he was just marvelous. We all loved him and loved everything he had to say. He represented this quintessential moment, when I saw how different and exciting sociology could be.[97]

As could be expected, Stein used the opportunity to criticize "Columbia sociology" which he felt was dominating Chicago. After that talk, some students and faculty left Chicago for Brandeis. According to Donald Light ('70):

> I originally chose Chicago for the Chicago school. When I got out there I found that the Chicago school really didn't exist. Morris Janowitz was trying to keep it alive. He offered a course on the Chicago School of Sociology although he had not gone there.[98] Otherwise everyone was doing survey research. Rossi was the head of National Opinion Research Center [NORC]. I became a research fellow at the NORC. The old Chicago school was completely gone by 1964. There was only one person interested in field methods and that was a new assistant professor named Larry Rosenberg. Larry was a Chicago Ph.D. who had done a highly quantitative dissertation.[99] Then he went to Boston as a post-doc with Eliot Mishler and did some studies of becoming a psychiatrist and psychiatric sociology. In the process he had become more and more interested in field methods and ethnography. So I started taking qualitative field methods with Larry and he was very innovative and brilliant. All of this was leading me to try to find the Chicago school when it wasn't there. Larry Rosenberg was the only faculty member at Chicago who represented that tradition, and he left to go to Brandeis.[100]
>
> The graduate students at Chicago wanted the old school back. So they brought in Maurie Stein as a speaker from Brandeis! Everett was there. Larry became a kindred spirit and a

major support. . . . And of course I knew that Everett Hughes was at Brandeis and was the last remaining original member of the Chicago school. And Larry knew him. And Larry said, "Why don't you come along?" I had independent funding. I had taken my Ph.D. exams. And so I applied through Maurie who was chairman then. . . . And the faculty met and allowed me to transfer as a post-generals student. I came because of Everett as the central figure representing the Chicago school, but also [because of] Larry.[101]

After Rosenberg was hired at Brandeis, Hughes was influential in hiring Charles Fisher, who also had somewhat of a Chicago connection through his family relation with Anselm Strauss and his undergraduate training at Chicago (his Ph.D. was in mathematics, from Berkeley).[102] In 1967 Jerome Boime, a graduate student at the University of Chicago who had not finished his degree, was hired. By this date, six years after the founding of the graduate program at Brandeis, a preponderance of the faculty had come either directly from the University of Chicago or were sociologists who engaged in fieldwork or attempted to do sociology in a nonpositivist way. During these six years, socialization practices occurred that were strong enough to sustain the cultural diffusion even when profound changes began to take place at the end of the period.

SOCIALIZATION OF GRADUATE STUDENTS

Shortly after Hughes arrived at Brandeis, he and Weiss received a National Institute of Mental Health fieldwork training grant.[103] With this training grant, fieldwork became formally institutionalized at Brandeis and Chicago-style sociology became Brandeis-style sociology. Schwartz served as program director of the field methods training program and Weiss served as director of field training. A Field Training Committee was established with Hughes as chairman. Hughes had done the same thing at Chicago, according to French sociologist Jean-Michel Chapoulie:

> When he arrived in Chicago as a faculty member in 1938, Hughes initiated a beginning course in fieldwork . . . , which according to many people played a large part in orienting many members of the next generation to the use of this method.[104]

In Schwartz's view the diffusion of the old Chicago school to Brandeis was explicit, yet modified:

This training grant . . . represented Chicago and mobilized us around the Chicago perspective in terms of doing fieldwork and participant observation, although Chicago wasn't all about participant observation.[105] That was the minor part of it. It was the fieldwork and interviewing that was the major part. Being in the community. . . . [106]

Unlike at Chicago, where fieldwork was no longer the predominant method, at Brandeis it became the major socialization experience because *all* graduate students were required to take fieldwork courses. Moreover, nearly all the faculty members in the program were involved in fieldwork, although Hughes, Weiss, and Schwartz were the first to have formal roles for grant purposes.[107] Fieldwork training thus became a shared socialization experience for faculty and students.

Some of the fieldwork courses were direct diffusions from Chicago, but at Brandeis there was more supervision. For example, Morris Schwartz remembers that at Chicago:

They had quite a few fieldwork courses, you went out in the field, you got supervision as much as you could, although the faculty were not easily available, in part because there were so many students, but in part because that's the way the tradition was, you'd come during their office hours.[108]

Herbert Gans describes the same from his M.A. experience:

When I was a graduate student at the University of Chicago just after World War II, no one talked much about participant-observation; we just did it. Like many of my fellow sociology students, I enrolled in Everett Hughes' course "Introduction to Field Work," and like them, I found it a traumatic introduction; we were sent to a census tract in nearby Hyde Park and asked to do a small participant-observation study. Everett Hughes gave us some words of introduction and of instruction, but good father that he was, he quickly pushed us out of the nest and told us to fly on our own.[109]

Carrol Bourg ('67) remembers the deliberate inculcation of insecurity combined with the eventual payoff in the fieldwork courses at Brandeis:

Hughes was the principal figure, teaching courses in field methods and also about careers and occupations. He sent the students out into the city, beginning with the phone book, on the topic of schools. We chose a school and went there, not really

sure what we were doing. We were encouraged to take copious
field notes and not worry what they meant or might mean.
From the beginning to near the end the students were bewil-
dered and simply confused. But the encouraging word was to
continue and that meaning would begin to emerge after review
of the notes. Then most of us found that we had done far more
than we could have planned from the beginning and much
more than we realized as we went along week after week. . . .
The combination of what I recall to be a Chicago influence in
the sociology I learned at Brandeis . . . had the effect of making
me aware of how much I was or could be the source of sociological knowledge. Sociology, then, was not merely repeating
what others had done. It was doing in new, hopefully fresh,
and may be even creative, ways what some others had done in
their own distinct ways.[110]

Students at Brandeis learned about this tradition, the significance of
Hughes's role, and the importance of doing this work as graduate students.
They inherited a mantle and a responsibility, as Gaye Tuchman ('69)
infers:

It is clear that at the University of Chicago in the 1950s, Everett Hughes was the primary faculty proponent of participant
observation and graduate students were the main practioners
of this method. Both Herbert Gans [personal communication]
and I agree that extended participant observation is a method
for the young: When one is in one's 20s or 30s, it may be possible to observe for ten to sixteen hours and then type notes
before sleeping. Later in life such long hours pose problems.[111]

Brandeis students were taught explicitly that they were learning Chicago-
style fieldwork. For example, Ruth Jacobs ('69) speaks of the unadulter-
ated relocation of Chicago to Brandeis:

The faculty at the time were individuals who had worked in
Chicago and had studied with the seminal people and thus
were a direct conduit of social psychology, theory and fieldwork methods. They were good professors who studied with
the greats. I did not feel that ex-Chicagoans revised their
agendas when they came to Brandeis—just perpetuated
them.[112]

Paul Campanis ('66) describes the excitement of learning Chicago-style
sociology from these people:

I loved fieldwork. I went down and looked at garbage in the South End. I looked through people's rubbish. I would fly! I loved it. I still do. Tremendous excitement. That fieldwork was right out of the Chicago school. I did Chicago-style fieldwork on the South Side of Boston. The major issues were race, ethnicity, social class. They all came out of Chicago. The concern for the small person in the abstract. The concern for the woman's role in the family, all of my training that I did here in the 60's—I was here from '61 to December '65—was very clearly Chicago-style.[113]

Barrie Thorne ('71) recognizes the significance of having so many faculty participate in fieldwork training:

In my experience, the year-long fieldwork class was, in the late 1960s, the core of "Chicago school" sociology at Brandeis. But it was actually taught by a remarkable group with varied backgrounds. Everett was the spiritual leader (in the sense of having the "spirit" of years and years of fieldwork), and his pedagogy—sights and sounds, community study—was clearly at the core. Irv Zola, Phil Slater, and Sam Wallace also taught the course, so that was an interesting array. Their comments on our fieldnotes were very different.[114]

Gaye Tuchman ('69) similarly remembers the multitude of faculty involved and the techniques they taught:

The Brandeis fieldwork courses were completely organized like Chicago. We had two semesters of it in the first year. There were five faculty members (Hughes, Zola, Slater, Wallace,[115] Weiss) for 18 students. It was required.[116] Another time it was Stein, Seeley, and Schwartz. Each group had a different neighborhood in the South End. They picked a community to study and fanned out students. I went to Charlestown, the census tract included Bunker Hill. We had forms on which to record observations, to map, to keep the time in the left-hand column. The idea was to count the number of people we saw and to take as many notes as we could. This was defined as "Chicago sociology."[117] We didn't read books. We went out and collected information. We had discussions in class, particularly about problems in doing fieldwork. There was no product, just fieldnotes and a few short papers in which we drew some conclusions. I remember Steve Rosenthal turning in a diary about poor, dismal conditions, and being taken to task for premature conclusions. How did he know that this was the way they saw themselves?[118] I remember going to a bar with another student and taking notes. At that time most graduate students at Brandeis University, including me, saw themselves as having inherited the mantle of "old Chicago sociology."[119]

Alex Liazos ('70) appreciated the disciplined training:

> We had a fieldwork class, which was Hughes, Zola, and Fellman. And they broke us into 3 groups and assigned us to a community. Dorchester, Cambridge, and Watertown. I went to Watertown. . . . The last thing I wrote for the fieldwork course, which led to my getting a 3-year fellowship in fieldwork, which I think Zola liked a lot, and also Hughes, was a study of an old-age retirement home right across the street from here. We did a series of things. It was very well organized. They sent us out in teams to do a history of the community first. Then a specific thing, like the fall of '64 was an election, so we studied that, and we all had a series of assignments about families, a bar. Those things we did in teams. But the last thing we did was an individual project. I did a nursing home. Some were just short exercises. Since then I have never changed my mind about discipline and careful observation. I remember the example he gave—don't say it's a tall house, say it's 2 1/2 stories. Now, that's a little example, but I remember it. I did my Ph.D. on a home for juvenile delinquents, using participant observation. I'll always remember Hughes's point: "Just because you did participant observation doesn't mean you can't be precise." My career at Brandeis was pretty much fieldwork, because I got this 3-year fellowship from NIMH. I did a participant observation study of a home for juvenile delinquent girls in Watertown as my Master's thesis and Sam Wallace directed it.[120]

Through the field training program, graduate students at Brandeis developed an identity as sociologists who do fieldwork in the Chicago tradition. For example, Gaye Tuchman ('69) describes her dissertation research as follows:

> I employed classic old-style Chicago sociological observation [see Junker, 1960, including the introduction by Everett Hughes]. That is, I observed the activities of news staff both inside and outside of the newsroom, following stories' dissemination. (In the case of television, they were aired at 6:30 P.M. and 11:00 P.M.) At the newspaper studied, I attended morning

editorial meetings and sat in on the copy desk through the revision of the second edition at 11:30 P.M.). I attended events with general reporters, made the rounds with beat reporters (some identified by editors as their "best" and others as their "weakest"), and put in time at news bureaus. I did general open-ended interviewing as well. All observations and interviews were recorded in fieldnotes the day they were made.[121]

For some students, the socialization as "Chicago-style sociologists" occurred even before they arrived, because they chose Brandeis specifically for this purpose. Murray Davis ('69) is an example:

I'm the right person to ask about the late period of the University of Chicago sociology tradition because I was steeped in it, having had my first course in sociology from Everett Hughes at the University of Chicago and my last course in sociology from him at Brandeis. I left the University of Chicago sociology department after receiving my M.A. there because it had been taken over by positivists from Columbia. I . . . wanted to study "traditional Chicago sociology." Consequently, I sought out as many ex-Chicagoans as I could in the diaspora of its tradition—first Blumer and Goffman at Berkeley, then, after Berkeley blew up in 1964, Hughes and Schwartz at Brandeis.[122]

Additional graduate students who came to Brandeis to study "the Chicago tradition" with Everett Hughes were Charles Levy ('67), Donald Light ('70), and Jonathan Freedman ('73).[123]

Other students learned that they were "inheriting the mantle" only after they arrived. An example is Paul Campanis ('66), the first to earn a degree in the Brandeis program and one of several whose dissertations Hughes supervised.[124] These students learned the tradition by taking fieldwork classes and by listening to stories:

Reinharz: So you didn't come here to be with Hughes?
Campanis: I didn't know who he was. How would I know? But then Hughes spent hundreds and hundreds of hours telling me about his life. He was very lonesome. And he had come here from Chicago, which was like a high place. And he had come to another place which was sort of untried and untested. He was lonesome. And I'm a good listener. He befriended me, so I became a pal. I spent 4 1/2–5 1/2 years with "the old man." He was a little shaky in the sense that he was getting older, so he repeated himself. But I'm the kind of per-

son who loves to hear a story 30 times. He embellished it a little bit. I loved being in the office. . . . And sometimes I would come in and just sit there, and I just enjoyed being around. He loved Simmel like I did.[125] And he loved Park. And he'd tell me Simmel and he'd tell me Park, and then he'd go back to some term like "restriction of production," "control of production," that was right out of Max Weber.[126] And he'd grab up the damn book. And then he'd tell me all about that. Hughes read about everything, studied everything, pulled this in from here and that from there. That all came out of Chicago, because it came from Park. Park was not one of those sociologists who would plug a lot of stuff into a machine. Park was like me, Hughes was like Park, it's a direct descendentship. Chicago was like a famous situation, and when Hughes came here all he talked about was his background in Chicago.[127]

Similarly, Barrie Thorne ('71) vividly remembers Hughes's stories:

He told stories about the various sociologists . . . who studied the "taxi dance-hall girl," the furrier, Negro physicians, etc., many of them, of course, studying topics from their own family and community backgrounds. He had stories about Goffman's arrival at Chicago, about Becker's jazz-band playing, about his own graduate-student days with fellow student and close friend, Robert Redfield, in courses taught by Robert E. Park in the times before anthropology and sociology split.

It occurs to me that some sociologists feel much more part of a "school" than do others, and that some, like parents passing on a tradition, are more intent than others on drawing their students into feeling part of their "school." In large and small ways, Everett helped me feel part of the Chicago lineage. I listened to his stories. . . .

Everett sometimes talked about the bad treatment of W. I. Thomas, about the career of St. Clair Drake. I wish I'd recorded these stories—they drift up from my unconscious, but the point is that they made me feel part of a field and of an approach with a rich individual and collective history. Helen Hughes shared in the story-telling, and they invited me to their house to meet people like Lee Rainwater, Blanche Geer, and Talcott Parsons. Everett told many stories about the old days in Chicago, about the fieldwork course where they had students go out and observe the "sights and sounds" of a census tract, which is exactly what we did in our first-year fieldwork course at Brandeis—we did a community study of Charleston.[128]

Ruth Jacobs ('69) also has vivid memories of Hughes' story-telling that conveyed to students a sense of tradition:

> He told stories about William Foote Whyte and *Street Corner Society* which everyone loved.[129] It gave me confidence to know that Everett's students had done these studies. Another Chicago connection is my interest in Simmel. Park studied with Simmel, and Hughes studied with Park, and I studied with Hughes. Hughes did Simmel-type sociology, which was to make wise connections. Social forms come out of Simmel. I learned Simmel in part through this oral tradition. . . . Park sat in on his lectures. Everett Hughes made excellent connections between ideas. He did not believe in a sociology of anything, but rather in sociology. Sociology was a generalizing science and tackled almost anything. I teach general courses, as Everett Hughes did. I'm not specialized.[130]

Karl Pillemer ('85) was an undergraduate student of Ruth Jacobs at Boston University and remembers her drawing diagrams on the blackboard:

> Simmel to Park to Hughes to her. Karen Fields ('77) also taught at BU [Boston University] and left to go to Brandeis. It was because of these people that I went to Brandeis.[131]

From my interviews and correspondence with these early students of the Brandeis program, I have learned that the story-telling went both ways. For example, Barrie Thorne ('71) wrote:

> Everett liked that I reminisced about my Mormon background and sitting shoulder-to-shoulder in church, when I described sitting in a little Protestant congregation in that Catholic-majority community. He sought me out after those early notes to talk about my background, and that was the start of our friendship—he was ever one to help one understand and, in a sense, come to terms with one's own origins. He often told me about Nels Anderson—of the *Hobo* book—who was also a Mormon by origin. . . . [132]

Lynda Lytle Holmstrom ('70) was one of many students who appreciated Hughes's encouragement to examine her own life:

> While at Brandeis University, he influenced positively the careers of numerous female students. He helped supervise many

of their dissertations, many of which had to do with some aspect of work or careers, and a number of which had special relevance for women's lives. He was the inspiration of my own work on two-career families [Holmstrom, 1972]. He was a mentor for Nancy Stoller Shaw, whose dissertation dealt with childbirth and the interaction between female clients and male obstetricians [Shaw, 1974]. He also was a mentor for Barrie Thorne, whose dissertation dealt with the draft resistance movement. . . . [133]

Gaye Tuchman explains that Hughes learned this approach from Park:

According to the late Everett Hughes [personal communication circa 1965], in the 1920s Robert Park instructed graduate students to use their jobs and their communities as sources of data for term papers and theses. Hughes continued this practice during his tenure at Chicago. Some student papers, such as Howard S. Becker's work on dance musicians and Fred Davis's on taxi-cab drivers, were eventually published as articles; most were not.[134]

This mutual story-telling gave students a whole new image of themselves. Ruth Jacobs ('69) acquired a new sociological family and learned that she had a place in a distinguished lineage:

They would also bring people. For example, Goffman came a couple of times, and maybe Bill Whyte. I felt I knew Herb Gans although I didn't, so I invited him to BU [Boston University] when I worked there. I felt that these people were my cousins, I was connected to them. I tell my current students that Everett Hughes is their grandfather when I teach fieldwork. I say that my students are the great-grandchildren of Park, the fourth generation, because I learned from Everett. The students relate to that.[135] Everett Hughes had been doing fieldwork in Chicago for a long time. He observed institutions. He talked about catching "humanity on the hoof." Everett and Morrie Schwartz told Chicago stories that I can still remember. They told about the fieldwork that was done there.[136]

Barrie Thorne ('71) was also taught to internalize the lineage:

Everett Hughes and also Bob Weiss (who was a strong influence on me during my first year—1965–66—at Brandeis) brought a "Chicago School" presence into the Brandeis graduate program. . . . In his seminars and conversations, Everett conveyed a strong sense of lineage from Park to him to Becker-Strauss-Goffman-Gusfield-Fred Davis, etc., etc. I felt, and still feel, like part of a family tree, for example, with Howie Becker as a sort of older brother/uncle. Other students of Everett also feel that way—connected to his ideas, and through him to the old Chicago school, and to one another.[137]

Being part of a distinguished lineage was very exciting for the students. In the words of Gaye Tuchman ('69):

For me it was a formative experience, it's something I love to think about, it's something that few other sociologists had, a sense of mission, of perpetuating continuity.[138]

Many students of this period use the metaphor of lineage, and some recognize that the lineage extended to several places. For example, Gaye Tuchman believes the following:

When Blumer went to California, his students there thought they had inherited the Chicago school. Similarly, at Brandeis we did not have a sense of being pioneers in a new graduate school but rather of *carrying on a tradition.* We were just another group who took fieldnotes all the time.[139]

Finally, I believe that students were learning what was being defined as "better sociology," as Murray Davis ('69) suggests:

What I liked about the Chicago tradition [at Brandeis] was that it wanted to study a fuller conception of social life than did the positivist-behaviorist tradition that then dominated professional sociology. Chicago sociology taught me that my own perceptions of social life—properly disciplined by logic, rigor, and the sociological classics—were more insightful than quantitative screenings of the social world, which could describe only gross surface behavior.[140]

Barrie Thorne ('71) parallels this attitude:

I'm thinking now that . . . openness to and use of students' backgrounds—ethnicity, immigration, etc., provided an explicit interweaving of biography with sociology, which survey researchers, for example, don't have. . . . [141]

The invidious comparison with survey research was even contained in the fieldwork training grant proposal to N.I.M.H. and must have been part of the "hidden curriculum" of the courses, as evident below:

> Field research, more than other techniques, tends to develop understandings of patterned relationships among individuals, of the values in terms of which people act, the goals they attempt to reach, and the stresses they experience. Whereas quantitative research is often concerned with the association of isolated determinants and effects, field research is more frequently focused on broad patterns of behavior within a situation, and on the social setting which to an extent governs this behavior. The overall aim of the . . . training program was the development of sociologists who would contribute to our knowledge of social settings through the use of field research techniques.

All students were required to take an initial year of fieldwork courses, but only those judged to be particularly skilled were invited to join the training program and receive a fellowship. These students underwent three additional years of training. Gaye Tuchman received one of these fellowships:

> The training grant was different from the course in that you had to apply, and the faculty had to decide that you could do it. People on the grant had to take special seminars associated with the grant every semester, taught by Jack Seeley and Sam Wallace. There you just kind of talked about your work and what you were working on; you wrote papers on your experience; they pushed you into the field quickly; someone critiqued your paper.[142]

Fieldwork training was not confined to methods courses. According to Gaye Tuchman, for example, Hughes taught fieldwork in his other courses:

> Barrie Thorne, Janet Mancini, and I took a reading course with Everett. He had each of us doing fieldwork at a different church in Charlestown. All the churches were in trouble, except the Roman Catholic church. We would get together and talk to him. Janet is a Protestant married to a Catholic; Barrie is Mormon; and I'm Jewish. We were studying Protestant churches.[143]

Rogers Johnson ('68) similarly remembers that the Chicago orientation characterized fieldwork training and other courses:

> The Chicagoan influence was significant, perhaps central, to the methods course in particular and to the more general methodological orientation of the department. For me, this broke down in two ways. First, the methods course, under Maurice Stein and Bob Weiss . . . was heavily qualitative, humanistic, open to inventive strategies (e.g. use of photography as a record of street gatherings). Quantitative techniques and positivist strategies were present . . . but they occupied a secondary "support" role in the course. The other singular influence in this context for me was a course on Institutional Analysis with Everett Hughes. His emphasis on fieldwork and primary data was, I believed then, a reflection of his Chicago agenda.[144]

The fieldwork-affirming atmosphere in the program encouraged faculty and students to publish their research, in turn establishing the program's reputation.[145] As Maurice Stein said:

> *Stein:* At that time, the department had a terrific national standing.
> *Reinharz:* Why?
> *Stein:* Because by that time, community studies and the fieldwork tradition in the department had become public. I published a lot during that period. We all published a lot.[146]

Clearly, particular socialization processes abetted the diffusion of the Chicago school of sociology to Brandeis. Foremost among these were the inclusion of almost *all faculty* in collective teaching, the requirement that *all students* be involved, the availability of *funds* to support particularly gifted field-workers, the sharing of *stories* by faculty about their collective past in Chicago, the use of the metaphor of *lineage* and the placement of students in that lineage, the reinforcing of *students' personal lives* and worth, and the labeling of the inheritance as "better" sociology, rendering current students "special."

FROM DIFFUSION OF KNOWLEDGE TO THE EVOLUTION OF A NEW IDENTITY

The initial fieldwork training grant lasted five years and was not renewed. Although nonrenewal was a blow, it probably prompted the departmental identity to become more diversified. After 1967 fieldwork was still the method of choice, but it was no longer taught by *all* the faculty, and some who taught it had not been faculty or students at the University of Chicago. Some students began to work primarily on questions of theory, and for other students fieldwork was redefined as "interviewing without observation" or reformulated as "qualitative research."

By the late 1960s students were no longer required to take fieldwork courses. In line with the educational revolution that was part of the counterculture, by the early 1970s students were not obliged to take any required courses at all.[147] Seeley left in 1966; Weiss in 1967; Hughes in 1968; Coser in 1969; Stein left temporarily shortly thereafter to explore the counterculture; Rosenberg left permanently to work on Eastern religious practice;[148] Sam Wallace, who had been hired as the field training supervisor, did not stay long; and Slater left in 1971 to write poetry and plays. Schwartz, Fisher, Wolff, Fellman, and later Rosabeth Kanter remained and taught fieldwork, but, as Barrie Thorne notes, "when Everett left, the story-telling tie was gone."

With this shift, the Chicago tradition began to assume a smaller place in the emerging department. The view that Chicago/Brandeis sociology was "better than" other types of sociology "out there" changed to a competition among views *within* the department. In Murray Davis's ('69) words:

> The increasing dominance of the critical Marxist perspective at Brandeis in the late 1960s shifted the Chicagoans, like Hughes, and soon thereafter even the European socialists, like Lew Coser, into the right wing of the department. . . . after I graduated in 1969, I was under the impression that the sociology department's "we're all in this together" perspective was replaced by an "us against them" attitude; that its humanism, which embodied the dynamic tension between its American and European wings, disintegrated into cultural radicalism on the one hand and political radicalism on the other, which later splintered into feminism and other subgroup radicalisms.[149]

New faculty hires with a tie to fieldwork, but not specifically to the Chicago tradition (e.g., Egon Bittner, who arrived in 1968 as a full professor), helped sustain a version of the fieldwork-oriented methodological identity of the department. But the emerging identity broadened from fieldwork to become "all alternative forms of sociology." Rogers Johnson ('68) stresses this idea:

What does seem to me to have emerged, during my particular years in the '60's was a certain resonance or compatibil-
ity between the Chicago School's humanistic and qualitative
thrust and the socially, politically, and theoretically critical
stances shared by others in the department, ranging from Wolff
to Slater to Stein to Walter, for example. Immensely diverse as
individuals, each had his challenge to traditional sociology as
symbolized, for example, by Parsons and Lundberg. . . .

In fact, I was much attracted initially to Brandeis because
of the understanding that it presented a creditable alternative
approach to the discipline, and this perception was strongly
reinforced by the students whom I met while there. This sense
of openness and options had a number of facets for me: in
the theoretical orientations (Wolff, Slater, Walter, Coser); in
methodology, with Stein and Weiss; the extremely diverse—as
I think about it—and fairly close aggregation of fellow students; and even the departmental climate for graduate studies
which was at times quite consciously addressed by many of the
faculty—the desire to avoid the "factory product" syndrome
of some large university departments of the day. This alternative intellectual experience was crucial to my understanding
and appreciation of Brandeis at the time. It does seem to me
. . . that the Chicago School may have constituted one major
element in this mix.[150]

As a graduate student myself in the department from 1967 to 1970 I (SR)
felt shaped by all these streams of thought. By 1967 I was hearing stories
not only about the "old Chicago school" but also about the "old Brandeis
school"! Later I was surprised to learn that for a few years before I returned to Brandeis as a faculty member in 1982, fieldwork was not offered
at all. Currently, it is offered, but not required.

Looking back at the founding years of the program, Paul Campanis
('66) suggests that "the Chicago school" was *not* transplanted at Brandeis;
rather it was both sustained and transformed. These changes can be seen
only if cultural diffusion is understood in the context of the host's own development:

If the Chicago sociological tradition had been very midwestern, pragmatist,[151] and liberal,[152] the Brandeis environment
it encountered was European, phenomenological, and Marxist. In the 1960's, this juxtaposition was very exciting to the
students—especially me. The Europeans in the department,

especially Kurt Wolff and Lew Coser, grounded the philosophically shallow Chicago tradition in European philosophy. In particular, they sharpened its fuzzy pragmatism with more rigorous European phenomenology; on the other hand, the fieldworking Chicago tradition expanded the range of the armchair European phenomenologists to the actual perspectives of those at different social locations. Finally, the Chicago sociological tradition had always been more appreciative than critical, more wide-eyed with wonder that institutions could function at all than cynically squinting at what was wrong with their functioning.

The European Marxist tradition, epitomized by Herbert Marcuse at Brandeis, added a critical edge to Chicago sociology. Although Chicago sociology had always been slightly critical in the sense of recommending that this or that institution be changed somewhat to accommodate its participants' needs better, the European Marxist tradition recommended that the entire society be changed, both in actuality and in ideology—something that seemed possible in the 1960's.[153]

Professor emeritus Kurt Wolff agrees with this view:

Certainly the Chicago school is an important component; another important component is the political thrust of the sociology which is taught here and which in turn was greatly influenced by at least two people, Jack Seeley and Herbert Marcuse.[154]

Maurice Stein goes even further. He suggests that politically inspired sociology became an important feature of the program precisely *because* Chicago school sociology was politically inadequate:[155]

Looking back, we never looked at the politics of Chicago, which was very much liberal, assimilationist, and sexist. Chicago really stood for liberal, anti-intellectual ethnography. And it was really "value free." Park contributed to it. It was even reactionary.[156]

In addition, several faculty members who came after the founding period believe that the fieldwork characterization is overblown. Understandably, these individuals define the department in line with developments after their arrival.

Obviously, many histories can be written of the same phenomenon. This account has focused on the diffusion of a definition of sociology from the oldest graduate department in the country to one of the youngest. It is important to remember that the diffusion occurred in several other institutions to which Chicago-trained sociologists moved, and that new settings such as Brandeis were influenced by additional factors—the radical political climate of the 1960s (represented foremost by Seeley and Stein); the European theoretical tradition (represented primarily by Coser, Kecskemeti, Wolff, Stein, Bittner, and later Ralph Miliband, Gila Hayim); the social psychological interest (represented by Schwartz, Zola, Slater, and Fellman); and the feminist movement (introduced into the faculty by Rosabeth Moss Kanter, but developed primarily among students[157] in part because many female faculty did not earn tenure). The Chicago school of sociology did not remain intact at the University of Chicago; neither did it remain intact at Brandeis. The old "Chicago school" tradition, nevertheless, permeates the continuously evolving identity of both in subtle ways, as it does the continuously changing definition of U.S. sociology.

Fieldwork methods are a minority approach to sociological research and they remain connected in sociologists' minds to the early "Chicago school." So too, symbolic interactionism and social psychology are products of that early school and remain a minority theoretical approach. Yet such mid-century Chicago sociologists as Goffman and Strauss reframed both the fieldwork methods and the social psychology theory of the earlier period in modern terms, and thus made it possible for places like Brandeis University's graduate program in sociology to believe it was restoring an old, significant tradition, while at the same time engaging in the most important contemporary sociological work as practiced by young graduates of the "second school." For those departments around the country that were willing to develop a sociological approach that differed from the quantitative mainstream, this was a combination too good to pass up.

SOCIOLOGY FACULTY AT BRANDEIS UNIVERSITY BY YEAR: 1958–1978

	1958*#	59*	60*	61*	62	63	64	65	66
Coser, Lewis A.	3-1	3	2	2	2	2	2	2	2
Lerner, Max	2	2	2	—	—	—	—	—	—
Feldmesser, Robert	4	4	4	4	4	—	—	—	—
Himelhoch, Jerome	4	—	—	—	—	—	—	—	—
Frank, Lawrence	—	—	2	—	—	—	—	—	—
Stein, Maurice	4	4	3	3	3	3	3	3	3-1
Keller, Suzanne	D	4	4	4	—	—	—	—	—
Wolff, Kurt	—	2-1	2-1	2-1	2	2	2	2	2
Schwartz, Morris S.	—	2	2	2	2-1	2-1	2-1	2	2
Griff, Mason	—	4	—	—	—	—	—	—	—
Weiss, Robert	—	—	4	4	4	3	3	3	3
Sherwood, Edward	—	—	4	—	—	—	—	—	—
Hughes, Everett C.	—	—	—	2	2	2	2	2	2
Walter, E. V.	—	—	—	—	—	3	3	3	3
Vidich, Arthur	—	—	—	—	V3	A	—	—	—
Slater, Philip	—	—	—	4	4	4	3	3	3
Sobel, Bernard Z.	—	—	—	—	I	4	4	4	4
Seeley, John	—	—	—	—	—	V2	V2	2-1	2
Zola, Irving K.	—	—	—	—	—	4	4	4	4
Levinson, Dan	—	—	—	—	—	VL	—	—	—
Zelan, Joseph	—	—	—	—	—	—	L	L	—
Fellman, Gordon	—	—	—	—	—	—	4	4	4
Wallace, Sam	—	—	—	—	—	—	—	4	4
Zalinger, Alvin	—	—	—	—	—	—	—	VL	VL
Kecskemeti, Paul	—	—	—	—	—	—	—	—	VP
Abrahams, Fred	—	—	—	—	—	—	—	—	4
Rosenberg, Larry	—	—	—	—	—	—	—	—	4
Jones, Kenneth	—	—	—	—	—	—	—	VL	—
Total	6	8	10	7	12	14	13	16	17

SOCIOLOGY FACULTY AT BRANDEIS UNIVERSITY BY YEAR *con't.*

	1967	68	69	70	71	72	73	74	75
Peattie, Lisa Redfield			(VL-1966)						
Coser, Lewis A.	2	2	—	—	—	—	—	—	—
Stein, Maurice	2-1	2-1	2	2	2	2	2	2	2
Wolff, Kurt	2	2	2	2	2	2	2	2	2
Schwartz, Morris S.	2	2	2	2	2	2	2	2	2
Weiss, Robert	3	2	2	2	—	—	—	—	—
Hughes, Everett C.	2	E	E	E	E	E	E	E	E
Walter, Victor	3	3	3	—	—	—	—	—	—
Slater, Philip	2	2	2	2	2	—	—	—	—
Sobel, Bernard Z.	4	4	A	A	A	—	—	—	—
Zola, Irving K.	4	3	3	3	3	2-1	2-1	2	2
Fellman, Gordon	4	4	4	4	4	3	3	3-1	3-1
Wallace, Sam	4	4	4	4	3	3	—	—	—
Kecskemeti, Paul	VP	VP	VP	VP	VP	VP	VP	—	—
Abrahams, Fred	4	4	—	—	—	—	—	—	—
Rosenberg, Larry	4	4	4	4	4	4	4	—	—
Boime, Jerome	4	4	4	4	4	4	4	4	4
Fisher, Charles	4	4	4	4	4	4	4	3	3
Kanter, Rosabeth M.	4	4	4	4	4	4	4	3	3
Friedman, Neil	4	4	4	4	4	—	—	—	—
Bittner, Egon	—	2	2	2	2	2	2	2	2
Marx, Leo	—	—	VP	—	—	—	—	—	—
Sennett, Richard	—	—	4	4	4	—	—	—	—
Hicks, Calvin	—	—	L	4	4	—	—	—	—
Derber, Charles	—	—	—	4	4	4	4	4	4
Ross, George	—	—	—	4	4	4	4	4	4
Patterson, Michelle	—	—	—	—	—	4	4	—	—
Roby, Pamela	—	—	—	—	—	4	4	—	—
Jean, Clinton	—	—	—	—	—	L	L	L	L
Hayim, Gila	—	—	—	—	—	—	—	4	4
Rosenthal, Kristine	—	—	—	—	—	—	—	VA	VA
Weissberg, Charlotte	—	—	—	—	—	—	—	4	4
Total:	19	19	20	20	19	17	16	15	16

SOCIOLOGY FACULTY AT BRANDEIS UNIVERSITY BY YEAR *con't.*

	1976	77	78
Stein, Maurice	2	2	2
Wolff, Kurt	2	2	2
Hughes, Everett C.	E	E	E
Schwartz, Morris S.	2	2	2
Zola, Irving K.	2	2	2
Fellman, Gordon	3	3	3
Fisher, Charles	3	3	3
Kanter, Rosabeth M.	3	—	—
Bittner, Egon	2-1	2-1	2-1
Derber, Charles	4	4	4
Ross, George	4	3	3
Hayim, Gila	4	4	4
Weissberg, Charlotte	4	4	4
Rosenthal, Kristine	VA	4	4
Fields, Karen	—	4	4
Miliband, Ralph	—	VP	VP
Rayman, Paula	—	4	4
Yedidia, Michael	—	VA	—
Total	14	16	15

Key:
* = undergraduate program only
# = combined sociology and anthropology department
D = Doctor; A = Adjunct Associate; M = Mr.
VP = Visiting Professor; VL = Visiting Lecturer
E = Professor Emeritus
L = Lecturer
VA = Visiting Assistant
1 = Chair of Department
2 = Full Professor
3 = Associate Professor
4 = Assistant Professor

NOTES

I would like to thank Egon Bittner, Paul Campanis, Charles Fisher, Alex Liazos, Donald Light, Ruth Jacobs, Abram Sachar, Morris Schwartz, Maurice Stein, Gaye Tuchman, Robert Weiss, Kurt Wolff, and Irving K. Zola, all of whom I interviewed, and Carroll Bourg, Murray Davis, Rogers Johnson, and Barrie Thorne, who corresponded with me about this paper. Thanks also to Blanche Geer, Lynda Holmstrom, and Karl Pillemer. Lenore Weitzman, Wini Breines, Susan Ostrander, Andrea Walsh, Jeanne Guilleman and Diane Vaughan discussed my initial draft with me, as did all the contributors to this volume. Thanks also to Howard Becker, Peter Conrad, Gordon Fellman, Gary Alan Fine, Jennifer Platt, Anselm Strauss, Diane Vaughan, and Irving Zola for their extensive comments on an early draft.

1. Martin Bulmer, *The Chicago School of Sociology: Institutionalization, Diversity, and the Rise of Sociological Research* (Chicago: University of Chicago Press, 1984), p. 14.

2. Ibid., p. 15.

3. Ibid., p. 15.

4. Abram L. Sachar, *A Host at Last* (Boston: Little, Brown, 1976), p. 25.

5. Ibid., p. 32.

6. Ibid., p. 35.

7. Ibid., p. 39.

8. Ibid., p. 44.

9. See, however, Alan M. Sica, "A Question of Priority: Small at Chicago or Blackmar at Kansas?" *Mid-American Review of Sociology,* 1990, *14:* (1–12).

10. Bulmer, *Chicago School,* p. 26.

11. See Mary Jo Deegan, *Jane Addams and the Men of the Chicago School* (New Brunswick: Transaction Books, 1988).

12. Interview with Chancellor Emeritus Abram Sachar, June 26, 1991.

13. Sachar, *A Host,* p. 41. Marcuse stayed on to spend over a decade at Brandeis University and had many close ties with the Department of Anthropology and Sociology. See also Kurt Wolff and Barrington Moore, Jr., eds., *The Critical Spirit: Essays in Honor of Herbert Marcuse* (Boston: Beacon Press, 1967), with the assistance of Heinz Lubasz, Maurice Stein, and E. V. Walter. Other senior scholars included Ludwig Lewisohn; Albert Guerard, professor of French literature and civilization; Alfred Kroeber and Paul Radin in anthropology; Rudolf Kayser in philosophy; Kurt Goldstein in psychology; Max Lerner in American civilization; Aron Gurwitsch in philosophy; and Eleanor Roosevelt in politics. See Lewis A. Coser, *Refugee Scholars in America: Their Impact and Their Experiences* (New Haven: Yale University Press, 1984); and David R. Holmes, *Stalking the Academic Communist: Intellectual Freedom and the Firing of Alex Novikoff* (Hanover, N.H.: University Press of New England, 1989).

14. In addition to Brandeis, some elements of the Chicago school migrated to the University of California at Berkeley, Indiana University, Northwestern University, and other universities whose faculties were joined by students of Everett Hughes and others.

15. See Eugene Uyeki letter to Gary Alan Fine, June 13, 1990 ("after Wirth died, the younger sociologists who came in were not-Chicago style"), and Annabelle Blum letter to Gary Alan Fine, June 12, 1990 ("the faculty of ex-Chicagoans was teaching at Indiana University: Ed Swanson, Anselm Strauss, Alfred Lindesmith, August Hollingshead, and Edwin Sutherland").

16. Barrie Thorne informed me that "Everett Hughes used to observe that we pick and choose which ancestors we claim, to evoke a present identity." Personal communication, September 10, 1992.

17. Personal communication, Howard S. Becker, July 29, 1991. "Yet [Everett was] a WASP with a sense of his own marginality as the ultimately non-believing and secularly-minded son of a Protestant minister. And also as a minister's child who had learned to keep to himself what Everett called 'guilty information' (the secrets his father learned and the household learned about.) That experience connected, I think, with his philosophical, wide-scope view of society—expecting sinners as well as saints, not surprised by anything." Personal communication, Barrie Thorne, September 10, 1992.

18. Bulmer, *Chicago School,* p. 205; see also Howard S. Becker, Blanche Geer, David Riesman, and Robert S. Weiss, eds., *Institutions and the Person: Essays Presented to Everett C. Hughes* (Chicago: Aldine, 1968).

19. Dorothy Ross, *The Origins of American Social Science* (New York: Cambridge University Press, 1991), p. 430.

20. Bulmer, *Chicago School,* p. 170.

21. Everett Hughes, ed., *Collected Papers of Robert E. Park:* Foreword, vol. 1, *Race and Culture* (1951); Foreword, vol. 2, *Human Communities* (1952); Foreword, vol. 3, *Society* (1955) (Glencoe: The Free Press); "Robert Park," *New Society* (December 31, 1964), pp. 18–19. See also Winifred Raushenbush, *Robert E. Park: Biography of a Sociologist* (Durham, N.C.: Duke University Press, 1979), with a foreword and an epilogue by Everett C. Hughes.

22. Helen MacGill Hughes, "News and The Human Interest Story: A Study of Popular Literature," Ph.D. diss., University of Chicago, 1940. See her "Robert Ezra Park," *International Encyclopedia of the Social Sciences,* 1968, *11:* 416–19; "Wasp/Woman/Sociologist," *Society,* 1977, *14* (5): 69–80; and "Robert Ezra Park: The Philosopher, Newspaperman, Sociologist," in *Sociological Tradition from Generation to Generation* (Norwood, N.J.: Ablex Press, 1980).

23. Jean-Michel Chapoulie, "Everett C. Hughes and the Development of Fieldwork in Sociology," *Urban Life,* 1987, *15* (3–4): 259–98, p. 263.

24. Bulmer, *Chicago School,* p. 188.

25. Jennifer Platt takes exception to some of the Adlers' views, which may result from their reliance on a single source for some of their interpretations. In contrast to the quotation below, Platt points out that Ernest Burgess continued to be an active researcher until he retired, obtained many grants, and was a leading figure on SSRC committees. Personal communication, Jennifer Platt, July 17, 1991.

26. He retired to Nashville, Tennessee, in 1934 but was already on leave in 1931 and 1932. See Bulmer, *Chicago School,* p. 205, for a discussion.

310   Shulamit Reinharz

27. Patricia A. Adler and Peter Adler, *Membership Roles in Field Research* (Newbury Park, Calif.: Sage, 1987), p. 10.

28. Roger Salerno, *Louis Wirth: A Bio-Bibliography* (Westport, Conn.: Greenwood Press, 1987), p. 27.

29. Actually William Ogburn died in 1959.

30. Ernest Burgess died in 1966.

31. Philip Hauser was a graduate student at the University of Chicago between 1929 and 1932 and an instructor in sociology between 1932 and 1934. He relocated to the Bureau of the Census in Washington, D.C., and returned to the Chicago faculty in 1947 where he remained. He did not actually chair the department until 1956. He served as chair until 1965. See Bulmer, *Chicago School,* p. 174.

32. James Short, letter to Gary Alan Fine, May 31, 1990.

33. Transcript of taped conversation between Fred Davis and Anselm Strauss, April 26, 1991.

34. Interview with Robert Weiss, February 1, 1991.

35. Interview with Morris S. Schwartz, January 3, 1991.

36. See Lee Braude letter to Gary Alan Fine, May 9, 1990. See also David Moore letter to Gary Alan Fine, June 19, 1990.

37. See Lee Braude letter to Gary Alan Fine, May 9, 1990; Charles Hawkins letter to Gary Alan Fine, May 18, 1990.

38. See Lee Braude letter to Gary Alan Fine, May 9, 1990.

39. See Harold Wilensky letter to Gary Alan Fine, May 22, 1990.

40. Chapoulie, "Hughes," p. 265.

41. Ibid., p. 264.

42. Howard S. Becker earned his Ph.D. from the University of Chicago in 1951. His dissertation was "Role and Career Problems of the Chicago Public-School Teacher."

43. Herbert Gans received his Ph.D. from the University of Pennsylvania in 1957 but he wrote, "Having been trained in sociology at the University of Chicago during the era when Everett C. Hughes and the late Louis Wirth—to name only two—were dominant influences in the Department of Sociology, I believed strongly in the value of participant-observation as a method of social research." Herbert J. Gans, *The Urban Villagers: Group and Class in the Life of Italian-Americans* (New York: The Free Press, 1962), p. 336.

44. Erving Goffman earned his Ph.D. from Chicago in 1953. His dissertation was "Rules Regarding Social Interaction in a Rural Community."

45. Anselm L. Strauss was a graduate student between 1939 and 1944, earning his Ph.D. in 1944. His dissertation was "A Study of Three Psychological Factors Affecting the Choice of a Mate in Marriage." He took no courses with Everett Hughes. Strauss was on the Chicago faculty from 1952 to 1958, during part of which time Hughes was department chair. While a faculty member, Strauss "was much influenced by Hughes and his students, personally and via writings." Personal communication, Anselm Strauss, August 1991.

46. Transcript of taped conversation between Fred Davis and Anselm Strauss, April 26, 1991.

47. Morris Schwartz earned his Ph.D. from Chicago in 1951. His dissertation was "Social Interaction in a Disturbed Ward of a Mental Hospital."

48. Assistant professor 1938–42; professorial lecturer 1943–49; assistant professor 1950; professor 1951–53; head of department 1954–56; professor 1957–61.

49. Adler and Adler, *Roles,* p. 10. See Everett Hughes, "Introduction: 'The Place of Field Work in Social Science,'" in Buford Junker, ed., *Field Work* (Chicago: University of Chicago Press, 1960), and "Natural History of a Research Project: French Canada," *Anthropologica,* 1963, pp. 225–39, reprinted in Arthur Vidich, Joseph Bensman, and Maurice Stein, eds., *Reflections on Community Studies* (New York: John Wiley, 1964; and Harper & Row, 1971), pp. 71–84.

50. Hughes participated in supervising numerous fieldwork doctoral dissertations at Brandeis. Of the 136 Ph.D.'s produced by the program until 1990, at least 43 (31%) were based on fieldwork.

51. All dates indicated in this way indicate the year of receipt of the Ph.D. in sociology.

52. Robert Emerson, *Contemporary Field Research: A Collection of Readings* (Boston: Little, Brown, 1983). See also Robert Emerson, "Observational Field Work," *Annual Review of Sociology,* 1981, *7:* 351–78. Other examples are Barrie Thorne, "'You Still Takin' Notes?' Fieldwork and Problems of Informed Consent," *Social Problems,* 1980, *27:* 284–97; Barrie Thorne, "Political Activist as Participant Observer: Conflicts of Commitment in a Study of the Draft Resistance Movement of the 1960s," *Symbolic Interaction,* 1979, *2:* 73–88; and Shulamit Reinharz, *On Becoming a Social Scientist: From Survey Research and Participant Observation to Experiential Analysis* (San Francisco: Jossey-Bass, 1979; New Brunswick, N.J.: Transaction Books, 1984).

53. I do not claim that Brandeis was the only place to which the tradition migrated. Obviously, students of Everett Hughes at the University of Chicago brought the tradition wherever they went as faculty members, too.

54. These were embodied by faculty such as Herbert Marcuse at Brandeis and Barrington Moore at nearby Harvard; and by graduate students such as Martin Nicolaus, Steve Rosenthal, and Jeremy Shapiro who had recently studied with Adorno in Frankfort and was translating Habermas.

55. An example is Barrie Thorne, who worked for two years with Hughes on a Carnegie-funded book on professional education while also writing her dissertation. "We had a lot of daily contact; he was then at Boston College." Personal communication, Barrie Thorne, September 10, 1992.

56. Robert Heine-Geldern, "Cultural Diffusion," *International Encyclopedia of the Social Sciences,* edited by David Sills (New York: Macmillan, 1968), vol. 3, p. 170.

57. Together they hired Suzanne Keller, whom they knew from Columbia and who remained for four years as an assistant professor; and Robert Feldmesser, a Harvard social relations Ph.D. who was an assistant professor from 1958 to 1962 when the sociology department split from the anthropology-sociology department.

58. Lewis A. Coser, "Notes on a Double Career," in Mathilda White Riley, ed., *Sociological Lives* (Newbury Park, Calif.: Sage, 1988), pp. 65–70, pp. 67–69.

59. This work culminated in his 1952 publication, "Field Work Procedures: The Social Organization of a Student Research Team," the appendix to Alvin Ward Gouldner, *Patterns of Industrial Bureaucracy* (Glencoe, Ill: The Free Press, 1954). See also Maurice R. Stein, "The Eclipse of Community: Some Glances at the Education of a Sociologist," in Arthur Vidich, Joseph Bensman, and Maurice Stein, eds., *Reflections on Community Studies* (New York: John Wiley, 1964; and Harper & Row, 1971).

60. Brandeis University Course Catalogue, 1955–56, p. 151.

61. Ibid.

62. See Maurice Stein and Arthur Vidich, eds., *Sociology on Trial* (Englewood Cliffs: Prentice-Hall, 1963).

63. See Alfred H. Stanton and Morris S. Schwartz, *The Mental Hospital* (New York: Basic Books, 1954); Morris S. Schwartz and Charlotte G. Schwartz, "Problems in Participant Observation," *American Journal of Sociology,* 1955, *60:* 343–53; see also Morris S. Schwartz, "The Mental Hospital: The Research Person in the Disturbed Ward," in Vidich, Bensman, and Stein, *Reflections,* pp. 85–117.

64. Howard S. Becker considers the fieldwork emphasis and contribution of Lloyd Warner to be very significant, particularly on himself and on Erving Goffman. Lloyd Warner's encouragement of St. Clair Drake and Horace Cayton in their studies of race relations in the South, culminating in *Black Metropolis,* had a major impact on Becker. Personal communication, Howard S. Becker, July 29, 1991.

65. Interview with Morris S. Schwartz, January 3, 1991.

66. Mason Griff, Chicago Ph.D. '58, was hired and stayed one year as an assistant professor.

67. Howard S. Becker stresses the importance of Redfield in sustaining the fieldwork emphasis at the University of Chicago. Personal communication, July 29, 1991.

68. Interview with Kurt Wolff, January 8, 1991.

69. See Kurt Wolff, "The Collection and Organization of Field Materials: A Research Report," in Richard N. Adams and Jack J. Preiss, eds., *Human Organization Research: Field Relations and Techniques* (Homewood, Ill: Irwin, 1960), pp. 240–54; and "Surrender and Community Study: The Study of Loma," in Vidich, Bensman and Stein, *Reflections,* pp. 233–63.

70. Interview with Robert Weiss, February 1, 1991.

71. Ibid.

72. Ibid.

73. Ibid.

74. Sachar, *A Host,* p. 132.

75. Interview with Robert Weiss, February 1, 1991.

76. Howard S. Becker felt that Hughes was different from most other American sociologists of the day by being at home in the European literature, including philosophy. He read widely in German and French, and these skills were not common. "So he must have been at home with people like Coser and Wolff, and they

with him, in a way that would have been unusual and perhaps had something to do with them choosing him." Howard S. Becker, personal communication, July 29, 1991.

77. Interview with Maurice Stein, January 11, 1991.

78. Interview with Morris S. Schwartz, January 3, 1991.

79. A contrary view was offered by Egon Bittner in an interview on January 14, 1991. He says that the department was never monolithic and did not represent "the Chicago School," which itself was a myth. He does not see Brandeis as having a mission. (Bittner arrived at Brandeis in 1968, the year Everett Hughes became emeritus and left Brandeis for Boston College.) "I had never quite believed the myth of the department having a clear cut identity that distinguishes it from the rest of the world. I didn't perceive it then, and I never perceived it later on either. I came the year the grant ended. Morrie Schwartz came from Chicago but didn't represent that tradition; Charlie Derber, I think, belongs to the mythical tradition."

80. Interview with Kurt Wolff, January 8, 1991.

81. Because of a perceived need for "balance," faculty such as Frederick Abrahams were hired from Columbia University to teach quantitative methods. These individuals must have felt like "tokens" and did not stay long. Moreover, most students in the department took quantitative courses in other departments or other universities in the vicinity, if they took them at all.

82. Interview with Maurice Stein, January 11, 1991. Interview with Irving K. Zola, February 1991, expresses the same thought.

83. Interview with Morris S. Schwartz, January 3, 1991.

84. Blanche Geer received her Ph.D. in education from Johns Hopkins in 1956 after studying anthropology at Columbia University in 1946–47. There was no anthropology or sociology department at Johns Hopkins while she was there. She wrote: "I have never been Everett Hughes' student in the formal sense of attending his classes" but she coauthored two books with him: Howard S. Becker, Blanche Geer, Everett C. Hughes, and Anselm Strauss, *Boys in White: Student Culture in Medical School* (Chicago: University of Chicago Press, 1961); and Howard S. Becker, Blanche Geer, and Everett C. Hughes, *Making the Grade: The Academic Side of College Life* (New York: John Wiley, 1968). See Becker, Geer, Riesman, and Weiss, *Institutions and the Person,* p. 221.

85. Anthropologist Hanna Papanek was a research associate of Everett Hughes's the same year.

86. Community sociologist Arthur Vidich came for a year as a visiting professor, and Zvi Bernard Sobel, who studied the Jewish community, was hired as an assistant professor. He stayed until 1969, went on leave, and then relocated at Haifa University in Israel.

87. John R. Seeley, R. Alexander Sim, and E. W. Loosely, *Crestwood Heights: A Study of the Culture of Suburban Life* (Toronto: University of Toronto Press, 1956), and John R. Seeley, "Crestwood Heights: Intellectual and Libidinal Dimensions of Research," in Vidich, Bensman, and Stein, *Reflections,* pp. 157–206. What Seeley learned at Chicago was that "you gotta do fieldwork." Interview with Maurice Stein, January 11, 1991.

88. A larger goal was to ban the Selective Service from campus. Interview with Irving K. Zola, February 1991.

89. Ibid.

90. Ibid.

91. Interview with Maurice Stein, January 11, 1991.

92. Joseph Zelan, Chicago Ph.D. 1964, taught at Brandeis from 1964 to 1966 as a lecturer. Jacob Feldman, Chicago 1965, is listed as having received his first job at Brandeis too.

93. Stephen J. Miller had worked with Hughes and Becker at Chicago, though his Ph.D. was from St. Louis University.

94. Stephen J. Miller, *Prescription for Leadership: Training for the Medical Elite* (Chicago: Aldine, 1970). While at Brandeis, Hughes received an NIMH grant jointly with the Heller School, listing himself and Howard Freeman as co-principal investigators. This grant funded fieldwork studies in medical settings. Steve Miller was the Heller School project director, later replaced by Irving K. Zola.

95. Irving Kenneth Zola, "Observations on Gambling in a Lower Class Setting," *Social Problems,* 1963, *10:* 353–61.

96. Interview with Irving K. Zola, February 1991.

97. Interview with Donald Light, January 22, 1991.

98. This is an error. Morris Janowitz *did* have a Chicago Ph.D.

99. Larry Rosenberg, "Communication Styles and Learning—A Factor-Analytic Study of Teacher-Student Interaction," Ph.D. diss., University of Chicago.

100. Joseph Zelan, Chicago Ph.D. '64, also came to the Brandeis graduate program in sociology briefly as a lecturer.

101. Interview with Donald Light, January 22, 1991.

102. Interview with Charles Fisher, February 1991.

103. Ruth Jacobs reported: "Bob Weiss was seduced; he came to teach statistics and then stopped. He was changed after being involved in the fieldwork course." Telephone conversation.

104. Chapoulie, "Hughes," n. 18.

105. For a discussion of these terms, see Jennifer Platt, "The Development of the 'Participant Observation' Method in Sociology: Origin Myth and History," *Journal of the History of the Behavioral Sciences,*" 1983, *19:* 379–93. Platt reminds us that the equation of the Chicago School with fieldwork is a misleading but conventional characterization. Bulmer, *Chicago School,* attempts to revise this characterization by presenting information about the role of quantification. See also Lee Harvey, *Myths of the Chicago School of Sociology* (Brookfield: Avebury, 1987), chap. 3.

106. Interview with Morris S. Schwartz, January 3, 1991.

107. Members of the Field Methods Training Program were Morris S. Schwartz, Robert Weiss, Everett Hughes, Sam Wallace, Larry Rosenberg, Maurice Stein, and Lewis Coser.

108. Interview with Morris S. Schwartz, January 3, 1991.

109. Herbert J. Gans, "The Participant-Observer as a Human Being: Obser-

vations on the Personal Aspects of Field Work," in Howard S. Becker, Blanche Geer, David Riesman and Robert S. Weiss, eds., *Institutions and the Person: Papers Presented to Everett C. Hughes* (Chicago: Aldine, 1968), pp. 300–317.

110. Personal communication, Carroll Bourg, April 15, 1991.

111. Gaye Tuchman, "Qualitative Methods in the Study of News," in Klaus Jensen and Nick Jankowski, eds., *A Handbook of Qualitative Methodologies for Mass Communications Research* (London: Routledge, 1991), pp. 79–92.

112. Interview with Ruth Jacobs, March 3, 1991.

113. Interview with Paul Campanis, January 10, 1991.

114. Personal communication, Barrie Thorne to Shulamit Reinharz, September 10, 1992.

115. Samuel E. Wallace (Minnesota Ph.D. '60) was hired in 1965 as an assistant professor with the role of program supervisor, Field Methods Training Program. He was a member of the Field Training Course, and a course instructor in the Field Methods Course at Brandeis. While a student at the University of Minnesota, he was the field supervisor of a fieldwork research project on homeless men, which appeared the year he came to Brandeis: *Skid Row as a Way of Life* (Totowa, N.J.: Bedminster Press, 1965). Before coming to Brandeis, he was a project director at the University of Puerto Rico and then at Columbia University's Bureau of Applied Social Research. Samuel Wallace was on leave at least two of the years he was on the faculty at Brandeis and left in 1973.

116. According to Gaye Tuchman, "We needed special permission to take a methods course that wasn't fieldwork, including a woman who needed permission to take statistics at Harvard." Interview, January 1991.

117. Tuchman, "Qualitative Methods," pp. 79–92, n.2.

118. Gordon Fellman suggests that this incident reflected the desire to separate fieldwork and political commitments. Personal communication, July 14, 1991.

119. Interview with Gaye Tuchman, January 10, 1991.

120. Interview with Alex Liazos, January 12, 1991.

121. Tuchman, "Qualitative Methods."

122. Personal communication, Murray Davis '69, February 12, 1991.

123. See interview with Maurice Stein, January 11, 1991.

124. Others whose dissertations he directed were Charles Levy, Jean Binstock, Linda Holmstrom, Donald Light, Lily Offenbach, and Barrie Thorne. He served on the dissertation committees of Robert Emerson, Ruth Jacobs, Gaye Tuchman, Alice Stewart Carloni, J. Starr, Natalie Alon, Norman Mirsky, Barbara Carter, Nancy Stoller Shaw, Rolland H. Wright, Jeanne Guilleman, Rachel Kahn-Hut, Fran Portnoy, and Doug Harper.

125. See Charles Hawkins letter to Gary Alan Fine, May 9, 1990; Charles King letter to Gary Alan Fine, May 24, 1990; Don Levine letter to Gary Alan Fine, June 27, 1990. Eugene Uyeki says, "Hughes made extensive use of Simmel and Weber—largely in the context of his formulations of sociological theory as applied to social institutions, race and ethnic relations, work urbanism, etc." Eugene Uyeki to Gary Alan Fine, June 13, 1990.

126. See Charles Hawkins letter to Gary Alan Fine, May 18, 1990.

127. Interview with Paul Campanis, January 10, 1991.

128. Personal communication, Barrie Thorne, September 10, 1992.

129. William Foote Whyte did the research for *Street Corner Society* while a junior fellow at Harvard University (1936–40), shortly after he received his B.A. from Swarthmore College in economics. He then went to the University of Chicago and received his Ph.D. in sociology under W. Lloyd Warner and Everett Hughes. *Street Corner Society* appeared while Whyte was on the faculty of the University of Oklahoma (1942–43). See William Foote Whyte, *Learning from the Field* (Newbury Park, Calif.: Sage, 1984).

130. Interview with Ruth Jacobs, March 3, 1991.

131. Brief telephone interview with Karl Pillemer.

132. Interview with Barrie Thorne, September 10, 1992.

133. Lynda Lytle Holmstrom, "Everett Cherrington Hughes: A Tribute to a Pioneer in the Study of Work and Occupations," *Work and Occupations,* 1984, *11* (4): 471–81, esp. pp. 466–67.

134. Tuchman, "Qualitative Methods."

135. Barrie Thorne makes the same point. Gaye Tuchman says that Barrie Thorne thought of Hughes as a father. Interview with Gaye Tuchman, January 10, 1991.

136. Telephone Interview with Ruth Jacobs, March 3, 1991.

137. Personal communication, Barrie Thorne, September 10, 1992.

138. Telephone interview with Gaye Tuchman, January 10, 1991.

139. Ibid.

140. Personal communication, Murray Davis, February 12, 1991.

141. Personal communication, Barrie Thorne, September 10, 1992.

142. Telephone interview with Gaye Tuchman, January 10, 1991.

143. Ibid.

144. Personal communication, Rogers Johnson, February 5, 1991.

145. In her first semester, Ruth Jacobs wrote two papers which were published in *The Gerontologist* and the *Family Coordinator,* called "The Friendship Club," and "Social Club for Elderly Armenian Men." She published her second-semester papers in *The Geriatric Digest*—"Mobility Pains" and "One Way Street"—concerning the Hebrew Home for the Aged.

146. Interview with Maurice Stein, January 11, 1991.

147. In essence, this is the case today.

148. Shortly after he arrived at Brandeis in 1966, Larry Rosenberg told students that he had thrown his (quantitative) dissertation from the University of Chicago into Lake Michigan. He left Brandeis in 1973, and in 1985, after studying meditation in Korea, Japan and Thailand, founded the Cambridge Insight Meditation Center.

149. Personal communication, Murray Davis, February 12, 1991.

150. Personal communication, Rogers Johnson, February 5, 1991.

151. See Tamotsu Shibutani letter to Gary Alan Fine, May 19, 1990.

152. See Charles Hawkins letter to Gary Alan Fine, May 18, 1990.

153. Interview with Paul Campanis, January 10, 1991.

154. Interview with Kurt Wolff, January 8, 1991.

155. Gordon Fellman suggests that he may not have been perceived as a fieldwork "insider" because his fieldwork studies were explicitly political. The department may have differentiated between method and politics, and the charged political era of the late 1960s and early 1970s may have revealed the limitations of fieldwork. Personal communication, July 14, 1991.

156. Interview with Maurice Stein, January 11, 1991.

157. For extensive documentation, see Barrie Thorne, "Feminist Sociology: The Brandeis Connection," Talk given at the 25th anniversary of the graduate program of the Brandeis University Sociology Department, April 11–12, 1987.

BIBLIOGRAPHY

BOOKS AND ARTICLES

Adler, Patricia A. and Adler, Peter. *Membership Roles in Field Research.* Newbury Park, Calif.: Sage, 1987.

Becker, Howard S.; Geer, Blanche; Hughes, Everett C.; and Strauss, Anselm. *Boys in White: Student Culture in Medical School.* Chicago: University of Chicago Press, 1961.

Becker, Howard S.; Geer, Blanche; and Hughes, Everett C. *Making the Grade: The Academic Side of College Life.* New York: John Wiley, 1968.

Becker, Howard S.; Geer, Blanche; Riesman, David; and Weiss, Robert S., eds. *Institutions and the Person: Essays Presented to Everett C. Hughes.* Chicago: Aldine, 1968.

Bulmer, Martin. *The Chicago School of Sociology: Institutionalization, Diversity, and the Rise of Sociological Research.* Chicago: University of Chicago Press, 1984.

Chapoulie, Jean-Michel. "Everett C. Hughes and the Development of Fieldwork in Sociology." *Urban Life,* 1987, *15* (3–4): 259–98.

Coser, Lewis A. "Notes on a Double Career." In Mathilda White Riley, ed., *Sociological Lives.* Newbury Park, Calif.: Sage, 1988, pp. 65–70.

Coser, Lewis A. *Refugee Scholars in America: Their Impact and Their Experiences.* New Haven: Yale University Press, 1984.

Deegan, Mary Jo. *Jane Addams and the Men of the Chicago School.* New Brunswick, N.J.: Transaction Books, 1988.

Emerson, Robert. *Contemporary Field Research: A Collection of Readings.* Boston: Little, Brown, 1983.

Emerson, Robert. "Observational Field Work." *Annual Review of Sociology,* 1981, *7:* 351–78.

Gans, Herbert J. "The Participant-Observer as a Human Being: Observations on the Personal Aspects of Field Work." In Howard S. Becker, Blanche Geer, David Riesman, and Robert S. Weiss, eds., *Institutions and the Person: Papers Presented to Everett C. Hughes.* Chicago: Aldine, 1968, pp. 300–317.

Gans, Herbert J. *The Urban Villagers: Group and Class in the Life of Italian-Americans.* New York: The Free Press, 1962.

Harvey, Lee. *Myths of the Chicago School of Sociology.* Brookfield: Avebury, 1987.

Heine-Geldern, Robert. "Cultural Diffusion." *International Encyclopedia of the So-*

cial Sciences, edited by David Sills. New York: Macmillan, 1968, vol. 3, pp. 169–73.

Holmes, David R. *Stalking the Academic Communist: Intellectual Freedom and the Firing of Alex Novikoff.* Hanover, N.H.: University Press of New England, 1989.

Holmstrom, Lynda Lytle. "Everett Cherrington Hughes: A Tribute to a Pioneer in the Study of Work and Occupations." *Work and Occupations,* 1984, *11* (4): 471–81.

Hughes, Everett, ed. *Collected Papers of Robert E. Park:* foreword, vol. 1, *Race and Culture* (1951); foreword, vol. 2, *Human Communities* (1952); foreword, vol. 3, *Society* (1955). Glencoe, Ill: The Free Press.

Hughes, Everett. "Robert Park." *New Society* (December 31, 1964), pp. 18–19.

Hughes, Everett. "Introduction: 'The Place of Field Work in Social Science.'" In Buford Junker, ed., *Field Work.* Chicago: University of Chicago Press, 1960.

Hughes, Everett. "Natural History of a Research Project: French Canada." *Anthropologica,* 1963, pp. 225–39, reprinted in Arthur Vidich, Joseph Bensman, and Maurice Stein, eds., *Reflections on Community Studies.* New York: John Wiley, 1964; and Harper & Row, 1971, pp. 71–84.

Hughes, Helen MacGill. "Robert Ezra Park." *International Encyclopedia of the Social Sciences,* 1968, *11:* 416–19.

Hughes, Helen MacGill. "Wasp/Woman/Sociologist." *Society,* 1977, 14 (5): 69–80.

Hughes, Helen MacGill. "Robert Ezra Park: The Philosopher, Newspaperman, Sociologist." In *Sociological Tradition from Generation to Generation.* New York, Ablex Press: 1980.

Miller, Stephen J. *Prescription for Leadership: Training for the Medical Elite.* Chicago: Aldine, 1970.

Platt, Jennifer. "The Development of the 'Participant Observation' Method in Sociology: Origin Myth and History." *Journal of the History of the Behavioral Sciences,* 1983, *19:* 379–93.

Raushenbush, Winifred. *Robert E. Park: Biography of a Sociologist.* Durham: Duke University Press, 1979, with a foreword and an epilogue by Everett C. Hughes.

Reinharz, Shulamit. *On Becoming a Social Scientist: From Survey Research and Participant Observation to Experiential Analysis.* San Francisco: Jossey-Bass, 1979; New Brunswick, N.J.: Transaction Books, 1984.

Ross, Dorothy. *The Origins of American Social Science.* New York: Cambridge University Press, 1991.

Sachar, Abram L. *A Host at Last.* Boston: Little, Brown, 1976.

Salerno, Roger. *Louis Wirth: A Bio-Bibliography.* Westport, Conn.: Greenwood Press, 1987.

Schwartz, Morris S. and Schwartz, Charlotte G. "Problems in Participant Observation." *American Journal of Sociology,* 1955, *60:* 343–53.

Schwartz, Morris S. "The Mental Hospital: The Research Person in the Disturbed Ward." In Arthur Vidich, Joseph Bensman, and Maurice Stein, eds., *Reflections on Community Studies.* New York: John Wiley, 1964; and Harper & Row, 1971, pp. 85–117.

Seeley, John R.; Sim, R. Alexander; and Loosely, E. W. *Crestwood Heights: A Study of the Culture of Suburban Life.* Toronto: University of Toronto Press, 1956.

Seeley, John R. "Crestwood Heights: Intellectual and Libidinal Dimensions of Research." In Arthur Vidich, Joseph Bensman, and Maurice Stein, eds., *Reflections on Community Studies.* New York: John Wiley, 1964; and Harper & Row, 1971, pp. 157–206.

Shaw, Nancy Stoller. *Forced Labor: Maternity Care in the United States.* New York: Pergamon Press, 1974.

Sica, Alan M. "A Question of Priority: Small at Chicago or Blackmar at Kansas?" *Mid-American Review of Sociology,* 1990, *14:* 1–12.

Stanton, Alfred H. and Schwartz, Morris S. *The Mental Hospital.* New York: Basic Books, 1954.

Stein, Maurice R. "Field Work Procedures: The Social Organization of a Student Research Team." Appendix to Alvin Ward Gouldner, *Patterns of Industrial Bureaucracy.* Glencoe, Ill: The Free Press, 1954.

Stein, Maurice R. "The Eclipse of Community: Some Glances at the Education of a Sociologist." In Arthur Vidich, Joseph Bensman, and Maurice Stein, eds., *Reflections on Community Studies.* New York: John Wiley, 1964; and Harper & Row, 1971, pp. 207–32.

Stein, Maurice R. and Vidich, Arthur, eds. *Sociology on Trial.* Englewood Cliffs: Prentice-Hall, 1963.

Thorne, Barrie. "Feminist Sociology: The Brandeis Connection." Talk given at the 25th anniversary of the graduate program of the Brandeis University Sociology Department, April 11–12, 1987.

Thorne, Barrie. "'You Still Takin' Notes?' Fieldwork and Problems of Informed Consent." *Social Problems,* 1980, *27:* 284–97.

Thorne, Barrie. "Political Activist as Participant Observer: Conflicts of Commitment in a Study of the Draft Resistance Movement of the 1960s." *Symbolic Interaction,* 1979, *2:* 73–88.

Tuchman, Gaye. "Qualitative Methods in the Study of News." In Klaus Jensen and Nick Jankowski, eds., *A Handbook of Qualitative Methodologies for Mass Communications Research.* London: Routledge, 1991, pp. 79–92.

Vidich, Arthur; Bensman, Joseph; and Stein, Maurice, R., eds. *Reflections on Community Studies.* New York: John Wiley, 1964; and Harper & Row, 1971.

Wallace, Sam. *Skid Row as a Way of Life.* Totowa, N.J.: Bedminster Press, 1965.

Whyte, William Foote. *Street Corner Society: The Social Structure of an Italian Slum.* Chicago: University of Chicago Press, 1943.

Whyte, William Foote. *Learning from the Field.* Newbury Park, Calif.: Sage, 1984.

Wolff, Kurt and Moore, Barrington, Jr., eds. *The Critical Spirit: Essays in Honor of Herbert Marcuse.* Boston: Beacon Press, 1967, with the assistance of Heinz Lubasz, Maurice R. Stein, and E. V. Walter.

Wolff, Kurt. "The Collection and Organization of Field Materials: A Research Report." In Richard N. Adams and Jack J. Preiss, eds., *Human Organization Research: Field Relations and Techniques.* Homewood, Ill: Irwin, 1960, pp. 240–54.

Wolff, Kurt. "Surrender and Community Study: The Study of Loma." In Arthur Vidich, Joseph Bensman, and Maurice R. Stein, eds., *Reflections on Community Studies.* New York: John Wiley, 1964; and Harper & Row, 1971, pp. 233–63.

Zola, Irving Kenneth. "Observations of Gambling in a Lower Class Setting." *Social Problems,* 1963, *10*: 353–61.

INTERVIEW TRANSCRIPTS: SHULAMIT REINHARZ, INTERVIEWER

Bittner, Egon, January 14, 1991.
Campanis, Paul, January 10, 1991.
Fisher, Charles, February 14, 1991.
Liazos, Alex, January 12, 1991.
Light, Donald, January 22, 1991.
Jacobs, Ruth, March 3, 1991.
Sachar, Abram, June 26, 1991.
Schwartz, Morris, January 3, 1991.
Stein, Maurice, January 11, 1991.
Tuchman, Gaye, January 10, 1991.
Weiss, Robert, February 1, 1991.
Wolff, Kurt, January 8, 1991.
Zola, Irving Kenneth, February 10, 1991

INFORMAL INTERVIEWS

Geer, Blanche
Holmstrom, Lynda
Pillemer, Karl

CORRESPONDENCE

Becker, Howard S., to Shulamit Reinharz, July 29, 1991.
Blum, Annabelle, to Gary Alan Fine, July 12, 1990.
Braude, Lee, to Gary Alan Fine, May 15, 1990.
Bourg, Carroll, to Shulamit Reinharz, April 15, 1991.
Davis, Fred, and Anselm Strauss to Gary Alan Fine, April 26, 1991 (transcript of audiotape).
Davis, Murray, to Shulamit Reinharz, February 12, 1991.
Fellman, Gordon, to Shulamit Reinharz, July 14, 1991.
Hawkins, Charles, to Gary Alan Fine, May 18, 1990.
Johnson, Rogers, to Shulamit Reinharz, February 5, 1991.
King, Charles, to Gary Alan Fine, May 24, 1990.
Levine, Donald, to Gary Alan Fine, June 27, 1990.
Moore, David G., to Gary Alan Fine, June 19, 1990.
Platt, Jennifer, to Shulamit Reinharz, July 17, 1991.

Shibutani, Tamotsu, to Gary Alan Fine, May 19, 1990.
Strauss, Anselm, to Shulamit Reinharz, August 1991.
Thorne, Barrie, to Shulamit Reinharz, September 10, 1992.
Uyeki, Eugene, to Gary Alan Fine, June 13, 1990.
Wilensky, Harold, to Gary Alan Fine, May 22, 1990.

CHAPTER NINE

THE SECOND SEX AND THE CHICAGO SCHOOL: WOMEN'S ACCOUNTS, KNOWLEDGE, AND WORK, 1945–1960

Mary Jo Deegan

Sociology is embedded in society: this is a highly problematic fact for a discipline that studies society. It creates an irreducible tension in the profession between being a part of society and claiming to be outside its rules. One of the most burdensome and embarrassing challenges to sociological assertions of disinterest is the incorporation of inequality within its practice, ideas, networks, and fundamental social processes. This injustice undermines sociologists' avowal of "objectivity," "expertise" in interpreting social problems, and "difference" from the groups they study. Furthermore, like members of other groups, sociologists do not want to examine their biases, patterns of discrimination, and failure to meet their ideals. Unlike those in other groups, however, sociologists generate the tools to critique inequality and empower the victims to understand victimization as a social process.

In this chapter I examine this convoluted professional problem within a specific context, institution, and cohort: the women who were trained in sociology at the University of Chicago between 1945 and 1960. These women are crucial to understanding this particular institution, practice, and era, and its hegemonic role in the larger definition of gendered labor and inequality in the profession. A number of our most eminent, contemporary women in sociology were being trained or employed in marginal positions at the University of Chicago during this era.[1] (The names of the women who earned doctorates there during this era are listed in table 9.1. The names of women on the instructional staff from 1892 to 1960 are listed in table 9.2.) This gendered era was part of a larger pattern affecting both sexes at the university, when the Chicago school of sociology underwent major transitions from its earlier, more famous years. These changes affected the social construction of sociology itself through the institutionalized power of Chicago sociologists.[2]

It is almost impossible to use sociology to discuss sociology as biased, because the concepts hide the professional practice of sexism. Doro-

TABLE 9.1. DISSERTATION TITLES FOR SOCIOLOGY DOCTORATES EARNED BY WOMEN AT THE UNIVERSITY OF CHICAGO, 1945–1960

Author	Title	Year
Sarma, Jyotirmoyee	"The Social Categories of Friendship"	1946
Whitridge, Eugenia Remlin	"Art in Chicago"	1946
Lee, Rose Hum	"The Growth and Decline of Chinese Communities in the Rocky Mt. Region"	1947
Miller, Vera	"The Areal Distribution of Tax Delinquency in Chicago and Its Relationship to Certain Housing and Social Characteristics"	1947
Burnet, Jean	"The Problem of Community Instability in East Central Alberta"	1948
Cohen, Lillian	"Factors Associated with Home Ownership in Twenty-Two Metropolitan Districts"	1948
Bernert, Eleanor H.	"The Chicago Labor Force, 1910–1940"	1949
Shanas, Ethel	"The Personal Adjustment of Recipients of Old Age Assistance: With Special Consideration of the Methodology of Questionnaire Studies of Older People"	1949
Williams, Josephine J.	"The Professional Status of Women Physicians"	1949
Motz, Annabelle Bender (Blum*)	"Conceptions of Marital Roles in Transition"	1950
Quinn, Olive Westbrooke	"Racial Attitudes and the Conforming Personality"	1950
Rogoff, Natalie (Ramsay*)	"Recent Trends in Occupational Mobility"	1950
Ross, Aileen D.	"Ethnic Relations and Social Structure: A Study of the Invasion of French-Speaking Canadians into an English Canadian District"	1950
Star, Shirley Ann	"Interracial Tension in Two Areas of Chicago: An Exploratory Approach to the Measurement of Interracial Tension"	1950
Kitagawa, Evelyn	"Differentials in Total and Marital Fertility, Chicago, 1920–1940"	1951
Buckman, Rilma	"Interaction Between Women's Clubs and Institutions"	1952

324   Mary Jo Deegan

TABLE 9.1. (*cont.*)

Author	Title	Year
Kimura, Yukiko	"A Comparative Study of the Collective Adjustment of the Isei, the First-Generation Japanese, in Hawaii and in the Mainland, U.S., since Pearl Harbor"	1952
Nelson, Leona Bernice	"The Secularization of a Church-Related College"	1953
Amerman, Helen Ely	"The Impact of Intergroup Relations on Non-Segregated Urban Public Education"	1954
Goldstein, Rhoda Louis (Blumberg*)	"The Professional Nurse in the Hospital Bureaucracy"	1954
Huang, Lucy	"Dating and Courtship Innovations of Chinese Students in America"	1954
Lang, Gladys Engel	"A Study of Politics on Video: Viewers. Content and Definitions of the 1952 Convention"	1954
Lopata, Helena Znaniecka	"The Functions of Voluntary Associations in an Ethnic Community: Polonia"	1954
Lyman, Elizabeth Latimer	"Similarities and Differences in Emphasis Given to Certain Aspects of Work"	1954
Lilienthal, Daisy (Mrs. Taglizcozzo)	"The Meaning of Unionism: A Study of the Perspectives of Members of the Plumbers' Union, the United Mine Workers and the United Automobile Workers of America"	1956
Duncan, Beverly	"Population Distribution and Economic Activity"	1957
James, Rita (Simon*)	"Jurors' Reactions to Definitions of Legal Insanity"	1957
Helper, Rose	"The Racial Practices of Real Estate Institutions in Selected Areas of Chicago"	1958
Carter, Wilmoth Annette	"The Negro Main Street of a Contemporary Urban Community"	1959
Cassidy, Sally Whelan	"A Study of Lay Leadership"	1959
Moore, Joan Willard	"Stability and Instability in the Metropolitan Upper Class"	1959
Verdet, Paula	"Inter-Ethnic Problems of a Roman Catholic Parish"	1959

*Present last name.

TABLE 9.2. FEMALE SOCIOLOGISTS WHO WERE MARGINAL FACULTY MEMBERS IN
SOCIOLOGY BETWEEN 1892 AND 1960

Name	Title	Years as Faculty
Marion Talbot	Assistant to full professor of Sanitary Science*	1892–1920
Mary E. McDowell	Special instructor	1894–1930?
Annie Marion MacLean	Extension assist. prof.	1900–1934?
Edith Abbott	Special lecturer	1914–15
	Instructor	1916–18
	Lecturer	1919–20
Ruth Newcomb	Assistant	1932
Josephine Williams	Instructor	1947–49
	Assist. prof.**	1950
	Research associate	1951
Evelyn Kitagawa***	Instructor	1949–50
	Research associate	1951–60
Shirley Star	Research associate	1951–56
	(Associate professor**)	1957–60
Ethel Shanas	Research associate	1951–56
	(Associate professor**)	1958–65
Rita James (Simon)	Research associate (Assistant professor**)	1959–61
Joan Moore	Research associate (Assistant professor**)	1960–61

*Talbot's precise relation to the sociology department during these years was ambiguous and changed several times. She was also the dean of women.
**Nontenured.
***The first women to be tenured in the Department of Sociology and to chair it, in 1975, when she was promoted to full professor. She is listed differently in Appendix Two below.

thy E. Smith has described this dilemma in considerable detail, and her writings are a sophisticated resource for the invisibility of women in sociological theory and practice (e.g., 1977, 1987, 1988). I leap over these epistemological problems here to examine specific lives and patterns. These issues are amply illustrated in the self-reports of over thirty male sociologists in this cohort. These sociological critiques of this school and era were written in 1990 for Gary Fine and the authors in this book. *In these male accounts, there are almost no references to the 15% of their cohort who were women.* The men's reflections on their training and careers, and their celebration of sociology, continue the patriarchal patterns embedded in the wider society, their profession, and their specific training. These men, moreover, were specifically asked to comment on gender as part of their experiences as students and professionals, so they actively rejected such an analysis. Generally, gender and sexism were not discussed.

SEXISM IN SOCIOLOGY; THE PROBLEM THAT HAS NO NAME

In 1963, three years after this cohort had graduated, Betty Friedan—a housewife who was not trained as a sociologist—rocked a complacent society by noting that women were dissatisfied with their traditional roles in the home and family. She called this challenge to sexism "a problem that has no name." Thus a woman outside sociology claimed "the power to name" (Laws and Schwartz 1977) discrimination against women a social problem: a task that was within the professional domain of sociologists who could not—and often cannot—see the problem.

Furthermore, Simone de Beauvoir's penetrating text on women as "other" was available in English after 1952. According to de Beauvoir, women's otherness permeates society. It becomes, therefore, the basis for social interactions, knowledge, and professional expectations in sociology.

De Beauvoir defined women as the "second sex" with these words: "She is the incidental, the inessential as opposed to the essential. He is the Subject, he is the Absolute—she is the Other" (1952: xvi). The intellectual woman, moreover, is doubly doomed, by her failure to be blind to her situation and by her desire to speak about it (de Beauvoir 1952: 685). "To be situated at the margin of the world is not a position favorable for one who aims at creating anew" (de Beauvoir 1952: 132).

This marginality to intellectual work appears in myriad ways. Women, for example, are not seen as embodied authority (Kristeva 1977). They are not the creators of knowledge: they are its objects. They do the invisible tasks of clerical labor, library research, and data collection. They teach undergraduates, correspondence students, or they grade examinations. Their invisible work needed for the production of sociological knowledge is "shadowwork" (Illich 1982; Deegan 1989a): it is "women's work" in sociology. It is a counterpart to their shadowwork in the home and family. Such shadowwork, moreover, takes a particular historical form in sociology: female sociologists often marry male sociologists and reproduce the double shadowwork of home and profession. The women's reflection in the work of their husbands elaborates a series of paradoxes.

Helen MacGill Hughes (Ph.D. from the University of Chicago in

1937; hereafter the degree and year are noted only for Chicago graduates) wrote of these complex patterns in her reflections on herself as "Maid of All Work or Departmental Sister-in-Law?" (1973a). From 1944 to 1961 she was the managing editor at the *American Journal of Sociology* (*AJS*), a position previously held only by graduate students. Her life at the University of Chicago embodied a series of contradictory statuses.

> I was a graduate of the department and a fellow student, though junior to them, of three of the editors, Blumer, Wirth, and Hughes: a student of a fourth, Burgess; and as if that were not enough to upset the customary relationships in the office, wife of one of them (Hughes 1973: 9).

Her reflections on this state were like echoing, "mirrored images" (Cooley 1902) limiting her ideas and actions within gendered parameters.

The axis polarizing the women's lives during this era was a gendered line drawn between the family and society. Jane Addams (1910) called it the struggle between "family" and "social" claims, while Alva Myrdal and Viola Klein (1956) analyzed it as women's "two roles."[3] As Erving Goffman (Ph.D. 53)[4]—insightfully wrote in 1977:

> In modern industrial society, as apparently in all others, sex is at the base of a fundamental code in accordance with which social interactions and social structures are built up, a code which also establishes the conceptions individuals have concerning their fundamental human nature. (P. 301)

Most appropriately, Robert Park's concept of the "marginal man" can be used to analyze the women's status. Park, a Chicago sociologist (Hughes 1968, 1980), used the concept to refer to immigrants and African Americans who were outside the dominant Anglo-Saxon society in America. Women, however, were "marginal men" not only to society but also to Park (Deegan 1994). Thus the women of the Chicago school were "marginal women" through their training by an expert in marginality who trained others, primarily men, to continue his peculiar legacy. A further irony in this paradoxical situation is that Park was mentored by a significantly less sexist man, W. I. Thomas (Klein 1948; Deegan 1988a: 202–8), who was part of the earliest Chicago school of sociology.

Many women "transcended" the limits surrounding their gender, however, and they used sociological ideas, mentors, and jobs to do so.

CONTEMPORARY CHICAGO REFLECTIONS ON
"THE PROBLEM THAT STILL HAS NO NAME"

A major barrier to women's professional success was their invisibility. Their absence is a "negative space": something that does not exist where it should. Thus, women comprised half of society, yet no woman was a tenured or even a tenure-track member of the faculty in the era studied here. This blatant exclusion of women was not seen as problematic by these supposedly observant experts on society. For example, one man (Ph.D. in the late 50s) writes:

> Almost all the students and teachers were men. I don't think that there was sexism within the Department; rather this was due to outside influences. On the other hand, there was no feminism among the female students. (18 May 1990, p. 3)

This man's continuing denial of sexism in the past and in contemporary reflections is also found among some women who were students. Thus, Annabelle (Bender) Blum (Ph.D. '50) writes:

> I personally was not conscious of discrimination against women students in the department. I was awarded scholarships and a fellowship and I was asked if I'd like to have my name referred to teaching positions. I know that one other woman received a coveted fellowship at another university. I was aware that some of the male students felt that they were being bypassed. (12 July 1990)

Blum's retrospective account conflates the experiences of male and female students, glossing over real differences in professional opportunities and accomplishments.

An anonymous male even lauds the university for being "strongly anti-discriminatory in its approaches and policies with regard to social differentiation in racial, ethnic, religious, and political characteristics and orientations." This man holds this belief despite the department's failure to maintain any Marxist voice; to hire tenure-track women and/or men of African-American background; or to support a sociology critical of the status quo. Chicago sociologists remain silent to this day about the development of nuclear weaponry at the University of Chicago.[5]

This contemporary denial is found in yet a third, anonymous male account:

So far as I could see, there was no difference in the treatment of students by any imaginable difference in ascribed or achieved characteristic. Rumors of preferential treatment abounded—but these were attributed to specific intellectual and research preferences of particular faculty, not to race, class, or ethnicity, or even gender.

This male sociologist denies, even in the 1990s, the patterns of blatant structural inequality within sociology.

"Graduate student dialogues," wrote Robert A. Dentler (Ph.D. '60), "did not go to questions of how to redesign the existing social order" (1987: 177). The Chicago students were expected to lead their colleagues in a world torn by economic chaos, war, nuclear armaments, sexism, and racism, but as Dentler notes: "Our horizon was limited to better evidence, better analysis of it, to questions such as interpersonal environments, social climates, attitude change, community conflict, and to program evaluation" (1987: 177). This sociological emphasis trained students to look at others, but not at each other. Thus, sexism at Chicago became invisible and difficult to articulate.

The complicated nature of women as the second sex at Chicago is revealed in Margaret Peil's (Ph.D. '63) account that displays simultaneously both insight into and denial of sexism:

The main gender issue was the absence of women teachers: they were ok for research, but we heard more than once, "A Sociology Department is excellent in inverse ratio to the number of women therein; Chicago hasn't any." Thus, while top men might be taken on—or traded with the University of Michigan—women would have to look elsewhere. Still, Chicago was top of my list partly because it gave scholarships to women, whereas North Carolina was known not to. I never experienced any problems with staff or students in women being treated differently than men. Friendships arose from mutual interests or common employers, not from gender. Age was another factor in friendship, though not a determining one. Another male friend was supporting himself and family by working at NORC. Our "core" study group (all female) noted once that we included Catholic, Protestant and Jew, black and white, middlewesterners and easterners, straight through school and several years employment or marriage/family. (9 May 1990, p. 2)

In this remarkable passage, Peil reveals her knowledge of women's exclusion from the faculty, differential gender placement in academia, Chicago's relatively lower sexism, the gender segregation in her study group, and a denial of any personal experience of sexism. She compares herself to a male who was supporting himself and his family, but not to the men on fully funded fellowships. She appears unaware of her exclusion from the "old boy network" formed in graduate school.

Peil later reflected on this passage and my interpretations of it. First, like many other women in her cohort, she acknowledged that sexism occurred, but it was invisible in interpersonal relationships. Her doctoral training, moreover, occurred over a busy nineteen months. She had friends and advisors inside and outside of sociology, and "I was in my 30s and socialized to accept that men ran things, though it never occurred to me that I couldn't compete on fairly equal grounds given the appropriate education" (23 May 1991). Understanding sexism from her perspective involved issues embedded in memory, evaluation, biography, and professional performance.

Jean Burnet (Ph.D. '48) also found this tangle of sexism problematic and presented a vivid example of this complexity. In 1974, Burnet had an unsettling sexist response to a paper she wrote on belonging to three minority groups: sociologists; Canadians; women. After she shared her paper (published in 1981) with her mentor Everett Hughes, he replied:

> The great thing which your piece taught me, however, was that we males have so little appreciation of the female handicap and of how that handicap combined with others such as being in a subject of low prestige enhanced the minority status in some high geometric degree. It isn't just women plus sociology, but women times sociology.

Burnet was startled by this response because she had been taught by Hughes how to understand the situation of women. Although Helen Hughes was an expert on sexism in sociology (e.g., Hughes 1973b), Burnet's account was still a revelation to Everett Hughes.

Thus, we can extend Goffman's insight on society as organized by a sex code, to one where sociologists have a sex code based on denial of sexism within the profession. This sociological sex code affects all the sociology they produce. Friedan's "problem that has no name" has been named by her and large segments of society, but it has not been named by many Chicago sociologists.

"WINDOWS" OF OPPORTUNITY FOR WOMEN

There were several less sexist institutional opportunities in sociology at Chicago in comparison to everyday practice. These "windows" of opportunity were located in the undergraduate college and practiced by the few, usually marginal, men who actively supported women in professional—not student—activities.[6] The distinction between student and professional support is important, for women were often challenged and sometimes welcomed as students. The most important barriers occurred after graduation. Each small "window" of opportunity supported women within the larger, hostile, professional universe.

The Undergraduate College

The Department of Sociology was engaged in an elitist, patriarchal practice of the profession. It was oriented to scholarly production instead of student-teacher interactions. The undergraduate college, especially with its interdisciplinary course "Social Science II," challenged this way of doing sociology.

> Tension between these two modes of doing scholarly work was hard to avoid. One mode—that of the professional sociologist—constrained and bound the scholar close to the empirical world of his/her direct observation; to the tools and limits of craft. The other—that of the interpreting mind—was impatient with such limitations and with the very specialization inherent in the idea of craft itself. (Gusfield 1982: 5)

Although faculty from the sociology department were involved in various stages of administering the course, Robert Hutchins, the president of the University of Chicago, drew a strict line between the college and the graduate divisions (Riesman 1990: 62).

The better treatment of women students within the college reflects this difference. Women such as Rosalie Hankey (Wax) (Ph.D., anthropology, '50, teaching assistant, 1947; member of the Social Science II faculty, 1950–57; denied tenure in 1957 [Murray Wax 15 June 1991]) and Sylvia Thrupp (Ph.D., history '60?, associate professor of social sciences in the college, 1960–61) were on the staff of the college.[7] The Department of Sociology, however, kept women and their more flexible way of doing sociology out of its administrative domain.

Male Mentors Who Supported Women as Students

I could not find any male faculty member who supported female students to become full-fledged faculty at eminent doctoral departments of sociology in universities from 1945 to 1960, despite diligent efforts to do so.[8] There were, however, varying degrees of support and opposition to women as students. Few male faculty are mentioned by any former female student at Chicago. Two men—W. Lloyd Warner, the cultural anthropologist/sociologist, and David Riesman, a lawyer turned sociologist/lawyer—were discussed very positively.[9] Warner, in particular, supported African-American students and white women. Wilmoth A. Carter noted Warner's helpfulness as well as an internal grapevine about other, unspecified faculty to avoid (28 August 1990). Similarly, Murray Wax described Riesman's structural support of Rosalie Wax as a faculty member (15 June 1991).

Riesman, however, was not well accepted by several Chicago men and spent the majority of his highly productive career at Harvard, not Chicago. Riesman was himself a marginal man at Chicago. For example, Kimball Young, a respected scholar of the Chicago school, dismissively wrote that Riesman was "a popular writer. He ha[d] no training." According to Young, Robert Maynard Hutchins hired Riesman without consulting the department.

> Louis Wirth just about had little kittens when he discovered, as other people did, that they put Riesman into the department of sociology with a full professorship. Nobody had ever been consulted about him. They didn't even know who he was. Well, he's a very charming guy. I knew Riesman quite well on a social level, but even his charm didn't win over people such as Louis Wirth and Blumer. (1988: 305)

Despite Riesman's difficulties with some sociologists, he befriended others, notably Everett Hughes.

In 1954, Hughes, then chair of sociology, and Morton Grodzins, the dean of the Division of the Social Sciences, proposed that Riesman join the department staff. A bitter fight ensued, led by Philip Hauser. A compromise between the factions resulted in Riesman's appointment as a "professor of social sciences" in the department instead of a position as a "professor of sociology." The enmity towards Riesman continued during his remaining years at Chicago, spilling over to his relations with graduate students. This repressive atmosphere led to Riesman's recollection:

> I sometimes had the dismal experience of having as a doctoral candidate someone who had been a spirited undergraduate and watching that person become more timid and less original as time went by. (Riesman 1990: 63)

Riesman's problems with the department were significant and emerged from a number of factors. Riesman's openness to women students was one difference from departmental norms. He was also committed to a form of inquiry that was considerably more freewheeling and exploratory than that of some other sociologists on the faculty, and he was not single-mindedly devoted to sociology as a "profession" and discipline (Riesman 1990). The more rigid worldviews of the male network in the Department of Sociology were not supported by Riesman or Warner.

THE GENDERED ERAS

Women's acceptance at Chicago is further complicated by a long tradition of women's work in the profession. The conventional history of the department, though, presents only a male pattern. "Chicago sociology" has been told, therefore, as a "male story." Women's distinct history must be grasped, however, to understand the Chicago women trained between 1945 and 1960.

As I document elsewhere (e.g., 1978, 1987, 1988a,b, 1991a), the earliest years at the University of Chicago, from 1892 to 1920, were a "golden era" for women in sociology. Women's work centered on political activism and emphasized democracy and human rights, especially for women, the poor, and the immigrant. Their powerful role in the profession was followed by "the dark era of patriarchal ascendancy" (Deegan 1991a) extending from 1920 until 1965.

This "first era" was an illustrious age for the men, too: they established the first graduate Department of Sociology in 1892; they founded the most important sociological journal, *AJS,* in 1895; they helped form and lead the major professional organization, the American Sociological Association, in 1905; and they trained a considerable proportion of the first cohort of Ph.D.s in the profession prior to 1920. This distinguished first era for men is "unnamed."

The next era, between 1920 and 1940, saw the birth of international recognition for the "Chicago school of sociology," a school characterized by ethnographic studies and by an intellectual emphasis on human ecology, the city, crime and delinquency, and immigration. By 1930 almost half of all sociologists in the world had been trained at Chicago, and the school exercised hegemonic control over the discipline. For women, this was the end of their golden era.

By 1945, the department's epistemology, staff, and institutional control had vastly changed. This new, "male" era is often seen as a "decline," but this evaluation emerges only in comparison to the department's previous, hegemonic power. Its influence was now shared with a more heterogeneous and positivist profession. This new era is only now being examined intensely as an institutional power with its own unique patterns. Women from this era had careers and ideas that exhibit patterns quite different from those of the men.

The Golden Era of Chicago Women in Sociology (1890–1920)

A powerful network of Chicago women flourished between 1892 and 1920. They recruited each other into the profession; helped each other find employment; supported each other through hard times; documented women's lives; shared a vision of a more egalitarian society; lobbied for legislation; founded massive social organizations; and wrote books, pamphlets, articles, and broadsides together. They were friends, allies, and colleagues in a new profession. They critiqued each other's work, elaborating and extending their intellectual corpus. They were part of the "first wave of feminism," and sociology was integral to their work and lives. Their network was international in scope and linked to women's demands for higher education. Changing women's roles in society were linked to the emerging social sciences, especially sociology (Klein 1948).

Two generations of women entered sociology during the golden era. The first generation, born generally between 1855 and 1870, was made up of "pioneers" who established a place for "women's sociological work" in a society with distinct spheres for each sex. This gender-segregated ideology, the doctrine of the separate spheres, allowed for the growth of a separate women's network in sociology. It was led by women who emphasized the study of the home, women, children, and the family. Because women were assumed to have higher "emotional and cultural sensitivity" than men, the women were deemed ideal professionals to improve society and make it more humane. The men's network was more abstract, intellectual, and academic (Deegan 1978, 1981, 1987, 1988a, b). The second generation was made up of women who were born between 1870 and 1890. They were "professionals" who obtained male credentials in the academy but who sometimes chose and sometimes were forced to operate in the distinct women's world within sociology (Deegan, 1988b, 1991a).

The pioneers in the golden era battled for women's right to higher education, suffrage, and work outside the home. They used social science to document women's restricted lives and opportunities. The professionals combined the role established by the pioneers with formal training in the academy. This second generation was often mentored by the pioneers and by sympathetic male sociologists such as George H. Mead and W. I. Thomas. Female students were not accepted as equal faculty members in the male academy, however. The women struggled on the margins of soci- ology departments (see table 2). *This established an early pattern of encour- aging women students to perform at their peak, but discriminating against women graduates as professional colleagues.*

Some of these early, Chicago-trained professionals included Edith Abbott (Ph.D., political economy, '05), Sophonisba Breckinridge (Ph.D., political economy, '01; J.D. '04), Katharine Bement Davis (Ph.D., political economy and sociology, 1900), Amy Hewes (Ph.D., sociology, '03), and Jessie Taft (Ph.D., philosophy, '13). Some willingly turned to social work as a more inviting profession for women. Others entered social work be- cause they felt pressured by unemployment and limited professional op- portunities in sociology. Thus, the female faculty in sociology at the Uni- versity of Chicago (Edith Abbott, Sophonisba Breckinridge, Mary McDowell, and Marion Talbot) was transferred en masse from sociology to social work in 1920 (Deegan 1978; for a discussion of shifting, gendered definitions of women's work, see Deegan 1988a, pp. 309–23). The male sociologists did not want the women in the department. Simultaneously, the women wanted to end their second-class status as sociologists.

Powerful "founding sisters"—doctorally trained, prolific writers, and active in the American Sociological Society—virtually disappeared from male academies in sociology departments after 1920. Male sociolo- gists erased their ties to these founding sisters and began a new era. Jane Addams (University of Chicago Extension faculty 1896–1912?; frequent visiting lecturer, Chicago School of Civics and Philanthropy, 1904–20) was a central figure in this sociological drama, especially in the areas of ap- plied sociology and the social thought generated by the Chicago school. Hull-House, the social settlement house she headed, was located in Chi- cago, and it was the major women's sociological institution. It generated a new model of professional work, where the home and workplace were combined: a kind of intellectual commune and salon. Some of the brilliant female sociologists who lived and worked there were Edith Abbott, Emily Greene Balch, Sophonisba Breckinridge, Charlotte Perkins Gilman, Florence Kelley (Extension faculty 1894–1896?), Frances Kellor (sociology graduate student, 1898–1902), Julia Lathrop (co-founder, Chicago School of Civics and Philanthropy, 1904), Mary McDowell, Annie Marion MacLean (Ph.D. 1900), and Ida B. Wells-Barnett. Dozens of other women sociologists, including Beatrice Webb and Alice Mazaryk, visited it (Deegan 1991a).

Both the pioneers and the professionals looked to Jane Addams for international and professional leadership. Her intellectual legacy to sociology is a function of two major streams of thought: cultural feminism and critical pragmatism. "Cultural feminism" is a theory of society that assumes that traditionally defined feminine values are superior to traditionally defined male values. "Critical pragmatism" (Deegan 1988a) is a theory of society that emphasizes the need to apply knowledge to everyday problems based on radical interpretations of liberal and progressive values. The successful combination of these two theories is called "feminist pragmatism." This unique theory applies traditional female values to eliminate or ameliorate everyday problems (Deegan 1993).

Addams's work was firmly grounded in the "male Chicago Schools" of pragmatism and of sociology (especially the ideas developed by John Dewey, George Herbert Mead, and W. I. Thomas; see Deegan and Hill 1987). During World War I, Addams experienced a dramatic fall from grace as a public figure in this country and around the world. This vilification arose from her defense of the feminine values of cooperation and nurturance as superior to the masculine values of conflict and aggression. These male values supported war and its attendant devastation of people, nations, and physical resources. Her political censure as a pacifist coincided with a professional judgment of her "failure" as a sociologist, and for many years she remained an outcast in society and the discipline (Deegan 1988a).

The elimination of Addams as a leading sociologist was tied to the elimination and erasure of her female cohort. The power of the separatist world of the golden era also made it vulnerable to its thorough removal by more powerful men. Few students, colleagues, institutions, and texts championed their sociology after 1920. Women who survived in sociology worked in a narrowly redefined patriarchal profession. The first wave of feminism receded in power in sociology and in the wider society. A "dark era of patriarchal ascendancy" began in sociology in 1920 and lasted until 1965 (Deegan 1991a).

The Professionals Trained in a Redefined Male Profession (1920–1929)

Simultaneously with the dispersion and destruction of the women's network in American sociology, a dramatic loss of power and visibility for women in the profession occurred throughout the world. England, France, Germany, Czechoslovakia, and the Soviet Union, major sociological centers prior to the Great War, were in turmoil. European countries were devastated by the war, and most sociology programs were greatly undermined.

Despite this upheaval, the men of the Chicago school of sociology flourished. As noted earlier, they dominated the profession worldwide from the end of World War I until the beginning of World War II (Faris 1967; Kurtz 1984). They also spearheaded the elimination of women in sociology. Women who were trained in sociology in the 1920s entered a male world, discourse, and institutional structure. They were second-class citizens without the earlier, powerful women's network. This was the world of such Chicago women as Ruth Shonle Cavan (Ph.D. '26), Frances Donovan (Ph.B., English, '18), Helen MacGill Hughes (Ph.D. '37), Fay Berger Karpf (Ph.D. '24), Ellen Winston Black (Ph.D. '28), and Vivien Palmer (Ph.D. '32). Generally, if these women did not have a powerful male sponsor they suffered professionally. Women during this dark age of patriarchal ascendancy learned to survive in a male world with male rules. They often wrote textbooks instead of monographs, taught at less prestigious colleges, and received minimal research funds. In short, they were the "second sex" in the discipline. *This cohort established a pattern of professional participation that frequently shaped the careers of women trained at Chicago between 1945 and 1960.* During the 1920s the women who had flourished during the golden age were thrust out of professional networks, recognition, and legitimation in sociology. Most of them realigned professionally with another field, especially with social work.

The Professionals Trained During the Great Depression (1929–1939)

The grim, worldwide, economic collapse that characterized the 1930s had a profound impact on sociology. Sociologists increasingly justified their withdrawal from the study of a society by claiming that it was "natural" for scientists who studied "facts" to search for "social regularities" outside of and unaffected by the turmoil in the economic order. They retreated into "value-free" scientific rhetoric, a popular political position that continues in the 1990s. At Chicago this movement elicited a controversial fight between William F. Ogburn, who represented the positivist position, and Robert E. Park, who represented a qualitative, more humanist orientation.[10] Their ideological conflicts continued into the 1950s when the "quantitative" supporters gained ascendancy after considerable conflict and a redefinition of "good sociology" (Riesman 1990).

Originally, mathematical work was defined as part of women's work in sociology (e.g., see Edith Abbott's title in table 2). It was denigrated as "technical" (versus innovative), "repetitive," and "uninteresting." In the 1950s, however, men's quantitative work was increasingly defined as "creative" and powerful because it used "hard" science. This quantitative versus qualitative debate raged at Chicago, but many men at Chicago supported qualitative work. In fact, they held an important line in the profession by linking qualitative methods to definitions of male work. One of the ways of maintaining this line was keeping women out of the powerful inner circle of qualitative, male sociologists.

After the Great Depression, however, mathematical work was increasingly lauded as "sophisticated" male labor and claimed as men's special interest. One type of statistical work still legitimated for women, however, was demography. Counting births and death was defined as more "feminine" than counting armaments, industrial stockpiles, and the number of friends in social networks. Despite the men's redefinition of sociology and quantitative methods, women trained in sociology in the 1930s were oriented generally to the community and the solution of social problems. Almost all the women pioneers from the golden era had died or retired. The first professionals were rarely active in sociology during the 1930s, although they often did groundbreaking work in other disciplines and outside the academy. Thus, they rarely mentored the next generation of women in sociology.

The Professionals Trained During World War II and Its Immediate Aftermath (1939–1950)

Two academies trained a number of women in sociology during the dark era: the University of Chicago and Columbia University in New York City. The latter institution, moreover, gained ascendancy in the training of women in sociology in the 1940s. Robert Merton and Robert Lynd, in particular, established a relatively open context for women students.

One indicator of this more favorable Columbia setting is the fact that a Chicago woman from this era has never been the ASA president, while nineteen of the men who were Chicago faculty or students at this time have held that position (see table 9.3). Alice S. Rossi, Mirra Komarovsky, and Dorothy Swaine Thomas, three of the six women ASA presidents, received major portions of their graduate training at Columbia (see table 9.4).

Unlike the women in the golden era of sociology, this new cohort tended to marry. Many of the husbands of these eminent women became or were eminent sociologists (e.g., Helen MacGill Hughes and Everett C. Hughes; Carolyn Rose and Arnold Rose; Alice S. Rossi and Peter Rossi; Rose Laub Coser and Lewis Coser). In a juggling act that continued until the mid-1960s, this new generation of women usually combined marriage, motherhood, and careers in a hostile discipline. They did not operate within a strong female network, however. In fact, three eminent female sociologists—Jessie Bernard (interview, 1978), Elizabeth Briant Lee (interview, 1986), and Irene Diggs (interview, 1989)—noted that there was often tension between female professionals during these years, particularly at professional meetings.

Immediately after World War II, veterans returned to graduate schools to "pick up" their civilian lives. Leo Bogart (Ph.D. '50) recalls how the veterans formed a distinct, bonded group:

> What made our particular crop of graduate students unique, of course, was the war experience, and the opportunities opened up by the G.I. Bill. This set an immediate dividing line between the veterans, who I believe were in the majority, and everyone else. The veterans were not necessarily an older group, since the others included a number of people in their thirties and forties who were entering or returning to graduate school to advance their careers in teaching or government service. (Bogart, 29 May 1990, p. 1)

Bogart did not remark that most, if not all, of the women were not veterans. In this way, the sex-segregated combat veterans were seen as a "natural" rather than a gendered group.

Bevode McCall (Ph.D. '54) recalled that many veterans were children of the Depression. They were spouses and parents more frequently than the other graduate students. This "meant there were strong pressures to go along, get along, get out and get on a payroll" (May 1990: 1). "Women's issues" were not a high priority in such a cohort.

TABLE 9.3. MALE SOCIOLOGISTS WHO WERE FACULTY OR STUDENTS AT THE
UNIVERSITY OF CHICAGO BETWEEN 1945 AND 1960 AND BECAME PRESIDENTS OF
THE AMERICAN SOCIOLOGICAL ASSOCIATION (ASA).

Name	Year of ASA Presidency	Years at Chicago
Ellsworth Faris	1937	1911–14(S), 1917–45(F); 1946–53(PE); Ph.d '14, Psychology
Ernest W. Burgess	1934	1916–52(F+S); 1952–60(PE); Ph.D. '13
William F. Ogburn	1929	1927–52(F); 1952–60(PE)
Louis Wirth	1947	1926–51(F); Ph.D. '26
E. Franklin Frazier	1948	Ph.D. '31
Talcott Parsons	1949	1937–72(F)*
Cottrell, Leonard S.	1950	Ph.D. '33
Herbert Blumer	1956	1926–52(F); Ph.D. '28
Everett C. Hughes	1963	1938–60(F); Ph.D. '28
Phillip M. Hauser	1968	1947–60**(F+S); Ph.D. '38
Ralph H. Turner	1969	Ph.D. '48
Reinhard Bendix	1970	Ph.D. '47
Peter M. Blau	1974	1954–59(F)
Peter H. Rossi	1980	1956–60(F)
Erving Goffman	1982***	Ph.D. '53
James F. Short, Jr.	1984	Ph.D. '51
Kai T. Erikson	1985	Ph.D. '47
Stanley Lieberson	1991	Ph.D. '60
James S. Coleman	1992	1957–60(F)

*Intermittent Visiting Professor
**Appointment continued after 1960
***Died in office
PE = Professor Emeritus
F = Faculty
S = Student
There are many male Chicago sociologists who were presidents of the ASA who were not active at the University of Chicago between 1945 and 1960. This table underestimates the male leadership in this organization if the entire period of the ASA presidencies from 1905 until the present were included. In addition, Kimball Young (U. of C. graduate student, 1917–1919) was an ASA president in 1954.

The Professionals Trained During The Years When
"The Woman Problem" Had No Name (1950–1960)

Between 1950 and 1960, women's proper place was in the home, together with her family. During these years, few women entered sociology. As we have seen, Betty Friedan sparked a tinderbox of unrest in 1963.

TABLE 9.4. FEMALE SOCIOLOGISTS WHO WERE FACULTY OR STUDENTS BETWEEN 1945 AND 1960 (NONE AT THE UNIVERSITY OF CHICAGO) AND BECAME PRESIDENTS OF THE AMERICAN SOCIOLOGICAL ASSOCIATION (ASA).

Name	Year of Presidency of the ASA	Year of Ph.D. and University
Dorothy S. Thomas*	1952	Ph.D.,** London School of Economics, 1924
Mirra Komarovsky	1973	Ph.D., Columbia University, 1940
Alice S. Rossi***	1983	Ph.D., Columbia University, 1950
Matilda White Riley****	1986	ABD, Harvard, 1937
Joan Huber*****	1989	Ph.D., Michigan State University, 1967

*Thomas was married to W. I. Thomas, U. of C. Ph.D., 1894, and faculty, 1893–1917. He was president of the ASA in 1928. She was the first woman to hold this office.

**Thomas earned her M.A. at Columbia University, the most important institution for training women who have been presidents of the ASA.

***Rossi is married to Peter H. Rossi, U. of C. faculty, 1956–60. He was president of the ASA in 1980.

****Riley is married to John W. Riley, Jr., a sociologist who worked for the ASA for many years, as did Matilda White Riley.

*****Huber is married to William F. Form, a sociologist who plays major roles in the ASA, such as his editorship of the *American Sociological Review.*

Women's haunting yet unspoken problem permeated the lives of many Chicago women, for example, Helena Z. Lopata (Ryan 1991), Helen Mac-Gill Hughes (Deegan 1991c), and Caroline Rose (Howery 1991). Many of the women in sociology, moreover, married men in academia during an era when nepotism rules banned the hiring of both spouses (e.g., Rosalie and Murray Wax experienced this difficulty; Wax 19 June 1991). The husband was the one hired in tenure track positions while the wife sought employment elsewhere. Although a number of Chicago women were writing and surviving, few were flourishing professionally. Virginia Olesen (M.A. '56) and Rita Simon (Ph.D. '57) were among the few young women scholars to survive this age of repression. Perhaps more women trained during this period will emerge as leaders of American sociology in the near future. As this cohort enters their 60s and 70s, they may experience the spurt of creativity reflected in the lives of several women trained in the dark era (Deegan 1991a).

THE EPISTEMOLOGY OF THE CHICAGO WOMEN

Although Chicago women tend to actively support women's issues, I do not assume they are all feminists. They share a fundamental

worldview and social location, nonetheless. Regardless of their specializa-
tions, they are women in a man-made world and profession (Gilman
1911). They share a major system of relevance that constructs their life-
world (Schutz 1970). This gendered location leads to a particular body of
knowledge that is identifiably female. This gendered knowledge is both
chosen by them and shaped by others. It emerges from a process of choice
and coercion.

AUTOBIOGRAPHICAL ACCOUNTS BY THE WOMEN WHO STRUGGLED AS "THE OTHER"

White male sociologists who graduated from the University of Chicago frequently write autobiographies and are the subjects of biographies.
(Examples of this literature are noted both in this chapter and in other
chapters in this volume.) The men's accounts stress male colleagues, graduate students they trained, the male network, invisible colleges, and their
control over funding, journals, and professional associations. Their professional success, mentors, organization building, and other "public" aspects of their careers dominate their narratives. Their lives as husbands,
fathers, sons, lovers, and professional "failures" are a "background" to
the central public story. Their private lives are distinct and minor in comparison to their "patriarchal careers." They rarely discuss conflicts in
decision-making or emotions (Deegan 1980, 1991a).

The women share this autobiographical and biographical tradition
but with a marked divergence of style, content, and critique. Their accounts are characterized by extreme struggle and triumph. Their fascinating lives, often unusual for women, encourage them to reflect about their
experiences and knowledge. Their literature of biography and autobiography emerges from their experiences of social change and professional challenges. They unite ideas, experiences, and views that are dichotomized,
sanitized, and simplified by a predominately white, male elite in sociology.
The gendered nature of the women's accounts is discernible when the writings are viewed collectively.

As noted above, the women from Chicago tend to actively support
their alma mater and exhibit great loyalty to it. When discussing the university they tend to emphasize the comparative lack of sex discrimination
there. Their original letters to Gary Fine barely touched on inequality.
This "invisible" discrimination is discussed more openly, even at the university, in their autobiographical accounts.

Helena Znaniecka Lopata, for example, related in several accounts her complex relationship to the men of the Chicago school, due to her father's affiliation with them (Maines 1983; Ryan 1991; e.g. her father, Florian Znaniecki, co-authored with W. I. Thomas *The Polish Peasant in Europe and America,* 1918–1920).

> Although her father's name gained her respect and opened some doors, it also limited her explorations of new areas of study. Even her dissertation topic was constrained by her committee's expectations of Znaniecki's daughter. She originally wanted to do a theoretical piece, but her professors told her to "go back and find out why your Father predicted the Polish community in America would die, and it hasn't." She reluctantly did what they expected. (Ryan 1991: 265)

Lopata's father was a "ghost" following her career and ideas throughout the 1950s and into the mid-1960s (Bentz 1989).

Lopata also thought her evaluations at Chicago were inflated due to her father's influence.

> I thought everybody had *given* me my Ph.D. and that Blumer had *given* me my honors in social psych because they all liked daddy. (Emphasis in source, Maines 1983: 7)

> People always introduced me as Znaniecki's daughter. That's why I reacted so violently when you [David Maines] said let's build the interview on that, actually. Oh yes, that's always bothered me, and still does. (Maines 1983: 5)

This self-doubt was hidden through her immersion in the traditional roles of wife and mother during the 1950s. She worked on the margins of the academy, teaching part-time, in evening courses at DePaul University from 1956 to 1960 and at Roosevelt University from 1960 to 1964. Roosevelt students signed a petition asking for her appointment as a full-time assistant professor in 1965, reflecting the changes initiated by the second wave of feminism (Ryan 1991).

Alice Rossi's career at Chicago displayed another male-influenced pattern. Rossi followed her husband, Peter, to Chicago in 1960, after they had earned degrees at Columbia. She was pregnant with their first child, and she quickly bore two more in the ensuing four years. Trying to combine her professional and traditional roles led to superwoman standards. "She found herself with insomnia and neuritis misdiagnosed as arthritis" (Deegan and Hill 1991: 343). Rossi has described this stressful time in a series of publications (1983, 1988; Rossi in Bermant 1972). A crucial turning point in her conflicting career occurred when she was fired by a Chicago anthropologist from a study that she

> had designed, supervised the fieldwork for, and was happily analyzing at the time my draft of a proposal for continued support was funded by the National Science Foundation. I was "let go" within days of receiving word of the grant's approval, when the principal investigator decided the study was a good thing he wished to keep to himself. (Rossi 1988: 45)

This blatant discrimination "provided the stimulus for a first venture into a sociological study of gender, and a first publication on sex equality in 1964" (1988: 45). This article (1964), in turn, caused other women to critically examine gender inequality, particularly within their own lives. It was a catalyst for change in the profession and affected the lives of all the Chicago women.

A very different account of gender and sociology is presented by Rosalie Wax (1971). In her innovative account of fieldwork as methodology and autobiography, she combined personal and private information. She showed how being a female and a specific age changed her data and relationships to the population she studied. Her trenchant "Chicago school" text on qualitative methodology is rarely cited in the writings of Chicago men.

Women's professional careers from 1945 to 1960 are often similar, although there are few accounts of female networks. One of the most notable accounts of a female colleague from this cohort was written by Helen MacGill Hughes, who analyzed the career of Caroline Baer Rose (Chicago graduate student 1942–52?). Hughes documents that Arnold Rose consistently had professional jobs, publications, and offices several years before Caroline (see also Howery 1991: 337–38). Hughes found Rose to be an exemplar of women in sociology from 1925 to 1975:

> Her professional career took the old pattern characteristic of women in academic life. She gave correspondence courses in sociology through the Department of Independent Study; she held night sessions in the Extension Division. (Hughes 1975: 469)

These "indispensable functions" remain hidden in men's accounts.

Similarly, Ethel Shanas worked on the margins of the Department of Sociology at the University of Chicago for many years. In the 1930s, Faris discouraged her from entering the graduate program:

When I, a Phi Beta Kappa, applied for admission to graduate
studies, Professor Faris said: "Little girl, why don't you go
home and get married?" This was said in all seriousness and I
still remember my shock and bewilderment. (Shanas 1984: 4)

Saner opinions prevailed, and she was admitted to the program. She also
recalled a male-only informal organization:

Within its ranks were many of my fellow students, Edward
Shils, John Clausen, and others. Their meetings were reported
to me at "cram sessions" for the Ph.D. They also discussed
other topics of sociology interest. (Shanas 1984: 5)

These sexist practices were balanced by many other opportunities to interact with the male faculty and students, too.

Shanas enjoyed the support of her nonsociological husband, unlike
many female sociologists married to men in sociology.

From 1947 through 1952 she was research associate and instructor for the Committee on Human Development at the
University of Chicago. . . . After five years as an instructor she
worked for the city of Chicago from 1952 to 1953 as senior
analyst, Office of the Housing and Redevelopment Coordinator. From 1954 to 1956 she was a lecturer in social science
at the University of Illinois at Chicago. She returned to the
University of Chicago, and from 1956 to 1961 she was a senior
study director, National Opinion Research Center, and research associate (associate professor), department of sociology.
Then from 1961 to 1965 she held the position of research associate (associate professor) in both the department of sociology
and the Committee on Human Development. (Streib 1991:
351–52)[11]

In her sociology position, Shanas had a prestigious title but not a tenure-
track position. In 1965 the University of Illinois at Chicago hired her as a
full professor.

AUTOBIOGRAPHICAL ACCOUNTS BY CHICAGO WOMEN IN SOCIOLOGY WHO WORKED PRIMARILY BETWEEN 1892 AND 1945

These conflictful, albeit fascinating, accounts of Chicago women on
campus between 1945 and 1960 are dramatically different from those written by women from the golden era. The earlier women found adventure,

excitement, and fulfillment in each other. The men were peripheral figures, often viewed as engaged in competitive and petty status issues and generating "ivory-tower" ideas. Marion Talbot's powerful documentation of sex discrimination at the University of Chicago, for example, is a highly critical analysis of her experiences there (1936). The moving autobiographies of Jane Addams (e.g., 1910, 1930) have no counterpart in the women's accounts from the dark era.

The first cohort of professionals from the University of Chicago often experienced dramatic lives that empowered themselves and others (e.g., Abbott 1950; Davis 1933; and Jessie Taft 1962). The late Ruth S. Cavan (Ph.D. '26) also wrote an account of her sociological career that differs from that of the generation that followed her. Cavan unequivocally supported the Chicago men of the 1920s and 1930s and affirmed her choice to follow her husband to his job in out-state Illinois (Moyer 1991). Her traditional home was combined with a long commute to Chicago for her work as Burgess's assistant. Her choices were apparently less stressful for her than similar choices by many women who graduated twenty or thirty years after her.

Black male sociologists often blended the white male and female styles of autobiography. For example, Horace Cayton's (1970) tumultuous life is brutally revealed in his searing autobiography, including his "failure" to complete a Chicago doctorate. Anthony Platt has similarly written a reflexive account of E. Franklin Frazier, combining tales of his public career with a few peeks at its private dimensions (1991). Since Wilmoth Carter (Ph.D. '59) was the first African-American woman to graduate in sociology from the University of Chicago, there is no comparable literature for this group (see Deegan and Steans 1991). Thus, the Chicago literature reflects both gender and race patterns that are rarely examined, a point extended below.

"Women's" Topics in the Chicago School of Sociology

There are numerous gendered themes in the work of Chicago women. In this section I briefly compare the two genders' ideas. I rely heavily on the women's published accounts, their vitas, and published scholarship on them, thereby overemphasizing an eminent portion of the cohort. In order to represent more of the total group, I also use their dissertations, while acknowledging the limitations of the dissertation as a source of professional reputation. Many of these dissertations were rewritten as books and articles, however.

"Women" are a topic of study that runs throughout their bibliographies. "Women's issues," such as children, marriage, family, divorce, childbirth, paid labor, and the social construction of women's lives, are analyzed repeatedly through various voices. Lopata has personally established the specialization of studying widows, both in this country and internationally. She also was an early sociologist to study housework and homemakers (see Ryan 1991 for a thorough bibliography). A number of dissertation titles reveal this pattern, as well (e.g., Buckman, Ph.D. '52; and Blumberg, Ph.D. '54). Men very rarely studied "women" as a special topic during this era, with Joseph Gusfield (Ph.D. '54, 1963) a notable exception. Following a tradition established by Burgess, many women studied marriage and the family (e.g., Goldstein, Ph.D. '54; Blum, Ph.D. '50; Peil, Ph.D. '63). Many of these "women's" topics were examined by Chicago demographers, too (e.g., see Evelyn Kitagawa, Ph.D. '51, or Ethel Shanas, Ph.D. '49; on Shanas, see Streib 1991).

Another long-established literature is found in the "Chicago school of race relations" (see Wacker, this volume). Scholarship in this area almost entirely cites the work of men, both black and white. Carter's important contributions to this literature are singularly overlooked (see Deegan and Steans 1991). Helen Hughes's joint work with her husband is similarly invisible (see discussion in Deegan 1991c). Aileen Ross's (Ph.D. '50) study of French-speaking Canadians reflected the Hughes interest. Rose Hum Lee (Ph.D. '47) has received some marginal recognition for her work on Chinese-Americans (Phillips 1991), but Lucy Huang (Ph.D. '54) has not received even this modicum of attention. Helen Ely Amerman (Ph.D. '54), Rose Helper (Ph.D. '58), Shirley Star (Ph.D. '50), Margaret Peil (Ph.D. '63; vita), and Jean Burnet (Ph.D. '48) are also systematically understudied in accounts of this "school." Rosalie Wax's work on Native Americans has been similarly neglected (Grana 1991).

Other "minority issues," such as the study of the poor, are emphasized in the women's literature (e.g., Peil, Ph.D. '63). Female deviance is examined by Helen Hughes, too, although she is rarely noted as part of the Chicago school of criminology and deviance (Deegan 1991c). Ruth Cavan, from an earlier generation, shares some of Hughes's obscurity, albeit to a lesser degree (Moyer 1991). Rita Simon (Ph.D. '57) and Joan Moore (Ph.D. '59, 1991) show the significant change in the acceptance of women's work in criminology and deviance after 1965.

The women of this Chicago era systematically altered the assumptions of symbolic interaction and its generally male-defined worldview.

The women tended, for example, to examine the impact of biology on social interaction. This embodied female self changes through aging (See Streib 1991 on Shanas; Ryan 1991 on Lopata); childbirth (Kitagawa, Ph.D. '51); and particular women's roles, such as being a widow who is aging, poor, and socially isolated (Ryan 1991). Analyzing the role of biology in shaping women's lives alters the theoretical apparatus used to describe them. The importance of lived experience, emotion, and the mix of public and private spheres systematically influences the women's scholarship. *This epistemology is often closer to the writings and symbolic interaction theory of the first cohort of Chicago women in the golden era than it is to the epistemology of the men who were teaching and being trained from 1945 to 1960.* Despite the epistemological similarity between the Chicago women, the men are recognized as teachers, mentors, and experts overwhelmingly more often than the early women are. Thus a vicious cycle of understudying women's ideas and overemphasizing men's ideas is perpetuated.

A similar pattern of understudying women's contributions is found in other specialty areas, especially the quantitative tradition. This obfuscation of women's work reaches an extreme in Martin Bulmer's book examining the early tradition of quantitative work at Chicago (1984; Deegan 1985). He totally ignores the significant roles of Abbott and Breckinridge in sociological research and teaching there. He searches for men in departments other than sociology in order to find a quantitative tradition based in men's rather than's women's work. Indeed, the often marginal status of quantitative analysis in the work of Park can be traced to his opposition to women scholars at the University of Chicago (Deegan 1988a).

Between 1945 and 1960, the Chicago women and men often shared common interests but enacted them differently. Everett C. Hughes, for example, emphasized the study of occupations. Virginia Olesen studied nurses, however (see Olesen's bibliography in Deegan 1991d), while most Chicago men studied physicians (i.e., Eliot Freidson, Ph.D. '52, or Howard Becker, Ph.D. '51). These gendered distinctions are only trends, nonetheless, and not rigid lines. Thus, Fred Davis (Ph.D. '58) studied nurses while Josephine Williams (Ph.D. '49) studied physicians, and Natalie Rogoff (Ph.D. '50) studied occupational mobility.

Although few women from this era cited the earliest women from Chicago, they often shared common interests. For example, Eleanor Bernert (Ph.D. '49) analyzed labor, and Daisy Lilienthal (Ph.D. '56) studied labor unions (See Addams 1910, 1930). Caroline Rose, who did not complete her doctorate, had a life-long interest in labor unions as well (Howery 1991). Housing was also a common interest (e.g., Lillian Cohen '48; Abbott, with the assistance of Breckinridge 1936).

"Women's specialties" such as an interest in art is reflected in both groups, too (Whitridge, Ph.D. '46; Tuchman 1975). Kurt Lang (Ph.D. '53) and Gladys Engel Lang (Ph.D. '54) have co-authored a book on British and American printmakers reflecting this continuing heritage and, in this case, its interest for both sexes (1990). Women's clubs were the focus for Buckman's dissertation (Ph.D. '52), and a major interest of the earliest Chicago women (Addams 1910, 1930; Breckinridge 1933). The study of friendship similarly reveals a "gendered" interest (Sarma, Ph.D. '46; Addams 1910, 1930). Joan Moore also examined upper-class women and their work in voluntary associations (Ph.D. '59), reflecting the scholarly interests of Breckinridge (e.g., 1933).

These Chicago women often found work and research interests in the area of applied sociology, again like their female predecessors. This was sometimes by choice, and sometimes a consequence of being unable to find jobs in the academy. The separation between sociology and community interests is often problematic, therefore. Elizabeth L. Lyman, for example, draws a distinction between being a sociologist and a political activist, and chooses to be an activist in her retirement (4 May 1990).

Topics chosen by Chicago men, such as the military, bureaucratic organizations, governmental politics, nation-states, violent crime, technology, international markets, and suicide are more rarely found in the women's corpus. The sexes did share a number of concerns, nonetheless. Thus, the city (Miller, Ph.D. '47), news-making (H. Hughes 1940), communication (Lang, Ph.D. '54, vita), the institutional church (Nelson, Ph.D. '53; Verdet, Ph.D. '59; Cassidy, Ph.D. '59), and deviance were explored by both sexes.

The women, in their publications after 1965, were profoundly more critical of education and the discipline of sociology than the men (e.g., see section on autobiographies above). The women tended to work outside the academy or on its margins, particularly during the dark era. Applied sociology was one of their most viable options, and this emphasis on practical, community uses of sociology structured their work as a group. Similarly, their careers were shaped by their husbands' careers, childbirth, and children's needs. It appears that as a group, as these women aged, their freedom tended to increase. Their years after child-rearing were an exciting time for growth, to a far greater degree than for men in their cohort.

A Feminist Critique of Women's Work in Epistemology

Female scholars often challenge patriarchal "paradigms" or dichot-omies. Feminist epistemology, moreover, requires a new vision of doing theory: an approach that is more discursive and convoluted than most male sociology. Feminist sociology, by definition, transcends patriarchal boundaries (Deegan 1988b). Sisterhood is integral to its epistemology and praxis.

Unfortunately, the rich, feminist heritage from the golden era of Chi-cago women is rarely cited by sociologists (Deegan 1988a, 1991), and the female generations remain isolated from each other. In this way, contem-porary women from Chicago are separated from their own rich traditions. Clearly their work emerges from a system of patriarchal education that disconnects each women's generation from earlier ones. The women's fun-damental divergence from patriarchal ways of thinking partially accounts for their general failure to be included in the annals of sociology. Their work, to greater and lesser degrees, only approximates the worldview of men.

The very tools of criticism, moreover, need to be altered. For ex-ample, I have suggested that critiques of scholarly work be considered "conversations" rather than antagonistic "comments" (Deegan 1989a), and I have offered a "multilectic" rather than a dialectic model elsewhere (Deegan 1980). With a multilectic model, ideas, practices, and groups are analyzed as sometimes complementary, sometimes in conflict, and some-times isolated and indifferent to each other. This more flexible and com-plex model fits women's epistemologies better than more established, com-partmentalized distinctions do, and it challenges traditional ways of defining knowledge. This type of epistemological assumption is frequently found, moreover, in the thought of other female sociologists. For the de-velopment of such a conceptual apparatus, however, a "second wave" of feminism was necessary.

Chicago-Trained Women as the Second Sex and Their Partial Transcendence of This Status Between 1965 and 1995

In 1964, at the beginning of the second wave of feminism, Alice Rossi raised one of the first voices in sociology to call for "an immodest proposal": equality between the sexes. This ideal and a snowballing women's movement in the wider society resulted in the famous 1969 caucus of women in sociology and the establishment of a new organization: Sociologists for Women in Society (SWS). A new era for women in sociology emerged.

Their organized network has met with only mixed success, however. Clearly, individual women, particularly Chicago women, are flourishing and establishing precedents. For example, in 1978 Rita Simon became the first woman to edit the *American Sociological Review*. Women's acceptance as "tokens" is vastly different from their inclusion in everyday patterns of legitimation as professionals (Kanter 1977). Women as a group have not penetrated the powerful structural positions in the profession (e.g., see tables 3 and 4; see the appendix to Reinharz's chapter, this volume, for changing employment patterns for women).

Women in sociology have not made significant in-roads in tenured positions in prestigious graduate institutions, in obtaining well-funded grants and fellowships, or in pay and promotions (Helen MacGill Hughes 1973b; Rossi and Calderwood 1973; Dorothy Smith 1977, 1987, 1988). The dozens of women who were denied tenure in the 1970s and 1980s and the unchanging demographic data on women in prestigious, graduate-training institutions reveal how very radical and fragile these gains are (Blum 1991). All the Chicago women discussed here remain on the frontier of establishing women in a patriarchal profession.

The female Chicago graduates in our cohort assumed major leadership roles in the profession during the 1970s and 1980s: as scholars, mentors, professional leaders, journal editors, and community voices. They, like their male counterparts, became preeminent leaders, but they often held tenure-track positions in the academy ten or twenty years after the males did. They led professional organizations, edited journals, wrote books, and trained students, but on this same differential schedule (Hughes 1975b). Thus, Evelyn Kitagawa became a member of the Chicago staff in 1951 but she was promoted to professor only in 1975, more than a decade after the "second wave" of feminism started. In 1975 she also became the first woman to chair the Department of Sociology.

Despite this "female delayed career" pattern, these women succeeded when many other men and women did not.[12] They became professionals when the larger society, not the profession, was demanding changes in women's opportunities. Specific women, such as Hughes, Rossi, and Lopata, actively changed gender patterns in sociology, but many women from Chicago did not. The whole female cohort, however, benefited from the increased opportunities for women.

The recent proliferation of women in sociology has generated a number of outstanding women whose lives need to be documented and shared. Kathryn P. Meadow Orlans and Ruth Wallace's book on Berkeley women sociologists (1994) illustrates how fascinating this information is. Only two of the sixteen women included in their anthology graduated before 1960, however, so their lives were influenced by the second wave of feminism more than were the lives of the cohort studied here. In one respect the Berkeley women shared a training similar to that of the women studied here. Many of the Berkeley women were taught by Chicago-trained faculty, such as Herbert Blumer, Erving Goffman, and Tamotsu Shibutani. This Chicago influence is similar to that found at Brandeis during the 1960s (Reinharz, this volume). Their book illustrates how we can retrain and reconnect ourselves to the whole range of our hidden and powerful heritage. We can then share this new knowledge with each other, our students, and our successors (Schutz 1967; Deegan 1988b).

There are some early signs that Chicago women who entered professional life during and after the 1970s may have benefited from the groundwork established by the women who proceeded them. Thus, in 1992, Marta Tienda (Ph.D., University of Texas-Austin, '77), a tenured professor at the University of Chicago, became the first Hispanic person and the first woman to edit *The American Journal of Sociology*. In 1994, Tienda became the first Hispanic person and the second woman to chair the Department of Sociology at the University of Chicago. In 1994, Maureen Hallinan became the first female Chicago graduate (Ph.D. '72) to be elected president of the American Sociological Association. Both professional achievements mark a changed opportunity path for Chicago women who are part of a later cohort than the one studied here.

Despite these accomplishments, Helen MacGill Hughes's groundbreaking documentation of how women were kept out of tenured positions in prestigious graduate institutions until 1973 reveals a pattern that continues in the 1990s (Blum 1991). Stinging blows to affirmative action programs were delivered by the Supreme Court in 1989, and many women did not receive tenure during the economically constrained years in the academy from the late 1970s and throughout the 1980s. The women examined here continue to lead a struggle for a permanent place for women in sociology. Their courage, vision, and intellectual power are fundamental to the progress of all women in the profession. These Chicago women clearly shine as scholars, producing hundreds of books and articles. Despite this stellar productivity, they are rarely included in Chicago school accounts or networks. This is the next "invisible ceiling," one that blocks entry into the everyday accounts of the profession, theory groups, and social stock of knowledge in sociology (Schutz 1967).

As I noted earlier, discrimination against Chicago women remains problematic, even "invisible," to many sociologists from this cohort. This complexity is found in the responses of those from the cohort who read this chapter and commented upon it.

THE FEMALE COHORT'S REFLECTION ON SEXISM IN THE PAST: A FEMINIST METHODOLOGICAL NOTE

I mailed an earlier draft of this chapter to all the women graduates for whom I had an address (twenty-six women; three men from the cohort provided specific information in response to inquiries from me; another two men sent information, but I had not requested them to do so.) This procedure, to allow one's subjects to critique the sociologist's interpretation, is advocated by feminist sociologists whenever feasible (Reinharz 1992; Nebraska Sociological Feminist Collective 1981, 1989). Many of these graduates responded in detail (over 130 pages of information was sent by twenty alumni—sixteen women and four men), often explaining their understanding of sexism, providing information on their careers, and correcting errors in the text. I gratefully acknowledge their help, and their correspondence is listed in the bibliography.

Five correspondents unequivocally supported the interpretation of this paper. They noted the extreme difficulty of addressing sexism in their cohort and in their careers. This type of response is expressed in the following passage:

> I could not help but admire your vivid portrayal of the truth on the condition of graduate women. I used to be a teaching assistant in Chicago for two years, but I did not get anywhere near the next step.

A second woman found the paper "fascinating" and sent an autobiographical statement elaborating on some points I had discussed. Another woman supported a series of passages. She commented on the general sexism of the era, the lack of citation of her work in the writings of her male cohort, and the significance of marriage in shaping the options of women in her cohort. She also noted the changes that occurred after the second wave of feminism.

The largest response (7) acknowledged this pattern of discrimination but found it difficult to do so. They perceived Chicago as relatively non-sexist, or pointed out the invisibility of sexism. If a person does not experience sexism consciously, they asked, does it exist? With their generous permission, I have included some of their reflections in the body of this paper.

A small cohort of Chicago alumni—composed of four white women and two white men who had been sent portions of this earlier draft by an anonymous person—"vehemently denied" that any sexism existed in the past or in their reflections upon the past. The men wanted their answers to the original questionnaire made anonymous, and of course they are. As a result of these requests for anonymity by the two men, I decided to make all such vehement denials anonymous in this paper.

An example of the position of this group is found in one woman's comment:

> At no point, not at home, not in school, not in (X), was I made
> to feel that I belonged to a "second sex." I was a free, search-
> ing, engaged human being.

This sociologist completely denied any gendered stratification in sociology. "There was not," she wrote, "an 'old boy' network from which we were excluded."

This cohort is obviously articulate and passionate. They often sent extremely helpful critiques as well as some vitriolic ones. I have included information from all the respondents to correct the present text and to add information wherever relevant. The use of this feminist methodology improved this chapter substantially, although it made its completion considerably more complex. This chapter is only an opening view on a vast and talented group and a controversial topic.

CONCLUSION

Female Chicago sociologists have been significant leaders for both sexes in sociology, and pioneers for women in sociology. Despite their overwhelming achievements, many Chicago women remain disconnected in analyses of this tradition. Regrettably, professional barriers against women are an often invisible thread weaving together their various approaches and times, but these women were not powerless victims. They used the power of knowledge to observe themselves and the world around them. Many of them applied this knowledge, and they often met with remarkable success.

Their situation as women generated a perspective that frequently emphasized the study of women, children, marriage and the family, female occupations, female delinquency, oppressed peoples, applied sociology, and social justice. During the golden era of women in sociology this intellectual commonality was often acknowledged and overtly coordinated. Feminist pragmatism created a common intellectual heritage. The later, dark era showed both more diversity and less shared intellectual power. Nonetheless, as individual scholars, women trained during the era of patriarchal ascendancy made major contributions to sociology. These Chicago-trained women were often forgotten by their male colleagues who were frequently leaders in the profession.

This situation is changing, and this new consciousness is visible in the inclusion of these women in this volume. In this way, this chapter is part of a more liberated history of Chicago sociology. In this new corpus, race, sex, religion, politics, physical disability, and sexual preference will not be barriers to professional recognition. This diversity will mirror the rich and varied contributions made by this multidimensional community. On a more pessimistic note, the Department of Sociology at the University of Chicago still had only four tenured women and twenty tenured men in 1993–94 out of a faculty of twenty-seven. (There were six additional "associated faculty," all men. See *Graduate Studies in the Department of Sociology, University of Chicago,* 1994–95.) There are *no* untenured women in the department, although women now comprise almost half of all graduating Ph.D.s in the profession.

Despite the loyalty many women continue to feel toward the Chicago school, these graduates and the contemporary faculty lag behind major social changes in gender inequality. Most sociologists trained at the University of Chicago still find it hard to acknowledge that women were the second sex between 1945 and 1960. Discrimination against women in sociology remains for many professionals a problem that has no name.

NOTES

Many people have granted interviews, corresponded with me on this and other projects, and supplied unpublished materials. If they wanted to be identified, I have noted their names in the references.At my request, Gary Fine included questions on gender in the correspondence he sent concerning this project. His unfailing support of this project included an exciting meeting of the contributors that helped me formulate this paper. Finally, Michael R. Hill was a constant colleague and companion throughout this work.

1. In addition to these eminent female graduates from the Department of Sociology, many other eminent women were influenced by this institution and structure of knowledge. Thus, Dorothy Swaine Thomas, the wife of a former Chicago sociologist and the first woman to become president of the ASA, in 1952, is not considered as part of this school, yet she was part of its extensive informal network during these years. Similarly, Elise Boulding became a sociologist instead of a social worker because of her contacts with the group of Chicago-trained sociologists at Fisk University who were influenced by Robert Park, who retired there after 1934. Thus, the circle of gendered influence was wider than the women on campus with direct ties (professional and/or marital) to the department. This fascinating wider sphere is not addressed here.

2. Major statements on the "school" can be found in Steven Diner (1975); Robert E. L. Faris (1967); Ernest W. Burgess and Donald J. Bogue (1964); James F. Short, Jr. (1971); and Mary Jo Deegan (1988a).

3. Although Myrdal was from Sweden and Klein from Austria, they shared Chicago women's status as "the second sex."

4. The late Erving Goffman said he was a blatant sexist prior to a major transformation in his consciousness in the mid-1970s. He thought all the men in his age group and cohort were similarly biased against women to greater or lesser degrees. He said this during an intense discussion we had at the American Sociological Association meetings in New York City, in August 1982. Goffman had prepared a three-page, single-spaced, typed critique of a paper a group of us had prepared on his sexism that he had read prior to this hour-and-a-half interview/meeting/confrontation (Nebraska Feminist Sociology Collective 1981).

5. Compare this silence on the Manhattan Project to the criticism by Irving Louis Horowitz of Project Camelot, 1968. Despite the faculty's apolitical stance, some of them were subjected to political scrutiny by the government and organizations on the far right, particularly during the McCarthy era. For example, a book by Archibald B. Roosevelt and Zygmund Dobbs (1964) depicts some Chicago sociologists as dangerous communists, e.g., Albion Small, Louis Wirth, and William F. Ogburn.

6. David Riesman was spontaneously mentioned as supportive by Virginia Olesen, an M.A. student at Chicago (1954–56), and by Rose Laub Coser, a "faculty wife" from 1948 to 1950 who later earned a doctorate in sociology from Columbia University. M.A. students and faculty wives are important female populations generally overlooked in this and other accounts of sociology as a discipline. I engaged in lengthy face-to-face talks with Virginia Olesen and corresponded with the late Rose Laub Coser, documented in Deegan 1991b, d.

7. The sociology students were represented by Sally Cassidy (Ph.D. '59), as a teaching assistant from 1955 to 1959, and by Paula Verdet (Ph.D. '59), from

1956 to 1959, although they were not listed as faculty in the college catalogs I read. Their appointments were in Human Development, not Sociology (Murray Wax, 15 June 1992).

8. Helen MacGill Hughes, trained before the generation examined here, was one of the few women actively mentored by men. She fondly recalled William F. Ogburn (1959) and Robert E. Park (1968, 1980). This mentoring was highly limiting, nonetheless, and sustained her marginal role at *AJS* for seventeen years. It did not result in the faculty status her husband enjoyed.

9. Several women noted Wirth's support after reading an earlier draft of the paper; e.g., Rhoda Blumberg, 27 May 1991.

10. This was a long battle, since Ogburn arrived at the University of Chicago in 1927 and Park retired in 1934.

11. These dates and titles conflict with those found in college catalogs used to compile table 9.2.

12. The female delayed career pattern is often due to "family claims" on women, their lower income in the marketplace, and gender socialization. Jennifer Platt (p. 2, 4 June 1991; 17 December 1992) sent me information to document the relatively older age of the women who completed their doctorates (37.2 years) in comparison to a "younger" male model (34.2 years). The men's ages were elevated, too, as a result of their being veterans of the Korean War and the Second World War. The women, nonetheless, were an older cohort (two women graduated at fifty) than the men (the oldest male graduate was forty-three). These women would have been subject to greater age discrimination after graduation, too.

REFERENCES

Published Works

Abbott, Edith. 1950. "Grace Abbott and Hull-House, 1908–20," Parts I & II. *Social Service Review* 24 (September): 374–94; 24 (December): 493–518.

Abbott, Edith, assisted by Sophonisba Breckinridge. 1936. *The Tenements of Chicago, 1908–1935.* Chicago: University of Chicago Press.

Addams, Jane. 1910. *Twenty Years at Hull-House.* New York: Macmillan.

———. 1909. *The Spirit of Youth and City Streets.* New York: Macmillan.

———. 1930. *The Second Twenty Years.* New York: MacMillan.

Beauvoir, de, Simone. [1949] 1952. *The Second Sex.* Tr. and ed. by H. M. Parshley. New York: Modern Library.

Becker, Howard S. 1963. *The Outsiders: Studies in the Sociology of Deviance.* New York: The Free Press.

Bentz, Valerie. 1989. *Becoming Mature: Childhood Ghosts and Spirits in Adult Life.* Chicago: Aldine.

Bermant, Gordon. 1972. "Sisterhood is Beautiful." *Psychology Today* 6 (August): 40–46, 72, 74–75.

Bernard, Jessie. 1964. *Academic Women.* University Park: Pennsylvania State University Press.

———. 1968. *The Sex Game.* Englewood Cliffs: Prentice-Hall.

————. 1972. *The Future of Marriage.* New York: World Publishers.

————. 1981. *The Female World.* New York: The Free Press.

Blum, Debra E. 1991. "Environment Still Hostile to Women in Academe, New Evidence Indicates." *The Chronicle of Higher Education* 38 (October 9): 1, and A20.

Breckinridge, Sophonisba P. 1933. *Women in the Twentieth Century.* New York: McGraw-Hill.

Burgess, Ernest W. and Donald J. Bogue, eds. 1964. *Contributions to Urban Sociology.* Chicago: University of Chicago Press.

Bulmer, Martin. 1984. *The Chicago School of Sociology.* Chicago: University of Chicago Press.

Burnet, Jean. 1981. "Minorities I Have Belonged To." *Canadian Ethnic Studies* 13 (1): 24–36.

Cayton, Horace. 1970. *Long Old Road.* Seattle: University of Washington Press.

Cooley, Charles H. 1902. *Human Nature and the Social Order.* New York: Scribner's.

Davis, Katharine Bement. 1933. "Three Score Years and Ten." *University of Chicago Magazine* 26 (December): 58–62.

Deegan, Mary Jo. 1978. "Women in Sociology: 1890–1930." *Journal of the History of Sociology* 1 (Fall): 11–34.

————. 1980. "Feminist Sociological Theory." Paper presented at the meeting of the Midwest Sociological Society, Milwaukee, Wis.

————. 1981. "Early Women Sociologists and the American Sociological Society." *The American Sociologist* 16 (February 1981): 14–24.

————. 1983. "Sociology at Wellesley College, 1900–1919." *Journal of the History of Sociology* 6 (December): 91–115.

————. 1985. "Book Review of Martin Bulmer's *The Chicago Tradition.*" *Contemporary Sociology* 14 (May): 365–66.

————. 1986. "The Clinical Sociology of Jessie Taft." *Clinical Sociology Review* 4: 33–45.

————. 1987. "Symbolic Interaction and the Study of Women." Pp. 3–15 in *Women and Symbolic Interaction.* Boston: Allen and Unwin.

————. 1988a. *Jane Addams and the Men of the Chicago School, 1892–1918.* New Brunswick, N.J.: Transaction Press.

————. 1988b. "Transcending a Patriarchal Past: Teaching the History of Early Women Sociologists." *Teaching Sociology* 16 (April): 141–59.

————. 1989a. "Sociology and Conviviality: A Conversation with Ellenhorn on Convivial Sociology." *Humanity and Society* 13 (February): 85–88.

————. 1989b. *American Ritual Dramas: Social Rules and Cultural Meanings.* Westport, Conn.: Greenwood Press.

————. 1991a. "Great Women In Sociology." Pp. 1–28 in *Women in Sociology,* ed. by Mary Jo Deegan. Westport, Conn.: Greenwood Press.

————. 1991b. "Rose Laub Coser." Pp. 110–17 in *Women in Sociology,* ed. by Mary Jo Deegan. Westport, Conn.: Greenwood Press.

————. 1991c. "Helen MacGill Hughes." Pp. 191–98 in *Women in Sociology,* ed. by Mary Jo Deegan. Westport, Conn.: Greenwood Press.

————. 1991d. "Virginia Olesen." Pp. 313–19 in *Women in Sociology,* ed. by Mary Jo Deegan. Westport, Conn.: Greenwood Press.

————. 1992. "The Genesis of the International Self: Working Hypotheses Emerging from the Chicago Experience (1892–1918)." Pp. 339–53 in *Non-European Youth and the Process of Immigration: For a Tolerant Society,*" ed. by Luigi Tomasi, Trento, Italy: The University of Trento.

————. 1993. "Consciousness-Raising: The Personal Is Public and Political." Paper presented at the Fifth International Interdisciplinary Congress on Women, San José, Costa Rica.

————. 1994. "'The Marginal Man' as a Gendered Concept." Pp. 55–71 in *Robert E. Park, and the "Melting Pot" Theory,* ed. by Luigi Tomasi and Ruberto Gunzo. Trento, Italy: The University of Trento.

Deegan, Mary Jo and Nancy A. Brooks, eds. 1985. *Women and Disability: The Double Handicap.* New Brunswick, N.J.: Transaction.

Deegan, Mary Jo and Michael R. Hill, eds. 1987. *Women and Symbolic Interaction.* Boston: Allen and Unwin.

————. 1991. "Alice S. Rossi." Pp. 342–49 in *Women in Sociology,* ed. by Mary Jo Deegan. Westport, Conn.: Greenwood Press.

Deegan, Mary Jo and Edith Steans. 1991. "Wilmoth A. Carter and the Better Half of Chicago Sociology." Manuscript.

Dill, Bonnie Thornton. 1987. "Race, Class and Gender: Prospects for an All-Inclusive Sisterhood." Pp. 159–75 in *Women and Symbolic Interaction,* ed. by Mary Jo Deegan and Michael R. Hill. Boston: Allen and Unwin.

Diner, Steven. 1975. "Department and Discipline." *Minerva* 8 (Winter): 514–53.

Donovan, Josephine. 1985. *Feminist Theory: The Intellectual Traditions of American Feminism.* New York: Frederick Ungar.

Faris, Robert E. L. 1967. *Chicago Sociology: 1920–1932.* Chicago: University of Chicago Press.

Fish, Virginia. 1991. "Frances R. Donovan." Pp. 131–39 in *Women in Sociology,* ed. Mary Jo Deegan. Westport, Conn.: Greenwood Press.

Friedan, Betty. 1963. *The Feminine Mystique.* New York: Norton.

Gilman, Charlotte Perkins. 1911. *The Man-Made World.* New York: Charlton Co.

Goffman, Erving. 1977. "The Arrangement Between the Sexes." *Theory and Society* 4 (Fall): 301–31.

————. 1959. *The Presentation of Self in Everyday Life.* Garden City: Doubleday.

Graduate Studies in the Department of Sociology, University of Chicago, 1994–1995. 1994. Pamphlet distributed by the Department of Sociology, University of Chicago.

Grana, Sheryl. 1991. "Rosalie H. Wax." Pp. 417–24 in *Women in Sociology,* ed. by Mary Jo Deegan. Westport, Conn.: Greenwood Press.

Gusfield, Joseph R. 1963. *Symbolic Crusade.* Urbana: University of Illinois Press.

————. 1982. "The Scholarly Tension: Graduate Craft and Undergraduate Imagination." Paper presented at the 40th Anniversary of Social Sciences II. November 1982.

Harvey, Lee. 1987. *Myths of the Chicago School of Sociology.* Aldershot, England: Avebury.

Horowitz, Irving Louis. 1968. *Professing Sociology.* Chicago: Aldine.

Howery, Carla. 1991. "Caroline Baer Rose." Pp. 335–41 in *Women in Sociology,* ed. by Mary Jo Deegan. Westport, Conn.: Greenwood Press.

Hughes, Helen MacGill. 1940. *News and the Human Interest Story.* Chicago: University of Chicago Press.

———. 1959. "William Fielding Ogburn-1886–1959." *Social Forces* 38 (October): 11–12.

———. 1968. "Park, Robert E." Pp. 416–18 in *International Encyclopedia of the Social Sciences,* vol. 11, ed. by David L. Sills. New York: Macmillan and The Free Press.

———. 1973a. "Maid of All Work or Departmental Sister-in-Law? The Faculty Wife on Campus." *American Journal of Sociology* 78 (January): 5–10.

———, ed. 1973b. *The Status of Women in Sociology, 1968–1972: Report to the American Sociological Association of the Ad Hoc Committee on the Status of Women in the Profession.* Washington, D.C.: American Sociological Association.

———. 1977. "Wasp/Woman/Sociologist." *Society* 14 (August): 69–80.

———. 1980. "Robert Ezra Park: The Philosopher-Newspaperman-Sociologist." Pp. 67–79 in *Sociological Traditions from Generation to Generation,* ed. by Robert K. Merton and Matilda White Riley. Norwood, N.J.: Ablex.

Illich, Ivan. 1982. *Gender.* New York: Pantheon.

Kanter, Rosabeth Moss. 1977. "Some Effects of Proportions on Group Life." *American Journal of Sociology* 82 (March): 965–90.

Klein, Viola. 1948. *The Feminine Character: The History of an Ideology.* New York: International Universities Press.

Kristeva, Julia. [1974] 1977. *About Chinese Women.* Translated by Anita Barrows. New York: Marion Boyars.

Kurtz, Lester R. 1984. *Evaluating Chicago Sociology: A Guide to the Literature, with an Annotated Bibliography.* Chicago: University of Chicago Press.

Lang, Kurt and Gladys Engel Lang. 1990. *Etched in Memory: The Building and Survival of Artistic Reputation.*

Laws [Long], Judy, and Pepper Schwartz. 1977. *Sexual Scripts: The Social Construction of Female Sexuality.* Washington, D.C.: University Press of America.

Maines, David. 1983. "Coming to Grips: Aspects of the Life History of Helena Z. Lopata." *Midwest Feminist Papers* 4: 112–24.

Manis, Jerome and Bernard Meltzer, eds. 1967. *Symbolic Interaction,* 1st ed. Boston: Allyn and Bacon.

———. 1973. *Symbolic Interaction,* 2d ed. Boston: Allyn and Bacon.

Marx, Karl and Friedrich Engels. [1846] 1970. *The German Ideology.* Ed. and intro. by C. J. Arthur. New York: International Publishers.

Moore, Joan. 1991. *Going Down to the Barrios: Homeboys and Homegirls in Chicago.* Philadelphia: Temple University Press.

Moyer, Imogene. 1991. "Ruth Shonle Cavan." Pp. 90–99 in *Women in Sociology,* ed. by Mary Jo Deegan. Westport, Conn.: Greenwood Press.

Myrdal, Alva and Viola Klein. 1956. *Women's Two Roles: Home and Work.* London: Routledge & Kegan Paul.

Nebraska Sociological Feminist Collective, eds. 1981. "A Feminist Critique of the Writings of Erving Goffman." Manuscript.

————. 1989. *A Feminist Ethic for Social Science Research.* Lewiston, N.Y.: Edwin Mellen Press.

Orlans, Kathryn P. Meadow and Ruth Wallace, eds. 1994. *Gender and the Academic Experience: Berkeley Women Sociologists.* Lincoln: University of Nebraska Press.

Phillips, Terri. 1991. "Rose Hum Lee." Pp. 256–62 in *Women in Sociology,* ed. by Mary Jo Deegan. Westport, Conn.: Greenwood Press.

Platt, Anthony. 1991. *E. Franklin Frazier Reconsidered.* New Brunswick, N.J.: Rutgers University Press.

Publications of the Members of the University, 1902–1916. 1917. Chicago: University of Chicago Press.

Reinharz, Shulamit. 1992. *Feminist Methods in Social Science Research.* New York: Oxford University Press.

Riesman, David. 1990. "Becoming an Academic Man." Pp. 22–74 in *Authors of Their Own Lives,* ed. by Bennett M. Berger. Berkeley: University of California Press.

Roosevelt, Archibald B. and Zygmund Dobbs. 1964. *The Great Deceit: Social Pseudo-Sciences.* West Sayville, N.Y.: Veritas Foundation.

Rossi, Alice S. 1964. "Equality Between the Sexes: An Immodest Proposal." *Daedelus* 93 (Spring): 607–52.

————, ed. 1973. *The Feminist Papers: From Adams to de Beauvoir.* New York: Columbia University Press.

————. 1983. *Seasons of a Woman's Life.* Amherst, Mass.: Hamilton Newell.

————. 1988. "Growing Up and Older in Sociology, 1940–1990." Pp. 43–64 in *Social Change and the Life Course,* ed. by Matilda White Riley. Newbury Park, Calif.: Sage.

Rossi, Alice and Ann Calderwood, eds. 1973. *Academic Women on the Move.* New York: Russell Sage Foundation.

Rossiter, Margaret. 1982. *Women Scientists in America.* Baltimore: Johns Hopkins University Press.

Rubington, E. and M. Weinburg, eds. 1973. *Deviance: The Interactional Approach.* New York: Macmillan.

Ryan, Barbara. 1991. "Helena Z. Lopata." Pp. 263–72 in *Women in Sociology,* ed. by Mary Jo Deegan. Westport, Conn.: Greenwood Press.

Schutz, Alfred. [1932] 1967. *The Phenomenology of the Social World.* Trans. by George Walsh and Frederick Lehnert, with an intro. by George Walsh. Evanston: Northwestern University Press.

————. 1970. *Reflections on the Problems of Relevance.* Ed., annotated, and introduced by Richard M. Zaner. New Haven: Yale University Press.

Schwendinger, Herman and Julia Schwendinger. 1974. *The Sociologists of the Chair.* New York: Basic Books.

362   Mary Jo Deegan

Short, James F., Jr. 1971. *The Social Fabric of the Metropolis.* Chicago: University of Chicago Press.

―――. 1969. "A Natural History of One Sociological Career." Pp. 117–32 in *Sociological Self-Images: A Collective Portrait,* ed. by Irving Louis Horowitz. New York: Russell Sage.

Smith, Dorothy E. 1977. *Feminism and Marxism—A Place to Begin, A Way To Go.* Vancouver: New Star Books.

―――. 1987. *The Everyday World As Problematic: A Feminist Sociology.* Boston: Northeastern University Press.

―――. 1988. "The Deep Structure of Gender Antithesis: Another View of Capitalism and Patriarchy." Pp. 23–36 in *A Feminist Ethic for Social Science Research,* ed. by the Nebraska Sociological Feminist Collective. Lewiston, N.Y.: Edwin Mellen.

Spender, Dale. 1983. *Feminist Theorists: Three Centuries of Key Women Thinkers.* New York: Pantheon.

―――. 1988. *Women of Ideas (and What Men Have Done to Them): From Aphra Behn to Adrienne Rich.* Boston: Pandora.

Stone, Gregory and Harvey Farberman, eds. 1971. *Studies in Symbolic Interaction.* Waltham, Mass.: Xerox.

Streib, Gordon. 1991. "Ethel Shanas." Pp. 350–58 in *Women in Sociology,* ed. by Mary Jo Deegan. Westport, Conn.: Greenwood Press.

Taft, Jessie. 1962. *Jessie Taft: Therapist and Social Work Educator,* ed. and intro. by Virginia Robinson. Philadelphia: University of Pennsylvania Press.

Talbot, Marion. 1936. *More Than Lore.* Chicago: University of Chicago Press.

Thomas, W. I. and Florian Znaniecki. 1918–20. *The Polish Peasant in Europe and America,* 5 vols. Boston: Badger.

Tuchman, Gaye. 1975. "Women and the Creation of Culture." In *Another Voice,* ed. by Marcia Millman and Rosabeth Moss Kanter. New York: Anchor.

Wax, Rosalie. 1971. *Doing Fieldwork: Warnings and Advice.* Chicago: University of Chicago Press.

Whyte, William F. 1943. *Street Corner Society.* Chicago: University of Chicago Press.

Young, Kimball. 1988. "Kimball Young on the Chicago School: Later Contacts," ed. by Fred B. Lindstrom and Ronald A. Hardert. *Sociological Perspectives* 31 (July): 298–314.

Unpublished Materials

Correspondence

With Mary Jo Deegan:
    Blum, Annabelle Motz, 24 May 1991; 13 August 1991
    Blumberg, Rhoda L., 27 May 1991; 28 May 1992.
    Burnet, Jean, 17 May 1991
    Carter, Wilmoth A., 28 August 1990; August 1991; 6 October 1991.
    Jammes, Reverend Jean-Marie, 23 May 1991

Lopata, Helena Z., 4 June 1991, 8 June 1991, 23 May 1991; letter to parents,
    Florian and Ellen Znaniecki, March 1950, included in 4 June 1991
Lyman, Elizabeth, 3 June 1991; 20 May 1991
Moore, Joan, 22 May 1992
Peil, Margaret, 23 May 1991
Platt, Jennifer, 4 June 1991; 17 December 1992
Sarma, Jyotirmoyee, 1 July 1991
Shanas, Ethel, 10 June 1992
Wax, Murray, 15 June 1991; 15 June 1992
Plus ten letters from six Chicago alumni who are anonymous in this paper.

With Gary Fine:
Blum, Annabelle (Bender) Motz, 12 July 1990
Bogart, Leo, 29 May 1990
Carter, Wilmoth A., 8 June 1990.
Lyman, Elizabeth L., 4 May 1990
McCall, Bevode, n.d. (May?), 1990
Peil, Margaret, 9 May 1990
Sarma, Jyotirmoyee, 1 June 1990
Plus six letters from three Chicago alumni who are anonymous in this paper.

Papers

Deegan, Mary Jo. "Feminist Sociological Theory." Midwest Sociology Society,
    Milwaukee, Wisconsin, April 1980.
Dentler, Robert A. 1987. "Secrets of a Sociologist."
Freeman, Jo. "Women on the Social Science Faculties Since 1892." Paper pre-
    sented at the annual meetings of the Political Science Association, Winter
    1969.
Käsler, Dirk. 1981. "Methodological Problems of a Sociological History of Early
    German Sociology." Paper presented at the Department of Education, Uni-
    versity of Chicago, 5 November.
Shanas, Ethel. 1984. "The State of American Sociology During the Decade Prior
    to World War II—the University of Chicago." Paper presented at the Mid-
    west Sociological Society, 20 April.

Vitas (current as of 1990 unless otherwise noted)

Burnet, Jean Robertson
Carter, Wilmoth A.
Coser, Rose Laub
Hughes, Helen MacGill (1980)
Lang, Gladys Engel
Peil, Margaret
Sarma, Jyotirmoyee
Simon, Rita James

Olesen, Virginia
Wax, Rosalie H. (1992)

Interviews

Bernard, Jessie, 29 June 1978
Blumer, Herbert, 28(?) August 1979
Cavan, Ruth Shonle, October 1978
Diggs, Irene, 8 January 1989;
Goffman, Erving, 28(?) August 1982
Lee, Elizabeth Briant, 15(?) November 1988

Telephone Interviews

Diggs, Irene, 1 November 1989; 27 November 1989; 7 May 1989

Other Sources

Extensive correspondence and telephone conversations with Jessie Bernard and
the late Ruth Shonle Cavan between 1978 and 1992. Several telephone interviews and correspondence in 1989 and 1990 with Virginia Olesen.

Helena Znaniecka Lopata

I have been asked to contribute a postscript about some aspects of life at the University of Chicago during the "Second School" years and some contributions to sociology of graduates who developed in different directions than those highlighted in the other chapters of this volume. I have not attempted to write a definitive piece, but only to present some informal notes by a participant for some of those years. I feel that the organization of the book along selected field or specialty lines, while intellectually justified, camouflages the interweave of university life and neglects contributors to other important fields. Furthermore, the chapter on "women's accounts, knowledge, and work" needs some contextual explanation.

THE UNIVERSITY OF CHICAGO IN THE POSTWAR YEARS

The years immediately following World War II drew an enormous group of sociology students to the University of Chicago—enormous in comparison both to previous cohorts and to the size of the faculty. Until the 1950s, only seven full professors were on staff in the Department of Sociology: Burgess, Wirth, Blumer, Ogburn, Hauser, Hughes, and Warner. Whyte and Goldhammer were junior faculty, Shaw and Lohman were lecturers and did not carry major responsibilities for training graduate students. In addition, the major professors were often on leave or away from campus. For most of the postwar years, over 200 students were registered in either the M.A. or Ph.D. programs. These students overwhelmed the faculty by the 1950s with preliminary examinations and dissertations. While only four Ph.D.'s were granted in 1946, the number ballooned to twenty-eight in 1954. It tapered off to less than ten as the GI Bill students completed their work, increasing in 1959 to fifteen.

Not all of the students completed their degrees, but the 272 Ph.D.s that were awarded in the twenty-year span from 1946 to 1965 demanded extensive processing by the department, even if individual students did not receive extensive help with their dissertations, as several have commented.

Joseph Gusfield (1990) points out in his autobiographical essay in Berger's *Authors of Their Own Lives* that many students were older than typical graduates, veterans attending school through the GI Bill, beginning to marry and raise families. Their backgrounds were socioeconomically varied, although a disproportionate number were Jewish (Gusfield 1990). Leo Bogart defined the students as a mixed bag, with the dividing line between veterans, in the majority, and everyone else (letter to Fine, May 29, 1990). Actually, even the nonveterans tended to be older, bringing with them a variety of experiences.

Many of the respondents to Gary Alan Fine's inquiry fondly recall their years at the University of Chicago. At the same time, there is frequently expressed irritation over the limited contact with the faculty. As Gladys Lang documents (letter to Deegan, July 1991), the students were active politically, on the local race relations scene, although the McCarthy era kept much of the activity quiet. Some of the graduate students had been involved in labor unions and formed a student grievance committee focused on the neglect of students by the faculty (Gladys Lang, letter to Deegan, 1991, p. 2). The committee met in 1947 with Burgess, then the chair. Burgess received the representatives politely, but explained that the basic goal of the university was research and that the students benefited from the reputation of the school and research opportunities, so they could not expect much individual attention (Leo Bogart, May 29, 1990; Robert Stone, May 28, 1990, letters to Gary Fine).

During this period, the *American Journal of Sociology* listed activities of sociology departments in various schools in its "News and Notes" section. The University of Chicago news provided a picture of extensive departmental vitality, in conjunction with other scholars in related fields. These notes, coupled with a set of detailed letters, offer a feeling for the heterogeneity of ongoing academic endeavors.

The faculty was involved in four levels of scholarly activity: on the international and national levels; in major, usually interdisciplinary research centers and committees on campus, in specific projects organized by professors, and in "special events," often taking place in the summer. Many students who became major contributors to sociology participated in these projects.

Several interesting instances reveal how the department operated as a university without walls, cooperating with other scholars nationally and internationally. The first of these involved the University of Frankfurt in Germany. Everett Hughes was one of seven professors chosen from different departments of the university who went there with funding from the Rockefeller Foundation. The group had as its goal:

to restore communication between the academic world of Germany and the United States. For the next two years the University of Chicago plans to send teams of professors who will teach for three months at a time at the University of Frankfurt. It is proposed, if eventually feasible, to bring German professors in exchange to the Chicago campus. ("News and Notes," May 1948)

Another major venture involved faculty and students in a study of aging, and later in adult education such as medical training in Kansas City. Several members of the Department of Sociology and the Committee on Human Development developed a long-term association with Community Studies, Inc., in Kansas City, Missouri. Community Studies was organized with funds from Homer Wadsworth, director of the Kansas City Association of Trusts and Foundations, and provided the University of Chicago research teams a base of ongoing studies with which faculty and students could connect. The project was directed by Robert Havighurst, then chair of the Committee on Human Development, and included Bernice Neugarten, W. Lloyd Warner, Everett Hughes, David Riesman, Allison Davis, William Henry, Ethel Shanas, and the executive director of Community Studies, who was then Martin Loeb ("News and Notes," September 1952, p. 203). Warren Peterson, a student when the project began, later took over the directorship of Community Studies. Richard Coleman, identified as Warner's student, became involved in some of the projects, as did Howard S. Becker, Eugene Friedmann, Dan Lortie, and Irving Deutscher. Howard Becker, Blanche Geer, and Everett Hughes conducted a study of the medical school that eventuated in the famous *Boys in White.* Elaine Cumming and William Henry contributed *Growing Old: The Process of Disengagement.*

Another example of interuniversity cooperation that expanded the walls of the University of Chicago included:

A plan of cooperative sociological research on the "changing community and family" was developed by the department of sociology of the University of Chicago and Southern Illinois University. The program, involving exchanges of graduate students and materials, consultation, conducting of joint research projects, and pooling of research data, will provide faculty and students from the U of C an opportunity to study the essentially rural way of living in the thirty-one southern counties of

the state and will give SIU personnel an opportunity to become familiar with the metropolitan areas of Chicago. ("News
and Notes," November 1949)

The fourth example of the connection between the University of
Chicago and external scientific groups was the National Opinion Research
Center (NORC). Through NORC the University of Chicago became
affiliated with five other institutions for a "year of experimental work."
The center's board of directors included Professors Hauser of Chicago,
Merton of Columbia, Williams of Cornell, Cahalan of Denver, Stouffer
of Harvard, and McCormick of Wisconsin. NORC had moved the previ-
ous year from the University of Denver and was placed under the director-
ship of Clyde W. Hart; Peter Rossi assumed that position in later years.
The Department of Sociology made a point of having the sociologists at
NORC contribute to graduate instruction.

These cases indicate that University of Chicago was not isolated
but participated in the world of knowledge in national and international
arenas. In the meantime, many other research centers bloomed with which
students could be affiliated and which brought in new researchers. These
centers involved cooperation within the department as well as across departments.

For example, the January 1945 "News and Notes" reported the creation of the Industrial Relations Center:

The Industrial Relations Center, to provide University-wide
services in industrial relations for management executives,
union leaders, government officials, faculty members and students, was established in January, 1945.

The IRC did not confer degrees in industrial relations, but students in a
variety of disciplines could specialize in three areas: labor relations and
labor economics, government and industrial relations, personnel management and human relations. Harold Wilensky, Orrie Melville Dalton, Edward Gross, Robert Dubin, Jack London, Louis Kriesberg, and many others worked in these fields for their dissertations and continued to build
upon these interests throughout their careers.

An interdisciplinary Committee on Communication utilizing "the
resources of the Division of the Social Sciences" and related professional
schools was formed in 1949. It combined the departments of political science, psychology, and sociology, as well as the National Opinion Research
Center. As part of its program, Morris Janowitz studied the community

newspaper in the metropolitan center, and much of the work of Gladys and Kurt Lang was in this area of research.

In 1948 Louis Wirth formed the Committee on Education, Training, and Research in Race Relations, with the help of a five-year grant from the Carnegie Corporation and the Rockefeller Foundation. Its aims were:

> fundamental research in race relations and minority problems in order to build a scientific foundation for policies and methods of operation and to provide advanced professional training for leaders in the field. ("News and Notes," January 1948)

The program published a quarterly bulletin, the *Inventory of Research in Racial and Cultural Relations,* jointly with the American Council on Race Relations, also under Louis Wirth's chairmanship. Both the Goldsteins (Bernard and Rhoda Blumberg Goldstein) obtained experience as research assistants in these centers and wrote dissertations with Wirth's guidance (Blumberg, letter to Lopata, September 1, 1993). Gladys Lang contributed to the committee's research on intercultural relations in public schools.

Robert Dentler (1987) devoted a chapter to "The Chicago School" in his *Secrets of a Sociologist,* describing some of the work at the Family Study Center, organized and run by Burgess and later by Nelson Foote. Bruno Bettelheim, the Duncans, the Blaus, and Peter Rossi were involved in a study of the middle years of marriage. The students during Dentler's fellowship included Peter Pineo and Kai Erikson. Gerald Handel, a graduate student affiliated with the Committee on Human Development and with strong sociological interests, was very active in this center and elaborated on the Burgess view of the family as a unit of interacting personalities, as evident in his *Psychosocial Interior of the Family* (letter to Lopata, September 14, 1993).

In 1947 Philip M. Hauser was appointed director of the Chicago Community Inventory, which had a long history, with several name changes:

> The inventory is a service designed to secure facts of community conditions needed for the efficient operation of the civic and welfare agencies of the city. It plans to conduct surveys, to maintain a clearing house and reference library of pertinent data. It will utilize standard methods of random sampling, opinion surveys, and attitude interviewing. The inventory was

established by a three-year grant received from the Wieboldt
Foundation. ("News and Notes," January 1948)

William F. Ogburn, in the meantime, had begun a project on the social
aspects of technology, with a three-year grant. NORC, the Chicago Community Inventory, and Ogburn's research reflected the new quantitative
approaches in the department that attracted students different from those
of its more humanistic and symbolic interactionist past. Some combina-
tions of qualitative and quantitative research existed in the past, but with
a greater emphasis on the qualitative. The new trend was reflected in an
announcement in "News and Notes" (pp. 262–63) of November 1953:

> Three $4,000 postdoctoral fellowships in statistics are offered
> for 1954–55. The purpose of these fellowships, which are open
> to holders of the Doctor's degree or its equivalent in research
> accomplishment, is to acquaint established research workers
> in the biological, physical and social sciences with the role of
> modern statistical analysis in the planning of experiments and
> other investigative programs and in the analysis of empirical
> data. The development of the field of statistics has been so
> rapid that most current research falls far short of attainable
> standards, and these fellowships (which represent the fourth
> year of a five-year program supported by the Rockefeller Foun-
> dation) are intended to help reduce this lag by giving statistical
> training to scientists whose primary interests are in substantive
> fields rather than in statistics itself.

As a result of several changes the sociology department of the University
of Chicago established itself at the forefront in giving "statistical training"
to scientists in "substantive fields." This is what some of the faculty valuing
qualitative thought and methods, especially the symbolic interactionists,
found difficult to accept, as their interests appeared squeezed out by what
was called the "takeover" from the "Columbia cohorts."

Several other centers for research were operating, including the Population Research and Training Center set up in 1954 under the leadership
of Philip Hauser with Otis Dudley Duncan, Donald Bogue, and Evelyn
Kitagawa, that trained students in demography and offered a program
leading to a Ph.D. Quite different was the Committee on Social Thought,
with Edward Shils as its sociological member. Courses could be taken
there as well as from the Committee on Human Development. The Industrial Relations Center drew students, as did Joseph Lohman when elected
sheriff of Cook County in 1949.

Individually organized and more limited research projects included Fred Strodtbeck's Social Psychology program, devoted for many years to the study of the jury system in light of group dynamics. Rita Simon was an important participant in this venture. Some research programs were so tied to the faculty who started them that they vanished when the person left. This was true of David Riesman's Sociability Center. Of course, it is often hard to determine the extent to which a center is so institutionalized as to survive the leaving, for any reason, of its founder. The Population Center has had a longer life than did Riesman's Sociability Center, at least at the University of Chicago.

The fourth type of activity throughout these years included "special events," many of which took place during the summer or had unusual characteristics. An "annual conference for teachers of the social sciences in high schools and junior colleges" was held summers, starting in 1940. Also in summers, the annual Institute of the Society for Social Research, begun in 1923, offered students opportunities for presenting scientific papers. An Institute on Problems of Old Age was held during the summer for several years. A Chinese Sociological Society was organized in 1945 for the purpose of promoting social research in the problems of China and of establishing connections with the Chinese Sociological Society in China. A committee consisting of Everett C. Hughes, Robert Redfield, and Louis Wirth arranged for the publication of Robert E. Park's papers, and another committee organized an Advanced Fellowship for Studies in Urban Living in the name of Louis Wirth after his death.

Some graduate students were involved in teaching in the college, a very exciting experience while Robert Hutchins was president of the university. Joseph Gusfield (1990, p. 112) describes the intellectual stimulation derived from weekly seminars of the faculty teaching "Social Science 2." The staff included Milton Singer, Daniel Bell, Rose and Lewis Coser, Morton Grodzins, Rosalie Hankey (Wax), Martin Meyerson, C. Wright Mills, Benjamin Nelson, Philip Rieff, David Riesman, Sylvia Thrupp, and Murray Wax. Other students taught at Roosevelt University or, like Wolf Heydebrand, taught nurses at St. Luke-Presbyterian Hospital, in courses organized by Hans Mauksch. Research positions were available at the Institute for Juvenile Research, and at Social Research, Inc., organized and managed by Burleigh Gardner. Through Social Research, Inc., one of the most famous books on the family, *Workingman's Wife* was coauthored by Lee Rainwater, Richard Coleman, and Gerald Handel (1959).

Not all graduate students who could identify with the second-school

372 Helena Znaniecka Lopata

cohort did so. As with all organizations, levels of involvement depend on time commitments and competing social roles. In this case, commitments could be to sociology as learned at the university, the university itself, the department of sociology, the cohort, and so forth. Some members identified themselves, or were identified by others, as in the core, others now place themselves as having been in various circles surrounding the core, or in peripheral and transient membership. Daniel Glaser, who obtained his Ph.D. in 1954, explained that he did not identify himself closely with the department because his education was interrupted by the war. He, with his wife and children, lived away from Chicago the year when he returned to complete his Ph.D. work and was employed full-time at the Pontiac and Joliet prisons (letter to Fine, May 4, 1990). Paul Hare (Ph.D. 1951) "did not have much time to identify with the cohort" but initiated and edited a newsletter called *The Participant Observer* (letter to Fine, June 10, 1990).

Everyone with whom I have talked over the years—at the annual breakfasts, and the more recent (but, as far as I am concerned, less enjoyable) cocktail parties, meetings, or all kinds of other social events—recalls the atmosphere of the 1945–55 decade as exciting, full of talk, study, and play (Gusfield, 1990, p. 114). Those without such memories do not come to such events or remain silent. There were so many of us, and the faculty had so little time to pay attention, that we divided into study groups in the fields for which we decided to take preliminary examinations. I studied with those interested in theory, social psychology, and race and ethnic relations. (I remember taking Simmel as my theoretician and have never lost my liking for his ideas.) We sat around, at teas and lunch, in bars and bookstores, and talked and argued, and we did play. Living near to each other, we partied frequently. My husband and I had a television set early on, and fellow students brought beer and popcorn, and sat on the floor or on borrowed furniture, watching favorite shows. We organized softball games and picnics with families. We academics also did a good job of painting each other's apartments and moving books and furniture. Chicago had an active chapter of Zeta Phi, the sociology Ph.D. honorary society. Dan Lortie remembers when there was a hot debate over letting women into this society, probably around 1947 (personal conversation, October 1993). That passed and Gladys Lang later became Zeta Phi president. The meetings were more parties than business, discussion was rampant, and Katy Blumer often played the guitar.[1] We read the university paper, *The Participant Observer,* the *American Journal of Sociology* and, of course, the class notes from Blumer, Wirth, or Hughes, many of which were mimeographed.

WOMEN IN SOCIOLOGY

Mary Jo Deegan (this volume) defined the years 1892–1920 as the "golden era" of women in sociology at the University of Chicago and the 1945–60 years as the "dark era." Several characteristics of these times may have led to these conclusions. A group of women connected with Jane Addams and Hull-House blossomed into prominence in the early years. They combined unique features absent in later eras. First, they were closely associated with each other, often unmarried, and strongly focused on their reform work. Second, they emerged from middle- or upper-class backgrounds and shared a lifestyle, in addition to their scholarly similarities. Third, they were not integrated into the male world of the University of Chicago sociology department. Albion Small was allegedly determined to exclude them. In fact, their academic connection was within the newly formed Social Service Administration department.

The post–World War II cohort of women was very different. We came into the department individually, or in some cases as marriage partners. Most of us were determined to become sociologists. We did not form an isolated or segregated group of women. We had faced, and would in the future face, societal and academic discrimination, but many of us felt integrated, some more than others. Our roles were quite similar to those of the men in the cohort.

Helen MacGill Hughes edited a pamphlet on *The Status of Women in Sociology 1968–1972,* based on data collected by the Ad Hoc Committee on the Status of Women in the Profession and published by the American Sociological Association, that documents the extent to which women were absent in sociology as late as 1972.[2] This absence started with graduate school, and went on with a "diminishing flow" of numbers as one went up the status ladder. Thus, in 1969, women made up 37 percent of M.A. candidates and 30 percent of Ph.D. candidates. At that time, women constituted 27 percent of lecturers and instructors in full-time faculty, 14 percent of assistant professors, 9 percent of associate professors, 4 percent of full professors, and 1 percent of departmental chairs. There were no women full professors in five "elite institutions," as defined by the ASA (Hughes 1973, p. 6). Women graduate students in 1971–72 received 36 percent of the fellowships, and 39 percent each of research and teaching assistantships. One reason for the low numbers was the failure of many women to apply for financial assistance (Hughes 1973, p. 22). During earlier years, women who wanted to enter graduate school fought against the tide of the two-sphere ideology, as Deegan demonstrates (this volume and elsewhere). Gary Fine and Lori Ducharme note (this volume) that American society was in the midst of the feminine mystique and the McCarthy era during the training of the "second school" generation.

It is hard to imagine today the pressures suppressing open protests on campuses among what became known as the "silent generation" of students. As many autobiographies reflect, this does not suggest a lack of concern for social issues. Gladys Lang notes:

> In 1952 we supported Burgess, Don Horton and the scientist Anton Carlson in defending themselves against attacks from the House Un-American Activities Committee. (Letter to Mary Jo Deegan, July 1991, p. 5)

Often the same people later became deeply involved in the civil rights and antiwar movements (see Rhoda Blumberg's many publications).

The question is, of course: Why did so many of the women at the University of Chicago in the years under observation feel comfortable in these surroundings? It is difficult to explain the incongruity between the obvious fact of inequality in sociology between men and women (even now) and the fact that so many of the women in the second-school cohort declared that they did not face discrimination in that situation. Deegan calls this "denial," but there are more complex reasons for such responses. In the first place, second-wave feminism had not begun its activities of consciousness-raising and reality reconstruction until the 1960s (Sociologists for Women in Society was not formed until 1970). Many women who went to the University of Chicago in the post–World War II years had unusual backgrounds or independence-encouraging experiences, much as had the male veterans. In fact, Gladys Lang (1991, p. 2) describes us as veterans in our own way,

> quite able to speak up for ourselves and well prepared to look out for our own interests. . . . Lopata had fled Warsaw with her mother; Goldstein [Blumberg] taught at a leading "all Negro college" [Fisk], a hardly usual career choice [she came from a New York Jewish family]; Daisy Lilienthal, a "mischling" rescued after the war by her American father had worked as a

laborer in Nazi Germany; Maggie Blough had been a test pilot for Boeing and a union organizer in the Northwest Canning industry; Paula Verdet and Sally Cassidy . . . lived in France and French Canada and were active in resistance and left-Catholic circles. . . . As for myself, [I] worked in D.C., England (during the buzzbomb days), Italy and China. (Letter to Mary Jo Deegan, July 1991, pp. 2–3)

We selected Chicago because of its reputation as less discriminating than other schools, relatively accepting of women, and maintaining no visible sexist barriers.

A third reason for the frequent "denial" of serious problems was the sharing of marginality by all the graduate students we knew. Reading the autobiographies in Berger's (1990) book or those several of us have written for a variety of sources, we can find numerous references to individualizing feelings of being marginal, due to the social class, foreign, ethnic, or religious backgrounds of our families, many of which did not understand (and still do not) what on earth we wanted to do in graduate school and with sociology (I was lucky, coming from a family of sociologists). Being a woman was just one of these marginalizing factors, not especially different from those affecting others within this academic setting.

Finally, all of us had experienced the less congenial "outside world." Although various forms of discrimination were present at the university— sexism, anti-Semitism, anti-Polishness, elitism, ageism—these were so much less than we experienced elsewhere as to be relatively insignificant. We were surrounded by like-minded people and it was better inside than outside. I felt this very strongly in each contact with my husband's traditionalist business community; Becker (1951) felt similarly in front of the dance musician's audience.

Once we finished our degrees, we women faced the outside sexist world again. Those who were married to academics and wanted academic positions were hit by a nepotism rule in most institutions of higher education. Women could not be hired, often for even low-status positions, if they had a relative, usually a husband, in the organization. As Gladys Lang states:

it is hard to convince students nowadays what it was like "then." None of us would have thought of demanding that our wives or husbands be given a job at the same university as a condition of recruitment. (Letter to Deegan, July 1991)

Most of our careers were slowed for reasons obvious during the feminine mystique days. We invested in the careers of our husbands, who agreed to such an arrangement on practical grounds: they found jobs with greater ease and faster than we could, or their jobs paid better at the stage of the life course when we wanted to start or raise families. If married to men in other vocations, we still followed them into locales in which we could not get the jobs for which we worked for so long. Married to a businessman, I was restricted to Chicago. Kimball Young, chair of the Department of Sociology at Northwestern University, did not even turn around from his desk, facing a wall, when he rose to inform me that he had never hired a woman and never would! Besides, as Mirra Komarovsky (1953) made apparent in *Women in the Modern World: Their Education and Their Dilemmas,* the 1950s were not conducive to the careers of women. There were no established ways of meeting the needs of "greedy families" with small children and the "greedy" academic world (Coser 1974; Coser and Coser 1974).

Until secure in academic positions, we could not get grants or the opportunities to do independent research. However, I believe, and other women of this era believe, that the University of Chicago provided us with excellent backgrounds and encouraged intellectual independence, enabling us to become increasingly and visibly productive, as Deegan predicts.

By examining the careers of six women of this cohort of University of Chicago Ph.D.'s, I wish to illustrate the blossoming contributions of some of these women. I rely on the autobiographical notes that several women have written as to the actual support they did receive while in graduate school, as well as their curriculum vitae.

Rhoda Blumberg

Rhoda Blumberg wrote twice to Mary Jo Deegan and then to me (September 1, 1993) about the supports, emotional, financial, and in terms of research experience that she and her then husband, Bernard Goldstein, received from Louis Wirth. Wirth, giving a guest lecture at Fisk University, where the Goldsteins were teaching, was approached by them about the possibility of obtaining their Ph.D.'s at Chicago despite limited financial resources. Wirth arranged for both of them to move from Fisk, providing summer research assistantships. They worked under his direction at the American Council on Race Relations and the Committee on Research, Education and Training in Race Relations. Rhoda received the Sigmund

Livingston Fellowship in Race Relations and then obtained an assistantship for further work. She found Hughes extremely supportive:

> The Chicago years were great, not only because we were at a fine institution, but also because of the unusual cohort of which we became a part.[3]

After delaying full-time involvement in academic sociology due to raising a family, following Bernard, and pursuing her activities in the civil rights movement, Rhoda has contributed in major ways to the literature of race relations and the civil rights movement through books including *Black Life and Culture in the United States* (1971), *Interracial Bonds* (1978), *Civil Rights: The 1960s Freedom Struggle* (1984 and 1991), and *Women and Social Protest* (1990). As any good sociologist, she has capitalized on her interests and experience to broaden a field that had been a major focus of the University of Chicago's sociology department: race and ethnic relations. One of her major contributions has been the study of interracial interaction, friendship, and co-involvement in social movements. She has also analyzed women's roles, as in two studies of women in India: *Indian Women in Transition: A Bangalore Case Study* (1972) and *India's Educated Women: Options and Constraints* (1980). Blumberg has held major leadership positions in the ASA Section on Racial and Ethnic Minorities.

Gladys Lang

Gladys Engel Lang is the most frequently mentioned woman sociologist of this University of Chicago cohort in this volume, for her work in the general subject of collective behavior. She won one of the two Social Science Research Council predoctoral fellowships that was almost withdrawn when the national selection committee heard that she had not mentioned in her application that she was pregnant and "would have a two-month old baby by the time the fellowship year would begin" (letter to Deegan, July 1991, p. 4). This was an outside attempt at discrimination, but she defended her position, and became the first fellowship recipient to give birth after the award.

Gladys reports strong support and opportunities from such social psychologists at Chicago as Tamotsu Shibutani, friendships with members of the cohort (she married one of them, Kurt Lang), and a generally exciting environment. She found her biggest career obstacle to be the nepotism rule, but does not consider her positions at the New York State Commission Against Discrimination or at the Center for Urban Education to be marginal. Her record reveals frequent positions as "visiting" faculty. Despite this, she has accomplished much, and continues to do so, as evidenced by the recent award-winning *Etched in Memory: The Building and Survival of Artistic Reputation* (1990). Her contributions to the sociology of mass communication include three volumes: *Politics and Television* (1968), *Politics and Television Re-Viewed* (1984), and *The Battle for Public Opinion: The President, the Press and the Polls during Watergate* (1983). Her *Collective Dynamics* (1961), acknowledging indebtedness to Blumer and Shibutani, is a classic. One of Gladys' interests has been in fashion, long before the subject reached its current popularity.

Joan Moore

Joan Moore attended the University of Chicago from her undergraduate years through graduate training, finding support from people at the Committee on Human Development, with W. Lloyd Warner chairing her Ph.D. committee, while Everett Hughes chaired her M.A. committee. She notes that in terms of graduate colleagueship, "Lou Kriesberg was my real mentor" (letter to Lopata, August 31, 1993). Her most influential professional role model was Bernice Neugarten. Joan's work has focused on Mexican-Americans, especially on gangs and drugs within the Chicano community in Southern California and Milwaukee. Her *Homeboys* (1979) won numerous awards. Other books on related topics include *Mexican American People: The Nation's Second Largest Minority* (1970), *Mexican Americans* (1970 and 1975), *Hispanics in the United States* (1985), *Drugs in Hispanic Communities* (1990), and *Going Down to the Barrio: Homeboys and Homegirls in Change* (1992). She has received the Spivack Fellow Award, the Lee Founder's Award of the Society for the Study of Social Problems, and has been a president of SSSP and the Pacific Chapter of the American Association of Public Opinion Research.

Ethel Shanas

Although a few years senior to the second school as defined in this volume, Ethel Shanas is referred to by others, including men, as an important mentor. She has achieved the highest position in her field, presidency of the Gerontological Society of America:

> I don't think being one of the few women in the Sociology Department at the U of C blighted my career. Actually, the faculty, except Ellsworth Faris, were very decent. I took my AB

in 1935 and the Department elected me to Phi Beta Kappa. In 1940, when I came back for my Ph.D., I received a U of C Fellowship and in 1941 the Charles Richmond Henderson Fellowship, one of the two endowed fellowships that the Department had available. (Letter to Lopata, September 6, 1993)

As to her career, she summarizes it as follows:

*I have been president of a national society—The Gerontological Society of America.
*I have received an honorary degree—Hunter College, CUNY.
*I have spent a term as an Academic Visitor in the Department of Social Administration at the London School of Economics.
*In 1979–80 I was elected to membership of the Institute of Medicine of the National Academy of Sciences. At the time of my election, no member of *any* of the campuses of the University of Illinois, including the Medical School, had been so honored.
*I have served on two National Research Council Committees and have been a consultant to the United Nations, the World Health Organization, and the Social Science Research Council of Britain. (Letter to Helena Z. Lopata September 6, 1993)

Ethel Shanas has been a major developer of social gerontology, a field largely unknown in the post–World War II years. She has been involved in most of the important books, national and international conferences, and social events connected with her field, and, along with Bernice Neugarten and Matilda Riley, is the most widely known social gerontologist. All three of these leaders are women who managed to pursue marital and parental roles. Shanas has published eight pathbreaking books on health and family relations of older people and has contributed to methodology. Her contributions span medical and family sociology, as well as social gerontology and have been the basis of her numerous honorary and active positions in national and international, governmental and academic arenas.

Rita Simon

Rita Simon, now University Professor at the American University, moved into sociology from law, as did several of the other University of Chicago sociologists. She held a research fellowship in law and the behavioral sciences at the law school of the University of Chicago in 1957–58, followed by a position as research associate. She then became an assistant professor in the Department of Sociology. She has held Ford Foundation and Guggenheim fellowships and has been a fellow at the Center for Advanced Study of the University of Illinois. She has contributed to sociology in several areas: (1) criminology, studying the jury system (she started with Fred Strodtbeck in the 1950s), later expanding into a special emphasis on the insanity defense; (2) gender, studying women and crime, publishing *The Crimes Women Commit, the Punishments They Receive* (1991), *Women's Movements in America* (1991), and *Rabbis, Lawyers, Immigrants, Thieves: Women's Role in America* (1993); (3) ethnicity and racial relations, studying adjustment of Soviet immigrants and refugees in the United States and Israel, and interracial and intercountry adoption (1977, 1981, 1987, 1992, and in press). The latter set of studies also contributes to sociology of the family.

Helena Znaniecka Lopata

I believe that I have also contributed to sociology in ways other than those cited by Deegan. Combining Florian Znaniecki's theory of social roles with symbolic interactionism, I focus on the roles of American women in a way that is beginning to be accepted in occupational and gender studies. I see a social role as a set of negotiated, interdependent relations between a social person and a social circle. This moves role from the Lintonian and functionalist emphasis on behavior in a position or office to a set of relations between the central person and those toward whom duties are directed and from whom rights are received (see Colomy and Brown, this volume). This frees social roles from the rigidity of the prior definitions. I applied this definition of social role to the study of women, as in *Occupation: Housewife* (1971), taking homemakers as managers of households.[4] This was followed by *City Women: Work, Jobs, Occupations and Careers* (volume 1, *America,* and volume 2, *Chicago* [1984, 1985]) and *Circles and Settings: Role Changes of American Women* (1994b). Another line of emphasis has been upon gender as a pervasive identity that enters role relationships more or less significantly, rather than as a "sex role." Barrie Thorne and I appear to have influenced the section of the ASA called "Sex Roles" to change its name to "Sex and Gender." A third contribution has been the concept of support systems, used first in *Women as Widows: Support Systems* (1979).[5]

My University of Chicago committee of Everett Hughes, Herbert Blumer, and Louis Wirth rejected the theoretical dissertation I had in mind when arriving with a M.A. from the University of Illinois (this was not sexist, in that it happened to many, if not most, Chicago students) and insisted that I go to Polonia, the Polish-American community in Chicago to find out why it had not become totally disorganized, as predicted by *The Polish Peasant in Europe and America*. It took not only the dissertation, but a repeat study of Polonia in the 1970s, to let me realize that what was seen as disorganization was actually a complex system of status competition that, in combination with a highly developed system of organizations, held the community together and added enough *joie de vivre* to incorporate new immigrant cohorts and generations (see *Polish Americans: Status Competition in an Ethnic Community*). This theme is expanded in the revised edition of *Polish Americans* that incorporates the changes in Poland and Polonia during the last decade.

I have served as president of the Midwest Sociological Society, the Midwest Council for Social Research on Aging, the Society for the Study of Social Problems, and Sociologists for Women in Society. I have also received the Burgess Award of the National Council on Family Relations, the Distinguished Scholar Award of the Section on the Sociology of Aging of the American Sociological Association, and the George Herbert Mead award of the Society for the Study of Symbolic Interaction.

* * *

Several letters by the men of the second-school cohort mention the absence of women in the Department of Sociology and related centers. Such comments appear to be a consequence of invisibility rather than actual absence. For example, the 1954 graduating class had seven women out of twenty-eight Ph.D.s. The Thirty-first Annual Institute of the Society for Social Research, held in 1954, included papers by Beverly Duncan, Shirley Star, Rhoda Goldstein, Ruth Shonle Cavan, Evelyn Mills Duvall, and Lillian Ripple. Thus, women were "around."

My discussion of the six women Ph.D.s attending the University of Chicago during the years 1946 to 1960 indicates two peculiarities of this volume: the relative absence of women in the main chapters, and the questionable assumption of Mary Jo Deegan that our cohort lived in the "dark era" that so discriminated against these passive recipients that they were unable to contribute to sociology in later life.

What has made the contributions of women of the second Chicago school so invisible to their colleagues in later years? There are several possible answers:

1. There was a special bond of having gone through the armed forces

among the male cohort of graduate students that carried on into later life, magnified in memory. The women shared it less (for example, my being a refugee from the Nazis did not create the same bond as having shared life in the American armed forces). While on campus, the women felt integrated, and cross-gender friendships have lasted, yet the men's memory of the cohort is predominantly male.

2. The women dispersed, often following their mates, while the men became the main members of faculties.

3. Many women, although on equal terms during their university years, had "disorderly careers," due to the asymmetry of parenting and gender discrimination. Faculty wives were treated as such and their own careers were invisible. Faculty husbands experienced the same invisibility, but there were few of them in our cohort.[6]

4. By the time the women began catching up in their research and publication productivity, the men were already established. The men who are so often mentioned in this volume had already developed their reputations and mutual admiration networks, quoting each other and building upon each other's ideas. Younger women sociologists, often students of the second-school cohort, have a better chance of being visible earlier on than did our older cohort, tied to disorderly careers, but with expanded academic involvement in later years. Indeed, it appears that many late bloomers are not "burned out" to the extent of their male colleagues.

5. Many of the women worked in fields not in the "mainstream" of sociology, as evidenced by the chapters in this book. For example, the men who went into such fields as the family, as did Gerald Handel (a Human Development Ph.D.) and Bernard Farber, are also not covered in this volume.

In total, the department granted 272 new Ph.D.'s from 1946 to 1965: 154 the first decade, 116 the second. Women formed 12.90 percent of the first decade, 14.65 percent of the second. Thus, the total of thirty-seven women formed an average of 13.60 percent of the 272 Ph.D.s (see Appendix 1). While over thirty male sociologists in this cohort contributed "self-reports and sociological critiques of this school and era," in response to Gary Fine's requests, most male sociologists did not respond. Many male sociologists are also "neglected" in this volume because of limitations of space and choices of authors. Some University of Chicago sociologists, men and women, have made major contributions to collective behavior, racial and ethnic processes, deviance research and ethnography. Others took many different paths.

I believe that the answer to the question, "Was there a Second Chicago school?" is "Yes," but that the editor and authors of *A Second Chicago School?* have selected only a few directions of its development, especially as they relate to symbolic interactionism and qualitative sociology. That was their goal. My intent was to point out other directions present on campus and in the work of other contributors to sociology who attended the University of Chicago during the postwar era. No history is ever as complete as it needs to be.

NOTES

1. Gladys Lang turned over the Zeta Phi minutes to the University of Chicago archives, where they are available for researchers.
2. The members of the committee were: Elise Boulding, chair, Lenore Weitzman, James Sweet, Shirley Nuss, Cora Marrett, Paul Glick, and Rose Laub Coser, with Kurt Finsterbusch and Maurice Jackson, ex-officio.
3. Shulamit Reinharz quotes Lynda Lytle Holmstrom's experience with Hughes at Brandeis University:

> he influenced positively the careers of numerous female students. He helped supervise many of their dissertations, many of which had to do with some aspect of work or careers, and a number of which had special relevance for women's lives. He was the inspiration of my own work on two-career families. He was a mentor for Nancy Stoller Shaw, whose dissertation dealt with childbirth. . . . He was also a mentor for Barrie Thorne, whose dissertation dealt with the draft resistance movement. (Reinharz, this volume)

4. I was criticized, patronized, and laughed at for this choice of topic early in the research.
5. One form of sexism that is only now becoming less fashionable with the entrance of feminist literature into mainstream sociology is the neglect by male sociologists of contributions to theory and concept construction if they arise from studies done by women. For example, I do not study widows, but role modifications produced by widowhood, social class differences in social life spaces, forms and components of loneliness, and time in constructed memory.
6. This may be wrong, but I agree with Lewis Coser (1984) in his *Refugee Scholars in America: Their Impact and Their Experiences* that the "Eastern Establishment" in sociology is more supportive of "deviant" scholars, such as refugees or women. I also agree with Deegan that Columbia pushes its products more than the relatively dispersed academic world between the coasts.

REFERENCES

American Journal of Sociology, University of Chicago "News and Notes," 1945–60.
Becker, Howard S. 1951. The professional dance musician and his audience. *American Journal of Sociology* 57: 136–44.

Becker, Howard S., et al., 1961. *Boys in White*. Chicago: University of Chicago Press.

Berger, Bennett, ed. 1990. *Authors of Their Own Lives: Intellectual Autobiographies by Twenty American Sociologists*. Berkeley: University of California Press.

Blumberg, Rhoda, ed. 1971. *Black Life and Culture in the United States*. New York: Thomas Y. Crowell (under the name of Rhoda Goldstein).

Blumberg, Rhoda. 1972. *Indian Women in Transition: A Bangalore Case Study*. Metuchen, N.J.: Scarecrow Press (under the name of Rhoda Goldstein).

Blumberg, Rhoda and Wendell J. Roye, eds. 1979. *Interracial Bonds*. Bayside, N.Y.: General Hall.

Blumberg, Rhoda, with Leela Dwaraki. 1980. *India's Educated Women: Options and Constraints*. New Delhi: Hindustan.

Blumberg, Rhoda. 1984. *Civil Rights: The 1960s Freedom Struggle*. Boston: G. K. Hall.

Blumberg, Rhoda and Guida West, eds. 1990. *Women and Social Protest*. New York: Oxford University Press.

Carey, James. 1975. *Sociology and Public Affairs: The Chicago School*. Beverly Hills: Sage.

Coser, Lewis. 1973. *Greedy Institutions: Patterns of Undivided Commitment*. New York: The Free Press.

Coser, Lewis A. 1984. *Refugee Scholars in America: Their Impact and Their Experiences*. New Haven: Yale University Press.

Coser, Lewis and Rose Laub Coser, 1974. "The Housewife and Her 'Greedy Family.'" Pp. 89–100 in *Greedy Institutions: Patterns of Undivided Commitment*, edited by Lewis Coser. New York: The Free Press.

Cumming, Elaine, and William E. Henry. 1961. *Growing Old: The Process of Disengagement*. New York: Basic Books.

Deegan, Mary Jo, ed. 1991. *Women in Sociology: A Bio-bibliographical Sourcebook*. New York: Greenwood Press.

Dentler, Robert. 1987. "Secrets of a Sociologist." Manuscript

Gans, Herbert J. 1990. "Relativism, Equality and Popular Culture." Pp. 432–51 in *Authors of Their Own Lives*, edited by Bennett Berger. Berkeley: University of California Press.

Gusfield, Joseph. 1982. The Scholarly Tension: Graduate Craft and Undergraduate Imagination. Presented at the 40th Anniversary of Social Sciences II, University of Chicago College. November.

Gusfield, Joseph. 1990. "My Life and Soft Times." Pp. 104–29 in *Authors of Their Own Lives*, edited by Bennett Burger. Berkeley: University of California Press.

Handel, Gerald, ed. 1967. *The Psychosocial Interior of the Family*. Chicago: Aldine.

Hughes, Helen MacGill. 1973. *The Status of Women in Sociology 1968–1972*. Washington, D.C.: American Sociological Association.

Komarovsky, Mirra. 1953. *Women in the Modern World: Their Education and Their Dilemmas*. Boston: Little, Brown.

Lang, Kurt and Gladys E. Lang. 1961. *Collective Dynamics*. New York: Thomas Y. Crowell.

Lang, Kurt and Gladys E. Lang. 1968. *Politics and Television.* New York: Quadrangle.

Lang, Kurt and Gladys E. Lang. 1983. *The Battle for Public Opinion: The President, the Press, and the Polls during Watergate.* New York: Columbia University Press.

Lang, Kurt and Gladys E. Lang. 1984. *Politics and Television Re-viewed.* Beverly Hills: Sage.

Lang, Gladys Engel and Kurt Lang. 1990. *Etched in Memory: The Building and Survival of Artistic Reputation.* Chapel Hill: University of North Carolina Press.

Lopata, Helena Znaniecka. 1971. *Occupation: Housewife.* New York: Oxford University Press.

Lopata, Helena Z. 1973. *Widowhood in an American City.* Cambridge, Mass.: Schenkman.

Lopata, Helena Z. 1976. *Polish Americans: Status Competition in an Ethnic Community.* Englewood Cliffs: Prentice-Hall.

Lopata, Helena Z. 1979. *Women as Widows: Support Systems.* New York: Elsevier.

Lopata, Helena Z., Cheryl Allyn Miller and Debra Barnewolt. 1984. *City Women: Work, Jobs, Occupations, Careers.* Volume 1, *America.* New York: Praeger. Reprinted in 1986 as *City Women in America.*

Lopata, Helena Z., Debra Barnewolt and Cheryl Allyn Miller. 1985. *City Women: Work, Jobs, Occupations, Careers.* Volume 2, *Chicago.* New York: Praeger.

Lopata, Helena Z. 1994a. *Polish Americans.* New Brunswick: Transaction. Second, revised edition.

Lopata, Helena Z. 1994b. *Circles and Settings: Role Changes of American Women.* Albany: SUNY Press.

Moore, Joan, with Leo Grebler and Ralph Gusman. 1970. *Mexican American People: The Nation's Second Largest Minority.* New York: Macmillan and The Free Press.

Moore, Joan, with Alfredo Cuellar. 1970. *Mexican Americans.* Englewood Cliffs: Prentice-Hall. Revised, second edition with Harry Pachon, 1975.

Moore, Joan. 1979. *Homeboys: Gangs, Drugs and Prison in the Barrios of Los Angeles.* Philadelphia: Temple University Press.

Moore, Joan, with Harry Pachon. 1985. *Hispanics in the United States.* Englewood Cliffs: Prentice-Hall.

Moore, Joan and Ronald Glick, eds. 1990. *Drugs in Hispanic Communities.* New Brunswick: Rutgers University Press.

Moore, Joan. 1992. *Going Down to the Barrio: Homeboys and Homegirls in Change.* Philadelphia: Temple University Press.

Rainwater, Lee, Richard Coleman and Gerald Handel. 1959. *Workingman's Wife.* New York: Oceana.

Riesman, David, Nathan Glaser and Reuel Denney. 1950. *The Lonely Crowd.* New Haven: Yale University Press.

Simon, Rita. 1967. *The Jury and the Defense of Insanity.* Boston: Little, Brown.

Simon, Rita and Jean Landis. 1991. *The Crimes Women Commit, the Punishments They Receive.* Lexington, Mass.: Lexington Books.

386   Helena Znaniecka Lopata

Simon, Rita and Gloria Danziger. 1991. *Women's Movements in America: Their Achievements, Disappointments and Aspirations.* New York: Praeger.

Simon, Rita. 1993. *Rabbis, Lawyers, Immigrants, Thieves: Women's Role in America.* New York: Praeger.

Simon, Rita. 1977. *Transracial Adoption* (with Howard Altstein). New York: Wiley-Interscience.

Simon, Rita. 1981. *Transracial Adoption: A Follow-up* (with Howard Altstein). Lexington, Mass.: Lexington Books.

Simon, Rita. 1987. *Transracial Adoption: A Study of Their Identity and Commitment* (with Howard Altstein). New York: Praeger.

Simon, Rita, 1992. *Adoption, Race and Identity* (with Howard Altstein). New York: Praeger.

Simon, Rita. In Press. *The Case for Transracial Adoption* (with Howard Altstein and Marygold Melli). Lanham, Md.: The American University Press.

Thomas, W. I. and F. W. Znaniecki. 1918–20. *The Polish Peasant in Europe and America.* Boston: Richard G. Badger.

Correspondence

Blumberg, Rhoda, letter to Helena Z. Lopata, September 1, 1993, with reference also to two letters to Mary Jo Deegan and including an autobiographical account

Bogart, Leo, letter to Gary Fine, May 29, 1990

Glaser, Dan, letter to Gary Fine, May 4, 1990

Gusfield, Joseph, transcript of taped cassette to Gary Fine. June 4, 1990

Handle, Gerald, letter to Helena Z. Lopata, September 14, 1993

Hare, A. Paul, letter to Gary Fine, June 10, 1990

Lang, Gladys, letter to Helena Z. Lopata, August 7, 1993

Lang, Gladys, letter to Mary Jo Deegan, July 1991

Moore, Joan, letter to Helena Z. Lopata, September 11, 1993

Shanus, Ethel, letter to Helena Z. Lopata, September 6, 1993

Simon, Rita, letter to Helena Z. Lopata, September 11, 1993

Stone, Robert, letter to Gary Fine, May 28, 1990

PH.D. Degrees in the Department of

Sociology at the University of Chicago,

1946–1965

1946

Hill, Mozelle C.
"The All-Negro Society"

LaViolette, Forrest
"Americans of Japanese Ancestry: A Study of Assimilation in the American Community"

Sarma, Jyotirmoyee
"The Social Categories of Friendship"

Whitridge, Eugenia Remlin
"Art in Chicago"

1947

Bendix, Reinhard
"The Public Servant in a Democracy"

Breese, Gerald William
"The Daytime Population of the Central Population District of Chicago with Particular Reference to the Factor of Transportation"

Campisi, Paul John
"A Scale for the Measurement of Acculturation"

Clark, Robert Eugene
"The Relationship of Occupation and Various Psychoses"

Dubin, Robert
"The Grievance Process: A Study of Union-Management Relations"

Ericksen, Ephraim Gordon
"Protest Society: Social Irrationality in the Extraterritorial One-Sex Company Town"

Freedman, Ronald
"Recent Migration to Chicago"

Lee, Rose Hum
"The Growth and Decline of Chinese Communities in the Rocky Mountain Region"

This list was compiled from information made available by the Alumni Office of the University of Chicago.

Miller, Vera
"The Areal Distribution of Tax Delinquency in Chicago and Its
Relationship to Certain Housing and Social Characteristics

Rose, Alvin Walcott
"A Socio-Psychological Analysis of the Ambition Patterns of a Sample of
Industrial Workers"

1948

Burnet, Jean
"The Problem of Community Instability in East Central Alberta"

Bowerman, Charles Emert
"The Measurement of Areas of Adjustment in Marriage"

Cohen, Lillian
"Factors Associated with Home Ownership in Twenty-two Metropolitan
Districts, 1940"

Duncan, Hugh Dalziel
"Chicago as a Literary Center: Social Factors Influencing Chicago
Literary Institutions from 1885 to 1920"

Faw, Volney Emmert
"Vocational Interests of Chicago Negro and White High School Junior
and Senior Boys"

Janowitz, Morris
"Mobility, Subjective Deprivation, and Ethnic Hostility"

Klapp, Orrin
"The Hero as a Social Type"

Meltzer, Bernard N.
"Preprofessional Career and Early Publication as Factors in the
Differential Productivity of Social Scientists"

Milne, David Spencer
"Juvenile Delinquency and Youth Services in War-time California"

Ni, Ernest In-Hsin
"Social Characteristics of the Chinese Population: A Study of the
Population Structure and Urbanism of a Metropolitan Community"

Rosenthal, Erich
"Jewish Population of Chicago, Illinois: Size and Distribution as Derived
from Voters' Lists"

Shibutani, Tamotsu
"The Circulation of Rumors as a Form of Collective Behavior"

Swanson, Guy Edwin
"Emotional Disturbance and Juvenile Delinquency"

Turner, Ralph Herbert
"Some Factors in the Differential Position of Whites and Negroes in the
Labor Force of the United States in 1940"

1949

Bernert, Eleanor H.
"The Chicago Labor Force, 1910–1940"

Bonner, Hubert
"Paranoia and Paranoid Condition: A Social-Psychological Study of the Paranoic Personality"

Clausen, John
"Soldiers' Plans and the Prediction of the Post-Separation Activities of Veterans"

Cothran, Tilman C.
"Negro Stereotyped Conceptions of White People"

Dalton, Orrie Melville
"A Study of Informal Organization among the Managers of an Industrial Union"

Dee, William L. J.
"The Social Effects of a Public Housing Project on the Immediate Community"

Duncan, Otis Dudley
"An Examination of the Problem of Optimum City Size"

Gross, Edward
"Informal Relations and the Social Organization of Work in an Industrial Office"

Hale, William Henri
"The Career Development of the Negro Lawyer in Chicago"

Hormann, Bernard Lothar
"Extinction and Survival: A Study of the Reaction of Aboriginal Populations to European Expansion"

Killian, Lewis Martin
"Southern White Laborers in Chicago's West Side"

Klassen, Peter
"Internal Migration in Relation to Literacy and Language"

Lunday, George Albert
"A Study of Parole Prediction"

McKeown, James Edward
"The Dynamics of the Childhood Families of Small Highly Selected Groups of Male and Female Schizophrenics: Behavior Problems and Normals"

Nelson, Charles Wego
"Development and Evaluation of a Leadership Attitude Scale for Foremen"

Reiss, Albert John, Jr.
"The Accuracy, Efficiency, and Validity of a Prediction Instrument"

Shanas, Ethel
    "The Personal Adjustment of Recipients of Old Age Assistance: With
    Special Consideration of the Methodology of Questionnaire Studies of
    Older People"

Smith, Harvey Liss
    "The Sociological Study of Hospitals"

Stone, Robert Clarence
    "Vertical Mobility and Ideology: A Study of White-Collar Workers"

Thomas, John L.
    "Some of the Factors Involved in the Breakdown of Catholic Marriage"

Williams, Josephine J.
    "The Professional Status of Women Physicians"

Willkening, Eugene A.
    "The Acceptance of Certain Agricultural Programs and Practices in a
    Piedmont Community of North Carolina"

Wray, Donald
    "The Foreman and Managerial Functions"

1950

Bogart, Leo
    "The Comic Strips and Their Adult Readers: A Study of Male Workers in
    a New York City Neighborhood"

Calhoun, Donald Wallace
    "The Reception of Marxian Sociological Theory by American Academic
    Sociologists"

Fitchett, Elijah H.
    "The Free Negro in Charleston, South Carolina"

Goldman, Nathan
    "The Differential Selection of Juvenile Offenders for Court Appearance"

Harlan, William Harrell
    "Isolation and Conduct in Later Life: Study of Four Hundred and Sixty-
    four Chicagoans of Ages Sixty to Ninety-five"

Henry, Andy Fred
    "The Nature of the Relation between Suicide and the Business Cycle"

Ikle, Fred C.
    "The Impact of War upon the Spacing of Urban Population"

Lee, Shu-Ching
    "Social Implications of Farm Tenancy in China"

Lindstrom, Fredrick B.
    "The Military Mind and the Soldier Press"

Lu, Yi-Chuang
    "A Study of Dominant, Equalitarian, and Submissive Roles in Marriage"

Marcson, Simon
"The Prediction of Intermarriage"

Mayer, Albert J.
"Differentials in Length of Life, City of Chicago: 1880–1940"

Miyamoto, Shotaro Frank
"The Career of Intergroup Tensions: A Study of the Collective
Adjustments of Evacuees to Crises at the Tule Lake Relocation Center"

Motz, Annabelle Bender
"Conceptions of Marital Roles in Transition"

Pan, Ju-Shu
"A Comparison of Factors in the Personal Adjustment of Old People in
the Protestant Church Homes for the Aged and the Old People Living
Outside of Institutions"

Quinn, Olive Westbrooke
"Racial Attitudes and the Conforming Personality"

Reitzes, Dietrich
"Collective Factors in Race Relations"

Rogoff, Natalie
"Recent Trends in Occupational Mobility"

Rosenstein, Joseph
"Small-Town Party Politics"

Ross, Aileen D.
"Ethnic Relations and Social Structure: A Study of the Invasion of
French-Speaking Canadians into an English Canadian District"

Schmidt, John F.
"Patterns of Poor Adjustment in Persons of Later Maturity"

Stafford, Alfred B.
"Trends of Invention in Material Culture: A Statistical Study of the Class-
wise Distribution of Inventive Effort in the United States as Determined
by Patents Granted During the Period 1914–45"

Star, Shirley Ann
"Interracial Tension in Two Areas of Chicago: An Exploratory Approach
to the Measurement of Interracial Tension"

1951

Becker, Howard S.
"Role and Career Problems of the Chicago Public-School Teacher"

Elkin, Frederick
"A Study of the Relationship between Popular Hero Types and Social
Class"

Haimowitz, Morris L.
"The Development and Change of Ethnic Hostility"

Hare, Alexander Paul
"A Study of Interaction and Consensus in Different-Sized Discussion Groups"

Ireland, Ralph
"The Aging Industrial Worker: Retirement Plans and Preparation with Some Reference to the Meaning of Work"

King, Charles
"Factors Making for Success or Failure in Marital Adjustment among 466 Negro Couples in a Southern City"

Kitagawa, Evelyn Mae
"Differentials in Total and Marital Fertility, Chicago, 1920–1940"

Lewis, Hylan G.
"The Social Life of the Negro in a Southern Piedmont Town"

Schwartz, Morris
"Social Interaction in a Disturbed Ward of a Mental Hospital"

Short, James F., Jr.
"An Investigation of the Relation Between Crime and Business Cycles"

Westley, William A., Jr.
"The Police: A Sociological Study of Law, Custom, and Morality"

1952

Al-Tahir, A. J. A.
"The Arab Community in the Chicago Area: A Comparative Study of the Christian-Syrians and the Muslim Palestinians"

Benson, Purnell
"The Interests and Activities of Engaged and Married Couples in Relation to Their Adjustment"

Blackiston, Don
"The Judge, the Defendant, and Criminal Law Administration"

Buckman, Rilma
"Interaction Between Women's Clubs and Institutions"

DePoister, Marshon
"Trends in Theological Beliefs within Selected Denominations"

Dornbusch, Sanford
"The Family in the Labor Force: A Study of Supplementary Workers in U.S., 1940"

Edwards, Gilbert Frank
"Occupational Mobility of a Selected Group of Negro Male Professionals"

Freidson, Eliot
"An Audience and Its Taste: A Study in Mass Communication"

Keyfitz, Nathan
"Urban Influence on Farm Family Size"

Kimura, Yukiko
"A Comparative Study of Collective Adjustment of the Isei, the First
Generation Japanese, in Hawaii and in the Mainland, U.S., since Pearl
Harbor"

Linn, Erwin
"The Correlation of Death Rates from Selected Causes with the Business
Cycle, 1919–1947"

London, Jack
"A Case Study of a Local Union"

Reeder, Leo
"Industrial Location in the Chicago Metropolitan Area with Special
Reference to Population"

Roy, Donald
"Restriction of Output by Machine Operators in a Piecework Machine
Shop"

Solomon, David
"Career Contingencies of Chicago Physicians"

Wilson, Everett
No Title Available

Winget, John
"Teachers Inter-School Mobility Aspirations"

1953

Adams, Samuel Clifford, Jr.
"The Changing Organization of Negro Plantation Society: With Attention
to Implications for the Pattern of Race Accommodation"

Chan-Paang Siu, Paul
"The Chinese Laundryman: A Study of Social Isolation"

Farber, Bernard
"Evaluation and Revision of Burgess-Wallin Rating Scale"

Friedmann, Eugene
"Voluntary Retirement and the Meaning of Work"

Goffman, Erving
"Rules Regarding Social Interaction in a Rural Community"

Gold, David
"The Influence of Religious Affiliation on Voting Behavior"

Kornhauser, William Alan
"Some Factors in the Cohesion and Disintegration of Unpopular Political
Movements"

Kriesberg, Louis
"Steel Distributors and the American Government: A Study in National
Cohesion"

Lang, Kurt
   "McArthur Day: A Study in Political and Observational Perspectives"
Nelson, Leona Bernice
   "The Secularization of a Church-Related College"
Rinder, Irwin Daniel
   "Jewish Identification and the Race Relations Cycle"
Schietinger, Egbert F.
   "Racial Succession and Changing Property Values in Residential
   Chicago"
Scott, John C.
   "Race and Culture Contact in a Southeastern Alaskan Community"
Uyeki, Eugene Shigemi
   "Process and Patterns of Nisei Adjustment to Chicago"
Warriner, Charles
   "Leadership and Society: Social Change and Changing Leadership in
   Three Small Communities"
Yeracaris, Constantine Anthony
   "Differential Mortality, General and Cause-specific, Buffalo, 1940"
Zadrozny, John
   "The Development of Nationality"

1954

Amerman, Helen Ely
   "The Impact of Intergroup Relations on Non-Segregated Urban Public
   Education"
Dadrian, Vahakn Norair
   "A Comparative Study of Modern Nationalism: A Sociological Effort of
   Analysis of the Cases of Modern England, France, and Germany by Way
   of Typology with Historical and Political Data"
Fisher, Herbert
   "Bias and Error in the Coding of Free Answer Responses"
Floro, George K.
   "The City Manager in the State of Michigan: A Sociological Study of
   Manager Careers"
Glaser, Daniel
   "A Reformulation and Testing of Parole Prediction Factors"
Gold, Raymond Leonard
   "Toward a Social Interaction Methodology for Sociological Field
   Observation"
Goldstein, Rhoda Lois Blumberg
   "The Professional Nurse in the Hospital Bureaucracy"
Gorden, Raymond Lowell
   "An Interaction Analysis of the Depth-Interview"

Gray, Robert
"A Study of the Personal Adjustment of the Aged Members of the Mormon Church"

Gusfield, Joseph Robert
"Organizational Change: A Study of the WCTU"

Habenstein, Robert Wesley
"The American Funeral Director: A Study in the Sociology of Work"

Huang, Lucy
"Dating and Courtship Innovations of Chinese Students in America"

Jammes, Jean Marie
"The Priest's Clientele: Expectations, Criticisms, Mistakes"

Junker, Buford Helmholz
"Room Compositions and Life Styles: A Sociological Study of Living Rooms and Other Rooms in Contemporary Dwellings"

Lagey, Joseph Chiozza
"Relationship of Social Factors to Attitude Change"

Lang, Gladys Engel
"A Study of Politics on Video: Viewers, Content and Definitions of the 1952 Convention"

Lopata, Helena Znaniecka
"The Functions of Voluntary Associations in an Ethnic Community: Polonia"

Lyman, Elizabeth Latimer
"Similarities and Differences in Emphasis Given to Certain Aspects of Work"

McCall, Bevode Chalmus
"Georgia Town and Cracker Culture: A Sociological Study"

McDowell, Harold
"The Principal's Role in a Metropolitan School System: Its Functions and Variations"

Maynard, Albert Douglas
"Modern Methods of Management Opposition to Union Organizing Activities in the Georgia Textile Mills"

Moore, David Graham
"Managerial Strategies and Organization Dynamics in Sears Retailing"

Ohlin, Lloyd E.
"The Validity and Stability of Parole"

Pfautz, Harold
"Christian Science as a Social Movement and Religious Sect: Its Ecology, Demography and Social Psychology"

Sahib, Hatim Abdul Al-Ka'bi
"Social Psychological Analysis of Arab Nationalist Movement in Iraq"

Singleton, James Winslow
"The Meaning of Work and Attitudes Toward Retirement Among Steelworkers"

Sorensen, Robert
"The Role of the Public Sentiment and Personal Prejudice in Jury Trials of Criminal Cases"

Taylor, Stanley
"Conceptions of Institutions and the Theory of Knowledge"

1955

Bradford, Alvin Priestly
"The Tactics and Methods of Labor Organizing: The Role of Agitation in the Development of a Social Movement"

Dreer, Herman
"Negro Leadership in St. Louis: A Study in Race Relations"

Gilman, Glenn William
"Industrial Relations in the Georgia Piedmont"

Karsh, Bernard
"The Labor Strike in a Small Community: A Study of Industrial Conflict"

Lawson, Lawrence Breslin
"The Protestant Minister in Chicago"

Lawton, William Cranston
"The DuPonts: A Case Study of Kinship in the Business Organization"

Royer, Donald Mark
"The Acculturation Process and the Peace Doctrine of the Church of the Brethren in the Central Region of the United States"

Wilensky, Harold L.
"The Staff 'Expert': A Study of the Intelligence Function in American Trade Unions"

1956

Breen, Leonard Zachary
"A Study of the Decentralization of Retail Trade Relative to Population in the Chicago Area, 1929 to 1948"

Lilienthal, Daisy
"The Meaning of Unionism: A Study of the Perspectives of Members of the Plumbers' Union, the United Mine Workers and the United Automobile Workers of America"

Peterson, Warren Alfred
"Career Phases and Inter-Age Relationships: The Female High School Teacher in Kansas City"

Reid, John Daniel
"The People of St. Simon Island"

Shapiro, Leopold Julius
"The Opinion Poll"

Trutza, Peter George
"The Religious Factor in Acculturation: A Study in Assimilation and Acculturation of the Roumanian Group in Chicago"

Wilkins, Arthur H.
"The Residential Distribution of Occupation Groups in Eight Middle-sized Cities of the U.S. in 1950"

1957

Duncan, Beverly
"Population Distribution and Economic Activity"

Flapan, Harry Mark
"Empathy in the Marital Relationship"

Glick, Ira Oscar
"A Social Psychological Study of Futures Trading"

Goldstein, Bernard
"Unions for Technical Professionals: A Case Study"

James, Rita
"Jurors' Reactions to Definitions of Legal Insanity"

Levine, Donald Nathan
"Simmel and Parsons"

Mugge, Robert Herman
"Negro Migrants in Atlanta"

Phillips, William McKinley, Jr.
"Labor Force and Demographic Factors, 1940–1950"

1958

Carey, James Thomas
"The Development of the University Evening School in Urban America: An Aspect of Institutionalization in Higher Education"

Chow, Yung-Teh
"Status Mobility of the Chinese Gentry"

Davis, Fred
"Polio in the Family"

Griff, Mason
"Role Conflict and the Career Development of the Commercial Artist"

Helper, Rose
"The Racial Practices of Real Estate Institutions in Selected Areas of Chicago"

Lortie, Dan Clement
"The Striving Young Lawyer: A Study of Early Career Differentiation in the Chicago Bar"

Seymour, Sam Frederick
"The Labor Force in Kansas City: 1950"

1959

Bain, Robert Ketcham
"The Process of Professionalization: Life Insurance Selling"

Baum, Bernard Helmut
"Decentralization of Authority in a Bureaucracy"

Bolton, Charles Dewey
"The Development Process in Love Relationships"

Carlin, Jerome
"The Lawyer as Individual Practitioner"

Carter, Wilmoth Annette
"The Negro Main Street of a Contemporary Urban Community"

Cassidy, Sally Whelan
"A Study of Lay Leadership"

Ferron, Alfred Lewis
"Background and Trends in the Development of a Residential Treatment Center: A Structural-Functional Analysis"

Mehta, Surinder Kumar
"The Labor Force of Urban Burma and Rangoon, 1953: A Comparative Study"

Moore, Joan Willard
"Stability and Instability in the Metropolitan Upper Class"

Quarantelli, Enrico
"The Dental Student"

Redekop, Calvin Waldo
"Sectarianism: Tension With the World"

Stone, Gregory Prentice
"Clothing and Social Relations: A Study of Appearance in the Context of Community Life"

Verdet, Paula
"Inter-Ethnic Problems of a Roman Catholic Parish"

Wager, Leonard Wesley
"Career Patterns: A Study of Airline Pilots in a Major Airline Company"

Wax, Murray Lionel
"Time, Magic, and Asceticism: A Comparative Study of Time Perspectives"

1960

Cutright, Phillips
"Party Organization and Voting Behavior"

Dentler, Robert A.
"Attitude Change in Work Groups: Group Composition Solidarity and Environment as Sources of Conformity"

Gottlieb, David
"Processes of Socialization in the American Graduate School"

Hawkins, Charles
"Interaction and Coalition Realignments in Consensus-Seeking Groups: A Study of Experimental Jury Deliberations"

Kauffman, J. Howard
"A Comparative Study of Traditional and Emergent Forms of Family Life among Midwest Mennonites"

Lamson, Robert
"Scientists and Congressmen"

Lieberson, Stanley
"Comparative Segregation and Assimilation of Ethnic Groups"

Mauksch, Hans O.
"The Nurse: A Study in Role Perception"

Pappenfort, Donnell M.
"A Study of Births in Hospitals and Technology"

Pineo, Peter Camden
"Dyadic and Change Analysis in a Study of Marriage and Divorce"

Stanton, Howard R.
"The Assessment, Valuation and Reinforcement of Autonomy: An Exploration of Concern with a Critical Skill"

Vajd, Emil
"Burmese Urban Characteristics: A Size-of-Place Study of a Southeast Asian Urban Population"

1961

Bloomberg, Warner
"The Power Structure of 'Stackton': Patterns of Status, Reputation, and Perception among the Leaders of an American Industrial Community"

Brazeau, Jacques
"The Training of French-Canadian Ground Crew Personnel in the Royal Canadian Air Force (1953–1957)"

Broel-Plateris, Alexander
"Marriage Disruption and Divorce Law"

Bucher, Mary Rue
"Conflicts and Transformations of Identity: A Study of Medical Specialists"

Erbe, William W.
"Student Integration and Departmental Cohesiveness in American Graduate Schools"

Johnstone, John W. C.
"Social Structure and Patterns of Mass Media Consumption"
Mathur, Prakash C.
"Internal Migration in India, 1941–1951"
Mitra, Samerendranath
"The Future of Population, Urbanization and Working Force in India"
Redick, Richard Warren
"A Demographic and Ecological Study of Rangoon, Burma: 1953"
Scott, William R.
"A Case Study of Professional Workers in a Bureaucratic Setting"
Spaeth, Joseph L.
"Value Orientations and Academic Career Plans: Structural Effects of the Careers of Graduate Students"
Winsborough, Halliman H.
"A Comparative Study of Urban Residential Densities"
Zakuta, Leo
"A Becalmed Protest Movement: A Study of Change in the CCF"

1962
Beale, Lathrop Vickery
"Religiousness and Integration into the Community"
Beltran, Anita K. G.
"Social Origins and Career Preparation Among Filipino Students in American Universities"
Gouveia, Aparecida Joly
"Student Teachers in Brazil"
Greeley, Andrew M.
"The Influence of Religion on the Career Plans and Occupational Values of June 1961 College Graduates"
Hare, Nathan
"The Changing Occupational Status of the Negro in the U.S."
Hashmi, Sultan
"Trends and Factors in Urban Fertility Differences in the U.S."
Jillani, Mahmud S.
"Resettlement Patterns of Displaced Persons in Pakistan"
Marcus, Philip M.
"Trade Union Structure: A Study of Formal Organization"
Matras, Judah
"Israel: Absorption of Immigrants, Social Mobility and Social Change"
Richter, Maurice N.
"A Study of Cognitive Inconsistency"
Risler, Walt
"A Study of Parent-Linked Delinquency"

Seaton, Richard W.
"Hunger in Groups"
Taeuber, Alma F.
"A Comparative Urban Analysis of Negro Residential Succession"

1963

Arnold, William Robert
"The Adjustment of Adolescent Males on Parole"
Concepcion, Mercedes B.
"Fertility Differences among Married Women in the Philippines"
Crain, Robert Lee
"Inter-City Influence in the Diffusion of Fluoridation"
Erikson, Kai T.
"Wayward Puritans: A Study in the Sociology of Deviance"
Gordon, Robert A.
"Values and Gang Delinquency"
Hajda, Jan
"An American Paradox: People and Books in a Metropolis"
Hamilton, Herbert
"Social Bases of Opinion in the Cold War American Army"
Nishi, Setsuko Matsunaga
"Japanese American Achievement in Chicago: A Cultural Response to Degradation"
Peil, Margaret
"The Use of Child-Rearing Literature by Low-Income Families"
Raphael, Edna E.
"Welfare Activity in the Local Union: A Study in the Sampling of Organizations"
Scherer, Rose
"Ministers of the Lutheran Church—Missouri Synod: Origins, Training, Career-Lines, Perceptions of Work, and Reference"
Wallace, Walter L.
"Bringing Up Intellectuals: Changing Student Values, Aspirations, and Achievement in College"
Zinser, Raymond Edward
"Sectarian Commitment and Withdrawal"

1964

Biderman, Albert D.
"American Prisoners of War in Korea: Reinterpretations of the Data"
Blum, Alan
"Family Structure, Peer Culture and the Learning of Political History"

Braude, Lee
    "The Rabbi: A Study of the Relation of Contingency Situations in
    Differential Career Structure"
Colfax, John David
    "The Big-City Voter: A Study of Political Participation in Chicago"
Farley, Walter Reynolds
    "Negro Cohort Fertility"
Finestone, Harold
    "A Comparative Study of Reformation and Recidivism among Italian and
    Polish Criminal Offenders"
Heise, David R.
    "Effects of Motivation on Word Choice in Verbal Behavior"
Kurup, R. S.
    "Recent Trends in World Mortality and Their Implications for a Revised
    System of Model Life Tables"
Nosanchuk, Terrance A.
    "A Multivariate Analysis of the Acquaintance Process"
Roberts, Bryan Rees
    "The Effects of College Experience and Social Background on
    Professional Orientations of Prospective Teachers"
Rosenberg, Larry
    "Communication Styles and Learning—A Factor-Analytic Study of
    Teacher-Student Interaction"
Vazquez, Jose Luis
    "The Demographic Evolution of Puerto Rico"
White, Rodney Francis
    "Female Identity and Work Roles: The Case of Nursing"
Zelan, Joseph
    "Recruitment in the Legal Profession: A Study of College Student Career
    Choice"

1965

Cherry, Frank Talley
    "Southern In-Migrant Negroes in North Lawndale, Chicago, 1949–59: A
    Study of Internal Migration and Adjustment"
Cho, Lee Jay
    "Differential Fertility in the United States: Based on the 1940 and 1950
    Census"
Choldin, Harvey M.
    "First Year in the Metropolis: A Study of Migration and Adjustment"
Feldman, Jacob J.
    "The Dissemination of Health Information: A Case Study in Adult
    Learning"

Friedell, Morris
"A Laboratory Experiment in Retaliation"

Haerle, Rudolf K., Jr.
"Catholics and Mixed Marriage: A Comparative Analysis of Types of Interfaith Marriages and Their Consequences for Mate Selection and Religious Adjustment in Marriage"

Heydebrand, Wolf V.
"Bureaucracy in Hospitals: An Analysis of Complexity and Coordination"

Kantrowitz, Nathan
"Pre–Civil War Political Realignment"

Masse, Jaqueline Cloutier
"Interpersonal Attraction and Similarity of Nationality, Tenure and Location"

Misra, Bhaskar D.
"Correlates of Males' Attitude towards Family Planning: A Study of the Low Socio-Economic Status Negro Males of Chicago"

Parkman, Margaret A.
"Identity, Role, and Family Functioning"

Pinto, Leonard
"Social and Cultural Determinants of Anxiety in a Crisis Situation"

Potter, Robert
"Interpersonal Ties and Interaction"

Queeley, Mary Albertha
"Innovation in an Urban Slum School"

Renck, Richard T.
"Industrial Organization and Employee Morale"

Stelling, Joan G.
"Religious Behavior: Some Aspects of Religious Participation and Religious Change"

FACULTY IN THE DEPARTMENT OF SOCIOLOGY AT THE UNIVERSITY OF CHICAGO, 1946–1960

E. Burgess
Professor, 1946–1952
Emeritus Professor, 1952–1960

E. Faris
Emeritus Professor, 1946–1953

C. Shaw
Lecturer, 1946–1958

L. Wirth
Professor, 1946–1951

H. Blumer
Professor, 1946–1952

W. F. Ogburn
Professor, 1946–1952
Emeritus Professor, 1952–1960

P. Hauser
Professor, 1947–1960

J. D. Lohman
Lecturer, 1947–1957

W. L. Warner
Professor, 1946–1960

E. A. Shils
Associate Professor, 1946–1948
Professor, 1958–1960

E. C. Hughes
Professorial Lecturer, 1946–1950
Assistant Professor, 1950–1951
Professor, 1951–1960

H. Bonner
Lecturer, 1946–1947

W. F. Whyte
Assistant Professor, 1946–1947
Associate Professor, 1947–1949

J. J. Williams
Associate Professor, 1950–1951

M. Goldhammer
Associate Professor, 1947–1951

A. J. Reiss
Assistant Professor, 1950–1952

L. Goodman
Assistant Professor, 1950–1954
Associate Professor, 1954–1956
Professor, 1956–1960

D. G. Moore
Assistant Professor, 1950–1955
Associate Professor, 1955–1956

O. D. Duncan
Assistant Professor, 1951–1958

E. R. Kitagawa
Assistant Professor, 1951–1955

N. Foote
Assistant Professor, 1952–1957

H. Wilensky
Assistant Professor, 1951–1953

W. Bradbury
Assistant Professor, 1951–1953
Associate Professor, 1953–1959

M. B. Loeb
Assistant Professor, 1951–1953

Material in this appendix is taken and rearranged from Appendix 1, tables 1d and 1e in Lee Harvey, *Myths of the Chicago School of Sociology* (Aldershot: Avebury, 1987), pp. 224–27. Harvey's material is from *The Official Publications of the University of Chicago*. Abbott and Gaziano note (this volume) that some of the ranks provided by Harvey may be incorrect, and that a more precise table would involve a detailed search of the university's personnel files—if those files still exist.

D. Riesman
   Assistant Professor, 1954–1959
D. Bogue
   Professorial Lecturer, 1954–1959
   Assistant Professor, 1959–1960
P. Blau
   Assistant Professor, 1954–1959
A. Strauss
   Assistant Professor, 1954–1958
E. Katz
   Assistant Professor, 1955–1960
P. Rossi
   Assistant Professor, 1956–1958
   Professor, 1958–1960

A. H. Barton
   Assistant Professor, 1957–1958
J. S. Coleman
   Assistant Professor, 1957–1960
J. A. Davis
   Assistant Professor, 1958–1960
R. Wohl
   Associate Professor, 1958–1959
C. A. Anderson
   Professor, 1959–1960
D. McRae
   Assistant Professor, 1959–1960

CONTRIBUTORS

ANDREW ABBOTT is Professor of Sociology and Master of the Social Sciences Collegiate Division at the University of Chicago.

J. DAVID BROWN is Assistant Professor of Social Sciences at Redrocks Community College in Lakewood, Colorado.

PAUL COLOMY is Associate Professor of Sociology at the University of Denver.

PHILLIP W. DAVIS is Associate Professor of Sociology at Georgia State University.

MARY JO DEEGAN is Professor of Sociology at the University of Nebraska, Lincoln.

LORI J. DUCHARME is a Research Associate at the Institute for Behavioral Research at the University of Georgia.

GARY ALAN FINE is Professor of Sociology at the University of Georgia.

JOHN F. GALLIHER is Professor of Sociology at the University of Missouri, Columbia.

EMANUEL GAZIANO is a graduate student in the Department of Sociology at Indiana University.

JOSEPH GUSFIELD is Professor Emeritus of Sociology at the University of California, San Diego.

HELENA ZNANIECKA LOPATA is Professor of Sociology at Loyola University, Chicago.

JENNIFER PLATT is Professor of Sociology and Director of the Graduate Research Centre in the Social Sciences at the University of Sussex.

SHULAMIT REINHARZ is Professor of Sociology and Director of the Women's Studies Program at Brandeis University.

DAVID A. SNOW is Professor of Sociology at the University of Arizona.

R. FRED WACKER is Professor of History at Wayne State University.

406

INDEX

Jacobs, Ruth, 291, 296, 297
Janowitz, Morris, 4, 87, 288, 368; career of, 223, 234, 236, 240, 242, 255; on collective behavior, 188, 213n.14; on race and ethnicity, 137, 150–51
Jehovah's Witnesses, 211n.2
Jewish heritage: at Brandeis University, 273–74, 276; of Gans, 154; of Goffman, 112, 115; of second Chicago school, xv, 89, 101, 233, 366
Jewish social types, 51–52
Joas, H., 42
Johnson, Chalmers S., 190
Johnson, Charles S., 136, 150
Johnson, Earl, 154
Johnson, Guy, 136
Johnson, Rogers, 300–302
Joint Commission on Mental Health, 88
Junker, Buford H., 28, 35, 82, 87, 252

Kansas, University of, 121–22
Kanter, Rosabeth Moss, 301, 304
Karpf, Fay Berger, 337
Karsh, Bernard, 86, 153
Katz, Elihu, 96, 222, 235–37, 239, 278
Kecskemeti, Paul, 304
Kelin, Viola, 327
Kelley, Florence, 336
Kellor, Frances, 336
Keyfitz, Nathan, 5
Killian, Lewis, 1, 86, 144; on collective behavior, 188–89, 195–96, 199, 203–8; on race and ethnicity, 137, 148–49, 154
Kimpton, Lawrence, 224, 226, 232–34, 238–39, 241
King, Charles E., 93, 144
Kitagawa, Evelyn, 3, 82, 99, 351, 370
Klapp, Orrin E., 52, 188, 197–98, 202–4, 207
Kogon, Eugene, 114
Komarovsky, Mirra, 339, 376
Kornblum, David, 240
Kornhauser, Ruth, 153
Kornhauser, William, 144–45, 188, 204, 207
Kriesberg, Louis, 225, 257, 368, 378
Kwan, Kian, 146

Labeling theory, 44, 182
Lal, Barbara Ballis, 137–38, 156
Lang, Gladys Engel, 349, 369; career of,

377–78; on collective behavior, 188, 193–96, 199, 201–7; on politics of students, 366, 374; on postwar cohort, 374–75
Lang, Kurt, 153, 349, 369, 377; on collective behavior, 188, 193–96, 199, 201–7
Lathrop, Julia, 336
Lazarsfeld, Paul, ix, 40, 140; career of, 228, 232, 235, 249, 256
Leaders, symbolic, 197–98
LeBon, Gustave, 191, 193
Lee, Alfred C., 257
Lee, Elizabeth Briant, 339
Lee, Rose Hum, 149, 347
Levine, Donald, 224–25
Levittowners, The (Gans), 155
Levy, Charles, 294
Lewis, D. J., 40
Liazos, Alex, 293
Lieberson, Stanley, 156
Liebow, E., 127
Life histories, 28, 93
Light, Donald, 288–89, 294
Lilienthal, Daisy, 348, 374–75
Lind, Andrew, 136
Lindesmith, Alfred R., 33, 35, 50, 51, 55, 170
Linton, R., 53
Lipset, Seymour M., 235, 236
Loeb, Martin, 367
Lofland, John, 39, 92, 98, 202
Lofland, Lyn, 98
Logical positivism, 27
Lohman, Joseph D., 8, 88, 365, 370; and criminology, 166–67, 171–72; on race, 145; research methodology of, 35, 95
London, Jack, 86, 144, 368
Lonely Crowd, The (Riesman), 111, 152, 155
Looking-glass self, 51
Lopata, Helena Znaniecka, 1, 149, 153, 257; career of, 341–43, 351–52, 372, 374, 380–81; on roles, 52, 55, 56; topics studied by, 347
Lortie, Dan, 90, 367, 372
Lu, Yi-Chuang, 87
Lundberg, George, 28
Luther, Martin, 175
Lyman, Elizabeth L., 349
Lyman, Stanford, 42, 156

reer of, 222, 225, 236, 238–41; research methodology of, 82, 96, 278, 368
Roth, Julius, 99; on social control in hospitals, 35, 111–12, 118–21, 125–26
Roy, Donald, 82, 86
Rumor, 193–97

Sachar, Abram, 274–75, 280, 284
St. Elizabeth's Hospital (Washington, D.C.), 113–14
St. Luke-Presbyterian Hospital, 371
Salerno, Roger, 277
Sampling, 34
Schatzman, L., 99
Schlesinger, Arthur, Jr., 236
Schools, in sciences, 1–2
Schumann, Karl F., 182
Schumpeter, Joseph, 255
Schwartz, C. G., 35
Schwartz, Morris S., 28, 35; at Brandeis University, 278–86, 290, 292, 294, 297, 301, 304; research methodology of, 88, 95
Second Chicago school, ix-xvi, 365–73; case for existence of, 1–10, 82–103; on collective behavior, 188–210 (*see also* Collective behavior); on criminology and deviance, 164–83 (*see also* Criminology and deviance research); "decline" of, 6, 9–10, 94–97, 102, 156, 222, 278; faculty changes in era of, 221–57; generalized discourse of, 20–42; on race and ethnicity, 136–57 (*see also* Race and ethnicity); role theory of, 49–57; on social control, 108–30 (*see also* Social control); as social scientific tradition, 17–20; women in, 322–55, 373–83 (*see also* Women); on work and occupations, 45–49. *See also* Chicago, University of; Research methodology; Sociology Department, University of Chicago
Secrets of a Sociologist (Dentler), 369
Seeley, John, 228; at Brandeis, 279, 286–87, 292, 299, 301, 303, 304
Seidman, Joel, 223
Self, 22, 38–39, 51, 54, 126
Selznick, Philip, 228
Sewell, William, 229, 232, 235, 256n.24
Sexism, 12, 322–55, 373–82; College and

Department contrasted in, 331; during patriarchal era, 333–34, 337–45; in sociology, 322–27, 337–41. *See also* Women
Shadowwork, 326
Shalin, D., 42
Shanas, Ethel, 87, 225, 344–45, 367, 378–79
Shaw, Clifford, 83, 88, 184n.1, 365
Shibutani, Tamotsu, x, 228, 352, 377, 378; on ambiguity, responses to, 120; on Blumer, 61n.6; on collective behavior, 188; interactionism of, 33, 35, 44; on race and ethnicity, 137, 146–48, 154, 157; role theory of, 51, 55
Shils, Edward A., 87, 156, 345; career of, 221–22, 224–25, 227, 234, 239, 370; on sociology, 137, 140
Short, James F., Jr., 239, 277; on criminology and deviance, 164–65, 168, 178–81; research methodology of, 88, 89; on role of theory, 183
Shosid, N., 56
Shott, S., 56
Simmel, Georg, 30, 295, 296, 372
Simmons, J. L., 35, 76
Simon, Rita, 341, 347, 351, 371, 379–80
Singer, Milton, 371
Slater, Philip, 287, 292, 301, 302, 304
Small, Albion, 243, 254, 274, 373
Smelser, Neil, 190, 202, 235, 242
Smith, Dorothy E., 322–25
Smith, R. L., 40
Snow, David A., 207–8
Sociability Center, 371
Social action, 20–24, 52
"Social Change and Status Protest" (Hughes), 141
Social class, 55, 165
Social control, 108–30; Becker on, 122–24; in criminology and deviance research, 172–73; Davis on, 116–18; Goffman on, 113–15; Janowitz on, 151; Roth on, 119–21; "third school" on, 126–29
Socialization: of Brandeis University graduate students, 289–300; medical school, 122–24; of mental patients, 173; in professions, 48; role, 54
Social movements. *See* Collective behavior studies
Social organization, debate on, 252–54

Whyte, William Foote, 8, 222, 297, 365; re-
search methodology of, 82, 86, 87, 91,
100; and second Chicago school, 46,
127, 153, 167, 296
Whyte, William H., 6, 111, 112, 255
Wilensky, Harold, 153, 222, 225, 368
Wiley, Norbert, 92
Williams, Josephine, 225, 228, 243, 348
Williams, R., 33–34
Williams, Robin, Jr., 144, 145
Winget, John, 87
Winkin, Y., 101
Wirth, Louis, 150, 327, 365, 371, 373; career of, 221, 223, 226–34, 257; and collective behavior studies, 188; death of,
9, 96, 221, 241, 243; and ethnography,
183; as influence on second Chicago
school, x, 1, 9; and Lopata thesis, 380;
on race and ethnicity, 137, 145–49;
and race relations program, 380; and
Riesman, 332; role theory of, 50–52; in
seminar debates, 244–55; on student-
faculty contact, 89
Wisconsin, University of, 164, 183
Wolff, Kurt, 277, 280, 282–85, 301–4
Women, 11, 12, 63n.14, 90, 322–55, 373–83;
accounts by individual, 342–49,
376–81; at Brandeis University,
296–97; epistemology of, 341–42, 350;
during "golden era," 333–37, 345–46,
348, 350, 355, 373; Hughes on status
of, 141, 330; male mentors to, 332–33;
number of, on faculties, 373; during pa-

triarchal era, 337–45, 373; and wom-
en's movement, 201; in Zeta Phi, 372.
See also Feminism; Sexism
Women's Christian Temperance Union
(WCTU), 174, 181
Wood, M., 42
Work and occupations: as influence on
criminology and deviance research,
167, 180; in racial and ethnic research,
140–41, 148; second Chicago school
on, 45–49
Working consensus, 36
Workingman's Wife (Rainwater, Coleman,
and Handel), 371
World War II, 109, 110, 123, 153; sociology
training during and after, 338–39. *See
also* G. I. Bill veterans

Yearning for Yesterday (Davis), 10
Young, Kimball, 332, 376
Yu, Henry, 150

Zakuta, Leo, 90
Zald, Meyer N., 190–91
Zeta Phi, 372
Znaniecki, Florian, 136, 139, 380; *Polish
Peasant* of, 46, 166, 343, 381; on roles,
50, 52
Zola, Irving, 287–88, 292, 293, 304
Zoot-suiters, 145, 197
Zurcher, Louis, 207–8
Zygmunt, Joseph, 211n.2